ABOUT ISLAND PRESS

THE COMPLETE GUIDE TO ENVIRONMENTAL CAREERS IN THE 21ST CENTURY

The next fifty years are a special time. Between now and 2050 we'll see the zenith, or very nearly, of human population. With luck we'll never see any greater production of carbon dioxide or toxic chemicals. We'll never see greater species extinction or soil erosion.

So it's the task of those of us alive right now to deal with this special phase, to squeeze us through these next fifty years. That's not fair—any more than it was fair that earlier generations had to deal with the Second World War or the Civil War or the Revolution or the Depression or slavery. It's just reality.

We need in these fifty years to be working *simultaneously* . . . on our ways of life, on our technologies, and on our population.

The period in question happens to be *our* time. That's what makes this moment special, and what makes this moment hard.

—Bill McKibben

THE COMPLETE GUIDE TO ENVIRONMENTAL CAREERS IN THE 21ST CENTURY

The Environmental Careers Organization

John R. Cook, Jr.
President

Kevin Doyle
Editor and Project Director

Kevin Doyle
Sam Heizmann
Tanya Stubbs
Writers

Meryl Brott
Dylan Murray
Research Assistants

ISLAND PRESS

Washington, D.C. • *Covelo, California*

Cover design and illustration by Lightbourne Images, copyright 1998.

Library of Congress Cataloging-in-Publication Data
Heizmann, Sam.
   The complete guide to environmental careers in the 21st century / the
Environmental Careers Organization ; Sam Heizmann, Tanya Stubbs, writers.
   Rev. ed. of: The new complete guide to environmental careers / the
Environmental Careers Organization ; Bill Sharp, principal author.
2nd ed. c1993.
   Includes bibliographical references (p.   ) and index.
   ISBN 1–55963–585–1 (Cloth). — ISBN 1–55963–586–X (Paper)
   1. Environmental sciences—Vocational guidance.   I. Stubbs,
Tanya.   II. Sharp, Bill, 1952– New complete guide to environmental
careers.   III. Environmental Careers Organization.   IV. Title.
GE60.H45   1999   98–39091
363.7'0023—dc21   CIP

Printed on recycled, acid-free paper

Manufactured in the United States of America
10 9 8 7 6 5 4 3 2 1

Contents

Preface

Each morning, the newspaper brings fresh reports from the front lines of environmental work. The issues—global climate change, habitat destruction, toxins in the environment, species extinction, air and water pollution, urban sprawl, loss of wetlands and agricultural land, energy conservation, and environmental injustice affect us all. Although great progress has been made in our efforts to understand, protect, and restore our common environment, immense challenges lie ahead.

Fortunately, concern about the environment, and a willingness to make a difference, is extremely high. As we enter the twenty-first century, over $400 billion is spent worldwide annually on conservation and environmental protection, supporting hundreds of thousands of fascinating jobs. People throughout the world are working on three impossibly large tasks simultaneously—restoring ecosystems damaged in the past to vibrant health; reducing the negative environmental impacts of today's actions; and building a truly sustainable way of life for the future. This is the world of environmental careers.

With so much to be done, there is literally something for everyone. Among scientists, the environmental world needs biologists, chemists, geologists, geographers, hydrologists, ecologists, oceanographers, meteorologists, botanists, health scientists, toxicologists, foresters, agronomists, and many more. A wide variety of engineers are required to solve our environmental problems. Computer professionals (programmers, modelers, geographic information systems specialists, website designers, database technicians) are in demand. Professionals from law, finance, business, accounting, management, public administration, and insurance have a major role to play. Planners, architects, landscape architects, and designers will help create an environmentally sound world. Teachers (from kindergarten through doctoral school) and journalists from every medium are crucial to environmental protection and conservation. Social scientists and people from the humanities are found in environmental careers everywhere. A virtual army of technicians and laborers is part of the environmental workforce. Finally, elected officials, activists, and citizen volunteers remain at the very center of our hope for a sustainable future.

HOW THIS BOOK CAN HELP YOU

The Complete Guide to Environmental Careers in the 21st Century is a resource, a celebration, and an invitation for anyone who cares about our future and longs for a career in defense of the environment.

As a resource, this book has the most comprehensive and up-to-date information available on environmental careers. In the first three chapters, we've summarized the current state of the field, drawn a statistical picture of jobs and employers, outlined the major trends driving the rapidly changing environmental job world, and offered advice and resources about educational choices, on-the-job experience, and achieving success in your environmental job search.

The rest of the book brings you detailed information about careers in environmental protection (e.g., air, water, hazardous waste, solid waste, and energy), natural resource management (e.g., land and water conservation, parks and recreation, forestry, and fish and wildlife), environmental education/communications, and planning. We'll tell you where the jobs are, what's growing, what's not, how much you'll earn, what kind of education you'll need, and much more.

Each chapter includes:

- *At a Glance.* A brief snapshot of employment in the field.
- *What is . . . ?* A definition of the career field for quick understanding.
- *History and Background.* Includes key laws that professionals need to know.
- *Issues and Trends.* The major forces creating the jobs you're looking for.
- *Career Opportunities.* Types of work available in government, business and at nonprofit organizations.
- *Salary.* Current earnings at the entry level and beyond.
- *Getting Started.* Educational needs and other advice.

In addition, every chapter includes a carefully selected group of Resources, with a focus on top Internet sites for the environmental job seeker. We have identified dozens of organizations and websites to help you find the environmental career of your dreams. Naturally, the resources listed here are only a tiny fraction of those available to aspiring environmental professionals. A comprehensive list of websites alone would fill volumes. Use the Resources section of each chapter as a starting point for your own, unique search.

Information about the current state of environmental career fields is important. The story of environmental work, however, is best told by the people who live it every day. That's why, in each chapter, we've included a

Case Study of environmental professionals at work, as well as Profiles of men and women from government agencies, businesses, and nonprofit groups throughout the nation who are making a difference.

More than a resource book, *The Complete Guide to Environmental Careers in the 21st Century* is a celebration of the people who devote their lives to ecological protection and conservation. For twenty-six years, the Environmental Careers Organization has worked with thousands of dedicated environmental professionals who do the work behind the headlines. We are proud to shine a light on park rangers, wildlife biologists, school teachers, journalists, recycling coordinators, air quality engineers, geographic information specialists, political activists, land trust directors, hazardous waste clean-up crews, water quality inspectors, marine ecologists, and all of the other people who collectively make up the environmental and conservation work force.

Whether you choose an environmental career or not, we hope that this book gives you an appreciation for the remarkable people who have helped make the modern environmental movement such an amazing success.

Finally, *The Complete Guide to Environmental Careers in the 21st Century* is, of course, an invitation. In these pages, we hope you will find information and inspiration for your own environmental career. Whether you choose the world of government service, nonprofit work, academia, or a career in business, this book invites you to learn, grow, and do something crucially important.

Naturally, we believe that environmental careers are the best careers around—challenging, important, rewarding, amazingly diverse, and worthy of a lifetime's devotion. The Earth is a source of wonder and delight, and environmental professionals are honored to earn a living through understanding it and protecting it from the worst excesses of our species' actions. This book is an invitation to join us.

ABOUT THE ENVIRONMENTAL CAREERS ORGANIZATION (ECO)

This is the third edition of *The Complete Guide to Environmental Careers* to be written by the Environmental Careers Organization (ECO), and published by our partners at Island Press, the nation's leading publisher of environmental and conservation resources. The first edition came out in 1989. It was completely updated in 1993, and now, again, in the fall of 1998. The third edition is completely revised and updated to reflect the rapid and fundamental changes that environmental careers have undergone in the last five years.

The Complete Guide to Environmental Careers in the 21st Century is a natural extension of ECO's work. Started in 1972, ECO is a national, nonprofit organization that "protects and enhances the environment through the development of professionals, the promotion of careers, and the inspiration of individual action." We are dedicated to helping the people who protect and conserve the environment.

Our core initiative is a national program of paid environmental "associate" positions at government agencies, nonprofit groups, and corporations. Through our offices in Seattle, San Francisco, Cleveland, and Boston, we employ 600 to 700 people every year in challenging, full time assignments that can last from twelve weeks to two years. ECO associates are current college students and recent graduates at the associate, undergraduate, graduate, and doctoral levels. Each associate is matched with a current environmental professional, who acts as the associate's project adviser. In many ways, associate positions are old-fashioned apprenticeships, which allow aspiring environmental and conservation professionals to learn from the talented professionals of today. Stipends range between $400 to $700 per week, and sometimes higher.

Over the last twenty-six years, ECO has placed more than 7,000 associates at hundreds of private and public sector environmental employers. ECO alumni can now be found as leading professionals, managers, academics, and activists throughout the nation, as well as in many parts of the world.

What do ECO associates do? They work on pollution prevention, toxins use reduction, range management, air and water pollution control, fish and wildlife management, environmental justice, brownfields redevelopment, global climate change, habitat preservation, land-use planning, alternative energy development, international policy, endangered species protection, environmental education, land preservation, sustainable development, coastal erosion, and much more.

Although ECO places associates in a wide variety of employment settings, we have a particularly large program with the federal government, including the U.S. Environmental Protection Agency, Bureau of Land Management, Geological Survey, National Park Service, Department of Energy, and National Oceanic and Atmospheric Administration.

An important feature of ECO, and the associate program, is our commitment to diversity in the development of new environmental professionals. In 1990, ECO launched The Diversity Initiative, an effort to create more opportunities for underrepresented people to begin environmental careers. Just as the natural world requires biological diversity for health and survival, so the world of environmental policy and action must have a vibrant human diversity if it is to prosper. The environmental community needs men and women, younger and older, the well off and the less fortunate, rural and urban people, residents of every state, and people from all parts of the educational spectrum. We are extremely proud that 37 percent of our 1997 associates were people of color, and that half were women. Here are two measures of The Diversity Initiative's success.

In addition to our flagship associate program, ECO offers other services to help the environmental career seeker. Our National Environmental Careers Conference, held annually since 1984, brings together hundreds of aspiring environmental professionals for a weekend of panels, speeches, workshops, field trips, and networking opportunities with today's leaders. The ECO website (http://www.eco.org) is a constantly updated source of information that provides news and links about environmental careers, attracts over 130,000 people every month (as of August 1998), and is growing very rapidly. ECO publications and research studies explore important issues involving environmental education, career preparation, diversity, and trends in environmental problem solving. And, ECO often offers scholarships and small grants in collaboration with charitable donors, government agencies, and academic institutions.

Through all of our activities, ECO empowers people to protect, conserve, and enhance the environment. Although laws, regulations, funds, and public support are crucial to success, it is ultimately the people—individuals such as those featured in this book and you as well—who must implement solutions, create innovations, enforce the law, and teach a new generation. ECO is about educating, assisting, and inspiring the people of the environmental community—wherever they work and volunteer.

We hope that you will join us and that this book will help.

John R. Cook, Jr.
Founder and President
The Environmental Careers Organization

For more information about ECO programs, events, and publications, contact us at our national headquarters: ECO, 179 South Street, Fifth Floor, Boston, MA, 02111. Phone: 617-426-4375, Fax: 617-423-0998. For a complete overview of ECO, as well as links to other environmental career resources, visit our website at http://www.eco.org.

Acknowledgments

It is impossible to thank all of the people who made *The Complete Guide to Environmental Careers in the 21st Century* possible. Dozens of professionals and educators shared their time, ideas, and stories with us. Staff people at professional associations in environmental and conservation fields provided invaluable assistance. In many ways, this is their book. You will meet many of these people throughout these pages, and we are honored to pass on their experience and advice to you.

This is the third edition of *The Complete Guide to Environmental Careers*. We owe a large debt to the teams that created the previous editions in 1989 and 1993. Creation of the original guide was managed by the Environmental Careers Organization's (ECO) former Great Lakes director, Lee DeAngelis, and written by Stephen Basler. The work of Lee and Steve is an inspiration to everyone involved with this book and we hope the current edition meets the standard they set.

Our thanks also go to the George Gund Foundation and the Pew Charitable Trusts for the financial support that made the first edition of *The Complete Guide to Environmental Careers* possible.

The 1993 edition was managed by Kevin Doyle and written by Bill Sharp, with assistance from Elaine Appleton, Catherine Pederson, Jean Anderson, and Lee DeAngelis. A heartfelt thank you to this superb team of writers and researchers. We stand on your shoulders.

This edition was managed, edited, and partially written by Kevin Doyle, ECO's director of development. After fifteen years at ECO, Kevin's passion about ecological protection and love for the people who pursue environmental careers is undiminished. We are thankful to have had a wonderful group of writers for this latest edition of *The Complete Guide to Environmental Careers*. Tanya Stubbs was a valuable part of the ECO team. As a first-time author with responsibility for nearly half of the book, Tanya did a wonderful job of bringing environmental careers to life. She brought to her work a thoughtful and meticulous approach that was much appreciated. Sam Heizmann did an excellent job of preparing the chapter on the planning profession. Dylan Murray and Meryl Brott provided valuable research assistance to the project, and the edits contributed by Deb Mapes improved the final manuscript.

Special thanks to Todd Baldwin at Island Press, who is everything one could want in an editor. Production editor Cecilia González did a wonderful job of copyediting, for which we are deeply grateful.

The Complete Guide to Environmental Careers in the 21st Century is a project of the Environmental Careers Organization and draws on the strength of the people who manage ECO's respected environmental intern program, national career conference, and other programs. Thank you to the 1997–1998 staff in Boston, Cleveland, San Francisco, and Seattle for their dedication to environmental career education. Your work is a source of daily inspiration to me.

Finally, I would like to dedicate this book to the more than 7,000 men and women who have begun environmental careers as ECO interns over the last twenty-five years, and to the generous and thoughtful environmental professionals who serve as project advisors and mentors. I started the Environmental Careers Organization in 1972 with a vision that college students and recent graduates could make a difference in their communities if they worked together with today's leaders on well-designed projects. Twenty-five years and thousands of interns later, that vision is alive and well. My thanks to everyone who has helped make my internship the best one of all.

John R. Cook, Jr.
President
The Environmental Careers Organization
September 23, 1998
Boston, Massachusetts

Part I

ENVIRONMENTAL CAREER AND EDUCATION OVERVIEW

1 Introduction to Environmental Careers

THE FIRST half of the 21st century will be a critical era in the evolution of environmental careers. It has been the task of the past thirty years to raise environmental awareness, control and reverse unregulated pollution, and create public and private organizations dedicated to conservation and environmental protection. The work has been difficult and expensive, but the current generation has made remarkable progress. In fact, it has been nothing short of a revolution.

In many ways, however, the next generation of environmental professionals faces challenges that are infinitely more difficult than those that have confronted the current one. The task at hand today is not only to control pollution, but to prevent it; to not only slow the rate of habitat and soil loss, but to reverse it; and to not only regulate unsustainable activity, but to create a sustainable way of life on a crowded planet.

Where will the human race find solutions to its environmental problems? We must find them *everywhere*, and at the same time. We need dramatic improvements in technology, protection of plant and animal habitats, energy conservation and development of renewables, creation of market incentives that complement government action, greater social and racial justice, and better education and ecological understanding. The new generation must pursue all these goals *and* protect the gains of the last half century.

We can safely say that there is enough work ahead to keep all serious environmental workers busy for a lifetime. Conservation, environmental protection, and creating a sustainable future are *the* work of the 21st century.

It's a sobering yet optimistic time that you've chosen to begin an environmental career. As you set out into this changing territory, you'll need a map. This book is designed to be a useful guide for your adventure. Congratulations on your commitment and interest! Let's get started.

MAPPING THE TERRITORY

The environmental world is a large one. There are careers for scientists, engineers, journalists, business people, activists, social scientists, accountants, computer specialists, educators, attorneys, health professionals, and more. Whatever your future interests (or current background), your environmental career will be influenced by trends that are dramatically changing the environmental world.

This chapter provides an introduction to "the big picture." First, we'll quickly review some of the largest environmental challenges facing the nation, and the world. Second, we'll examine the process of environmental employment creation in government, industry, academia, and the nonprofit sector. Third, we'll provide a statistical look at environmental employment today— How many environmental workers are out there? What do they do? Where do they work? Fourth, we'll describe twelve career tracks that are important now, or just coming into view.

ENVIRONMENTAL CHALLENGES FOR A NEW CENTURY

The environmental and conservation challenges before us are many, but some loom larger than others. Here are ten selected "mega-challenges" that will certainly engage the attention of environmental professionals as we enter the 21st century.

POLLUTION PREVENTION —WELCOME TO THE THIRD WAVE

The environmental movement in this country is just about one-hundred years old. The movement's first wave began in the 1890s and lasted until the early 1960s. It was characterized by the growth of a conservation movement that focused mainly on protection of wild and scenic areas and a general appreciation of nature in a rapidly urbanizing world. The second wave lasted from roughly 1964 until the early 1990s and focused primarily on pollution control and remediation—reducing "point source" emissions into the air, land, and water, and beginning to deal with the legacy of uncontrolled dumping. The environmental progress from 1970 to 1993 should be remembered as one of the most dramatic social achievements in our history.

We are now in the third wave of environmentalism, which emerges from the recognition that pollution is not simply industrial emissions, but a by-product of social demands—of the way we live. The by-word of the age is *pollution prevention*. Since the passage of the Pollution Prevention Act in 1990, Congress is on record as formally requiring that pollution prevention be our preferred method of dealing with environmental degradation. What can't be prevented is to be recycled. What can't be recycled is to be treated. Disposal is the last (and least preferred) option.

Your work will be done in the era of pollution prevention, and you should prepare for it now. If your education and experience prepare you primarily to *manage* pollution and clean up past mistakes, you will be behind the times.

GLOBAL CLIMATE CHANGE

Global warming is, perhaps, *the* environmental issue of the 21st century. The challenges are huge. In some ways, however, the diagnosis is straightforward. We must rapidly reduce energy use and develop alternatives to fossil fuels, which can be used by all the people of the world. We must stop (and reverse) the destruction of the world's forests. We must stabilize world population (although debates rage about acceptable levels). Bill McKibben reminds us that most environmental degradation affects a specific place, no matter how destructively. Global climate change, on the other hand, affects the whole planet, and for a long time. If there is a single piece of work for our generation, it lies here.

The challenges of global climate change create some obvious job opportunities for atmospheric scientists, air quality engineers, energy efficiency experts, and those who can commercialize renewable energy sources. The crisis will also require the creativity of policy analysts to draft international agreements, educators to help us change deeply ingrained behaviors, transportation planners who can get us out of our cars, and more.

INTEGRATING ENVIRONMENTAL COSTS AND BENEFITS INTO THE GLOBAL MARKET ECONOMY

We live in a global economy that is becoming more and more integrated every day. There are no holdouts. The old Communist bloc has collapsed and national boundaries (and environmental laws) mean less and less in a global marketplace. Treaties and regulations at the international level can help immensely. In some ways, however, these are merely holding actions. The real work lies in designing policies and institutions that make the market system take environmental degradation into account as a matter of course.

BIODIVERSITY AND MASSIVE SPECIES EXTINCTIONS

We are wiping out plant and animal species at astonishing rates, primarily through the destruction of habitats. Slowing the rate of habitat loss (and then reversing it) will require political will, scientific research and creativity in planning. It will require that we protect and manage lands effectively, as well as educate private landowners and users about the value of biodiversity. Environmental professionals will play a leading role throughout the world.

Marine scientists with the National Oceanic and Atmospheric Administration study and protect coastal zone ecosystems.

CREATING SUSTAINABLE COMMUNITIES

Many environmental issues are framed as a need to *stop harmful activities*. The creation of sustainable communities asks us to invent new realities and create environmentally sustainable ways of living our lives. The sustainable communities movement is less about "solving problems" than it is about creating entire communities that are more fulfilling and less destructive than the old ones. The movement asks fundamental questions, including: What does a sustainable way of life look like on a planet of more than six billion people? Eight billion? Ten billion? If not fossil fuels, then what? If not urban and suburban sprawl, then what? If not industrial farming, then what? If not ever greater levels of "growth," then what? In 1977, Wendell Berry wrote that we could not yet imagine what a real alternative to our present way of life looked like. In our time, examples will begin to take shape.

ENVIRONMENTAL JUSTICE

A clean and healthy environment is the birthright of *all* people, regardless of how much money they have, the color of their skin, where they live, or their nationality. This isn't how the world works today. People of color and the poor, both in this country and throughout the world, bear a disproportionate impact from environmental pollution. It does no good to "solve" an environmental problem for one group of people by displacing it onto another. We must build an environmental movement that addresses the needs of people of all races, classes, ethnic groups, and nationalities. We cannot have one environmental movement that is about protecting miles of beach for walks and wildlife, and another for people whose neighborhoods are ringed by toxic waste dumps.

Fortunately, an environmental justice movement has been rising steadily over the last ten years. Led by committed Hispanic, African, Asian, and Native Americans, environmental justice leaders are remaking the face of environmentalism for an era when Americans of European descent will be the minority. It remains to be seen, however, whether environmentalism will become a united movement involving all people or will fragment into factions based on class, race, and ethnicity.

ECOLOGICAL LITERACY

Education is no guarantee of environmentally sound action. A biologist with a Ph.D. can live as destructively as the next person. Nonetheless, understanding the systems that make up our natural world allows one to make choices on the basis of knowledge, and this is always to the good. People are less likely to be taken in by extremists of any stripe. For a democracy to have a discussion about environmental concerns, the citizens must have basic levels of ecological literacy. This is currently not the case.

MONITORING THE EARTH

One hundred years from now, at the end of another century, those who follow us may marvel that our greatest achievement was not that we reached zero emissions in pollution or that we broke our dependence on fossil fuels. These may be seen as accomplishments of the moment, brought on by pressing need. No, it's possible that our descendents will look in awe at us as the first generation that monitored the Earth in real time—that showed us the living Earth. Those who work in fields such as remote sensing and long-term monitoring projects are performing an immense service. They provide factual answers to politically charged questions about biodiversity, global warming, water pollution and use, illegal dumping, soil erosion, and toxics in the environment.

WATER

Clean water is an excellent barometer of ecological health, and water for human use is essential for community life. And yet 20 percent of the world's population—over one billion people—lack access to potable water. Demands for water far exceed its supply. We use almost seven times as much water today as we used in 1900, and economic improvements in less developed countries promise another sizable increase in the next few years. Our demands for water reduce flows, which affect fish and wildlife. How will we assure steady supplies of water for drinking, agriculture, industry, and the needs of other species on an equitable basis? This is a challenge that is at least as great as the water pollution issues, which faced the first generation of environmental professionals.

MULTIMEDIA, ECOSYSTEMS, AND "PLACE-BASED" APPROACHES TO ENVIRONMENTAL PROTECTION

When the Environmental Protection Agency (EPA) was formed in 1970, it set up departments for different environmental "media" (e.g., air, water, land), and for different types of waste (e.g., solid, hazardous waste). This structure was widely imitated and has had a major impact on environmental careers. The environment, however, isn't divided up this way. The natural world is a holistic system. In recent years, environmental management has moved toward integrated approaches that reflect the way nature works. Ecosystems management, "place-based" protection, strategic environmental management, watershed planning, and "multimedia" management are all part of this trend. Each chapter of this book shows examples of professionals crossing lines and working together to solve problems.

TAKING UP THE CHALLENGE: FOUR DRIVERS OF ENVIRONMENTAL EMPLOYMENT

Many of us have a basic understanding of employment in such fields as financial services, entertainment, food service, health care, retail sales, and education because we interact with these industries in our daily lives. The process by which these jobs come into being, and continue to be supported, is fairly clear.

In the environmental field, job creation is less clear. It's fair to ask a very basic question: Where do environmental jobs come from? Obviously, environmental employment is generated when government, industry, or the nonprofit sector spends money to hire people. But, what makes a business or agency spend money on environmental employees? What forces provide the funds for your career as an environmental professional?

Aspiring environmental workers would do well to ponder this question early and often. Environmental fields are undergoing rapid change. The sooner you get in touch with the underlying drivers that result in environmental expenditures and job creation, the sooner you will be able to see the waves of change that create and sweep away environmental careers.

In the environmental career world, there are four basic drivers: political agreement supporting legal and regulatory requirements, economics and the marketplace, environmental values, and technology. Let's explore each one of these.

DRIVER 1: CREATING ENVIRONMENTAL CAREERS THROUGH LAWS AND REGULATIONS

In 1970, fewer than 230,000 people were employed in "environmental" and conservation work on expenditures of around $32 billion. By 1998, nearly seven times as much—$200 billion—was being spent annually in the United States on environmental protection, supporting the jobs of nearly 2.5 million people. To put this in perspective, consider the size of some other parts of the economy. According to the *Environmental Business Journal*, 1994 revenues to the "environmental industry" were $172 billion in 1994. In the same year, the paper products industry generated $144 billion, petroleum refining $128 billion, aerospace $105 billion, and motor vehicles $198 billion. Environmental work, then, is *big*.

What happened to create such considerable environmental job growth in such a brief time?

In short, the environmental movement. American citizens decided that environmental protection was a serious priority. Over the last thirty-five years, citizens and legislators have created a large infrastructure of environmental laws and regulations that has, in turn, created millions of jobs.

Federal, state, and local laws create and define environmental jobs in several ways. First, and most importantly, the alphabet soup of laws *creates compliance responsibilities* that regulated entities must meet. Take the example of air quality. To comply with air quality regulations, the regulated spend money on lawyers, consultants, equipment manufacturers, installers and maintenance people, analytical laboratories, record keeping, public affairs staff, toxicologists, engineers, and research and development scientists.

Second, the passage of environmental laws *creates government employment* for enforcement, education, community involvement, monitoring, research, program management, information management, grant and contract administration, direct service delivery, and more. Behind every environmental worker in government there is a law that created the need for that person.

Third, government action may result in the *purchase and management of public land*, which is carried out by public employees, contractors, interns, and volunteers. Conservation workers at the state and local level eagerly watch budget appropriations for the purchase of new land for wildlife refuges, parks, recreation areas, forests, and other managed properties.

Fourth, environmental laws may require the distribution of funds in the form of *grants and loans*, which create employment, especially at the state government level and in the academic research community.

Finally, laws and regulations *create an industry* of lobbyists, citizen monitors, attorneys, journalists, and policy experts who bring lawsuits, advocate changes in regulations, argue for new (or fewer) laws, and inform the public.

Environmental law and regulation created the modern environmental professions and has been far and away the largest driver in employment creation.

It is difficult to overestimate the power of government action. For thirty years, in fact, environmental career monitoring has been synonymous with watching for changes in Washington, D.C., and the state capitals.

What *kind* of employment is created by law and regulation? It's a question worth exploring in depth, because the answer has had a major impact on the education, training, and career paths of environmental professionals.

Until recently, environmental law and regulation in the United States were largely a matter of "command and control"—a government agency would set out detailed rules to be met (sometimes with prescribed methods) and regulated businesses and governments would work to demonstrate that they were in compliance with the law. Help with funding was often the carrot that accompanied the stick. This style was the rule not only in the control of air and water pollution, but in land-use planning, fish and game management, and many other areas.

Command and control regulation creates a professional focus on knowing the rules, and staying within them. For years, the focus of environmental work has been as much about obeying environmental law as about solving our pressing problems. Environmental workers often felt like (and were treated like) the police. At its worst, command and control keeps the focus on better ways to *comply*, instead of on dramatic improvements in environmental quality and conservation.

Command and control approaches have a powerful upside, however. They worked for the first generation of environmental problems. Creating detailed requirements backed up by the power of law made things happen that would never have happened otherwise. We needed to spend billions on secondary treatment plants, and command and control measures made that happen. We needed to reduce emissions at millions of "point sources" throughout the nation, begin protection for endangered species, purchase large expanses for wilderness and refuges, and start to clean up our toxic waste sites.

Americans today owe a huge debt to the activists, environmental professionals, academics and everyday citizens who created our basic environmental laws and regulations. These command and control regulations (and outright bans) will continue to be used for many environmental problems. Some argue that we continue to need more, not less, regulatory intervention.

But the era of command and control as a guiding principle is fading away, both as the basis of environmental policy and as an employment generating "driver" for environmental professionals. This has immense implications for the next generation of environmental workers, in and out of government. Simply put, it's not enough anymore to know and follow the rules (if it ever was). It's not enough to wait for the next round of regulatory upgrades to create new work.

Today's environmental career seeker is being asked for new ideas, innovative technologies, and nonadversarial strategies. Citizens and businesses are looking for answers that cost less, can be implemented faster, are flexible and adaptable, and achieve dramatic levels of improvement for our investment. To respond, you must understand the legal and regulatory authorities at work in your field. But you must also seek answers that go far beyond compliance if you want to be competitive. You must have the skill and desire to solve problems.

DRIVER 2: ECONOMICS AND THE MARKETPLACE

We've seen that creating environmental careers through regulation has its limits. But if people are not forced by law to spend money on environmental protection, what else can induce them to do so?

In a market economy, one option is obvious. If people or corporations can save money, or (better still) make money by protecting the environment, many will do it. In recent years, we have seen how marketplace drivers can create innovative environmental career opportunities. Economic forces are becoming more and more powerful in environmental job creation, as this book will show.

Businesses are interested in operating profits, which can be enhanced as much by cutting costs as by increasing revenues. Even businesses whose products and services are not inherently "environmental" can improve their bottom line by producing less waste, which is expensive to deal with. In other words, environmental benefits are a by-product of the desire to reduce costs, improve productivity, and be more competitive.

The regulatory approaches discussed earlier play an interesting role in pushing businesses to invest in environmental solutions. By requiring businesses, and ultimately consumers, to pay to eliminate pollution, regulations bring more of the true cost of our way of life into the market system. These costs include polluted air and water, habitat loss, resource depletion, and damage to human health and safety.

It's useful to remember when regulations are attacked in favor of "the market" that regulation and taxation may be necessary to make the market respond at all. Why conserve energy if it's cheap? Why find substitutes for toxic chemicals if they are inexpensive, and legal? As the true costs are seen, the desire to reduce them grows, not only by preapproved means, but through other creative actions. Now, everyone—accountants, risk managers, process engineers, administrative assistants, marketing and sales people, fleet managers, contracting officers—can contribute to environmental solutions. The move to reduce waste, coupled with the legal necessity to do so, is producing talk about the possibility of zero emissions in some industries, a truly remarkable turn of events.

It's fairly easy to see how the drive to *save* money can produce environmental results and employment. Can whole businesses be built, however, on products and services that protect the environment and actually turn a profit?

Many businesses believe they can, and have, enhanced profits by appealing to customers who share their commitment to a clean environment. Of course, some companies engage in mere "green washing" (creating an ecofriendly image through colorful marketing alone), but a growing number are engaged in real change in their products and processes.

How? Think about your own buying and desires. Do you opt for organic food; 100 percent post-consumer recycled paper products; nontoxic cleaners; low-energy use appliances; wood certified as sustainably grown; ecotourism over the grand hotel; the string bag versus the plastic sack; curbside recycling; public transit over adding one more car to the road; renewable energy (if you could get it) over fossil fuels?

Multiply yourself by millions of others and add in the purchasing power of businesses and government agencies as well. Get the picture? All of the businesses that make ecofriendly products hire people, and although only a few of these people can be said formally to have environmental careers, they are making a large difference.

DRIVER 3: ENVIRONMENTAL VALUES

Protecting the natural world is a powerful value. Many of us don't need to be forced by law or lured by money to pursue it. We willingly spend time and money to create environmental and conservation organizations that, in turn, hire people and support careers. American individuals, foundations, and corporations gave over $4 billion in charitable donations to environmental, conservation, and animal welfare causes in 1997. Government agencies added to that amount with hundreds of millions in government grants and contracts to nonprofit groups.

Thousands of environmental professionals have jobs because people care about environmental quality and want to do something about it. This widespread citizen support is crucial to the growth of environmental careers (not to mention the protection of ecosystems). It's worth remembering that community support takes work to maintain, and that environmental professionals have a special duty to help broaden the circle of involvement.

The "values" driver gives us land trusts like The Nature Conservancy, The Trust for Public Land and hundreds of smaller groups. It's produced watershed organizations, dozens of environmental justice advocates, hiking and trail maintenance groups, animal rescue shelters, nature centers, big national activists (e.g., the Natural Resources Defense Council, the Environmental Defense Fund, the Sierra Club, and the National Wildlife Federation), and small neighborhood groups that fight local battles.

Our desire to understand, celebrate, and enjoy the natural world is also part of the driver that supports careers for nature writers, photographers, videographers, journalists, outdoor adventure leaders, environmental educators, scientists, academics, and more.

DRIVER 4: TECHNOLOGY

Technology is both a creator and a destroyer of environmental careers. Each new generation of remote sensing technology wipes out the need for some of the biologists who did field surveys. A new CD-ROM can do the work of a legal assistant. Water sampling that used to require two teams of chemists—one in the field and one in the lab—might now be done on-site by a couple of people in a van. Finding a replacement for a popular toxic substance can eliminate the need for people to store, ship, monitor, and dispose of hazardous waste. A talented geographic information system technician can develop in a day maps, that once would have taken a team of interns weeks to create.

Every single environmental career is being altered by technology, without exception. The obvious beneficiaries of this reality are not only the people who can use the new generation of technologies, but those who are exceptionally skilled in creating them in the first place.

Throughout this book, you will see examples of these four drivers at work. As you develop your own career, remember that no one driver exists alone. All four interact constantly to create new patterns of environmental and conservation jobs. Let's take a look at what that pattern looks like today.

WHERE THE JOBS ARE: AN ENVIRONMENTAL CAREER OVERVIEW

Hundreds of thousands of environmental professionals work for government agencies, from well-known players such as the National Park Service to the smallest local water district. Although overall growth in government employment has slowed, the public sector continues to be a dominant employer and a prime mover in the development of new policy directions for environmental problem solving.

PUBLIC SECTOR

Federal Government. The federal government is, by far, the largest single employer in the environmental career world. In late 1997, over 230,000 people worked for federal environmental and conservation agencies, according to a survey carried out by the Environmental Careers Organization (ECO) (see table 1.1).

The environmental agencies of the federal government employ (or fund) large numbers of professionals in certain fields. The Geological Survey employs more environmentally related earth scientists than anyone else. Nearly a quarter of professional foresters work at the Forest Service. The National Oceanic and Atmospheric Administration (NOAA) is probably the largest employer of oceanographers and atmospheric scientists, and helps fund many others. The field of range management is dominated by the Bureau of Land Management, and the park professionals who serve as superintendents at Yellowstone, Yosemite, Denali, and the Grand Canyon have reached a career pinnacle. The U.S. Fish and Wildlife Service is a major employer of biologists. The Department of Agriculture's Natural Resources Conservation Service employs a large number of the nation's soil scientists. Much of the nation's renewable energy

A wildlife biology survey crew in Oregon prepares for a day in the field.

research is done by the Department of Energy. Finally, the Environmental Protection Agency (EPA) has helped define modern environmentalism over the last twenty-eight years.

Throughout this book, you will find information about employment trends at the major federal agencies, as well as commentary about policy directions that influence other private and public sector employers, and website addresses to locate more information on your own.

Individual agencies change with new political climates and major legislation or executive orders. Generally, however, federal agencies are recasting their role in the direction of developing broad regulatory guidelines, conducting research, providing technical assistance and education to others, turning over authority to the states, and overseeing enforcement by state and local entities.

There are other trends you should be aware of. In general, the federal government workforce continues to shrink. It is hiring more consultants, private contractors, and temporary employees. Increasingly, federal employees manage nonfederal employees, who carry out much of the government's work. Finally, the workforce is growing older. A wave of retirees is inevitable. Whether or not this will generate an equal wave of new employment is questionable.

State Government. Although the federal government is large, nearly twice as many people work on environmental issues at the state level; 4,587,000 Americans worked for state government in 1996 (including 1,219,000 part-time employees), and roughly 10 percent of state employment involves envi-

Table 1.1 Federal Government Employment at Environmental and Conservation Agencies (1997)

Agency	Permanent	Temp/Seasonal	Total
National Park Service	15,729	6,000	21,729
Bureau of Land Management	8,760	1,900	10,660
Fish and Wildlife Service	7,000	500	7,500
U.S. Geological Survey	10,395	—	10,395
Other interior agencies	21,843	—	21,843
Environmental Protection Agency	18,165	—	18,165
USDA Forest Service	30,000	15,000	45,000
Other agriculture (enviro-related)	11,000	—	11,000
Department of Energy	16,983	—	16,983
Transportation (enviro-related)	12,610	—	12,610
National Oceanic and Atmospheric	7,500	—	7,500
Army Corps of Engineers	27,454	—	27,454
Other agencies	21,000	—	21,000
TOTAL	208,439	23,400	231,839

Source: Environmental Careers Organization.

ronmental work (broadly defined), producing an environmental workforce of 459,000 workers. Included are employees at state colleges and universities.

We have seen that the federal government is changing its role, from one of detailed management to broad goal setting, assistance, and oversight. This often means a transfer of authority to the states. Some even argue that ownership and management of many federal lands and forests might be given over to state governments. Unfortunately, transfer of responsibility is rarely accompanied by increased revenues. In addition, state legislatures may be trying to shrink *their* permanent workforces by transferring work to private contractors and local government.

In addition to increased responsibility for former federal programs, state governments create programs of their own that deal with citizenry concerns. State governments lead the way, for example, in the creation of laws to promote recycling and the protection of watersheds.

The structure of state environmental work is roughly the same throughout the United States. Although the names vary, most states have agencies in the following areas:

- Environmental protection
- Fisheries and wildlife
- Food and agriculture
- Parks and recreation
- Water resources
- Public health
- Public utilities
- Community and economic development
- Coastal zone management (if applicable)

- Emergency services
- Energy resources
- Planning (if state land planning is in force)

If you're interested in state government, be sure to look at the full range of agencies and not just the ones that are obviously "environmental."

Local Government. There are over 70,500 local governments in the United States, employing 5,948,000 people in 1996 (see table 1.2). Estimating the number of environmental workers at the local level is difficult. For one thing, employment counts for the "environmental industry" (see table 1.3) take in thousands of workers at publicly owned water supply and wastewater treatment plants, as well as those that are privately owned. After subtracting these workers, ECO estimates that roughly 8 percent of local government employees do environmental and conservation work, or 475,840 people.

Local government work is "hands on" environmental work. It's where recycling bins are picked up and the contents separated and sold, water and wastewater is treated, land-use plans are written and monitored, street trees are planted and trimmed, stormwater runoff systems are maintained, and community gardens are managed. Local government keeps the buses running and installs bike paths.

There is a lot of environmental work being done at the local level, but, ironically, jobs can be hard to find. A given town or city may have only a small handful of environmental professionals, and some of those may have a variety of nonenvironmental duties. In addition, "privatization" is a powerful movement at the local level, as towns and cities contract out work to business. The sheer number of employers can also work against the job seeker. Because employment is spread out over thousands of different jurisdictions, it's hard to keep track of more than a few at any one time.

Nonetheless, local government is a big part of the future of environmental-

Table 1.2 Local Government Employment in Environmental and Conservation Work (1996)

Municipal Government		*Towns and Townships*	
Entities:	19,279	Entities:	16,656
Full-time:	2,199,000	Employment:	410,000
Part-time:	440,000	Enviros:	32,800
Enviros:	211,120		
County Governments		*Special Districts*	
Entities:	3,043	Entities:	31,555
Employment:	2,251,000	Full-time:	497,000
Enviros:	180,080	Part-time:	151,000
		Enviros:	51,840

ism in this country. As Congress and the state legislatures shrink the govern-ment workforce while trying to increase environmental quality, more of the actual work is pushed to the local level. Local experiments are among the most creative in the environmental world.

To get an idea for the structure of local government where you live, simply take a walk through the Blue Pages of your telephone book.

Schools. There are at least 14,400 school systems in the United States, employ-ing 3,476,000 full-time and 1,107,000 part-time workers. Allowing for custo-dians, principals, bus drivers, administrators, secretaries, and so forth, the lion's share of this 4.6 million workforce is, of course, teachers.

It's impossible to make an accurate count of how many teachers could be categorized as "environmental" educators. Arguably, however, there is no "environmental" work more important than the education of our children. In many ways, it's the foundation upon which everything else rests. To everyone reading this book who chooses a teaching career and improves the nation's ecological literacy and commitment to citizenship, a hearty congratulations.

PRIVATE SECTOR

Private sector environmental employment is found throughout the economy—in the "environmental industry," at regulated companies such as electric utili-

Table 1.3   Estimated Environmental Industry Employment

Area	Entities	Jobs	Billions ($)
Services			
Analytical services	1,400	20,000	1.2
Wastewater treatment	27,000	113,700	25.9
Solid waste management	5,900	229,600	35.8
Hazardous waste management	2,500	53,300	5.6
Remediation/Ind. services	3,800	100,000	8.9
Consulting and engineering	5,800	162,800	15.6
Equipment			
Water (includes chemicals)	2,600	100,700	19.0
Instrument/Information system	500	24,800	3.4
Air pollution	800	83,300	16.2
Waste management	2,000	88,200	12.2
Process/Prevention technology	300	15,200	1.0
Resources			
Water utility	58,000	118,000	25.3
Resource recovery	2,000	128,300	16.9
Environmental energy	600	24,400	2.3
TOTAL	113,200	1,262,300	189.3

Primary source: Environmental Business International.

ties and manufacturers, at service businesses (e.g., law, architecture, insurance, finance, and so forth), and in a growing number of "green" businesses aimed at ecologically savvy consumers. More than ever before, the private sector is a source of job and entrepreneurial opportunities for those who care about the environment.

The Environmental Industry. The Environmental Business Journal estimates that there are over 113,000 "revenue producing organizations" in the environmental industry. These businesses and agencies supported nearly 1.3 million jobs on revenues of $189 billion in 1997. California, Texas, New York, Pennsylvania, and Florida are among the leading states for environmental industry employment.

From 1970 to 1988, the environmental industry grew rapidly. In the 1970s, growth was 9–11 percent annually. The 1980s saw even better growth, with around 10 percent in the early 1980s and more than 12 percent from 1985 to 1988, peaking in 1988 at 15 percent. Throughout the 1990s, growth has been flat to moderate, ranging from a low of 2 percent to a high of about 6 percent. Clearly, the industry has matured, although new growth spikes cannot be ruled out.

What activities make up the environmental industry? As table 1.3 shows, the industry can be roughly divided into *services, equipment,* and *resources.* Each sector deserves some explanation.

The services and resources areas are certainly the most visible part of the industry to the general public. The most prominent services are in solid waste (e.g., operating municipal and commercial recycling, landfill, and "resource recovery" facilities) and water (e.g., constructing and operating water utilities and wastewater treatment plants).

The area of consulting and engineering, which represents "environmental work" to many aspiring professionals, is a smaller part of the overall industry than many believe. The consulting field is an important barometer of environmental employment, however. Consulting firms are usually the first to unearth new trends and service needs. The consulting sector also hires a disproportionately large number of highly trained scientists and engineers, when compared with the other sectors.

Hazardous waste management and remediation activity is still a contributor to total employment, and clean-up activity on old military bases, Superfund sites, and Department of Energy lands can create sharp increases in jobs. Increased interest in "brownfields" redevelopment (see chapters 4 and 9) could create a boom if government and investors spend as expected.

Over 25 percent of all environmental industry employment is involved with designing, selling, installing, and servicing environmental equipment and chemicals, especially to water and wastewater treatment plants. The equipment sector uses large numbers of salespeople, technicians, and distributors.

As we enter the 21st century, the environmental industry is going through wrenching changes, brought on by shifts in the drivers we discussed earlier, and by general business trends in the economy. Until recently, the industry relied on new generations of government regulation and investment for its bread and butter. Government shifts in priorities from general pollution control (1970s), to hazardous waste remediation (1980s), to air pollution issues (early 1990s), to water concerns (late 1990s) have created roller-coaster employment rides.

New government actions are more uncertain today, as we saw earlier in our discussion of command and control regulation. Therefore, the industry is searching for ways to provide services to business and government that respond to marketplace needs that are not generated by government activity. This has proven to be a difficult venture, with as many failures as successes; however, four areas have emerged that hold promise. These are strategic environmental management, pollution prevention, environmental energy sources, and private management of water supplies. For more on these areas, see the waste, air, water, and energy chapters.

Mergers, acquisitions, and breakups have roiled the industry, as firms search for the right balance between size and flexibility to deliver environmental goods and services. Current trends point to an industry that will have a few dominant giants and many small "boutique" companies with fewer medium-size firms able to compete.

A major opportunity for private sector environmental employers lies overseas. The global market for environmental products and services is estimated at nearly $400 billion dollars annually, roughly 37 percent of which is in the United States. Overall growth in the U.S. at the end of the 1990s has, however, been extremely small. In contrast, other parts of the world are projected to experience an exploding demand for environmental work. Asia (not including Japan) is projected to grow at more than 15 percent annually (assuming recovery from the 1998 economic problems). Latin America will grow at 12 percent, and Africa at 10 percent. Although American industry faces heavy pressure from German, French, British, and Japanese firms, U.S. firms are competitive in most areas.

Regardless of these challenges, the environmental industry remains a great place for environmental professionals to build a satisfying career, especially for those with an entrepreneurial bent and a desire for fast-paced work environments that are focused on results.

OTHER PRIVATE EMPLOYERS

Beyond the environmental industry, the private sector is full of career opportunities. Although formal statistics are not available, here are a few of the places you will find environmental work being done.

Regulated Companies. Most larger companies have set up their own "environment, health, and safety" (EHS) departments to deal with regulatory compliance, pollution prevention, worker safety, risk management, and emergency services. Industries with well-staffed departments include electric utilities, mining, forest products, petroleum, chemicals, heavy manufacturing, metals, electronics, food products, transportation, hospitals, and consumer goods. Some companies also run their own analytical laboratories to test air, soil, and water samples.

Corporate environmental managers have noted considerable changes in their responsibilities in the last few years. The most challenging has been the attempt to integrate environmental concerns into the basic operations of the business; that is solving environmental problems through the mutual work of professionals in operations, product design, process manufacturing, finance and accounting, legal, and so forth. Environmental departments are no longer considered lonely backwaters that constantly bring bad news requiring expenditures that bring no financial returns.

Nonetheless, EHS professionals are still required to know the regulations and keep the company in compliance. Common professionals hired include engineers, chemists, environmental scientists, toxicologists, industrial hygienists, and technicians. Competition is often intense, and industry-specific experience is usually desired.

Law Firms. Environmental law is firmly ensconced as a specialty, both in law schools and in most law firms. The sheer bulk of case law on environmental concerns, and the risk of not knowing it, are so large (and change so fast) that legal employment will remain strong well into the next century. Competition, however, will certainly increase. Environmental law is a popular specialty for today's law students, even as demand has dropped somewhat.

The Financial and Insurance Industries. "Investment banking *is* social policy," says Allen Hershkowitz, senior scientist at the Natural Resources Defense Council. "Investment banking is more important to environmentalists, objectively, than nine out of ten things Congress is going to do."

In a similar vein, environmental writer Bill McKibben asks, "What does it mean that alone among the Earth's great pools of money and power, insurance companies are beginning to take the idea of global climate change quite seriously?" Environmental work is growing in both of these industries, as well as at accounting firms, business consulting outfits, and related companies.

Other Industries. Environmental employment is found in many other places throughout the private economy, including the health care industry, agriculture, media and entertainment, pharmaceuticals, and transportation. For dozens of examples of environmental work throughout the economy, see *Green at Work* by Susan Cohn (Island Press 1995), which is a great book that explores opportunities for people of all backgrounds who want to protect the environment while they pursue a business career.

NONPROFIT ORGANIZATIONS

No one knows how many environmental nonprofit groups there are in the United States. Estimates range as low as 4,000 and as high as 10,000 or more. There has been a large (and welcome) growth in small, local, grassroots groups in the last ten years. Many of these groups, however, have no staff. The number of nonprofit groups of interest to career seekers drops precipitously if one eliminates all volunteer groups. For example, the 1998–99 *EnviroDirectory* for New England lists about 200 environmental and conservation nonprofits in the six-state region, and it covers almost all of the well-known groups.

Although no comprehensive census has been done, we do know that there are:

- Over 1,200 land trusts;
- Over 2,000 water-related groups;
- 1,450 nature centers;
- Hundreds of chapters of national and regional groups, such as Sierra Club, Audubon Society, Izaak Walton League, and so forth;
- More than 200 environmental justice groups;
- Thousands of small neighborhood and community groups devoted to environmental improvement;
- Hundreds of animal rescue and rehabilitation groups;
- 90 aquariums; and
- Over 1,000 student groups on college campuses.

The list can go on to include church projects, garden clubs, scout troops, rails-to-trails organizations, summer camps, museums, and more.

The structure of staffed nonprofit organizations, wherever they are, is remarkably similar. Usually, there is an executive director who manages the organization, as well as an administrative assistant. In many cases, that's the whole staff. Larger organizations will also have a fundraising and membership department, program staff for major activities, finance and accounting personnel, education and communications people, lobbyists and attorneys, a volunteer coordinator, and project coordinators for grant-funded initiatives. Core staff are supplemented by interns and volunteers.

The largest environmental nonprofit group is certainly The Nature Conservancy, which employs over 2,500 people all over the world, as well as many seasonal employees and interns. Most groups are considerably smaller.

Thirty of the better-known groups in the nonprofit world include: American Farmland Trust, American Forests, American Lung Association, American Rivers, Appalachian Mountain Club, Audubon Society, Clean Water Action, Conservation Foundation, Defenders of Wildlife, Earth Island Institute, EcoTrust, Environmental Defense Fund, Friends of the Earth, Greenpeace, Izaak Walton League, Land Trust Alliance, League of Conservation Voters, National Parks and Conservation Association, National Wildlife Federation, Natural Resources Defense Council, Public Citizen, Public Interest Research

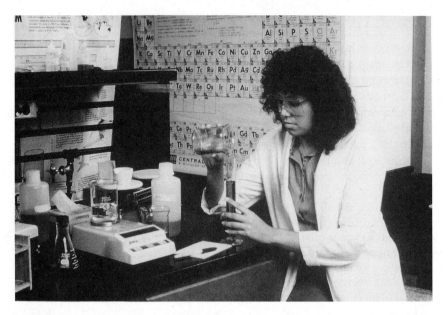

Analyzing air, water, and soil samples is an essential part of environmental protection work.

Group, Rails to Trails Conservancy, Resources for the Future, Sierra Club, Trust for Public Land, Wilderness Society, World Resources Institute, World Wildlife Fund, and Worldwatch Institute.

Taken together, these thirty influential groups employ perhaps 4,000 people, probably less. The Environmental Defense Fund (EDF), for instance, is one of the best-known environmental groups in the world. The paid staff at EDF numbers 160 people, and it is a big environmental group. It's not surprising that full-time staff positions at well-known environmental nonprofits are among the most competitive of all environmental career offerings.

The environmental nonprofit world is headquarted in a few major cities. Certainly, Washington, D.C., is the geographic center of nonprofit environmentalism. Many of the groups above have a heavy concentration of staff people in the nation's capital, as well as its Maryland and Virginia suburbs. New York City, Boston, San Francisco, Chicago, Denver, and Seattle are also popular centers for large nonprofits.

Nonprofit work in the late 1990s has a few consistent trends. First, management standards have increased. Boards are demanding that directors and managers have (or get) strong management and leadership skills. Passion and commitment are not enough. Second, revenue-generating ability is crucial. A lot of people can come up with good ideas, but fewer can make them pay through fee-for-service programs, membership, sales of supporting goods and materials, and fundraising. Those who can are in demand. Third, nonprofits are learning to work together. Funders (and the public) are asking that nonprofit managers learn to form effective alliances and collaborations. Fifth, nonprofit environmental groups are learning to diversify, creating an environmental movement that appeals to all Americans, regardless of class, race, and ethnicity. Finally, environmentalism is returning to the grassroots with the understanding that a concerned, involved, informed, and politically savvy citizenry is essential for environmental success.

ACADEMIA

There are more than 2,400 four-year colleges and over 1,400 two-year colleges in the United States. Almost all of them have programs that help prepare people for environmental and conservation fields, from basic biology, earth science, chemistry, and geography programs to the best-known graduate schools, such as the University of Michigan's School of Natural Resources.

The story of environmental employment at colleges, universities, and research institutes is a confusing one. On the one hand, environmental majors at the undergraduate level are extremely popular. Dozens of interdisciplinary environmental studies and environmental science degree programs have been created in the last few years, many of them in response to student demand as much as educational need. Within disciplines such as biology, chemistry, geography, earth science, political science, toxicology, and engineering, "environmental" foci are popular selections. In professional schools for journalism, law, and policy, the environmental track is a desirable one. Finally, large numbers of environmental technology (technician) programs have sprung up at community colleges and vocational schools.

Does all of this mean a booming market for full professors throughout the nation? Well, yes and no. Certainly, total employment is steady or rising. But, as everyone knows who has attended college recently, full professors remain a small core group, even at successful programs. The academic workforce is also made up of graduate assistants, part-time instructors, lecturers, and other nonpermanent positions. Landing a tenure track professorship in the environmental professions remains a fairly difficult task.

One might also think that environmental research grants to academics would be up substantially, fueling an increase in academic work at the scientific level. And research in some areas *is* up. Nonetheless, government funding for environmental research (still the overwhelming source of most research money) is erratic and subject to fads and political pressure. Many research workers report nomadic careers and constant grant writing. People pursuing a Ph.D. in environmental and conservation work with the idea of an academic or research career should plan carefully and develop skills in attracting funds to support their work.

DISCIPLINES IN DEMAND—THE MOST POPULAR ENVIRONMENTAL CAREERS

As we enter the 21st century, who is getting hired? What types of professionals are most in demand by environmental employers? The answers to these questions depend on which definition one uses for "in demand." People from some fields are "in demand" because of the sheer number of individuals employed in those fields, even if current growth rates are not high. Other fields may be growing rapidly but from a small base. Finally, a few fields are just starting to show up, but future growth will be needed soon. The descriptions that follow include a combination of all three definitions.

POLLUTION PREVENTION (P2) SPECIALISTS

Most pollution prevention (P2) work is done by engineers, chemists, and other scientists, but people from almost any profession can identify ways to reduce, reuse, and recycle. In addition, some of the most effective pollution prevention is achieved through education and training; that is, helping professionals understand what might be done in their industry through simple changes. To get a sense of the broad range of work being done by pollution prevention professionals, check out the National Pollution Prevention Roundtable's website at http://es.inel.gov/nppr. For information about education for P2, contact the National Pollution Prevention Center for Higher Education or visit their website at www.umich.edu/~nppcpub/.

GEOGRAPHIC INFORMATION SYSTEMS AND OTHER COMPUTER SPECIALISTS

The environmental community lives on data, especially data that can be shown visually and interactively by computer systems that demonstrate interaction between human activities and ecological systems. Geographic information systems (GIS) specialists are in demand at planning agencies, consulting firms, research centers, and throughout private industry. GIS, of course, relies on the existence of good data in the first place, which creates employment for sampling professionals and new technological developments in monitoring equipment and remote sensing from satellites. Finally, traditional database and information systems managers are also in demand. For more information about GIS careers and educational opportunities, visit http://ulysses.unl.edu/calmit/gisrs.html, which links to dozens of other related sites.

ENVIRONMENTAL COMMUNICATORS AND EDUCATORS

In recent years, the nation has seen a noticeable shift in environmental problem solving, away from a preference for secrecy, adversarial relationships, and litigation, and toward greater openness and a search for common ground.

Regulators depend on education as much as they do on enforcement. Non-profit leaders meet with corporate executives. "Right-to-know" laws require polluters to make available information that would have been carefully guarded just a few years ago. And institutions of all stripes seek to influence the hearts and minds of the general public.

The freer flow of information, and the desire for more voluntary actions, creates opportunities for communicators and educators who can help translate scientific and technical issues for the general public, and for those who can create venues (e.g., meetings, conferences, public hearings, and community gatherings) for an open exchange of opinions. Progressive land developers, for instance, now engage local governments and community residents in open dialogue long before approaching formal boards for permit approvals.

Simultaneously, the rapid growth in environmental information creates a pressing need for professionals to stay up-to-date. Continuing education is critical for success, and this has created opportunities for educators who provide rapidly changing seminars, workshops, short courses, safety trainings, and other learning opportunities.

ENGINEERING SPECIALTIES

Engineers of all kinds are at the center of the environmental careers world. Process and chemical engineers with industry-specific knowledge will be particularly in demand for pollution prevention projects. Consulting in this field is on the rise. Agricultural engineering is another rising position, and one that is tackling one of our most intractable environmental problems—raising food sustainably for six billion people (and growing). Environmental engineers with training in multimedia approaches to environmental concerns are certainly needed.

International work holds immense possibilities for environmentally related engineers of the future as less advanced countries spend billions to improve the basic water, wastewater, and pollution control infrastructure that wealthier nations have already constructed. Finally, engineers will have interesting challenges taking apart some of the engineering "solutions" of the past. See chapter 4 for information on how the Army Corps of Engineers is working to dismantle the dikes, levees, dams, and braces on the Napa River, allowing it to run free for flood control purposes. Aspiring engineers can start with information from the American Academy of Environmental Engineers (www.enviro-engrs.org), the American Institute of Chemical Engineers (www.aiche.org), and the American Society of Agricultural Engineers (www.asae.org).

ENVIRONMENTAL CHEMISTS

Chemists are found at every level of environmental work and in all parts of the economy. Education in chemistry remains one of the best baseline scientific backgrounds for an environmental professional career, including nonscientific ones. Chemistry training is particularly crucial in the environmental protection and waste management fields (e.g., water, air, solid waste, and hazardous waste, chapters 6, 7, 8, and 9, respectively). Chemists are found in the lab, on the remediation site, at treatment facilities, in the classroom, and on corporate and government regulatory compliance staffs. Finally, experiments in chemistry will bring us new, nontoxic chemicals that can be incorporated by engineers into pollution prevention strategies. If you are interested, you can get more information from the American Chemical Society (www.acs.org) or university chemistry departments.

FUNDRAISING PROFESSIONALS

If there is one constant in the nonprofit world, it is the need to raise funds. In fact, development directors are often among the best paid, and most sought after, professionals in nonprofit environmental work. Fundraising directors write grant requests, develop relationships with foundation and corporate donors, manage membership campaigns, pursue major donors, and carry out appeals and special events. Organizational communications involving newsletters, websites, public education, and marketing often fall in the development department as well. The National Society of Fund Raising Executives (www. nsfre.org) can help you get started.

The private sector corollary to fundraising professionals are "rainmakers"—professionals who can attract business to consulting firms and other environmental industry firms. If you can generate revenue, you will be in demand.

PLANNERS

Environmental management is looking for greater levels of integration. That's what "place-based" approaches, multimedia management, watershed planning, ecosystems management, and sustainable development are all about. Moreover, environmental problems call for a greater number of people whose professional background prepares them to combine human needs and ecological realities for the advancement of both within a framework of political and financial reality at the local level. Well-educated planners bring exactly this set of skills to the table, not only for jobs formally called "planner," but for a wide range of opportunities. Get in touch with the American Planning Association (www.planning.org) to learn more.

ENVIRONMENTAL TECHNICIANS

Environmental technicians are an immense part of the environmental career world, although they may go under different names. Technicians collect air, water, and soil samples. They carry out botanical and wildlife inventories. Technicians do the basic work at water and wastewater treatment plants, as well as at treatment, storage, and disposal sites. There are thousands of forestry, biological, range management, and remediation technicians.

The vast majority of technicians have undergraduate training. One of the themes of environmental employment over the last ten years has been a noticeable rise in the number of environmental degree programs at community college and vocational schools. As environmental work has matured, many employers have come to realize that a talented person with an associate's degree, trained in the latest technologies and regulations, can effectively do work that was once reserved for people with undergraduate degrees. Job oriented students have also realized that a two-year degree might be a more cost-effective way to enter the environmental professions.

Finally, if it's true that many people become environmental professionals to work outdoors, technician work is a great place to start. It's often true that the technicians are the ones out in the fields, streams, and work sites, while other professionals are back in the office.

TEACHERS

The nation needs a new generation of teachers. Shortages in many school districts are already a serious problem, and a large wave of retirees is about to make it worse. From our point of view, all teachers are prospective environmental educators. Talented educators use math, science, literature, theater, art, languages, government, and history to open the eyes of students to the natural world and environmental issues. Someone has probably figured out a way to use driver's education and gym class as well. And yet fewer people are entering the field. The arguments against teaching are well known—low pay, hard working conditions, considerable responsibility, and no guarantee of respect from your peers, to name a few. However, don't let this dissuade you. If you think that teaching is for you, go for it! You will find a world of opportunity. See chapter 5 for a wealth of resources on education careers.

CONSERVATION BIOLOGISTS

Environmental employment in biology has moved away from "single species" biologists to more broadly ecological scientists who study whole ecosystems. Within the ecosystems management approach, the field of conservation biology has emerged as a demand field. As the name implies, conservation biology focuses on conservation and protection of plants, fish, and wildlife. The rapid pace of species extinction, the need for practical ways to enforce the Endangered Species Act, and the general awareness that biological understanding does not lead automatically to workable conservation strategies has moved conservation biology into the spotlight. On a pure science front, many conservation biologists work in the field of population genetics, which is crucial to our understanding of extinction. Good places to learn more include universities that offer conservation biology specializations (including Minnesota,

Michigan, Maryland, Penn State, and Clemson) and associations such as the Ecological Society of America (www.sdsc.edu/~esa/esa.htm), the American Institute of Biological Sciences (www.aibs.org), and the Society for Conservation Biology (www.scb.org).

ENTREPRENEURS AND BUSINESS MANAGERS

Paul Hawken, in his influential book *The Ecology of Commerce*, makes a powerful case that the transformation of business into an inherently sustainable enterprise is perhaps the crucial task of our generation. This points to the need for a new kind of manager within business and for entrepreneurs who will start businesses that advance sustainability. On the first front, the rapid growth of environmental coursework within most of the leading M.B.A. schools is cause for hope. On the second, Gary Hirshberg, founder and president of Stonybrook Farms (known best for their yogurts) is an example. Hirshberg left the environmental nonprofit world to start his own company and demonstrate by example that the ideas he advocated could succeed in the "real world." The company has been an outstanding success. For regular examples of stories like this, check out *In Business: The Magazine for Environmental Entrepreneuring* (J.G. Press, 419 Stale Avenue, Emmaus, PA, 18049, 610-967-4135). To learn more about environmental business management at the Fortune 500 level, contact the Management Institute for Environment and Business (www. wri.org/meb/).

DUAL TRACK ENVIRONMENTAL MANAGERS

Integration of different fields—science, engineering, politics, law, information technology, project management, business administration, marketing, communications, and economics—is at the heart of the emerging environmental professions. Among the most popular careers are hybrids that combine two or more professional tracks. The Masters of Environmental Management program at Duke University's Nicholas School for the Environment is an example of an interdisciplinary program that weaves together different tracks to educate the environmental managers of tomorrow. Demand is also high for people who combine two traditional degrees. Engineers with an M.B.A., or scientists with a master's in public administration are two good examples.

These are just a few of the popular career fields in environmental and conservation work. There are many, many more. Let your own skills, talents, and dreams guide you.

2 Education and Internships for Your Environmental Career

LET'S SAY you are a college freshman with an interest in wildlife, or a career changer returning to school to pursue a watershed protection career. You're likely to ask, "What kind of degree should I get?" It's a commonsense question. After all, education is an expensive proposition in time and money, and you want to be sure that it leads to the right job for you.

While some careers (such as law, medicine, and accounting) have clear educational paths, the requirements necessary to pursue environmental careers are less clear cut. There are many educational paths to a satisfying environmental job. A quick review of undergraduate majors held by professionals at the U.S. Environmental Protection Agency reads like a college catalog in that almost every field in the humanities, social sciences, business, natural sciences, engineering, and the professions is included. In addition, environmental agencies are full of people who are doing work completely unrelated to their original college degree.

While it can be liberating to hear about a Spanish major who is now the director of a land trust, it doesn't help one decide which classes to take, which specialties to select, and which skills are most in demand. For, while it is true that the environmental career world remains remarkably open to a variety of academic disciplines, it's also true that there are more people with specialized education, advanced degrees, and experience competing for jobs. This reality increases the importance of making good choices.

To make things even more difficult, you are entering the environmental professions during an era of rapid and sweeping change, as chapter 1 indicated. It's easier to plan your education when you can predict that the future will be pretty much the same as the past, or at least that today's employment trend will continue long enough for you to spend four to six years preparing for it. The current generation of students faces a world in which the only known constant is constant change. It's a whole new ballgame.

Times of rapid change create some interesting contradictions. The hazardous waste management field provides a good example. Nearly all environmental leaders agree that the future of this field lies in pollution prevention (P2), and that a profession that "manages" waste will presumably decline as the waste itself decreases. Less waste produced, the fewer "waste managers" needed. And, indeed, the industry is declining. Today, however, there are still several times as many jobs in the treatment, storage, disposal, and remediation of hazardous wastes as there are in prevention. The field is in a transition from an existing structure of jobs (waste management) to an emerging one where standards are just coming into view (pollution prevention). These intriguing dilemmas are common throughout environmental careers.

Among the contradictions, however, there are many trends that seem clear and a great deal of good advice available to help you. This chapter aims to take some of the guesswork out of your educational decisionmaking by exploring: suggestions on how to think about education and careers; advice on selecting the right educational level (associate, undergraduate, graduate/professional, or doctoral), as well as information about each one; the crucial importance of volunteering, internships, and practical experience; and some thoughts about educational choices for career changers.

THINKING ABOUT EDUCATION AND CAREERS

Career advisers agree that the more specific you are about what you want, and the more information you have about employer needs, the easier it will be for you to plan your education. This is a commonsense observation, but one that is rarely acted on. Most of us make up our educational path as we go along, inspired or discouraged by the last class we took, the advice of a professor, or the results of a summer internship. Some serendipity is inevitable, even desirable. A steady diet of unplanned choices, however, and you will reach graduation day with a degree in hand but little idea about what comes next. You can avoid this outcome. Spend a little time right now thinking about the environmental work you would most like to do. Be as specific as you can. To prime the pump, read about the work of environmental professionals. Go to conferences. Surf the Web regularly for career information. Read the ads in environmental job listings like *Earth Work Magazine*, *Environmental Career Opportunities*, and *The Job Seeker*. Meet people who are doing the work you might want to do and don't be bashful about dreaming big. You may want to lead treks in Costa Rica or Nepal, start an environmental technology business, work with wildlife in Montana, or study the coastal regions of the South Pacific. There are already people making a good living in those areas. Why not you? Go for it!

As you meet environmental professionals, always ask, "What advice do you have for me about my education?" Ask about needed certifications and degrees and for opinions about schools. Ask professionals to rate different skills and abilities in priority order. What is crucial to know *now* and what can be picked up later? People who are actually doing work successfully in the field are the very best source of good advice. It's best to go straight to the practitioners. Better yet, combine many different information sources to get a complete picture.

Your education, of course, is not only about career preparation. Undergraduate work, in particular, is also about growing as a person, exposing yourself to new ideas, challenging your prejudices, fueling the fires of political involvement, and learning "how to learn." Your education is also a time for exploring visions of a better world that may seem impossible today. The ability to envision new realities and not be limited by today's constraints is one of the most valuable products of a good education. You must also allow for a social life and the part-time jobs that help pay for all this learning. Planning your education can be a daunting task, but you'll be glad you did it. There are very few people who create an educational plan that links school to clear career ambitions. Any amount of thinking you do will put you ahead of the pack. It also feels good to know *why* you're in school, and what you plan to do with your education.

As you review your educational choices, keep the following general trends in mind:

Jobs without college. Environmental employers offer some positions for people without a college degree, particularly in the fields of waste management, recycling, parks, and forestry.

More associate degree programs. Respect has grown for graduates from quality two-year degree programs, creating employment opportunities for environmental technicians and putting employment pressure on new undergraduates in fields such as chemistry and biology. Graduates of technician programs are competitive for entry-level positions, but will need additional education for career advancement.

Differing opinions on interdisciplinary undergraduate training. While there is general agreement about the need for skills and knowledge that cross many disciplines, judgments are mixed about the career preparation value of current interdisciplinary undergraduate programs in environmental studies and environmental science. (See the discussion on undergraduate education, later in this chapter.)

Graduate education often needed. Employment in scientific and engineering fields above the entry level almost always requires a master's degree. Within the sciences, those with MS degrees (and above) in fields like conservation biology, ecosystems management, industrial ecology, and other "multi-media" approaches are particularly in demand. Engineers with specialties in land restoration, industrial/chemical processes, and agricultural engineering issues are particularly in demand, although environmental and civil engineers are also needed.

Combination degrees are in demand. People who combine science with nonscience degrees (e.g., law, business, communications, and policy) are extremely competitive in all sectors. John R. Cook, Jr., president of the Environmental Careers Organization (ECO) sees degree combinations, especially at the master's level, as one of the most important educational trends in environmental and conservation fields. "Employers are looking for people who combine real expertise in more than one area," Cook says. He adds that, "Instead of choosing between someone who knows their science and someone who is good at business or politics, the best employers want people who can master both." Combining a science or engineering degree with an M.B.A. makes a particularly attractive package.

Skills everyone needs. You must have strong computer skills to be competitive. In addition, an ability to communicate well, in writing and through verbal presentations, is crucial to success in every field.

CHOOSING THE RIGHT EDUCATIONAL LEVEL

One of the first things you'll want to learn about different career paths is the educational level required to secure a full-time position in the field you choose to pursue. As you read through the chapters in this book, look for information on which jobs can be done by people with associate degrees and undergraduate diplomas and which require graduate a education.

Community Colleges and Vocational Programs. Associate degree programs help aspiring environmental professionals in two ways. First, two-year programs serve as final degrees for careers in a wide range of environmental protection and conservation fields. Second, community colleges prepare students for transfer to undergraduate schools for two more years of study.

If you are interested in an immediate, technician-level job in environmental fields such as hazardous waste management, water and wastewater treatment, air pollution control, geographic information systems, recycling, site remediation, and "environmental technologies," you should examine community colleges.

Community college programs are focused on preparation for today's jobs, which means curricula must be current to attract students. The best programs create employment relationships with local and regional employers and offer well-organized internships. They use adjunct faculty from employers and the most current technology and lab equipment. In addition, community college graduates often come to employers with certified training in health and safety procedures that companies would otherwise have to pay for themselves. Finally, staff and faculty at community colleges take very seriously the career placement aspect of their work and the best programs pride themselves on 100 percent job or college placement rates.

Community college graduates in technical fields come to employers with another perceived advantage—they have trained themselves in environmental technology fields as a career, as opposed to undergraduate students who may see technician positions as a short-term step on the career ladder. With community college graduates, turnover rates are expected to be lower and job satisfaction may be higher.

Two-year degree programs are not limited to environmental protection fields. They are also popular as career preparation for technicians in the conservation world. If a desire to spend time outdoors motivates you to consider an environmental career, then definitely look into two-year programs in fisheries, forestry, parks and recreation, wildlife, range management, and landscape architecture. Environmental professionals with a master's degree may find themselves back at the office dealing with paper and people, while a small army of technicians does the outdoor field work that drew them to the field in the first place.

If you think community college education might fit your career aspirations, there are a few questions to ask about any school you are considering. Is the school accredited? What is the placement rate of its graduates and where are they today? Are students really getting the jobs the school claims to train people for? Don't depend on information from the school alone. Talk to recent graduates and local employers before making any decisions.

Community colleges are, without question, becoming a more important part of the higher education scene in environmental careers. There is a downside, however. There is almost always a ceiling on advancement for two-year graduates. If you want to move up, you will almost certainly need an undergraduate degree or higher.

Many environmental programs at community colleges prepare students specifically for transfer to a four-year institution. Often there are arrangements with universities whereby acceptance is practically guaranteed and all credits earned transfer automatically. If attendance at a specific four-year school is already in your plans, check on transfer requirements so that you can make good class choices in your first two years.

Undergraduate Education. Community college programs are usually focused on preparation for an immediate job after graduation. Graduate, professional, and doctoral programs (when well designed) prepare people for career specialties. Then there is the undergraduate degree—the degree of choice for most new graduates. The relationship between undergraduate education and career preparation is much less clear.

People with newly minted undergraduate degrees are the most likely to complain that they can't find a permanent, entry-level environmental or conservation job in their field. Above them, the field seems crowded with more experienced people and graduate degree holders. Below them, are technicians, temporary and seasonal employees, interns, and volunteers. Around them are thousands of other new undergraduates from the nation's 2,400 degree granting institutions.

Newly graduated B.S. holders enter a world in which their new degree is necessary to be considered for a lot of openings, but not sufficient to land a job. Their diplomas say they are environmental scientists, but their training may be too general and the technology they use may not be "cutting edge." The number of good field courses their school offered was probably limited. They may be intelligent, passionate, and ready to work, but they can't find environmental jobs that pay a decent wage. People are already telling them to go to graduate school and spend more time and money on education.

Of course, many new bachelor's degree graduates avoid this fate. They move directly into a challenging job or graduate school without missing a beat. What can you do to increase your chances of being in this category? Good decisions along the way are crucial. Some of the most important decisions you will make involve the school you select, the academic major you choose, and the collection of courses and work experiences you develop. Below are some ideas gathered from employers and educators to help you with these critical decisions.

SELECTING A SCHOOL

Consider Schools with a Variety of Good Environmental Programs. Undergraduates tend to change their minds as quickly as their majors. You may have a better chance of landing on your feet if you select a school with more than one quality program in the environmental and conservation fields.

Consider Schools that Have Reputable Graduate Programs in Your Field of Choice. A school that has an excellent graduate department in, for example, ecology, can be a good place to pursue an undergraduate degree as well. If you know what major you want to pursue, the presence of graduate students, research facilities, and well-known faculty may help your education.

Linking School Location with Geographic Work Preference. It is often to your advantage to attend school in the region where you would like to work after graduation. In this way, you can begin to seek out potential employers while in school. It will be easy to search for internships and permanent positions, and the chances are good that your school will have alumni working for firms in the region. College faculty members may be researching issues in the region. Part-time faculty members may even have full-time jobs in firms or agencies that are potential or current employers of the program's graduates.

Researching Colleges and Programs. Over the past three decades, there has been a tremendous increase in the diversity of programs and the number of colleges offering them. Where should you start? A number of good college directories are listed in the Resources section at the end of this chapter to help you, and there is great information available on the Internet. To whet your imagination, run a few "keyword" searches using a good search engine such as AltaVista, at http://www.altavista.digital.com. If you are interested in wildlife biology, for example, run a search for "wildlife biology undergraduate programs."

SELECTING A MAJOR

A lot of environmental workers use scientific knowledge in their work. Many fewer, however, are working scientists who "do science" every day. If you want to be part of the latter group, especially in consulting or the academic world, you may want to choose a traditional major (e.g., biology, chemistry, ecology, and earth science), as opposed to an interdisciplinary degree. Right or wrong, many employers and graduate school selectors in traditional scientific fields question whether interdisciplinary programs are rigorous enough to prepare scientists for "their" field. Charlie Anderson, vice president of TRC (a national consulting firm) told job seekers at a 1998 workshop that, "We prefer people with science and engineering backgrounds. We like to know that they have a strong technical base." Don't let this keep you from interdisciplinary work within a traditional major. A person with a B.S. in chemistry may take many of the same courses as an environmental science graduate, however when the time arrives to look for a job, the person is a chemist and that still counts for something.

Find out now whether working professionals in your field generally require a graduate degree. Do you want to be a wetlands ecologist, conservation biologist, geneticist, marine ecologist, atmospheric scientist, agricultural engineer,

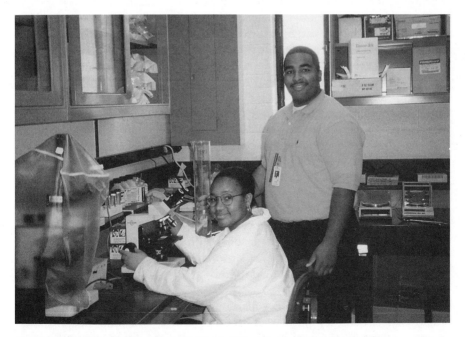

Interns at an air quality lab in Research Triangle Park, North Carolina. Knowledge of chemistry is an important part of an environmental science education.

wildlife scientist, process engineer, toxicologist, or environmental lawyer? Professionals in all these fields say that a graduate degree is essential. That's not going to change in the next few years. This means that an important goal for undergraduates in these fields is getting into a good graduate program. This will affect your class choices, internships, research projects, and faculty relationships.

Environmental chemistry, ecology, conservation biology, and engineering (environmental or chemical) are strong degrees for environmental employment on the technical side. Selecting a major is a personal decision. Only you can decide what's best for you. On a purely career basis, however, you couldn't go wrong with any well-planned curriculum in any of the four fields just mentioned if you are technically inclined. You will be well prepared for employment or graduate school.

For nonscientists, an interdisciplinary degree may be the best education. Quality varies, however, so research your options carefully. Over 250 colleges and universities offer environmental studies and environmental science degrees. The theory behind these programs is solid: Environmental issues involve complex interactions among economic, social, spiritual, political, legal, technological, and ecological variables. No one discipline can possibly claim to properly educate an environmental professional, so a new type of interdisciplinary education is required. This is fair enough. However, the problem is that there is little agreement on what an interdisciplinary environmental education should involve, and what career or graduate study such a degree prepares one for. This makes interdisciplinary programs hard to assess from the student's point of view. Many of these programs are a collection of already existing classes put together (and renamed) to take advantage of the intense interest undergraduates have shown in the environment. Others were begun by a particular department (e.g., geology, biology, and political science) and bear the imprint of that source. Still others are too new to judge accurately.

This doesn't mean that interdisciplinary degree holders don't get good jobs. Many government agencies and nonprofit organizations, in fact, prefer them. With each passing year, employers have more experience with interdisciplinary degrees, and academics learn more about how to structure learning that balances career requirements against other educational goals. If you are thinking of pursuing an interdisciplinary degree, ask the program office for information on where the last three years of graduates are working as well as the names of any employer contacts. Ask recent graduates directly whether they would have done anything differently. Then, sit down with an adviser early on and talk about your career goals. You should do this anyway, but in an interdisciplinary program it's essential.

Finally, take great care with your internships. With a traditional degree, employers feel that they know what they are getting. Graduates from interdisciplinary programs don't always get the benefit of the doubt. Demonstrating your abilities through job experience becomes even more important. You will be drilled to prove your actual skills.

If you choose a social science, humanities, or professional degree, don't worry too much about the "environmental" adjective. "Environmental" journalism is a good example. Yes, it is a professional specialty, and classes that address it specifically are a good idea. Employers of undergraduates, however, will be more concerned about whether or not you are, in general, a good journalist than in the specifically environmental background you bring to the table. Focus on becoming a good journalist first. The same is true for photographers, filmmakers, marketers, economists, computer scientists, political scientists, communicators, managers, and fundraisers.

SELECTING COURSES AND OTHER EXPERIENCES

Plan a multiyear collection of courses, field work, internships, and international opportunities as early as you can, even if you end up changing it. Don't make your class selections on a semester-by-semester basis. For four years your goal is to get the best education you can. A lot of that time will be prescribed for you by graduation and major requirements. A great deal of it, however, is up to you. Using the advice you've received from people in your field, and your own desires, try to plot out a plan for the whole multiyear experience. Do you want to take a semester abroad? Are there courses that are only taught at special times, but are required? It's hard to fit everything in. Your time at school is shorter than it might seem!

As soon as a field interests you, find a successful professional mentor. Don't depend on your teachers, career counselors, and fellow students to give you career guidance. Find someone in the field who is willing to help you. Have lunch with him or her once a month or so. Ask questions about your class choices, and share your concerns about what you're learning (or not).

While you're in school, put together a special project on the career experiences of recent graduates from your school and major. This is especially helpful for environmental undergraduates who are not pursuing science and engineering careers. Nothing is more informative than the real-life experience of recent students from your own, and related, departments. You will be doing yourself, and your classmates, a real service by researching the career paths of graduates from the last one to five years. If you can, bring them back to campus as guest speakers to talk about what they have learned. Put together a website that allows current students to interact with alums who are out there in the "real world." A project like this should be worthy of college credit. Talk to your adviser or a friendly professor about this option.

Work with employers or intern programs to create professionally challenging internships. See the section on internships and volunteering later in this chapter.

Selecting a good school, choosing the right major for you, developing a quality curriculum of courses and other experiences are all part of the formula for undergraduate success. However, if you are less than successful in following this advice, you can still emerge ready to pursue a satisfying career. No one expects an undergraduate to emerge from school perfectly prepared for the workforce or graduate school. If you founder a bit trying to find yourself, take a collection of courses that seemed like a good idea at the time, or focus too intently in one area at the expense of a more rounded education, don't worry about it too much. In three years, your undergraduate career will be ancient history, and employers will only want to know what you can do for them today.

GRADUATE SCHOOL

"Graduate school is hard work and is expensive. To be successful, you should have clear objectives and personal motivation," says Peter Otis, director of career services at the Yale School of Forestry and Environmental Studies.

By now the message is clear. Do your homework. Know yourself. Know the marketplace. Have a plan. Assuming you've taken this advice to heart, let's consider the most frequently asked questions about environmental and conservation graduate study.

Do I need a graduate degree to get a good job in my field? The best answer will come from hard data in your field. The best sources of information on hiring are employers, employment agencies, professional associations, and college departments or alumni associations. Don't accept just opinions. Find out about actual hiring realities.

Let's take an example—the field of toxicology. Two major professional associations for toxicologists are the Society of Toxicology and the Society of Environmental Toxicology and Chemistry. The National Institute of Environmental Health Sciences and the Extension Toxicology Network are also helpful. A 1996 job market survey from the Society of Toxicology reveals that 9,000 people in North America work as toxicologists. Forty-four percent are employed by academic institutions, where they teach and conduct research. A Ph.D. is essential for these positions and two-thirds of employers look for postdoctoral work in the candidate's specialty. Another 37 percent hold positions in the chemical, pharmaceutical, and food manufacturing industries. Federal and state government agencies employ 13 percent, and 6 percent work at consulting firms, research foundations, local governments, and nonprofit groups. Master's degrees are overwhelmingly preferred. Hiring trends are described as up for the chemical industry and at government agencies while those at consulting, pharmaceutical, and consumer products companies are described as down. University hiring will remain about the same. Salary levels from different degrees are given, and some of the most popular specialties are described (risk management is popular). Finally, a complete guide to academic and postdoctoral programs in toxicology is posted on the SOT website at www.toxicology.org, as well as information on the best undergraduate backgrounds to prepare one for graduate study.

With all of this information the aspiring toxicologist now has the answer about graduate study. He or she needs at least a master's degree, and a lot of jobs require a doctoral education. It took less than a day of Web surfing and phone calls to gather this information. To best learn about your field, we've listed many professional associations at the end of this chapter, as well as throughout this book.

What school should I go to? Rating graduate schools is a difficult task. Clearly, an individual can have a horrible experience at a top-rated school, and a wonderful one at a program with a limited reputation. Nonetheless, there is usually rough agreement on the top twenty programs in any discipline. Associations sometimes do surveys that ask professionals to rank programs based on reputation. These can be invaluable. More formal attempts, based on "objective" criteria, are made by *U.S. News and World Report* in its annual graduate school survey, and through *The Gourman Report* (available at most good libraries). Finally, look at the alma maters of prominent professors, academics, consultants and managers in your field. This can tell you a lot. For an excellent overview of environmental and conservation graduate programs, get *The Student Conservation Association Guide to Graduate Environmental Programs* (Island Press 1996).

Once you have a list of possible graduate schools in your field, obtain information on the program through the mail or on the Web. Be sure to ask for alumni career information. At the very least, any good program will have class and faculty information; the program's general philosophy; descriptions of special tracks of study; graduation requirements; data about application requirements (e.g., GRE scores, undergraduate grades, and so forth); and information about costs, scholarships, and financial aid.

A potential graduate student should look not only at the program, but at the department, school, or university that houses the program. Is this program strong compared with the other programs in the department or school? Is it growing or decreasing in importance? Are there other environmental graduate programs at the university besides the one that interests you? A university that has other such programs will present additional opportunities and resources.

Using this process, you should be able to select four to five programs that deserve closer scrutiny. If possible, visit these schools to talk with faculty members and students before applying. Also, talk with graduates, especially those who have jobs that interest you. Did their degrees help them obtain their positions? Where do they work? What is the range of starting salaries? Be wary of any program in which faculty members are hazy on this information or will not refer you to alumni.

Should I consider an interdisciplinary master's program? "Absolutely," says John Sigmon, associate dean of the Nicholas School of the Environment at Duke University in Durham, North Carolina. Duke offers a master of environmental management degree program with six different career tracks, including resource ecology, resource economics and policy, coastal environmental management, environmental toxicology/chemistry/risk assessment, water and air resources, and biohazard science. "The degree is designed to serve some of the same functions in the environmental field that an M.B.A. does in business or a J.D. in law—to prepare people for professional positions in government and industry," says Sigmon.

Sigmon points out that the master of environmental management is not for everyone. "This master's program is a professional degree. It is not the second leg of education on the way to a Ph.D.," he says. "It works best for a person with an undergraduate degree, some experience in the field, and a clear sense of career direction."

Another difference between the master of environmental management and traditional M.S. programs is cost. While many students in more academically focused master's programs earn scholarships and fellowships that pay for a good portion of their tuition, this is not the case with the M.E.M. Most students bear the full cost, which is another reason to plan carefully.

Employers seem to like the idea behind the Duke program. Graduates are snapped up quickly, as evidenced by the job titles of recent graduates highlighted on the program's website at http://www.env.duke.edu. Yale's School of Forestry and Environmental Studies and the University of Michigan's School of Natural Resources are two other well-known interdisciplinary master's programs, and there are many more.

Should I go to graduate school right after my undergraduate degree, or should I get some work experience first? "It's an age-old question," says Lisa Younger, director of career resources at The Student Conservation Association (SCA). "There's no single answer. I think in general, however, that people are better off getting some experience first. For one thing, you've been in school your whole life. Working gives you new perspectives that school just can't provide. You learn about the field, clarify your career thinking, gain some maturity, get a better understanding of what grad school can do for you, and save money for tuition." Duke's Sigmon says that getting work experience might make you a more competitive applicant for graduate study. "Working professionals can bring a more rounded level of understanding which helps them, the faculty and their fellow students," he says. "It's not essential to have work experience to get in, but it helps."

For those seeking academic or research careers, however, there is little incentive to wait. These tracks require a Ph.D., some postdoctoral work, and a strong network within your field. All three of those requirements are best met from within the academy. When you leave undergraduate school, you are looking at an additional five to six years of study. Getting started right away may be a good idea, once your decision is set. Deferring the Ph.D. dream can be as harmful as jumping in too soon. Career, family, and financial considerations may make it difficult to go back later. Even at the master's level, there may be little to gain in some fields by waiting. We discussed earlier how many scientific careers have little beyond technician work for undergraduates. If you're confident in your career choice, and that career choice requires a master's, go for it. You'll be competing for better jobs that much faster.

EDUCATIONAL OPTIONS FOR CAREER CHANGERS

Nearly everyone working today will change careers in their professional lives, and some will change several times. These career changes will not only be generated from external forces such as mergers, layoffs, business failures, and privatization of government services. If you are changing careers in the 21st century, you are just as likely to be doing so for greater satisfaction, more freedom, more money, a better balance between work and family, and a need to make a real difference through your work. Whether your career change is consciously chosen, or has been thrust upon you, you may be asking yourself, should I go back to school? The answer, of course, depends on what you want to do next and how well your current education and experience has prepared you for it.

Where are you on the career changer educational spectrum? The career changer's spectrum goes from easiest to hardest. At the easier end of the spectrum lie people who want to use their existing skills and knowledge at an environmental company or agency. In a real sense, these people are not changing careers at all. They are simply getting a new job in a different industry. Examples include accountants, fundraisers, marketing and communication professionals, information technology specialists, trainers, human resources staff, secretaries, bookkeepers, salespeople, and more. If you are an accountant in the insurance industry, and want to be an accountant at an environmental organization, your career change will be relatively easy. All the rules and most of the professional vocabulary is the same. There is certainly no need to go back to school.

At the other end of the spectrum is the person without a college degree who wants to be a marine biologist studying coral reef deterioration. There's no way around it. It's back to school for several years. This will be hard work, of course, but the educational decision is an easy one.

In the middle are professionals who have some transferable skills, but whose education and experience is in another discipline or specialty. These are the hard cases. Should a petroleum engineer go back to school for an environmental specialty? Can a chemist from the health care industry do environmental work without additional education? Can a tax attorney compete for jobs in environmental law? What is usually at stake here is not whether the career changer could do the job. Talented and ambitious engineers, chemists, and attorneys can certainly learn new subject matter quickly through reading, short courses, and on-the-job experience. The question, of course, is whether the person will be competitive enough to become a top candidate for the job.

Regardless of where you are on the career changers spectrum, the first step in your educational decision making is to do a quick "gap analysis" between your environmental career goal and your current skills, education, and experience. Your objective is to find out how big the gap is between where you are and where you want to go, and to determine the role that education might play in filling the gap. Don't assume you must go back to school. If you do have to go back, don't assume you will need a whole degree program. It's possible that a continuing education course, or a short training program, will be enough.

When conducting this research, go to employers and working professionals first, not colleges. It's only natural that educational institutions will define the gap between you and your dream in terms of formal education. Working professionals, especially senior managers at companies and agencies that interest you, can give you a more accurate assessment of your chances. Get as many interviews as you can, and ask the education question straightforwardly. Especially for older professionals, more formal education is often not the problem. The problem is getting the opportunity to tell your story and demonstrate how your experience is transferable. The interviews themselves can help you do that.

If your gap analysis leads you to the conclusion that formal education, especially a master's degree, is absolutely required for you to successfully change careers, don't delay! Do it as soon as you can. Educational requirements rarely diminish. If you really need that degree today, you will certainly need it tomorrow.

For people with undergraduate degrees, be wary of anyone who advises you to get a new, different undergraduate degree. Undergraduate degrees are usually not career advancers. If you have an undergraduate degree already and are changing careers, consider getting a master's in the new field, even if you must take some qualifying courses that lengthen the time of study.

Identifying the real gaps between you and your dream is a powerful experience for a career changer. The process gives you specific objectives to go after, and allows you to identify action steps that are tailored to your situation.

CONCLUSION

Your environmental career starts with a good education, supplemented by practical experience through internships and seasonal work. Although it is true that there are many educational paths to a successful environmental career, your college choices are important ones, and deserve careful thought and planning. Through a combination of self-awareness, goal-setting, good course selection, and well-designed internships, you will be prepared to launch your career in today's competitive environmental job marketplace.

THE SECOND HALF OF YOUR EDUCATION—ALL ABOUT INTERNSHIPS

"You can't learn how to be an environmental professional in the classroom," says Kathy Blaha, regional vice president of the Trust for Public Land. "You must get good experience while you are in school, and that means internships."

Armando Quintero, from the National Ocean Service, Gulf of the Farallones National Marine Sanctuary, reports that: "Your education isn't complete until you've proven what you can do through internships or seasonal work."

Searching for threatened and endangered botanical species in the Pacific Northwest. Skills such as this can only be learned through field study.

Practical experience is the other half of your environmental career education. You can gain the experience you need through:

- Volunteering
- Cooperative education
- Seasonal employment
- Part-time jobs
- Independent study
- Class projects
- Temporary jobs
- Apprenticeships
- Internships

Unfortunately, you can't depend on teachers, advisers, or employers to provide a work/learning experience that's right for you. You'll have to take charge of this part of your education yourself.

In this section, you will learn how to find (or create) quality internships that combine your learning goals with the needs of environmental and conservation employers. You will receive advice and suggestions about how to make your internships a success. Finally, we will review the importance of volunteers in the environmental movement and workforce.

Throughout this section, the word "internship" is used to cover a wide range of different work/learning experiences (see the list above). An internship is any work/learning experience that has an acknowledged learning agenda, with commitments from both employer and intern. This is what distinguishes an internship from any other kind of work experience. In an internship, the intern is required to work hard and produce results, but there is also an understanding that he or she is there to develop deeper knowledge and better skills for professional development. This mutual commitment may be extremely informal, but it must exist.

By this definition, many experiences that are called internships are not worthy of the name, and lots of seasonal field jobs with generous supervisors are amazing intern opportunities. The fact is, the word intern means different things to different people. To some employers it conjures up a negative image. At many organizations, interns are people with limited skills who can give only a few hours and who demand a lot of supervisory time for meager results. For others, interns are the people who make copies, file papers, get coffee, enter data, and run errands (e.g., Asok the intern from the comic strip "Dilbert"). Finally, there are those who see interns as creative, talented people who expand the organization's capacity to get things done while serving as professional apprentices. Fortunately, you can take positive actions to create meaningful internships in almost any environment, as we'll see next.

FOUR STEPS TO A GREAT INTERNSHIP

Although every internship is unique, there are some basic lessons that everyone can profit from. Use the four steps below to design and carry out an experience that gives you an edge and guarantees maximum learning. With a little planning, even a short experience can result in big benefits.

Step one: Know what you want from your internship. Over the last eight years, ECO and the U.S. Environmental Protection Agency (EPA) have placed over 1,100 students in EPA internships throughout the nation. Ethel Crisp and Bob Thayer manage one of the largest groups in the program (at EPA's regional office in Chicago) and have won national recognition for superior internships. "The best interns are usually the ones who know what they're after." Crisp says. "We know *our* project needs, but we don't know *your* desires. The summer tends to fly by, and we can help you much more if you have ideas of your own."

For many interns, this can be a frustrating request. After all, you may be using the internship to find out what you want and what you need to learn. It's fair to ask professionals and teachers such questions as, Why don't you tell me what I should want from my internship? You've been there. You're the professional. Help me out here!

Here's some help. Intern managers agree that there are at least four types of learning you should be seeking from your internship: skills, content knowledge, organizational knowledge, and information about professional life. Each one deserves some further exploration.

Skills. What skills do you want to learn or improve? Keep in mind that today's employers universally want people with good writing and verbal communication skills. Project management and scheduling skills are also in demand. Computer abilities are crucial, and anything you can do to improve those skills will be beneficial to your future. Competence on cutting-edge laboratory or field equipment is important for many entry-level jobs. Quantitative skills (such as statistical analysis) can help you immensely. Finally, creative problem solving is a critical skill. Check internships against this list, as well as your own skill-building needs.

Content knowledge. A good internship should improve your knowledge base. You should emerge from your experience with more knowledge of environmental justice, atmospheric chemistry, how toxins migrate in groundwater, or whatever issue your internship addressed. Compare your internship to a class. In a class, you start with little knowledge of the course content, and through planned activities, reading, and discussion you learn more. Tests, quizzes and papers are used to monitor your learning progress along the way. All of this curriculum has been put together for you by seasoned professors. In your internship, most of that learning structure is removed. You must be your own curriculum designer. For help, talk to professors and your intern supervisors. Ask for outside reading assignments and easy ways to test your learning progress. Finally, look for internships that incorporate some formal training with on-the-job learning.

Organizational knowledge and contacts. One of the reasons we pursue internships is to increase our chances of permanent employment at the same organization. If this is one of your goals, make it explicit to yourself and judge potential internships against it. Will you get a chance to meet people with hiring authority and show what you can do? Are interns incorporated into the organization's culture, so that you can make a decision about whether this employer is for you?

Learning about professional life. Perhaps the most important thing you can learn through an internship is what it feels like to be a working professional in your chosen field. Put this on your learning agenda. Is the internship a representative example of what daily life will be like as a geologist, chemist, journalist, biologist, webmaster, or policy analyst?

Obviously, there are many other things you'll want from your internship. You may want to spend a summer outdoors, meet new people, see a new part of the country, make a little money, have fun, or simply fulfill an internship requirement for your college degree. Get it all down on paper. You will be way ahead of the game when you examine specific intern opportunities.

Step two: Know what you have to offer. Although it's crucial for you to know what you want from your internship, it's important to realize that intern employers are more interested in what they want. Competition for internships has increased as more people realize how important practical experience is to career success. Internships have become more like entry-level jobs at many places, and you need to make a strong case for your selection. Environmental employers understand that you are at "intern level" and that your skills may be limited. Nonetheless, they need to know what you can do now to make an assessment of how you can help them. Be ready with an inventory of your existing abilities.

Step three: Identify organizations of interest. If you have completed the first two steps effectively, a picture of your preferred internship is starting to emerge. Carlton Eley is a two-time intern alumni of The Environmental Careers Organization, as well as a 1998 M.S. graduate from the University of Iowa geography department. "When I was an undergraduate at Hampton University, I was looking for an internship in my field of social work. Talking to a friend led me to the EPA Office of Environmental Justice," Carlton says. "That's where I discovered an internship in Seattle that essentially allowed me to do social work in an environmental context. I grabbed it!"

Linking your desires and skills to specific organizations is crucial. As we saw in chapter 1, there are tens of thousands of business, government, and nonprofit employers. It's time to narrow things down. For some people, this will be easy. If you want to work in a chemistry lab close to home, a few conversations with faculty and local professionals will narrow your search quickly.

To track down prospective employers and formal intern programs, start your search on the computer. See the list of environmental internship websites at the end of this chapter, as well as the names of print directories and employer listings.

As you identify organizations of interest to you, find out about the whole range of nonpermanent employment options and why the organization uses interns. In the environmental field, there are many different reasons to offer internships, and the underlying motivation of the employer can make a big difference in whether or not you are a realistic candidate. Using the nine options described below, ask employers directly about their own offerings.

Educational internships link employers with specific institutions, usually through cooperative education, and often involve formal eligibility and educational requirements. It can sometimes be hard to arrange an internship with an employer who has strong, formal promises to work with a specific college unless you are a student there. Check on this so that you'll know the odds. Other educational internships involve practicums for which one receives college credit.

Seasonal and part-time jobs can be made into internships, as we mentioned earlier, through commitments on both sides to be attentive to the learning needs of the intern. Land management agencies, parks, youth camps, nature centers, museums, and other seasonal employers have years of experience in managing short-term workforces of intern age.

Project internships are the most popular forms of internship at the undergraduate level and higher. The intern is expected to complete a specific project or set of projects (write a newsletter, complete a survey, build a database, gath-

A field researcher with EPA's Great Lakes National Program Office dons an immersion suit for work on Lake Erie, aboard the agency's research vessel, Lake Guardian.

er field samples, carry out a research assignment) before the end of the intern period. Project internships can be both paid and unpaid.

Recruitment internships are often found at larger, private companies and may target people from schools with elite reputations. These internships are used to draw new employees to the company under the assumption that a summer spent with the firm will increase the odds that you will accept a permanent offer when you graduate.

Diversity internships are offered to women and people of color as one part of an organization's strategy to increase racial, ethnic, and gender diversity (a crucial need in the environmental and conservation field).

Temporary jobs involve the use of contract temporary services for short-term assignments (sometimes as short as a few days). There are a growing number of firms with names like EnviroTemps and EcoTemps. Some of these firms have become quite sophisticated and offer additional training opportunities to temporary employees.

Part-time jobs can be great internships. While you're in school, a part-time job at an environmental agency or company gives you staff status and opens a wide range of assignments that may not be given to those whose work has a specific end date.

Fellowships are most often found in research fields and provide financial support that allows scientists to continue promising work. There are also a few fellowships in policy fields and for mid-career professionals. Fellowships are usually extremely competitive and application procedures are formal and demanding.

Community service internships are arranged through programs like the federal AmeriCorps initiative, Public Allies, Teach for America, GreenCorps, and conservation corps organizations throughout the nation. In these programs, participants agree to provide service on a variety of projects for terms that range from twelve weeks to two years. Some of these programs serve high school students, as well as those in college or advanced degree programs.

The final result of your employer research may leave you feeling a little overwhelmed. You probably have many more options to pursue than you thought would be the case. What's next? Most of us know by now that firing off lots of resumes and applications is *not* the best way to land a position, even if it is an internship. It's very rare that you will be able to send a few letters and wait for the offers to arrive. It's better to target your search to a few employers and tailor your approach to their needs. It's a tough job, but the sooner you get started, the sooner you will be able to move on to the next step.

Step four: Make your interest known and land the internship. You've done your homework. You know what you want and what you have to offer. You've identified some employers that are of interest to you. If the employer has a formal program of internships or seasonal opportunities, your next step is clear—let them know that you are available and interested. If you can make this contact in person, do so. In selecting interns, many employers opt for people they've met, or who have been recommended by friends and fellow employees. If you can't make your pitch in person, start with a letter and follow up quickly with a phone call or email. Email is a great communication tool for this purpose. You can compose your message carefully and present it in your own way. There is no need to wait to get the person on the phone (which can be difficult) and the receiving party can answer at his or her leisure. You can attach other materials (such as your resume, cover letter, and writing sample). Finally, you can follow up with a phone call and expect that the employer already knows something about you, or can readily get the necessary information with the click of a mouse.

If your employer of choice does not offer a formal intern program, and has no seasonal openings that meet your needs, you have an exciting opportunity—proposing your own tailored internship. To create a personalized internship, follow all of the steps above, and then meet personally with the person you would like to intern with. Use this meeting to learn about current projects of interest and tasks that are not getting done, but are of priority interest. Stay focused on the employer's needs during your meeting.

Immediately after the interview, prepare a short two- to three-page proposal on how you could help the organization through an internship. Your intelligence and initiative will almost always be rewarded. Even if the professional you have identified is unable to take you on, she will certainly be moved to share other ideas and contacts with you. If your proposal is accepted, you will almost certainly have a quality internship. After all, you and your supervisor designed the project together. What could be better?

DIFFERENCES IN INTERN USE: GOVERNMENT, BUSINESS, AND NONPROFITS

Internship use varies widely among different types of employers, both in the number of interns used and in the motivations for sponsoring them. Knowing something about how your targeted organizations operate can be crucial information for internship success.

PUBLIC SECTOR

Federal and State Government. Federal and state environmental agencies often have established internship, summer, and part-time programs. Contact these agencies during the fall for summer programs and at least three to six months in advance of when you are available. Consider regional and local opportunities, as well as those at the national headquarters. For example, if you want to work for the EPA or any other federal agency, contact its offices in Washington, D.C., but also contact regional offices, research laboratories, and other facilities. The agencies of the Department of the Interior (e.g., National Park Service, U.S. Geological Survey, Bureau of Land Management, U.S. Fish and Wildlife Service) have detailed requirements for interns, seasonal employees, and volunteers, while other agencies are more informal. Environmental agencies at the state level mirror this distinction, with land management and wildlife agencies usually having more formal programs. Most federal and state intern programs are well advertised on agency webpages.

Local Government. Some local governments have established internship programs. Usually, however, the process is much more informal, which means it is up to you to take the initiative. A mid-sized or large metropolitan area will have a number of different agencies, and a large municipality will have dozens of municipal and county units of government, commissions, and regional agencies. Start at home. Local governments like to hire their own citizens. Because local government is so close to the issues, it is an excellent place to gain practical work experience.

PRIVATE SECTOR

Large corporate institutions with thousands of employees and dozens of sites are completely different intern sponsors than small, owner-operated firms with a handful of employees. Match your intern desires with the right kind of private sponsor for maximum learning and career advancement.

Corporations. Although many companies have formal internship programs and seasonal opportunities, few of these programs focus on the environment. Notable exceptions exist in the outdoor recreation fields, tourism, forestry, and landscape architecture. Check with the company's human resources department, but do not stop there. If you are interested in a large corporation, seek out local facilities. See whether it has an environmental health and safety staff. At the plant level, you may find that the company has never used an intern and has not even considered the idea. Be prepared to assess the company's needs and create your own position. In these cases, specific projects with tangible end products will gain an employer's attention. A good question to ask is "What projects have been sitting on your back burner for more than three months that I could take the lead on?"

Consulting Firms. Only the largest consulting firms will have formal internship programs, and these programs usually recruit engineers and scientists from disciplines that the firm needs for its permanent staff. Of the hundreds of smaller firms, few have formal internship programs. Consulting companies are extremely dynamic operations, always looking for business and staffing for projects. If you call them the day after they land a big contract, you may be in luck; if you visit the day they finish that project, you might see laid-off staff members leaving the office. Consultants are accustomed to working with a variety of staffing situations and may be open to part-time and internship arrangements. The downside is that they rarely have a lot of time to train and manage interns. Your task, therefore, is to convince those who have the hiring power that you have a service to offer and are worth a small investment of their time.

Checking your local Yellow Pages under Environmental Conservation and Ecological Services will probably yield 15 to 20 firms in a large metropolitan area. Professors or contacts in professional associations will know about opportunities. See also the *EnviroDirectory* listings at the end of this chapter.

NONPROFIT SECTOR

Nonprofit organizations are one of your best options for internships. Literally hundreds of nonprofit organizations offer intern positions in which you will perform challenging work because the professional staff is so small. In major nonprofit groups, such as the National Wildlife Federation, the Natural Resources Defense Council, The Nature Conservancy, and so forth, competition for internships is intense. Unpaid internships are common in the nonprofit world, and those that are paid may provide an extremely small stipend. There are many nonprofit environmental organizations at the local level, and if you are a self-starter, you can do incredibly substantive work.

ABOUT THE ENVIRONMENTAL CAREERS ORGANIZATION

For those who would like to apply for several hundred environmental internships with one application, the Environmental Careers Organization (ECO) might be an option. ECO offers one of the nation's largest and most diverse environmental intern programs. Since 1972, ECO has placed over 7,000 students and recent graduates in professional-level internships of 12 to 52 weeks. Some ECO internships last up to two years. ECO places 450 to 600 new interns each year. All positions are paid, and 1998 stipends ranged from $400 to $700 per week.

ECO is headquartered in Boston, with regional offices in Cleveland, San Francisco, Seattle, and Boston. The organization serves the entire nation, including Alaska and Hawaii.

Sponsoring organizations include public agencies at the federal, state, and local levels, corporations, private consulting firms, activist groups, and other nonprofit organizations. Some grassroots nonprofit groups receive financial support for internships through ECO's project assistance fund, including twenty-five community groups in 1998.

ECO has a large federal government program and offers a wide range of opportunities at the EPA, Geological Survey, Bureau of Land Management, National Park Service, National Oceanic and Atmospheric Administration, and Department of Energy.

ECO positions span the entire spectrum of environmental and conservation careers, and the organization regularly has intern offerings for scientists, engineers, technicians, computer specialists, social scientists, journalists and educators, policy analysts, and generalists.

In 1990, ECO launched The Diversity Initiative, a multimillion-dollar effort to increase the presence and impact of Hispanic, African, Asian, and Native Americans in the environmental field. In that year, fewer than 5 percent of ECO's interns were people of color. By 1997, the percentage had exceeded 37 percent. Over 1,000 environmental professionals of color have graduated from the program in its first eight years.

ECO is not the only program that offers multiple internships through one source. Also check out the Student Conservation Association (SCA). A nonprofit organization, SCA has over forty years of experience in providing national and community conservation internship and volunteer opportunities. SCA annually recruits and fields more than 2,200 high school, college, and adult participants to help conserve our public lands and to further diversify the conservation workforce.

High school graduates (18 and older) are placed in 12- to 52-week internships with natural resource professionals. Positions come with a travel grant, housing provided by the host agency, a stipend for food and basic living expenses, and (in some cases) a monetary educational award upon successful completion of the position.

For individuals 16 to 19 years old, SCA offers the opportunity to spend 4 to 5 weeks, often in backcountry locations, performing hands-on conservation work and developing personal growth skills. Coeducational groups of 6 to 10 participants live and work together under the supervision of skilled crew leaders.

SCA also provides career resources through a number of publications and services, including *Earth Work*, a magazine for and about conservation professionals, and several excellent conservation career books, such as *Earth Work: Resource Guide to Nationwide Green Jobs* and *The Guide to Graduate Environmental Programs*. Finally, SCA offers the most complete listing of available conservation job opportunities in the nation on its website at http:\\www.sca-inc.org.

HOW TO MAKE THE MOST OF YOUR INTERNSHIP

Whether you create your own internship, get one through an organization's program, or find a position through ECO, it is what you accomplish with the opportunity that will determine how useful the experience is for you, your sponsor, and the environment. The following are some suggestions to help you make your internship useful and rewarding.

Make sure your employer is ready for your arrival. Communicate in detail with your intern employer before that first day. Interns are sometimes a low priority and some gentle prodding will help guarantee that you have a

All work and no play? Interns with the U.S. Bureau of Land Management (BLM) have some fun before heading out to the backcountry.

cubicle, desk, phone, computer, and some management time set aside for your orientation.

Develop a work/learning plan with your supervisor. Be wary of unstructured internships, especially short-term summer experiences. Ten to 12 weeks is not a long time, and you'll want a clear sense of what is expected of you and when. Developing a work plan together can also help you determine whether the expectations are realistic and what might get in the way of your success. If your supervisor seems slow or uninterested in this task, create a work plan of your own and see how that works.

Set regular meetings. Set up a regularly scheduled meeting with your supervisor, ideally once a week, to evaluate your progress. Insist on adhering to this schedule. If your supervisor misses a meeting, provide a brief written report of what you would have talked about at the meeting.

Work harder, longer, and better than you need to. Your internship is an opportunity, not an obligation. Treat each request as an opportunity to do something remarkable, and to learn as much as you can. Do things faster, better, cheaper, and more beautifully than anyone has a right to expect. Come in early and stay late. Put in a couple of weekends. Your time is short, so you can keep up a good pace while you're there. Go for the "wow" effect.

Keep records. Record your accomplishments and keep copies of your written work. Before you leave, request a letter of recommendation that you can use in future job applications. If possible, develop working relationships with more than one staff member so that if your supervisor leaves, there will still be someone who can speak to future employers about your accomplishments.

Get to know people. Meet people in your company and in related organizations. Ask them about their work and tell them about your professional aspirations. Start building a network of other talented professionals who care about the environment.

Stay in touch after the internship. You've spent several months working with professionals and other interns. Don't be a stranger! Stay in touch through email, phone calls, and letters. Let people know what you're doing. Ask for help occasionally, and offer help as well. Internships can be a source of new friends and colleagues that you'll have for the rest of your life.

SALARY

Here are two ads for environmental internships. The first is from a national environmental group in Washington, D.C.

CONSERVATION INTERN Assist program staff with habitat conservation policy, including national forest protection issues, funding for wildlife refuges, national forests and parks, and other public land issues. Salary: None. Qualifications: Must have bachelor's degree in relevant field. Advanced degree preferred.

The second is from an environmental education center in Ohio.

FIELD INSTRUCTOR Lead morning and afternoon instruction, both in the field and in the labs and activity areas, plus evening programs twice a week. Join students for all three meals in dining hall, and assist in upkeep of facilities and equipment. Contribute to food service operation on rotating basis. Teach day programs with National Park Service rangers. Participate in weekend use of center by rental groups. Attend professional development workshops. Position runs 50–60 hours per week. Salary: None. Housing, meals, health insurance provided. College credit possible.

The unpaid (or minimally paid) environmental internship is alive and well in the environmental world, especially at conservation employers and nonprofit organizations. At many agencies, the expression "paid intern" is an oxymoron. The word "intern" is a synonym for "volunteer." The practice is not universal, however. Intern pay has been creeping up toward entry-level wages at some environmental employers, and many seasonal environmental opportunities are competitive with other "summer job" opportunities. A recent edition of *Earth Work* magazine had intern listings that covered a spectrum from zero to $425 per week. In the middle were internships offering room and board, $250/week, $75/day, $1,000/month, and $100/week, including housing and transportation. If your financial situation allows you to accept unpaid, or poorly paid, internships, you will obviously have more opportunities. In making your decision, consider not only your checking account balance, but the checklist of skills, knowledge, and contacts you developed earlier. Internships are about learning and new experiences. If the quotient of learning and adventure are high enough, it may be worth it to accept unpaid positions.

What you want to avoid, of course, is accepting an internship with low learning potential and low money. Unfortunately, there are many of these types of internships. If you are preparing to accept an unpaid internship, know that you have some bargaining power. Be clear with your intern employer about what you need in return to make this worth your while. Chances are good that unpaid internships are rough around the edges, and that there is a lot of room to adapt the actual work plan to the skills and needs of the intern. Negotiate!

In a similar vein, don't assume that the stipend level advertised is all that the market will bear. It's highly unlikely that an employer will lose an intern they really want to save an inconsequential amount of money. Interns have been known to increase their pay $100 a week just by asking, especially on project-based internships where the product is really needed. Don't sell yourself short.

VOLUNTEERING FOR THE ENVIRONMENT

No book about environmental careers would be complete without acknowledging the nation's environmental volunteers, and the important role that volunteering plays in developing and sustaining your environmental career. The environmental world depends on volunteers at all levels. The U.S. Forest

Service, for example, estimates that volunteers log far more hours each year than the agency's permanent staff does. Tim Merriman of the National Association for Interpretation says that while there are roughly 10,000 full-time interpreters in the United States, there are over 250,000 interpretive docents at parks, museums, nature centers, zoos, and aquariums, most of whom are volunteers. Thousands of volunteers monitor water quality, serve on boards and commissions, organize protests and legislative campaigns, plant trees, restore land, build trails, and vote for environmentally aware candidates.

We are a nation of volunteers, and the environmental community is a perfect example.

Unpaid internships are a special kind of volunteer experience, but there are many others. Serving as a volunteer can be a valuable part of your environmental education and citizen service or it can be a waste of time for all concerned. Here are some things to think about as you consider the role of volunteering in your own education, environmental career, and personal life.

WHY PEOPLE VOLUNTEER

There are as many reasons for volunteering as there are individuals, but a few stand out.

To gain work experience, develop skills, explore careers, or find a job. You may be volunteering for all of the same reasons people seek out internships—seasonal employment and part-time jobs. If these are your goals, be sure to use the same process described earlier ("Four Steps to a Great Internship") and review the advice from intern professionals ("How to Make the Most of Your Internship"). Most volunteer experiences are designed with the goals of the organization, not the volunteer, in mind. Using the internship design method helps assure that your volunteer time achieves your educational and career development objectives.

To help environmental organizations with "nonenvironmental" skills. Environmental groups and government agencies need help, and there is never enough money to pay for all of the talent required. Volunteers make the difference. Examples include the banker who explores financing options for a new recycling program, and the public relations professional who designs a communications plan for a referendum campaign.

As a form of public service. Many environmental professionals serve on boards and commissions because they feel a duty to contribute their knowledge and experience to the solution of real-world problems in their communities. Smaller towns draw especially heavily on the volunteer contributions of engineers, scientists, activists, planners, lawyers, and designers as an integral part of the environmental "workforce."

To provide leadership in one's professional field. Look for volunteer opportunities in professional associations. Serving as an officer in association activities locally, regionally, or nationally can also be a great form of networking and finding new professional challenges.

To educate and inspire people of all ages. One of the most popular forms of professional volunteering is to serve as a speaker in the schools, at civic organizations, and at career fairs.

Out of a desire to "do something" about the environmental crisis. Millions of people volunteer simply because they are concerned—even outraged—about the deterioration of our environment. These people ask simply what they can do to improve environmental quality and reverse destructive trends.

How to Make the Most of Your Volunteering

In addition to the items listed earlier about effective interning, the following advice from volunteers and environmental staff members should help you in structuring your own volunteer position.

Find out if the organization you are interested in takes volunteers regularly. Managing volunteers effectively is a skill that is developed through practice. Organizations that have volunteer coordinators and experience with organizing volunteer projects may be the best place to start.

Decide how much time you have to give and when you are available. Environmental work, like all work, is planned ahead of time and needs to get on a schedule. If the organization you are working for knows that you are available every Tuesday and Thursday morning from 8 to 12, this helps immensely.

Be clear about your expectations and limitations. From the employer's perspective, you may be a name on a card (especially at first). It's important for them to know what kind of volunteering you are willing and able to do, and why you are volunteering in the first place. There are some people who are willing to do "whatever needs to be done." Others are available for specific types of volunteering only. Make sure people know when to call on you.

Work on group volunteering projects. These can be great fun, a wonderful way to meet people, and valuable for organizations who need a lot of people to volunteer at one time.

Meet your commitments. If you make a volunteer commitment, recognize it as such, just as you would a paid job. People are counting on you. Have some empathy for the staffer who manages volunteers. Show your enthusiasm, energy, and responsibility; these are the best foundation for a good working relationship.

Have fun. Good volunteer sponsors know that people who are giving freely of their time need to get some pleasure out of it. Have fun! Laugh and talk with your fellow volunteers and make some friends. Some of the best volunteer experiences are remembered for the great parties.

Volunteer Vacations and Travel Experiences

More and more people are taking advantage of programs that allow people to do something good for the environment while they travel and learn at the same time. Organizations such as Earthwatch, the Smithsonian Research Expeditions Program, and many others are an excellent way to combine vacations and volunteering. Most of these programs require you to pay the organization coordinating the trip and pay for your own travel as well. The growing numbers of people enjoying "environmental vacations," however, seem to indicate that many find such trips worthwhile. Information on how to find good programs is included in the Resource section for this chapter.

SUMMARY

Self-knowledge, good planning, and quality information have been stressed throughout this chapter because teachers, career experts, and employers all agree these factors are crucial to your preparation for an environmental career.

Creating the right mix of formal education and practical experience for your particular needs, however, is more art than science. As you read through the profiles and case studies in the *Complete Guide to Environmental Careers*, you'll find plenty of examples of successful professionals who had no idea what they wanted to do in college, happened into a variety of opportunities, met dead ends, experienced failures, and generally made up a wonderful career as they went along. The environmental field has matured in the last forty years, but it is still young and constantly changing. Who knows for sure what tomorrow will bring?

John R. Cook, Jr., founder of the Environmental Careers Organization and president since 1972, says: "Be persistent and keep learning. That's the best advice I've ever heard. If you are alive to learning and never give up, you'll find the education and experience you need." Cook likes to end his speeches to students around the country with a quote from the German poet and scientist Goethe, who wrote: "Whatever you can do, or dream you can, begin it."

"Get started," Cook advises. "The rest is details."

RESOURCES

Professional associations are one of the best sources of information on education for environmental fields. Many of those listed in this section are described in greater detail in other chapters. For information on internships, volunteering, colleges, and scholarships use these resources, and search the Internet for more specific information. For example, many employers have information about intern and volunteer opportunities on their company/agency websites. Almost every college has a website of its own.

PROFESSIONAL ASSOCIATIONS

Air and Waste Management Association, 1 Gateway Center, Third Floor, Pittsburgh, PA 15222. (412) 232-3444. Http://www.awma.org.
American Academy of Environmental Engineers, 130 Holiday Court, Suite 100, Annapolis, MD 21401. (410) 266-3311. Http://www.enviro-engineers.org.

American Chemical Society, 1155 16th Street, NW, Washington, DC 20036. (202) 872-4600. Http://www.acs.org.

American Epidemiological Society, 717 Delaware Street, Minneapolis, MN 55440-9441. (612) 623-5414.

American Fisheries Society, 5410 Grosvenor Lane, Suite 110, Bethesda, MD 20814. (301) 897-8916. Http://www.esd.ornl.gov/afs.

American Geological Institute, 4220 King Street, Alexandria, VA 22302. (703) 379-2480. Http://www.agi.org.

American Horticultural Society, 7931 E. Boulevard Drive, Alexandria, VA 22308. (703) 768-5700. http://www.ahs.org.

American Industrial Hygiene Association, 2700 Prosperity Avenue, Suite 250, Fairfax, VA 22031. (703) 849-8888. Http://www.aiha.org.

American Institute of Biological Sciences, 1444 Eye Street NW, Suite 200, Washington, DC 20005, (202) 628-1500. Http://www.aibs.org.

American Institute of Chemical Engineers, 345 East 47th Street, New York, NY 10017. (212) 705-7338. Http://www.aiche.org.

American Institute of Hydrology, 2499 Rice Street, Suite 135, St. Paul, MN 55113. (612) 484-8169.

American Meteorological Society, 45 Beacon Street, Boston, MA 02108. (617) 227-2425. Http://www.ametsoc.org/AMS.

American Ornithologists' Union, Smithsonian Institution, National Museum of Natural History, Division of Birds MRC-116, Washington, DC 20560. (202) 357-2051. Http://www.nmnh.si.edu/vert/birds/birds.html.

American Planning Association, 1776 Massachusetts Avenue, NW, Washington, DC 20036. (202) 872-0611. Http://www.planning.org.

American Society of Agricultural Engineers, 2950 Niles Road, St. Joseph, MI 49085. (616) 429-0300. Http://www.asae.org/people.

American Society of Agronomy, 677 South Segoe Road, Madison, WI 53711. (608) 273-8080.

American Society of Civil Engineers, 1801 Alexander Bell Drive, Reston, VA 20191. (703) 295-6000. Http://www.asce.org.

American Society of Landscape Architects, 636 Eye Street, NW, Washington, DC, 20001. Http://www.asla.org.

American Society of Naturalists, University of Kansas, Biological Sciences Division, Lawrence, KS 66045.

American Society of Sanitary Engineering, 28901 Clemens Road, Suite 100, West Lake, OH 44145. (216) 835-3040. Email to: asse@ix.netcom.com.

American Solar Energy Society, 2400 Central Avenue G-1, Boulder, CO 80301. (303) 443-3130. Http://www.ases.org/solar.

American Water Works Association, 6666 W. Quincy, Denver, CO 80235. (303) 794-7711. Http://www.awwa.org.

Association of American Geographers, 1710 16th Street, NW, Washington, DC 20009. (202) 234-1450. Http://www.aag.org

Association of Conservation Engineers, Arkansas Game and Fish Commission, 2 Natural Resource Drive, Little Rock, AR 72205. (501) 219-4300.

Association of Engineering Geologists, 323 Boston Post Road, Suite 2D, Sudbury, MA 01776. (978) 443-4639.

Association of Ground Water Scientists and Engineers, 601 Dempsey Road, Westerville, OH 43081. (614) 898-7791. Http://www.h2o.ngwa.org.

Crops Science Society of America, 677 South Segoe Road, Madison, WI 53711. (608) 273-8080. Http://www.crops.org/cssa.

Ecological Society of America, 2010 Massachusetts Avenue, NW, Suite 400, Washington, DC 20036. (202) 833-8773. Http://www.sdsc.edu/~esa/esa.html.

Environmental Engineers and Managers Institute, Association of Energy Engineers, 4025 Pleasantdale Road, Suite 420, Atlanta, GA 30340. Http://www.aeecenter. org.

Geological Society of America, 3300 Penrose Place, P.O. Box 9140, Boulder, CO 80301. (303) 447-2020. Http://www.geosociety.org.

Industrial Design Society of America, 1142 Walker Road, Great Falls, VA 22066. (703) 759-0100. Http://www.adsi.org.

Institute of Environmental Sciences, 940 East Northwest Highway, Mt. Prospect, IL 60056. (847) 255-1561. Http://www.iest.org.

National Academy of Sciences, Environmental Studies and Toxicology, National Research Council, 2001 Wisconsin Avenue, NW, Room HA-354, Washington, DC 20007. (202) 334-3060. Http://www2.nas.edu/besthome/.

National Association of Environmental Risks Auditors, 6645 Colerain Avenue, P.O. Box 53185, Cincinnati, OH 45253. (513) 674-1109.

National Environmental Health Association, 720 South Colorado Boulevard, Suite 970 South Tower, Denver, CO 80222. (303) 756-9090. Http://www.neha.org.

National Environmental Training Association, 3020 East Camelback Road, Suite 399, Phoenix, AZ 85016. (602) 956-6099. Http://www.ehs-training.org.

National Park and Recreation Association, 2775 South Quincy St., Suite 300, Arlington, VA 22206-2204. (703) 858-0784. Http://www.npra.org.

National Pollution Prevention Center for Higher Education, University of Michigan, 430 East University, Ann Arbor, MI 48109-1115. (313) 764-1412. Http:// www.umich.edu/~nppcpub/.

National Registry of Environmental Professionals, PO Box 2099, Glenview, IL 60025. (847) 724-6631. Http://www.nrep.org.

National Science for Youth Foundation, 130 Azalea Drive, Roswell, GA 30075. (770) 594-9367.

National Science Teachers Association, 1840 Wilson Blvd., Arlington, VA 22201-3000. (703) 243-7100. Http://www.nsta.org.

National Society of Fund Raising Executives, 1101 King St., Suite 700, Alexandria, VA 22314. (703) 684-0410.

North American Association for Environmental Education, P.O. Box 400, Troy, OH 45373. (937) 676-2514. Http://www.naaee.org.

Outdoor Writers Association of America, 2155 E. College Avenue, State College, PA 16801. (814) 234-1011.

Society for Conservation Biology. Http://conbio.rice.edu/scb/.

Society for Range Management, 1839 York Street, Denver, CO 80206. (303) 355-7070.

Society of American Foresters, 5400 Grosvenor Lane, Bethesda, MD, 20814. (301) 897-8720. Http://www.safnet.org.

Society of Ecological Restoration, 1207 Seminole Highway, Suite B, Madison, WI 53711. (608) 262-9547. Http://nabalu.flas.ufl.edu/ser/SERhome.html.

Society of Environmental Journalists, PO Box 27280, Philadelphia, PA 19118. (215) 836-9970.

Society of Toxicology, 1767 Business Center Drive, Suite 302, Reston, VA 22090. (703) 438-3115. Http://www.toxicology.org.

Soil and Water Conservation Society, 7515 Northeast Ankeny Road, Ankeny, IA 50021. (515) 289-2331. Http://www.swcs.org.

Soils Science Society of America, 677 South Segoe Road, Madison, WI 53711. (608) 273-8080. Http://www.soils.org/sssa.

Water Environmental Federation, 601 Wythe Street, Alexandria, VA 22314. (703) 684-2400. Http://www.wef.org.

BOOKS AND DIRECTORIES: VOCATIONAL, TWO-YEAR, AND UNDERGRADUATE EDUCATION

The Best 311 Colleges: 1998, by Edward T. Custard, Christine Chung, John Katzman, Zac Knower, Tom Meltzer (Princeton Review, 1997) $20.

Education for the Earth: The College Guide for Careers in the Environment (Peterson's Guides, 1996) $14.

The EnviroDirectory is updated annually. Regional editions are available for the New England, Mid-Atlantic, Great Lakes, and Southwest states. Includes hundreds of private environmental firms and reference listings for state government offices, regional nonprofit groups, and selected colleges. Contact Environmental Marketing Group, 1770 Massachusetts Avenue, Cambridge, MA 02140. (888) 784-9570 toll free or http://www.EnviroDirectory.com.

The Gourman Report: A Rating of Undergraduate Programs in American and International Universities (10th Edition), by Jack Gourman (Princeton Review, 1997) $21.

(Kaplan) What to Study: 101 Fields in a Flash, by Eric Freedman, and Edward Hoffman (Simon and Schuster, 1997) $18.

Peterson's Guide to Four-Year Colleges 1998 (28th Edition, includes CD-ROM) (Peterson's Guides, 1997) $24.

Peterson's Guide to Two-Year Colleges 1998 (28th Edition), by Joseph G. Emanski (Peterson's Guides, 1997) $21.

Peterson's Top Colleges for Science: A Guide to Leading Four-Year Programs in the Biological, Chemical, Geological, Mathematical, and Physical Sciences, by David Davis-Van Atta (Peterson's Guides, 1996) $24.

Peterson's Vocational and Technical Schools and Programs 1998 (Peterson's Guides, 1997) $34.

Researching Colleges on the World Wide Web, by Kerry Cochrane (Franklin Watts, 1997) $16.

BOOKS AND DIRECTORIES: GRADUATE AND DOCTORAL EDUCATION

The Gourman Report: A Rating of Graduate and Professional Programs in American and International Universities (8th Edition), by Jack Gourman (Princeton Review, 1997) $21.95.

The Guide to Graduate Environmental Programs (Island Press, 1997) $16.95.

Peterson's Graduate and Professional Programs: An Overview 1998 (Peterson's Guides, 1997) $34.95.

Separate editions of Peterson's Graduate Programs are available in *The Biological Sciences 1998* (Peterson's Guides, 1997) $49.95, *Humanities, Arts, and Social Sciences 1998* (Peterson's Guides) $42.95, and Business, Education, Health, Information Studies, Law and Social Work 1998 (Peterson's Guides, 1997) $34.95/each.

Student Advantage Guide to the Best Graduate Programs: 1997 (annual). The *Student Advantage Guide* comes in three volumes: Engineering ($20), Humanities and Social Sciences ($24), and Physical and Biological Sciences ($24). All from Princeton Review.

SCHOLARSHIPS AND FINANCIAL AID

There are a large number of good books on scholarships and financial aid available from Peterson's, Princeton Review, Prentice Hall, Sourcebooks Trade,

College Board, Ten Speed Press, and Career Press. Visit a good bookstore, or review them on the Internet at amazon.com. The largest of the annual guides for undergraduate study is *Peterson's Scholarships, Grants and Prizes 1998: The Most Complete Guide to College Financial Aid from Private Sources,* $24.95.

STUDY ABROAD

Peterson's Study Abroad 1998: Over 1,600 Semester and Year Abroad Academic Programs (Peterson's Guides, 1997) $29.95.

ENVIRONMENTAL AND CONSERVATION INTERNSHIP PROGRAMS

The Environmental Careers Organization (ECO), 179 South Street, Boston, MA 02111. (617) 426-4375. Http://www.eco.org. (See full description in this chapter.)

Student Conservation Association (SCA), P.O. Box 550, 689 River Road, Charlestown, NH 03603. (603) 543-1700. Http://www.sca-inc.org. (See full description in this chapter.)

INTERNSHIP DIRECTORIES

America's Top Internships, 1999, by Mark Oldman, and Samer Hamadeh (Princeton Review, 1998) $21.00.

The Internship Bible 1998, by Mark Oldman, and Samer Hamadeh (Princeton Review, 1997) $25.00.

Peterson's Internships 1998: More than 40,000 Opportunities to Get an Edge in Today's Competitive Job Market (Peterson's Guides, 1997) $24.95.

Sixth Annual Graduate Groups Internships in State Government (Graduate Group, 1996) $27.50.

SUBSCRIBER-ONLY JOB LISTINGS WITH INTERNSHIPS
AND SEASONAL OPPORTUNITIES

Earth Work Magazine. Monthly publication of The Student Conservation Association, P.O. Box 550, Charlestown, NH 03603. (603) 543-1700. Http://www.sca-inc.org.

Environmental Career Opportunities. Published every two weeks by Brubach Corporation, P.O. Box 560, Stanardsville, VA 22973. (804) 985-8627. Http://www.ecojobs.com.

The Job Seeker. Published every two weeks, Route 2, Box 16, Warrens, WI 54666. (608) 378-4290. Http://www.tomah.com/jobseeker.

National Environmental Employment Report. Monthly publication from Environmental Careers World, 100 Bridge Street, Building A, Hampton, VA 23669. Http://environmental-jobs.com.

ENVIRONMENTAL INTERNSHIPS ON THE INTERNET

Intern.net offers an environmental internship newsletter and a matching service for subscribers only at Http://www.intern.net.

Check the websites of all organizations above, and see also the extensive collection of Internet-based environmental employment sources in the next chapter.

Dozens of colleges and departments do an excellent job of providing environmental intern information for their students on the Internet. See Boston University's Center for Energy and Environmental Studies career website as one example at http://web.bu.edu/CEES/Careers.html.

VOLUNTEERING AND VOLUNTEER VACATIONS

Check directly with any organizations that interest you, or try the following:

Alternatives to the Peace Corps: A Directory of Third World and U.S. Volunteer Opportunities, by Phil Lowenthal, Stephanie Tarnoff, Lisa David, and Annette Olson (Food First Books, 1996) $9.95.

AmeriCorps, c/o Corporation for National Service, 1201 New York Avenue, NW, Washington, DC 20525. (202) 606-5000. Http://www.americorps.org.

The Back Door Guide to Short-Term Job Adventures: Internships, Extraordinary Experiences, Volunteering, Work Abroad, by Michael Landes (Ten Speed Press, 1997) $19.95.

The International Directory of Voluntary Work, by Victoria Pybus (Peterson's Guides, 1997) $15.95.

Volunteer Vacations: Short-Term Adventures That Will Benefit You and Others, by Bill McMillon (Chicago Review Press, 1997) $16.95.

Youth Service America, 1101 15th Street, NW, Suite 200, Washington, DC 20005. (202) 296-2992. Http://www.ysa.org. YSA operates a great Internet listing of organizations offering volunteer and service opportunities. Visit servenet.org.

RESOURCES FOR MINORITIES

Minorities in Agriculture, Natural Resources and Related Sciences (MANRRS). 418 Price Hall, Virginia Polytechnic Institute and State University, Blacksburg, VA 24061. (540) 231-6362.

National Action Council for Minorities in Engineering (NACME). The Empire State Building, 350 5th Ave., Suite 2212, New York, NY 10118. (212) 279-2626. Http://www.nacme.org.

National Association for Equal Opportunity in Higher Education (NAFEO).8701 Georgia Ave., Suite 200, Silver Spring, MD 20910. (301) 650-2440. Http://www.nafeo.org (under construction).

National Consortium for Graduate Degrees for Minorities in Engineering and Science, Inc. (GEM). The GEM Consortium Central Office, P.O. Box 537, Notre Dame, IN 46556. (219) 631-7771. Http://www.nd.edu/~gem.

RESOURCES FOR AFRICAN AMERICANS

National Association for Black Geologists and Geophysicists. U.S. Geological Survey, 2255 North Gemini Drive, Flagstaff, AZ 86001-1698. (520) 556-7220. Http://iapetus2.bgsu.edu:1003/nabgg.

National Council of Black Engineers and Scientists. 1525 Aviation Blvd., Suite C424, Redondo Beach, CA 90278. (213) 896-9779. Http:/www.blackscientists.org/ncbes.html.

National Organization for Professional Advancement of Black Chemists and Chemical Engineers (NOBCChE) Howard University, 525 College Ave., P.O. Box 5, NW, Washington, DC 20059. (202) 667-1699. Http://www.cantek.com/nobcche.

National Society of Black Engineers (NSBE). 1454 Duke St., Alexandria, VA 22314. (703) 549-2207. Http://www.nsbe.org.

National Technical Association, Inc. NTA National Headquarters, 6919 North 19th St., Philadelphia, PA 19126-1506. (215) 549-5743. Http://www.huenet.com/nta.

United Negro College Fund. 8260 Willow Oaks Corporate Drive, Fairfax, VA . (703) 205-3400. Http://www.uncf.org.

RESOURCES FOR HISPANIC AMERICANS

Center for Advancement of Hispanics in Science and Engineering Education (CAHSEE). P.O. Box 34520, Bethesda, MD 20827. (301) 299-0033. Http://www.seas.gwu.edu/student/cahsee/homepage.html.

Hispanic Association of Colleges and Universities. 4204 Gardendale St., Suite 216, San Antonio, TX 78229. (210) 692-3805. Http://www.hacu2000.org.

National Hispanic Environmental Council. 5909 N. Coverdale Way, 3rd Flr., Alexandria, VA 22310. (703) 922-2438.

Society for the Advancement of Chicanos and Native Americans in Science. SACNAS P.O. Box 8526, Santa Cruz, CA 95061-8526. Http://www.sacnas.org.

Society of Hispanic Professional Engineers (SHPE). 5400 E. Olympic Blvd., Suite 210, Los Angeles, CA 90022. (213) 725-3970. Http://www.shpe.org.

Society of Mexican American Engineers and Scientists (MAES). 3780 Kilroy Airport Way, Suite 200, Long Beach, CA 90806. Http://www.tamu.edu/maes.

RESOURCES FOR NATIVE AMERICANS

American Indian Higher Education Consortium. 121 Oronoco St., Alexandria, VA 22314. (703) 838-0400. Http://www.aihec.org (under construction).

American Indian Science and Engineering Society (AISES). 5661 Airport Blvd., Boulder, CO 80301-2339. (303) 939-0023. Http://www.aises.org.

First Nations Development Institute. The Stores Building, 11917 Main St., Fredericksburg, VA 22408. (540) 371-5615. Http://www.firstnations.org.

National Congress of American Indians. 1301 Connecticut Ave., NW, Suite 200, Washington, DC 20036. (202) 466-7767. Http://www.ncai.org.

National Tribal Environmental Council. 2221 Rio Grande Blvd., NW, Albuquerque, NM 87104. (505) 242-2175. Http://www2.ntec.org.

Native American Environmental Protection Coalition. P.O. Box 248, Valley Center, CA 92082. (760) 751-8686.

Native American Fish and Wildlife Society. 750 Burbank St., Broomfield, CO 80020. (303) 466-1725. Http://www.iex.net/nafws.org.

Native American Rights Fund. 1506 Broadway, Boulder, CO 80302. (303) 447-8760. Http://www.narf.org.

Native American Water Association. P.O. Box 511, Minden, NV 89432. (702) 782-6636.

3　The Environmental Job Search

"THE SUCCESSFUL job search begins long before you start applying for positions," says Bob Robitaille, national director of programs for the Environmental Careers Organization (ECO). "The most competitive people have a quality education, good skills and experience, some contacts, and a strong sense of direction. If you start with these things, the job search itself is much easier."

In the previous chapters, you received an overview of environmental careers today, as well as suggestions for getting your formal education and first practical experience. By now, the importance of self-knowledge, careful educational planning, and practical experience is clear. Let's assume, then, that you have these assets in place. You have some clear job options in mind, your skills and intern experience have positioned you to be competitive, you know a few people in the field who can help you, and you are motivated and full of passion about environmental problem solving.

In this chapter, you'll learn how to organize and implement a successful environmental job search. By definition, this is a general overview—Environmental Job Search 101. There are hundreds of good books about every aspect of the job search—resumes, interviews, cover letters, self-analysis, finding the "hidden job market," networking, using the Web, and so forth. Supplement the ideas presented here with the advice in more detailed career books and websites.

ALL ABOUT ATTITUDE

Job hunting is hard work, plain and simple. It can also be lonely and discouraging. If you are looking for work at a time when you are currently without steady revenue, job hunting can carry an undertow of fear as well. Are there any secrets that can help? The key to success may lie in your attitude about the process. Are you going to approach it with dread and apprehension or with excitement and creativity? Everything about looking for work encourages the former mind-set. After all, in the job hunt we enter the world of sales, and a few rejections are almost inevitable. Moreover, we are selling ourselves, which makes rejections all the more painful. When an employer says no, what he or she is rejecting is not a used car, or a mutual fund, but you.

Fear of rejection can cause us to delay, to wait for a magic "help wanted" ad to appear, or to fantasize about someone doing it for us or knocking on our door with a great job offer. Out of fear, we are tempted to take the first offer that comes our way, just to end the job hunt. Then, all we have to worry about is being miserable for at least forty hours a week.

However, there is an alternative. This is *your* life and *your* career. It really is true that with creativity and persistence you can do anything that you choose. Try to view all the decisions, telephone numbers, and contacts that lie before you not as an impossibly large list to be gotten through, but as proof of the unlimited possibilities available to you. You have chosen a career in an exciting and diverse field, one in which new options appear with increasing regularity. What could be more exciting than a job search—picking and choosing where and how you want to focus your unique creative energy? As for rejection, no one has found an answer to it yet. Getting through it is difficult, but if you allow it to stop you, it certainly will.

Why all this talk about attitude? Because environmental professionals have emphasized it over and over again as a key factor in breaking into the environmental field. To get and keep that winning attitude, consider the following advice from career advisor Melissa Everett, author of *Making a Living While Making a Difference*:

> If you don't have a full-time job right now, make sure that you are doing some kind of active professional work. Musicians don't stop being musicians between gigs. You shouldn't let the lack of a job keep you from your calling. Read environmental publications, participate in associations, talk to professional colleagues, take classes, and work on challenging projects, even if you have to volunteer or take on a poorly paid 'consulting' assignment. The difference in your attitude, and how you come across, is remarkable. On a purely tactical note, you'll have an interesting answer when people ask: What are you doing right now?

It's true. Environmental professionals tend to hire colleagues, not supplicants. Set up a situation that puts you in the flow of work getting done and you'll be more likely to meet people in "real" settings, instead of artificial ones such as "informational interviews" (more on those later).

Another way to keep your positive attitude is *to get help*. The single most important mistake that environmental job hunters make is the attempt to "go it alone." It doesn't work. Build a support network of friends, mentors, and fellow job seekers to carry you through.

Finally, make sure you use all of the resources available for your job search. We live in a remarkable time when access to people, information, and opportunities is at an all time high. Whether you are a newly minted undergraduate in Iowa, or an experienced policy analyst in Washington, DC, you have a world of environmental career help at your fingertips. Use it all.

RESOURCES FOR THE ENVIRONMENTAL JOB SEARCH

When you are looking for a job, you have a strong need for information concerning the following:

- What's going on in the environmental and conservation world.
- Employer needs at organizations that interest you.
- Changes in budgets and revenue streams that create (and destroy) jobs.
- "Who's who" in your part of the environmental world.
- The structure of employment (e.g., permanent, temporary, contract, intern, and volunteer) at organizations you've targeted.
- Current job openings (posted and unposted).

You can obtain this information by reading and talking to people. A dynamic job search is the interplay between these two activities. Everything you read leads you to more reading and more people to talk with. Everyone you talk with leads to additional people and more reading.

When job seekers are first starting out, there is a tendency to approach the search from an assumption of scarcity. Are there any jobs out there? Will people be willing to talk to me? Can I find good information about employers and opportunities? Before long, you will have a completely different problem— deciding how to make sense of the deluge of information, contacts, and advice that a good job search produces.

Sources of Written Information

Written information for your job search includes employer data, job postings, media stories about environmental professionals and issues, salary surveys, financial and budget information about environmental organizations, and more. Fortunately, there is no shortage of information, if you know where to look.

The Internet. The Internet is a great resource for the environmental career seeker. Today's career seeker can find more truly useful job search information in a single afternoon, than his or her counterpart of ten years ago could have located in two weeks. Look at the information listed above. Working the Internet helps you with all of them, and it does it quickly and inexpensively. If you have access to a personal computer and a phone line, you are well on your way to getting a lot of the information you need for your search. Best of all, more and more organizations are putting information online. Data that were once available only through the mail, or on a bulletin board in another city, is now just a click away.

There are any number of good resources with information about using the Internet in your job search (see the Resources section at the end of this chapter). These resources can help you with the details of on-line job applications and resumes, setting up your own homepage in a way that encourages interaction with employers, finding appropriate newsgroups and listservs for job seeking, locating the most popular job data banks on the Internet, and so forth.

There are also sites that are loaded with available job openings for environmental professionals in different fields. We've listed some of them in the Resources section, and they will automatically link you to many more.

For at least twenty-five years, career advisers have been reminding job seekers that only a small fraction of all available jobs appear in the "help wanted" ads, and have urged people to go digging in the "hidden" job market. The Internet has changed that somewhat. Many employers, including most government agencies, now automatically post all of their available jobs on their websites. Much of the hidden job market is not as hidden as it used to be. This is a tremendous benefit to you, and not to be underestimated.

The idea behind the advice about job ads is still true, however. Actual job postings, while incredibly valuable, are perhaps the least important types of information available to you on the Internet. After all, by the time a job is posted, a lot of people know about the position and have had time to talk to friends, classmates, colleagues, and family members. In addition, if you found the listing on the Internet, so did hundreds of others. Anyway, how many of those thousands of jobs on The Monster Board are right for you?

The real power of the Internet for job seekers lies in the opportunity it gives you to research an organization and get the information you need to contact real people for your search.

For example, suppose you live in North Carolina and you are interested in The Nature Conservancy (TNC). You're not exactly sure what you're looking for, but you know that TNC is certainly a big employer in the environmental world and you want to research them. You log on to your favorite Internet server (e.g., Yahoo, AltaVista, or Lycos) and do a search for "The Nature Conservancy." In an instant, you're logged onto their website at http://www.tnc.org. In less than an hour (depending on how fast you read and how fascinated you get while browsing around) the following are a few of the things you can find out:

- A detailed description of the organization and its programs.
- Where TNC nature preserves are located in the U.S. and around the world.
- Details of as many of them as you would like to visit.
- The names and job responsibilities of all TNC staff people in North Carolina, with telephone numbers and addresses.

- Current and recent job postings, broken down by category (e.g., science, fundraising, or administrative) and by location.
- Just about anything else you would like to know about the organization.

This is a revolution. A few years ago, up-to-date employer information about employee numbers, job titles, new programs, contracts and grants, budget size, and current news was difficult to come by. Job seekers often viewed the world of environmental employers as though it was a medieval map of the world—a few patches of relatively well-known territory surrounded by terra incognita. Now, a little time with the mouse paints a much clearer picture.

Finally, of course, looking for career information on the Internet offers you the incalculable advantage of instant interaction with environmental professionals at companies, agencies, and nonprofit groups. Through email links to websites you can ask questions and (usually) get better, quicker, and more targeted answers than you would have gotten through a blind phone call, or writing away for information. In addition, most good sites have links to other related sites, so a single research session can provide a journey through educational choices, good employers, current jobs, professional trends and debates, journals, magazines, and articles.

Where should you start? One good place is ECO's website at http:// www.eco.org. The ECO site has links to many others and should help launch you on your way. Check the resource listings at the end of each chapter in this book for numerous websites of special interest. Or, go directly to any agency, nonprofit, college, or company you know by name.

Newspapers. Read at least one major metropolitan newspaper, especially the newspaper that covers the geographic area in which you would like to work. Environmentally related stories will give you the names of important leaders and suggest major issues that are dominating the news. You will also get the names of agencies, corporations, and individuals to contact in your job search. The *Wall Street Journal, Washington Post,* and *New York Times* are excellent sources of information on national environmental issues.

Don't forget the "help wanted" ads, especially those in the Sunday editions. These ads are valuable not only as a source of job leads, but as a barometer of who is hiring and what kinds of people are most in demand. Employers take out paid ads when they are really looking for someone. This may mean that the place is booming and can't find people fast enough. It may also mean that the set of skills being sought is hard to find in your area. Retain any ads that look interesting, even if you could not hope to compete for them. They can lend clarity to the development of your personal job vision.

Free Publications. Government agencies, nonprofit organizations, trade associations, and some businesses offer free literature on environmental issues, programs, business developments, and laws. These are often good sources of contacts, job openings, and events. Professionals in the field are resourceful in finding these freebies to stretch their budget. Ask each person you meet for the names and addresses of their favorites. Some of the best of these for the job seeker are the internal newsletters of agencies such as the Environmental Protection Agency. Get on the mailing lists for these publications and you will have inside information that may never appear anywhere else. More important, you will have current names of people to talk to about priority projects.

Job Listings. There are a number of national, regional, and local environmental job listings. Some of these listings are specific to particular employers, and you must contact the agency's personnel department to check them out. You can receive other listings by getting on mailing lists through the employer, who will then send you relevant announcements. Finally, publications such as *Earth Work* and *Environmental Career Opportunities* are filled with current job openings and are available at reasonable subscription rates. Keep in mind, however, that many of these printed job listings are moving to the Internet, for an obvious reason. By the time the publisher has received a listing, printed it with others, and mailed it, it may be obsolete. On the Internet, the job can be posted in minutes and removed as soon as it is filled. If you are going to subscribe to an environmental job listing service, you may want to choose one that has an Internet option.

Conference and Job Fair Publications. These little-used resources are invaluable barometers of the times. Even if you are not able to attend events, retrieve copies of conference programs. Look over the lists of topics and speakers. Good conference organizers know what environmental professionals want to discuss and learn. People who speak at conferences are usually respected leaders in their field or people who hold key positions. In addition, they have already shown an interest in communicating what they know to others. Finally, scope out the display ads. Companies and agencies who pay for such ads are often the same ones who are hiring.

Magazines, Trade Journals, and Newsletters. There are over 1,000 journals and periodicals dedicated to environmental issues, science, technology, law, and careers in the Environmental Periodicals Bibliography at the Environmental Studies Institute in Santa Barbara, California. This number does not include many organizational newsletters at nonprofit organizations. There is absolutely no specialty or issue you can imagine that does not have a journal or newsletter, either on paper or on the Internet. These are an incredible source of information for the job seeker, not because they carry job listings (although many of them do), but because they keep you up to date about what is going on in the environmental world.

Journals, especially, are the major source of communication in most scientific and technical fields. Inevitably, your field will have one or two that are considered indispensable. Make it a point to visit a good university library, major consulting firm, and federal government regional library just to take in what's available (or do a Web search for "environmental journals"). Also, ask working professionals in your field about which periodicals they find most useful.

Annual Reports. Virtually all government agencies and nonprofit groups publish some kind of annual report. Public corporations publish annual reports and financial disclosure (10-K) reports, which are required by the Securities and Exchange Commission. You can find both at many university business libraries and some public libraries, or you can request them from the human resources or investor relations department of the organization you are interested in. Many organizations now post their annual reports on the Internet.

Both annual reports and 10-Ks can provide excellent snapshots of an organization. They usually discuss who owns and manages the organization, what the company does, issues the company is facing, strategic plans, and budgetary data. Even if annual reports do not directly discuss a company's environmental work, they identify facilities, plants, and all other company properties, as well as the top one or two officials in health, safety, and environmental affairs. Many larger companies now publish special reports that specifically address environmental concerns. Firms in the energy, chemicals, heavy manufacturing, electronics, and forest products industries are particularly likely to have such reports.

Realize, however, that organizations use annual reports to portray themselves in the best light possible. Although they are usually far drier, 10-Ks are sometimes more useful than annual reports. Reading either or both prior to a job or informational interview will arm you with knowledge that will help you formulate specific, insightful questions. Naturally, your current knowledge about an organization demonstrates initiative and commitment.

Directories. There is something encouraging about directories, about all those organizations, names, addresses, phone numbers, and websites in one place. And some directories are as helpful as they seem. In chapter 2, for instance, we highlighted some great directories of colleges, graduate schools, scholarships, intern programs, and adventure volunteering opportunities. Employer directories are a much more "hit and miss" proposition. A good place to start is with the environmental employer "directory" you probably have in your home right now. The phone book (with the Yellow Pages) will put you in touch with all environmental and conservation companies, agencies (local, state and federal) and nonprofit groups in your area. Check the Resources section at the end of this chapter for two directories that are particularly useful, as well as for employer listings on the Internet.

People. As we said earlier, written resources eventually lead you to people. No newspaper or website has hired a person yet. People are your best resource in the job hunt, be they neighbors, professionals, classmates, relatives, friends, experts, writers, or casual acquaintances. One of the cardinal rules of job hunting is to go out of your way to tell everyone you know or meet that you are looking for a job—and give them as much specific information as possible on the type of job you want. Most of us love to help others, especially when it is as easy as offering a name or making a telephone call. Each time you tell someone of your job search, your list of potential contacts expands logarithmically. To jog your creativity, the following are a few groups of people who can help.

College Faculty, Staff Members, and Students. Talk to current or former teachers, advisers, and fellow students. Many professors engage in outside research or consulting projects and know professionals in the field. They may be able to provide a recommendation to an employer they know personally. Students from smaller colleges should consider seeking advice from staff members at universities with larger environmentally related programs. Such programs often have at least one career counselor. Time permitting, these counselors will often accommodate nonstudents, especially if you express an interest in graduate study at their university. In addition, many state universities and community colleges employ general career counselors who are paid by the state and thus provide their services free to any state resident.

Alumni. This resource is probably the most underutilized by environmental job seekers. Think about yourself. If someone called you tomorrow who was a recent graduate from your college major department, wouldn't you talk with that person and try to help out a little? Many graduates of your institution are now working in your field of choice. Because they share the bond of having attended the same school, and because many have been through difficult job hunts themselves, they are often willing to help. To find alumni, ask whether your school's alumni relations department publishes a directory. Some programs actively track alumni careers for the benefit of current students and recent graduates. For example, the Cornell University Department of Agriculture and Biological Engineering has developed the Cornell Alumni Career Advisory Network. If your school does not conduct such a program, you might suggest it start one. In the meantime, at least get a few names from your major department. They are certain to be in touch with a few alumni informally.

Friends, Relatives, and Neighbors. Do not overlook the obvious. Think of how many successful job-hunting stories you know of that start this way: "My uncle put me in touch with my cousin, who knew a consultant who was hiring for a position. I called her, and . . . ."

Professional Societies and Trade Associations. Professional societies are as helpful in providing job leads as they are in giving you good information about educational requirements. Associations for people in a specific field offer journals, newsletters, job listings, placement services, and more. Using the staff at society headquarters is helpful, but active participation in your local chapter (or student chapter) is much better.

Temporary Employment Agencies. The demand for technical temporary employees in the environmental field has grown dramatically in the last few years, and working in a temporary position can be a great way to meet environmental employers. You are clearly showing what you can do, and you have an opportunity to talk as colleagues and professionals in a low-risk setting. Don't hesitate to ask your temporary employer for ideas on permanent employment, and to gather names of others you should talk to. For those outside of technical fields, temping can still be a good idea. Although the work you do may not be as "environmental" as you would like, working as a temporary still gives you entrée to the working professionals you would like to meet. Be careful, however. If the work you are looking for (legislative analysis) is too far removed from your temp responsibilities (answering the phone), it may be hard for you to be seen as capable of more responsibility.

Internships and Volunteering. These two opportunities were discussed in greater detail in chapter 2. Clearly, working with environmental professionals and leaders is one of the best possible ways to build the environmental network you will need for your job search.

Meeting People through Events. Conferences, trade shows, seminars, classes, fundraisers, receptions, and other events are a fantastic way to interact with the environmental professionals you want to know. Conferences can be a perfect opportunity to expand your network. You are meeting as professionals, the subject matter is related to your mutual environmental careers, and talk flows naturally toward work and careers. There are also a lot of people you want to meet together in one building at the same time.

Attending a conference allows you to meet people in a way that may be less intimidating than cold calls or visits. If, for example, you are looking for a career in brownfields redevelopment, you could probably benefit greatly from meeting people at an EPA conference on the topic. You can learn about key people and issues by attending panels and sessions. Not only would you make personal contacts, but you would also discover where some jobs might be created as a result of new grants and contracts. Moreover, simply mentioning to an interviewer something you learned at such a conference makes a good impression. You were there. You are a working professional.

Students and aspiring professionals attending these conferences have little competition from their peers, since most attendees are seasoned managers. They are usually impressed when they see students and job seekers at conferences.

There is, however, a catch. For many of us, the idea of approaching new people, introducing ourselves, striking up a conversation, and then doing it all over again with someone else, is a very difficult thing to do.

If you are shy, there are still ways to use conferences effectively for environmental professionals. People who speak on panels, for example, are usually glad to answer questions after the formal time is done. Ask your question and get a business card. You can follow up afterward via email, letter, or phone—at least a connection has been made. In a similar vein, make the rounds of the conference exhibit hall and collect as many business cards and as much promotional material as you can. Contact people later and express your regret that you missed them at the conference. They'll usually be glad to talk to you, and you may be more comfortable.

Informational Interviewing. Would you like to meet a marine biologist who is studying global climate change? Do you have some questions to ask about getting started and what the work is really like? Do you have the person's name and contact information? Then give him or her a call and set up an appointment! Sometimes the direct approach is the best one of all, and that's the basic idea behind informational interviewing.

Informational interviewing has received something of a bad name because it's been used as a manipulative technique by people who pretend to want information, but are really looking for a way to get past the secretary and ask for a job. Most hiring authorities are well protected against job seekers, and creative people are always looking for new ways to get past the screen.

Employers caught on to the informational interview ploy years ago, however, and are rightly suspicious of it. If you are sincere in your desire for information about a person and their work, don't use the expression "informational interview." Simply tell the truth—you are interested in the field and would like to ask a few questions.

The following are some tips to make these meetings a success:

- Talk to people who are doing the work that interests you, not to those who hire them. If you really want to know about that marine biologist, it does no good to talk to the personnel director at the lab. Go straight to the source.
- Tell your prospective interviewee that you will only need 20 or 30 minutes, and do not stay any longer.
- Do not waste your interviewee's time by asking questions that you could have answered on your own through research, or by talking to somebody below the person in the organization's hierarchy. In fact, if you find yourself looking for the "right" questions to ask in informational interviews, think carefully about what you're doing. The whole point of these meetings is for you to ask your questions. If you don't have any, don't bother. Otherwise, an artificial setting is created, where you are pretending to have questions in order to "network" and "make a contact," and the other person is pretending that your questions are sincere.
- At the conclusion of each interview, ask for the names of two people who do similar work and who might be willing to meet with you. Also ask this question if you are refused an interview.
- Thank your interviewee profusely. Thirty minutes is a big gift for a busy professional to give to a stranger.
- Always send a thank-you note, and, later, apprise the person of your progress.
- Finally, there is nothing wrong with coming back to the same organization

when you are looking for a job. Just be forthright about your request. The employer will probably already have a positive impression of you based on the initiative you have shown in your career search.

Résumés, Cover Letters, Interviews, and More. If you are a well-qualified job seeker who is searching the Web, meeting people, working on projects, and reading widely, you will find plenty of environmental jobs that interest you. Here are a few last pieces of advice from environmental employers that you will find useful as you apply for jobs, interview, and start the career that's right for you.

- *Take the time you need to find the right job.* Do not expect it to be a quick process. Career counselors note that the average career-related job hunt takes between six months and one year. One free-lance consultant from Seattle tells students: "You need to look at your career search as a long-term research project that always takes much longer and more effort than you want it to." If you possibly can, try to structure your life so that you are not forced by economics or anxiety to take the first thing that comes along. Lay some groundwork a few months before you actually want to start your job.
- *Work hard at the search.* This sounds obvious, but *What Color Is Your Parachute?* reports that two-thirds of all job seekers spend fewer than five hours a week on the process. At that rate, it takes two months to log just one week of full-time job hunting.
- *Shotgun approaches don't work.* A strategy of blanketing employers with résumés and to-whom-it-may-concern cover letters takes an enormous amount of time and almost never works. One study found that employers sent out one invitation to interview for every 245 résumés sent cold to their firm. Use résumés to cement a building process that begins with conversations, contacts, and reputations. Although résumés are not useful when sent out in a scattershot approach, they are nevertheless important.
- *Be brief and specific.* Although employers are usually pressed for time, they do want to know as much about you as possible. Be crisp. Also, become skilled at tailoring résumés to specific jobs so that an employer quickly reading your résumé can easily perceive pertinent experience and interests.
- *Master the art of the cover letter.* Cover letters are meant to highlight parts of your résumé that especially qualify you for the job, demonstrate that you have done your homework, and convey your enthusiasm for that particular line of work. A carefully written cover letter can go even further than your résumé in getting you an interview.
- *Use the spell check.* Never have a misspelling or a typographical error on your résumé, cover letter, or any other correspondence to an employer. He or she will inevitably ask, "If they can't even get it right on a job application, what kind of attention will they pay to important details after we hire them?"
- *Ask questions at job interviews.* This shows your interest and conveys the feeling that you have options, which immediately boosts your stock. Perhaps one of the biggest mistakes job seekers make during interviews is being so determined to come across as cool and professional that they do

not show any enthusiasm. Employers like to hire upbeat, excited, and motivated people.

- *Remember your manners.* Always send a thank-you note to the interviewer and anyone else you met, including support staff members. Employers often solicit input from everyone who met you, especially future colleagues. Reiterate any points you want to make about your interest and skills.
- *Close the deal.* Very close to the week when the employer will be making a decision, call to express your interest. Many times, a decision on whom to hire is a close call. Once the field is narrowed to a few qualified finalists, gut reactions are important. Showing interest in a professional manner could tip the balance in your favor.
- *Learn from your setbacks.* If you do not get the job, send a letter to the lead interviewer expressing interest in future positions. You may want to call and ask about other job leads and ask the interviewer to circulate your résumé if appropriate. In some cases it is appropriate to ask why you were not chosen. The answers may help you solve problems or address issues in later interviews.
- *Help others.* As you progress through your career, don't forget how hard the job search can be, and how lonely. Be a friend and mentor to others who have chosen an environmental career path. Speak at schools and career fairs. Be a source of names, contacts, internships, and volunteer opportunities. Do a little extra to create a new generation of environmental leaders.

RESOURCES

ENVIRONMENTAL EMPLOYERS ON THE INTERNET

Visit http://www.dbm.com/jobguide, which takes you to *The Riley Guide*, a short, well-written source of basic information with several great links on how to use the Internet for job seeking. The best way to find environmental jobs online is to go directly to individual companies, agencies, and nonprofits. Employer sites are usually the most updated of all job listings on the Web, which is crucial for the job seeker. Employer homepages will guide you to employment and job information.

Http://www.(the organization's name or acronym).org gives you nonprofit employers. Natural Resources Defense Council, for instance, is at http://www.nrdc.org.

Http://www.(the organization's name or acronym).com connects you to private companies. Browning Ferris, Inc. is found at http://www.bfi.com.

Http://www.(agency name or acronym).gov takes you to federal government agency websites. The Environmental Protection Agency is http://www.epa.gov. Be sure to explore the federal government sites for nonemployment information as well. They are a remarkable resource.

State government agencies are usually at http://www.state.(acronym of the state).us. The state of Massachusetts is http://www.state.ma.us.

See the list in chapter 2 for websites that link to environmental job listings for subscribers.

PROFESSIONAL ASSOCIATIONS ON THE INTERNET

Use the list of professional association websites and addresses in chapter 2.

OTHER SITES FOR ENVIRONMENTAL JOB SEEKERS

Http://www.usajob.opm.gov lists all current federal government openings (including seasonal positions and co-op education) in an easy-to-use search format. Don't miss it if you want to work for federal agencies.

Http://www.webdirectory.com takes you to "The Amazing Environmental Organization Web Directory." Click on "employment" for links to selected sites. Also good for nonemployment environmental information.

Http://www.cyber-sierra.com/nrjobs features a "natural resources job search," which groups jobs and career information under forestry, GIS, environmental, water resources, and so forth).

Http://www.mdc.net/~dbrier/jobs is called E-Jobs (Environmental Jobs and Careers) and has links to state government agencies, consulting firms, labs, law firms, nonprofits, and more. Especially good for job hunters in New England.

Http://www.fws.gov/r9mat/stategf.html connects people with the fish and wildlife homepages (and jobs) for all fifty states. Recently updated states are clearly marked.

Http://www.gisjobs.org, The Geographic Information Systems Jobs Clearinghouse, has a large number of active job listings for GIS technicians and professionals and other resources for people interested in GIS.

Http://eelink.ummich.edu/jobs.html, EELink: Environmental Education Server, has some listings and career information for environmental educators.

Http://www.environmentonline.com connects to information and job listings in water/wastewater fields, pollution control, and solid waste.

Http://www.enviroindustry.com is sponsored by the environmental industry website and has numerous links to employment-related sites, among others.

Http://ourworld.compuserve.com contains the Ubiquity Environmental Job Search Page, with links for job seekers.

Http://www.ies.wisc.edu/careers.htm is run by the Institute for Environmental Studies at the University of Wisconsin and is a good example of what college departments can offer and also connects you to similar sites at Texas A&M, Michigan, Boston University, Duke, Indiana, and so forth.

Http://enviro.mond.org/jobs/home.html, *Chemical and Industry* magazine, has an online job center for chemists, including a sort category for "environmental." Check the job links also for easy connection to many of the comprehensive on-line job services (see the section that follows).

Http://www.eco-web.com, the "Green Pages," connects you with dozens of environmental industry firms.

Http://www.gnet.org, the Global Network of Environment and Technology, was set up by the U.S. Department of Energy and has several interesting links and environmental industry news.

COMPREHENSIVE INTERNET JOB SERVICES

There are many large job and career websites, which have some environmental listings. America's Employers, America's Job Bank, *Career Magazine*, Career City, Career Mosaic, Career Site, Career Web, Online Career Center, The Monster Board, and more. Two notable ones are:

Http://www.careerpath.com groups "help wanted" ads from popular newspapers, giving you a chance to comb the Sunday ads in numerous cities from your computer.

Http://www.jobtrak.com is a particularly good career site for college students, and a good site to get an overview of job hunting on the Internet.

INTERNET SEARCHES

Search for information on environmental issues, careers and jobs by performing "keyword" searches using such popular search engines as AltaVista, Dogpile, Excite, HotBot, Infoseek, Lycos, Netscape, WebCrawler, and Yahoo.com, among many others. Use targeted keywords such as "wildlife biology careers." Most of them can be reached at http://www.(name of company).com. Yahoo, for instance, is http://www.yahoo.com.

ALSO OF INTEREST

Http://www.igc.org, the Institute for Global Communications, is home to "econet," with dozens of nonprofit members, as well as several links to environmental information and news.

Http://www.envirolink.org is another good source of links and information.

Http://www.islandpress.org is a good place to find great environmental books.

PRINT DIRECTORIES AND BOOKS ON ENVIRONMENTAL CAREERS

Books are listed by publication date, with the most recent ones first and no listings from before 1995.

Careers in the Environment, by Robert Fasulo and Paul Walker (Vgm Career Horizons, 1995) $17.95.

Careers in Environmental Geoscience, by Robert R. Jordan, Rima Petrossian, and William J. Murphy (American Association of Petroleum Geologists, 1996) $5.00.

Careers Inside the World of Environmental Science, by Robert Gartner (Rosen Publishing Group, 1995) $15.95.

The Conservation Directory is updated annually and published by The National Wildlife Federation. Order on the Internet at http://www.nwf.org or by phone (410) 516-6583. The 1998 edition is $61 and contains thousands of listings.

The EnviroDirectory is updated annually. Regional editions are available for the New England, Mid-Atlantic, Great Lakes, and Southwest states. Includes hundreds of private environmental firms and reference listings for state government offices, regional nonprofit groups, and selected colleges. Contact Environmental Marketing Group, 1770 Massachusetts Avenue, Cambridge, MA 02140. (888) 784-9570 toll free or http://www.EnviroDirectory.com.

Environment: Career in Focus, by Inc. Jist Works (Ferguson Publishing, 1998) $13.95.

Green at Work: Finding a Business Career That Works for the Environment, by Susan Cohn (Island Press, 1995) $17.95.

The National Green Pages is a directory published annually by Co-op America that lists 1,500 socially and environmentally responsible businesses and products. Co-op America, 1612 K Street, NW, Suite 600, Washington, DC 20006. (800) 584-7336, $6.95.

100 Jobs in the Environment, by Debra Quintana (Macmillan, 1997) $14.95.

Opportunities in Environmental Careers, by Odom Fanning (Vgm Career Horizons, 1995) $11.95.

TEMPORARY ENVIRONMENTAL EMPLOYMENT AGENCIES

Look in your local Yellow Pages. Temporary technical employment is a big business. A few agencies that you might want to contact are ETI, Inc. (http://www.sni.net/envirotemps), EnviroStaff (http://www.envirostaff.com), and OnSite Environmental (http://www.onsite.com).

Part II

PLANNERS, EDUCATORS, AND COMMUNICATORS

4 The Planning Profession

AT A GLANCE

Employment:
40,000 to 45,000 professional planners nationwide

Demand:
2 to 6 percent growth per year. High end of range in areas with strong population growth

Breakdown:
Public sector, 66 percent
Private sector, 15 percent (industry and consulting)
Nonprofit sector, 19 percent (including universities)

Key Job Titles:
Air quality planner
Building or zoning inspector
Community planner
Environmental planner
Geographic information systems specialist
Growth management planner
Historic preservation specialist
Land use planner
Planning consultant
Planning manager
Recreation planner
Regional planner
Rural planner
Site planner

Transportation planner
Urban planner
Watershed planner
Water resources planner

Influential Organizations:

American Planning Association (and the APA's American Institute of
Certified Planners)
Association of American Geographers
Association of Collegiate Schools of Planning
Land Trust Alliance
Urban Land Institute

Salary:

According to the American Planning Association, starting annual salaries for
planners are in the $29,000 to $32,000 range. In 1995 (date of the last survey), the median salary for all planners was $45,300. Planners with ten years
of experience were making $55,000 and higher annually. Federal government
and private firms offer the best salaries, followed by larger city planning agencies. Since 1985, planners' salaries have risen 3 to 5 percent annually.

WHAT IS PLANNING?

"Planning provides the framework to help communities address change to the
physical environment in which they live, work, and play. Planners use techniques such as economic and demographic analysis, citizen participation, land,
natural and cultural resource evaluation, goal-setting, and strategic planning,"
says Sarah Polster of the American Planning Association (APA).

"Planners use statistical and geographic information to provide a factual
basis for good decisions about future construction, recreation, and transportation," Polster notes. "And, they help convene different interest groups to work
toward consensus about what's best for the community."

According to the APA, most planners work at the local level, but
are concerned with issues that affect the whole world, such as the preservation
and enhancement of the quality of life in a community, the protection of the
environment, the promotion of equitable economic opportunity, and the management of growth and change of all kinds.

Polster believes that planning "provides the framework for tying together, in
an equitable and logical manner, individual choices affecting our towns, cities,
and countrysides."

Although planning draws from many wells (air quality, water quality, transportation, and so forth) contemporary planners must be capable of seeing their
work as tiles in a larger mosaic. They must understand the society and economy within which their plans will be implemented. Above all, planning is about
people.

Planners generally fall into two categories—those who concentrate on a specific geographical area (e.g., town, city, state, watershed, or ecosystem) and

those who specialize in a particular issue (e.g, air quality, hazardous waste management, water quality, or transportation). Regardless of where they work or what issue they specialize in, all planners have a similar agenda—to understand the key components of interlocking problems and to propose meaningful solutions to them.

What differentiates the professional planner from any other manager or scientist? "Three things set planners apart," according to a former city planning director. "First, our professional responsibility is to design systems which will solve multiple problems through one solution—a plan. Other environmental professionals tend to have narrower formal responsibilities, such as eliminating a specific discharge, preserving a wetland, or whatever.

"Second, our profession is *inherently* political, social, and economic, as well as technical, scientific, and environmental. A plan which cannot be approved by politicians, paid for by existing resources, supported by the public, and carried out with today's technology is no plan at all. Other ecological workers can consider politics and economics as obstacles to their 'real' work. For planners, mastering these 'obstacles' *is* the work.

"Third, planners receive a different training from other professionals. Lawyers often say that their law school education wasn't about the facts of case law. It trained them to *think* like a lawyer. Engineers, scientists, and politicians say the same thing. Planners receive certain tools, skills, and knowledge in their training, but basically we are trained to think like planners—that is, comprehensively and with a focus on setting up structures that will guide action and results in a desired direction predictably over time."

How does one tell if he or she would make a good planner? The Association of Collegiate Schools of Planning lists the following qualities that make for a good planner:

- The ability to envision what can be, rather than see only what is;
- The ability to analyze complex problems and develop workable solutions;
- The ability to communicate with others, particularly about ideas;
- A commitment to positive social, physical, economic, and environmental change; and
- The desire to work with people to develop a better future.

HISTORY AND BACKGROUND

Have you ever visited Washington, D.C., and marveled at its well-designed grid of streets and welcoming Mall? Or taken refuge from New York City's hubbub by ducking into Central Park? Perhaps you've relaxed on the banks of the Frog Pond in Boston Common. If so, then you've benefited from the vision of the pioneers of the modern planning movement. With great foresight, these early planners strove to strike a balance between burgeoning urban development and the desire of residents to maintain harmony with their environment. This spirit continues to guide the profession today.

As a formal occupation, the modern planning profession has as its origins the creation of the American City Planning Institute in 1917 and the forma-

Memorable urban spaces, such as the Charles River Esplanade in Boston, are the result of good planning and popular support.

tion of the Regional Planning Association of New York in 1929. These groups were the first to recognize that the protection of forests, waterways, wildlife habitats, and scenic areas was an integral part of a sensible plan for expansion of industry, transportation, and housing. Giants of the field included Frederick Law Olmsted and Sir Patrick Geddes, who believed that human beings can best develop in pleasant environments requiring careful planning and deliberate action.

The 1920s saw a mushrooming of local planning in the United States. The rapid growth of cities during this decade placed enormous pressure on public facilities. In response, many municipalities created planning commissions to oversee development. In 1920, roughly one hundred cities had such commissions. By 1930, the number neared five hundred.

With the 1930s came President Franklin Roosevelt and the New Deal programs, including a Public Works Administration and a National Planning Board, which tried to coordinate long-range projects. Sweeping initiatives such as the Tennessee Valley Authority sought to prove that professional planners could design and implement comprehensive plans that balanced physical development and job creation with environmental conservation.

Such balance, however, remained elusive. Planning was piecemeal or nonexistent. Little planning was done to curb growing urban sprawl. What planning there was often failed to protect the environment. In many cases, planning efforts actually facilitated the destruction of wetlands, open spaces, and wildlife habitats by encouraging expansive suburban and industrial communities that relied heavily on the automobile and highway development. A new approach was needed.

In 1970, help arrived in the form of the National Environmental Protection Act (NEPA), a milestone piece of legislation requiring that environmental impact statements (EIS) be prepared and approved before any federal projects such as building a highway or damming a river were undertaken. At least as important as NEPA itself was the *idea* behind it. From now on, it was assumed that the negative environmental consequences of development should be thought about in advance, planned for, and reduced.

State and local governments were quick to follow with their own EIS requirements, thus creating a demand for more, and better trained, "environmental" planners.

What is environmental planning? Dick Booth of the Cornell University City and Regional Planning Department says the field is concerned with "the utilization of the world's resources to ensure human needs are served in a context that allows for long-term stability of the environment." Larry Gerckens, national historian of the American Institute of Certified Planners says that environmental planners exhibit "a greater mastery of environmental science or engineering, and a commitment to environmental conservation that can inform general planning activity."

ISSUES AND TRENDS

Planners are addressing a wide array of issues as we enter the 21st century. Some are new and some are relatively timeless. The eleven concerns discussed below are among the greatest challenges facing the field today.

BROWNFIELDS REDEVELOPMENT

American cities and rural areas are full of abandoned former waste dumps (many of which are contaminated with toxic substances), industrial properties, and military bases. They are left undeveloped because the perceived risk involved in clean-up, redevelopment, and liability for the property's toxic past scares off investors. The U.S. Conference of Mayors has called brownfields "the number one environmental challenge for urban areas."

Brownfields have a powerful negative effect on community planning efforts. First, their existence reduces property values and promotes disinvestment in the inner city. Second, industries that fail to find reasonably priced land in the city move to the suburban and semirural "greenfields," which results in the destruction of agricultural lands and increased sprawl. Third, because brownfields properties are almost always in poor communities and communities of color, failure to develop them feeds injustice and racial tensions. (See the discussion of environmental justice concerns that follows.)

Planners are at the forefront of a national effort to bring brownfields back to productive life, as illustrated by the case study toward the end of this chapter.

ENVIRONMENTAL JUSTICE CONCERNS

Brownfields are only one planning issue that affects people of color and the poor disproportionately. Other issues include the siting of unpopular land uses (e.g., waste and recycling transfer stations, highway ramps, public transit parking lots, incinerators, and dirty industries) and food security, such as supermarket siting, public transportation scheduling, affordable housing, equitable siting of parks and green spaces, and more.

Demographic changes alone (in addition to social justice demands) are forcing these issues to the front of the planning agenda. Hispanic, African, Asian, and Native Americans make up the majority of the population in many American cities, and their environmental concerns must be addressed. Diversity within the planning field is also a crucial concern—planners of color are in demand.

REGIONAL PLANNING COORDINATION

Consider a typical, metropolitan area—home to over two-thirds of all Americans. How many planning units does it have? Certainly a city or suburban government exists. (There are 19,279 municipal governments and 16,656 towns and townships in this country.) Perhaps there is a county government (3,043 of them) that may (or may not) be contiguous with the city.

Because the metropolitan area has many towns and cities that abut one another, "special districts" have probably sprung up for schools, fire protection, police, water supply, wastewater treatment, parks, public tranportation, air quality, solid waste, land conservation, coastal protection, public health, senior services, soil conservation, emergency services, energy production, and more. Many of these special districts have their own distinct boundaries. There are 31,555 such districts in the United States.

A metropolitan area is nested within a state, which has planning boundaries, *and* within a variety of different regions, which are defined by natural features such as the Great Lakes, economic and cultural connections, and federal government jurisdictions.

In many metropolitan areas, *every one* of these overlapping entities has plans and supports planners. How does one create meaningful planning coordination that reflects both human activity patterns, ecological realities, and differing legal jurisdictions? This is an important issue for the planning profession.

INFORMATION MANAGEMENT, GEOGRAPHIC INFORMATION SYSTEMS, AND COMPUTER MODELING

Planners live on data. In order to plan, one must have information on land-use patterns, social demographics, soil types, housing prices, and dozens of other variables. Therefore, the computer has revolutionized environmental and land-use planning. Information management is one of the demand fields for planning agencies.

Within information management, people with expertise in geographic information systems (GIS) are especially needed. GIS allows planners to manipulate layers of data, which have been mapped to create visual descriptions that have great power. Through GIS, for instance, we can see the interactions between urban sprawl and loss of agricultural land, or view "cancer clusters" around polluting industries. A few years from now, all planners (and most environmental scientists) will have GIS computer skills as a basic part of their training and education. Software designers are trying to make GIS packages that are as easy to use as word processing and database programs. For now, however, high-level GIS ability remains a specialized field that is much in demand.

THE RISE OF WATERSHED PLANNING

Environmental managers have long sought a basic geographic unit around which to combine protection of the natural world and support of human activities. Watersheds are rapidly becoming the unit of choice. Watershed planning is supported at the federal level through the 1998 Clean Water Initiative (see chapter 6). It also has strong appeal to state managers and to grassroots activists who have produced a national watershed protection movement that has grown dramatically.

River Network, a national watershed movement group in Portland, Oregon, publishes a directory of over 3,000 listings of watershed organizations and agencies. Expect more states to pass legislation that puts watershed planning at the center of environmental and conservation policy.

RETHINKING ZONING

For the general public, zoning *is* planning. The idea of separating communities into residential zones of different lot sizes, with other zones for industrial, commercial, and agricultural activities, is assumed. Zoning also implies many rules about street widths, how close your house can be to the street, and so forth. In recent years, however, innovative planners, architects, and designers have shown that many of the environments we love the most would never pass zoning laws. Our best urban neighborhoods are often a jumble of different uses, shapes, and sizes crammed together in relatively small spaces, with

houses and shops that are close enough to the street for people to easily interact. Parking may be a little tight, but that doesn't stop people from seeking out
the great urban neighborhoods or the almost lost Main Streets and village
squares of our small towns. Some "new urbanists" claim that zoning has actively destroyed much of what was good and replaced it with strip development,
shopping malls, gated "communities," and barren subdivisions. Creative planners are rethinking zoning regulations and some talk dramatically of dropping
zoning altogether.

NATURAL HAZARDS PLANNING

Reimbursing people for flood damage costs about $5 billion every year in dis-
aster aid and related help. Dikes, levees, braces, and dredging are expensive
and, many say, environmentally destructive ways of dealing with the problem.
Megan Lewis of the APA tells us that "guiding development away from floodplain areas and protecting the natural functions of floodplains is a current concern of planners."

Some are going even further. In April of 1998, the people of the Napa Valley
in California voted to raise taxes to rip out flood control systems, which
allowed the Napa River to run free. The Napa plan is the most systematic effort
to try what is called the "living rivers" approach to improve flood control, and
has the active support of the U.S. Army Corps of Engineers.

Jason Fanselau of the Army Corps told the *New York Times* that tearing out
engineered flood control systems is "radically different from anything we have
ever done before. It's going to totally change the way we do business." Look
for planners to play a key role in new floodplain protection efforts.

SUSTAINABLE COMMUNITIES

Sustainable development is to environmental planning as pollution prevention
is to waste management. The idea, of course, is to create—through conscious
intention, planning, technology, regulation, incentives, education, and values—
an environmentally sound way of local community life that can continue "sustainably" over a long period of time. Advocates are also vocal in reminding us
that a "sustainable" community must guarantee higher levels of social justice
and equity than we have today.

The sustainable communities movement, although wildly eclectic, generally
envisions "green" factories, energy production, agriculture, transportation,
architecture, and so forth to be organized at the regional level into a somewhat
integrated system.

People in many cities and communities have launched "Sustainable *Our
Town*" programs. Towns such as Chattanooga, TN; Arcata and Davis, CA;
Ithaca, NY; and Burlington, VT, pursue policies that suggest what sustainable
community planning might look like.

As we approach the 21st century, it's unclear exactly what the push for sustainable communities will mean for professional planning opportunities. For now, the movement is a fertile arena for experiments that planners can adapt to local conditions.

GROWTH MANAGEMENT

Planners looking for job opportunities would do well to simply ask, Where is the population growing rapidly? That's where the jobs will be, as agencies try to simultaneously accommodate large numbers of new people *and* protect the natural areas, booming economies, and ways of life that attracted those numbers of people in the first place. There is no guarantee that the planners will succeed, and future generations may wonder whether any planning was done at all in areas where strip malls, subdivisions, and trophy homes are taking over agricultural lands and lake fronts.

When done well, however, growth management is a rewarding activity that puts planners at the leading edge of environmental protection. Characterized by one planner as "one of the noblest activities a planner can pursue," growth management planning is an intense professional challenge. In Florida, which must accommodate a growth of 900 new people *per day*, planners sometimes struggle simply to keep pace with the need for schools, subdivisions, roads, water, and sewer lines without overtaxing the environment. Planners in rapidly expanding areas and popular vacation spots face similar struggles.

FROM NIMBY TO BANANA

Local planners find it harder and harder to develop locations for undesirable facilities such as sewage treatment plants, incinerators, landfills, industrial sites, and highways. One EPA official says that we have gone from "not in my backyard" to "build absolutely nothing anywhere near anyone." Communities seeking to develop consensus on these politically charged issues need planners with strong skills in education, mediation, and communication.

LITTLE HELP FROM THE FEDERAL GOVERNMENT

It's been years since the federal government was the source of major funding for urban redevelopment efforts. With the exception of a few programs (see the brownfields case study toward the end of this chapter), local areas are on their own when it comes to the cost of community improvements and major planning efforts. Aspiring planners should focus serious attention on developing skills in innovative financing and partnerships with private investors. How will we pay for it? is often the first question asked of planners with a creative streak.

CAREER OPPORTUNITIES

The public sector dominates the employment picture in planning, but as governments pare down staffs, they increasingly rely on consultants from the private sector.

PUBLIC SECTOR

Federal Government. It's well known that land-use planning in the United States is a local affair, and that Congress generally keeps it that way. Just because federal agencies are not involved in the local battle over a subdivision, however, doesn't mean that federal agencies don't have jobs for planners. Far from it. A planning education is excellent preparation for many positions at federal agencies.

The Department of Housing and Urban Development hires planners to work on improving cities nationwide. The Department of Labor uses planners to collect and interpret employment patterns and their effects on specific regions. Those planners interested in finding alternatives to fossil fuels (a specialty of growing importance) can find employment with the Department of Energy. Transportation concerns under the auspices for the Department of Transportation create employment for large numbers of planners. In fact, the multibillion-dollar initiative known as the Intermodel Surface Transportation Act (ISTEA) requires planners for highway developments, mass transit, bike paths, greenways, and more. The Bureau of the Census also needs planners to analyze the avalanche of demographic information it receives regularly. Environmental planners are also hired by all of the agencies of the Department of the Interior (e.g., National Park Service, Fish and Wildlife Service, Bureau of Land Management, Geological Survey, and others), and by the Environmental Protection Agency, Federal Emergency Management Administration, and the National Oceanic and Atmospheric Administration.

State Government. A few states have state land-use planning agencies, which require communities to submit plans for state approval. Most state governments, however, mirror the federal government by hiring planners to work at environmental and conservation agencies and leave local planning to cities and towns.

Generally, two types of state agencies exist. First are those dedicated to specific environmental goals, such as forestry, fish and wildlife, water and air quality, solid waste and recycling, public health, and so forth. These agencies are often empowered with the authority to override local projects that threaten the integrity of overall state goals, or to require local governments to meet mandates created by the state legislature (e.g., recycling goals). Second are agencies that work with local planning organizations by acting as a mediator between communities (resolving conflict when necessary) and ensuring that local activities with other communities are well coordinated.

Regional Government. The Great Lakes, Cape Cod, the Chesapeake Bay, and the Colorado River are great natural features and are among our national treasures. However, because they cross boundaries—of cities, counties, states, even nations—these natural wonders are the source of fierce debate and contention. Regional planning grew out of the need to address the complexity of issues that are too large to be addressed by any one municipal planning agency. How can the City of Toronto alone protect Lake Ontario?

Regional planners are often expected to balance the demands of developers, conservationists, local governments, and private property owners. Because of the potential for conflict in their work, regional agencies seek out planners skilled in policy analysis, conflict mediation, and political savvy. They also require sophisticated GIS specialists.

Local Government. City and municipal planning agencies are, by far, the largest employers of planners in the United States today. Indeed, for many people "environmental planning" is synonymous with the local planning department at City Hall.

These departments are usually divided into "general" planners, inspectors, and more specialized planners for fields such as economic development or transportation. If the town is working on a new long-term strategic plan, there may be planners or consultants hired to help.

General planners govern day-to-day development activities by: ensuring compliance with zoning and building regulations; working with developers and the community on approval of permit requests; updating maps and files; meeting with citizen groups; and coordinating social services, transportation, resource development, and protection of ecologically sensitive regions. Planners examine proposed community facilities such as schools to ensure that these facilities will meet the demands of a growing population. They keep abreast of economic and legal issues, building codes, and state and federal regulations. They further ensure that builders and developers follow these codes, and have authority to stop development that fails to meet these standards.

Inspectors ensure that projects that are permitted for development are carried out in accordance with the law. For instance, inspectors determine that trees are not cut or wetlands filled without approval.

The position of municipal planning director is a crucial job in the field, and the end point for many career paths. Planning directors provide overall direction, prepare and manage budgets, work closely with elected officials and boards, and often make final decisions that will determine the look and feel of a community for decades.

Because local planners are so important, it's worth studying a local planning department in a little more detail. To do that, we visited Worcester, MA. Worcester, which is situated on a series of hills overlooking the Blackstone River in central Massachusetts, is the state's second-largest city and is an important center of manufacturing, insurance, and transportation. This city of 160,000 is currently undergoing what Alan Gordon, coordinator of the city's

Cartographic and geographic information systems skills are important tools for environmental planners.

planning department, calls a "dramatic revitalization." The $900 million project includes a new convention center, a downtown streetscape restructuring, and "Medical City"—a downtown, state-of-the-art medical facility. The city's Union Station is being upgraded into an intermodal transportation center. Worcester also expects its new outlet shopping center to attract crowds of visitors.

Undertaken alone, any one of these projects would require careful planning. Worcester, however, is working on them concurrently, and it is Mr. Gordon and his colleagues who are charged with overseeing the work. "A comprehensive plan is the key issue," says Mr. Gordon, stressing that with so many people and organizations involved in Worcester's facelift, the planning department must ensure that the participants hew to the city's final vision of itself. This vision is the result of a careful orchestration of various planning departments.

Worcester has six divisions involved in planning: traditional planning, economic development, housing, grants, finance, and public service. The traditional planning department has eleven members, of which only a few have general planning backgrounds. The others specialize in specific planning pursuits—landscape architecture, parks improvements, and GIS computer mapping. "The other departments have people who don't have traditional planning backgrounds," says Mr. Gordon. Instead, they approach planning issues from various and more specific angles. The economic development department, for example, employs people with banking or finance backgrounds.

Surprisingly, Mr. Gordon reports that the city of Worcester employs only four traditional planners, or "community planning generalists," as he calls them. Still, Mr. Gordon, who also teaches planning courses at Clark University, sees city planning as a growing field. Another arena in which Mr. Gordon sees increasing opportunity for planners, especially planning generalists, is in small suburban planning departments. "A lot of suburbs have one- to three-person planning offices. Those planners are expected to handle the whole range of things."

PRIVATE SECTOR

Although the public sector hires most planners, a growing number can be found in private practice or on staff at larger corporations.

Corporations. Any corporation that owns and manages land is likely to employ planners. Utility companies, forestry firms, railroads, mining corporations, real estate development companies, and ski areas are likely candidates. Planners at such companies are found in the "environmental, health and safety department" or in "facilities planning," and may have responsibilities for regulatory compliance concerns as well as planning.

Consulting Firms. Although there are some consulting firms that are exclusively devoted to planning, planners are more likely to be found at consulting companies that offer other services as well. Look for planners at architectural firms, engineering and construction companies, environmental consulting outfits, real estate development concerns, and law firms.

The use of planning consultants is on the rise, as government agencies seek to keep full-time employment (and costs) low. Planning consultants are especially popular on "one-time" planning projects with special funding sources, and on complex activities such as brownfields redevelopment.

NONPROFIT SECTOR

Environmental and conservation nonprofit groups will rarely put out a "help wanted" ad for a planner, but many find that planners have exactly the skills they need. Planners are well represented at land trusts (including The Nature Conservancy and the Trust for Public Land), activist and environmental justice groups, rail-to-trails organizations, local environmental organizations, foundations with environmental giving, policy institutes, and nonprofit legal defense groups. The nonprofit world and academia employ a small number of planners but have an influence far beyond their numbers.

Colleges and Universities. There are roughly fifty-five undergraduate and nine-ty graduate planning programs in the United States. Professors, instructors, and researchers at these institutions are a small but extremely influential part of the planning profession. Planners may also work as teachers in environmental studies, environmental science, landscape architecture, architecture, public administration, and political science. Professorships at most universities and colleges are highly sought after, and the application process is highly competi-tive. For nearly all positions a Ph.D. is required.

SALARY

The American Planning Association (APA) is an excellent source for informa-tion on salary trends in the planning field. Checking with federal and state agencies is also a good idea, since "planner" or "environmental planner" is usu-ally a listed job with specific salary requirements. In the private and nonprofit sector, salary information is much harder to come by.

According to the APA, starting annual salaries for planners are around $29,000 to $32,000. Some smaller planning departments may pay slightly less. Inspectors start in the low to mid-20s and sometimes higher. Adjusting APA data from a 1995 survey, the median annual salary for all planners in 1998 was approximately $51,000. Planners with ten years of experience regularly exceed $55,000. Planning directors can earn anywhere from $60,000 to 90,000 annu-ally. Successful entrepreneurs in the consulting field often earn more than $100,000 per year.

Overall, federal government agencies and the private sector offer the best salaries, followed by the larger city planning agencies. It is important to note that planners' salaries have risen 3 to 5 percent annually since 1985. A planner hired at $21,000 a year then would be making $40,000 in 1998.

GETTING STARTED

A career in planning begins with the right education, supplemented by problem-solving experience in the real world. Planners are remarkably consis-tent in their suggestions and advice for the would-be planner.

EDUCATION

A basic starting point for a planning career is a bachelor's degree in planning. A master's degree, although not currently required for all positions, is recom-mended and provides the potential planner with the most marketable back-ground. Those students possessing specialized training in such fields as geog-raphy, urban studies, political science, transportation, environmental studies, environmental science, biology, architecture, landscape architecture, or eco-nomics will find themselves in greater demand by employers. Of further help is some knowledge of environmental law, cartography, or urban design. At the graduate level, studies in public policy, public administration, natural resource management, or law make for excellent credentials for prospective planners.

In choosing a college, you may want to consider whether it has been certified by the Planning Accreditation Board (PAB), which is affiliated with the American Planning Association. Seventy-two graduate and undergraduate programs have been accredited by the board, which looks for course work in theory and history; an emphasis on physical planning, economic organization, administration, and government; communications; and a final project that ties the course work together. However, getting a degree from a school not accredited by the PAB does not prevent you from being a practicing planner.

No matter what formal education you receive, planners are unanimous on the crucial importance of practical experience in one's education. Megan Lewis of the APA tells us, "Internships are very important. Many M.A. programs require that students have an internship during the summer between their first and second years. It's also common for planning students to have internships during the school term. When looking for their first planning position, students with work experience have an advantage and are more competitive than those without. Many prospective employers expect applicants to have some professional experience."

Other planners offer the same advice but in different ways by stressing the importance of encouraging the use of volunteer positions, cooperative education, course work in college, and participation in advocacy groups such as the many public interest research groups (PIRGs) and independent study research projects that allow you to get involved with real-world problems.

As a final note, adding some weight to your credentials with a certification can be a good idea. The APA administers a day-long battery of tests by which you can earn the American Institute of Certified Planners (AICP) certification, which is the closest thing in the industry to a planning license. You do not need to have a planning degree to take the exam, and passing the test can add credibility to your planning career, especially if you come from an unrelated background.

ADVICE

Here is a collection of advice from experts in the planning field on how to get started and make the most of your opportunities.

Find an area that interests you. Most university planning programs require you to choose a specific area of interest. Take as many courses in your area of specialization as you can. Says one planner: "If you can show that you have extensive experience in a specific field, that really excites employers. All planners have a general planning background. Set yourself apart from the rest."

Learn to communicate your ideas. "Effective communication of your ideas is essential," says Worcester's Gordon. A great proposal is doomed if you're the only one who understands it. The ability to communicate effectively both verbally and in writing is a mandatory skill for anyone interested in this field.

Master computers, especially geographic information systems. Brant K. Scheideker, senior project director for the DuPage County (Illinois) Development Department sums it up best: "I can't stress enough the importance of computer literacy in the planning field today. Familiarity with basic computer skills, such as word processing and use of spreadsheets, is essential [and] additional skills and knowledge such as GIS, database systems, desktop publishing, even time-management/decision-making systems are excellent to possess as well." Master those computers!

Diversify your skills. Robert McNulty of the nonprofit group Partners for Livable Communities says: "There is a dearth of creativity in local planning departments today. There are too many report writers and pencil pushers who never take the lead. We need to create a new type of professional who knows how to manage change. This is done not by churning out planners who focus on computer modeling and data crunching but by training planners with a diversity of skills, including law, economics, environmental issues, coalition building, politics, historical preservation, architecture, and more."

Gain practical experience. Internships and volunteering are excellent ways for you, while still in school, to gain the practical experience employers look for in applicants. Says Kathy Sferra of the Cape Cod Commission: "I had two unpaid internships and an almost two-year, low-paying secretarial position at an environmental organization before I got a 'real' job in my field." You can gain experience by working in your college's planning department. Volunteer with your town's conservation commission. Internships for students are also available in your local planning office.

SUMMARY

The successful planner will have a strong scientific or technical background, perhaps in a planning specialty, coupled with well-developed skills in oral and written communication, mediation, management, and politics, as well as an ability to integrate the work of many different disciplines and the interests of different parts of the community.

The 21st century will see growth in land-use, urban, and environmental planning positions, especially in rapidly growing parts of the country. In addition, the skills and training of planners make them competitive for other kinds of environmental positions in both the public and private sectors. Good luck!

CASE STUDY

The Chicago Brownfields Initiative

It is planners who guide the development of land for one use or another. With increasing pressure on "greenfields," land not previously developed, planners are more and more aggressively seeking to redevelop "brownfields," which are usually

old, abandoned industrial sites in urban areas. There are over 450,000 brown-
fields sites in cities across the United States.

Most major cities have them: abandoned, crumbling factories, windows smashed, fallen brick scattered about, railroad cars rusting on long-unused spars. These sites are monuments to the bygone age of inner-city industry, the legacy of our flight to the suburbs, of declining U.S. manufacturing, and of the shift to corporate multinationalism and inexpensive labor abroad. The manufacturing jobs are largely gone. What remains is pollution and industrial blight. What's more, these abandoned tracts are, for complicated economic and demographic reasons, often found in neighborhoods of color, often dominated by the poor and the working class.

Of further concern is the fact that many of these sites are polluted by hazardous waste (e.g., heavy metals, oil, and chemicals), which under tightening federal and local laws must be removed before redevelopment can be started. The expense of such cleanup deters private industry from purchasing brownfield sites, especially because these sites are often abandoned property, meaning that there is no responsible owner to share clean-up costs with would-be developers.

Over the last decade, however, an encouraging trend has emerged. As federal and local government struggle to improve neglected inner-city neighborhoods, city planners and developers are aggressively reclaiming brownfields. Cities are realizing that brownfield redevelopment encourages environmental cleanup, brings jobs to underemployed communities, recycles infrastructure, and revitalizes deteriorating areas by counteracting suburban sprawl. Jim Bower, a former official of the EPA now with Chicago's Department of Planning and Development, puts it this way: "We are finally figuring out that urban economics and redevelopment, job creation, and cleaning up the environment are all fundamentally connected. Cleaning up the environment creates jobs and attracts development to the urban core." Most urban areas, especially older ones, are experimenting with brownfield redevelopment, but perhaps the most innovative is the city of Chicago.

In 1995, Chicago launched the Chicago Brownfields Initiative, which was aimed at examining and addressing brownfield redevelopment. An interdepartmental task began the search for suitable sites to be included as part of a pilot program. Funded in large measure by a grant from the U.S. Department of Housing and Urban Development, the city focused its search on Chicago's south and west sides, where residence and industry mix, and where abandoned industrial properties have created economic blight and hampered development.

One such property is the former site of the Burnside Steel foundry, which closed after a crippling 1979 explosion. Scavengers looted the site, removing any material of value, leaving only the dilapidated structures and a decaying smokestack. Bill Klapp of neighboring Verson Industries remembers the rotting foundry: "Just take something, a structure, slowly crumbling and disregard it for sixteen years. . . . It tends to attract things, things tend to grow, piles of rubbish tend to appear. . . . It was, basically, a wide open seven acres with no security around it." Local residents worried for their safety and the safety of their children, and local businesses felt they were losing customers through association with the gutted factory. The local alderperson, Lorraine Dixon, continued the work of her predecessor in trying to have the site cleared and redeveloped. She recalls working with the city to "try and pitch the site to a number of private industries," but says that "no industries were interested because they didn't know the level of contamination to the site."

Finally, local businesses employed the services of a private planning agency, the Southeast Chicago Development Commission (SCDCOM), to suggest remedies to the problems at Burnside. SCDCOM, recognizing that Burnside would be an ideal participant in the pilot program, contacted the city. The city agreed to include Burnside in the Initiative. Because Burnside Steel had declared bankruptcy after the explosion, the property had accrued substantial back taxes, and the city of Chicago was able to assume ownership of the parcel and begin the clean-up. Two hundred truckloads of debris and five barrels of hazardous waste were removed from the site. The total cost of the cleanup was more than $220,000.

Meanwhile, the Chicago Department of Planning and Development and SCDCOM worked on improving the surrounding area. SCDCOM's Jorge Perez remembers that, "The city, in addition to redoing the Burnside site, improved surrounding infrastructure, restructured streets, raised viaducts; generally they made it easier for local industries to move supplies in and products out." These improvements enticed Verson Industries, which had been considering a move to Indiana, to stay in Chicago. The Chrysler corporation recently awarded Verson a multimillion-dollar contract, securing 350 jobs and much-needed tax dollars for the city. As a result of the Chrysler contract, Verson purchased a parcel of the refurbished Burnside site, and is beginning a $31 million expansion, a move that is expected to create up to 150 new jobs. Alderperson Dixon is working with Verson to create a database of qualified local applicants for the new positions.

SCDCOM also strives to connect with local residents. Says Mr. Perez, "We're working to outreach with local church groups, block clubs, and with Alderperson Dixon's office to create linkages and relationships—so that when companies in the area engage in new planning, that it is not done in a vacuum." Ms. Dixon believes that the Burnside cleanup has led to what she calls "a general redevelopment in the area," such as the construction of a sorely needed senior center, which uses the only remnant of the old Burnside Steel foundry—its parking lot.

The Burnside redevelopment is a classic example of 90s-style planning—a comprehensive plan developed with local residents and businesses, using both public and private resources. The city of Chicago's Planning and Development Commission, Alderperson Dixon's office, SCDCOM, Verson Industries, Mayor Daley's office, and local residents all played a role in cleaning up

Burnside. Bill Klapp looks back: "I don't think any one person could have done what went on here. It really was a joint effort."

PROFILES

Kathy Sferra
Planner
The Cape Cod Commission
Barnstable, Massachusetts

Planners play a key role in preserving natural amenities and making them accessible to the public in such a way that they can enjoy them without damaging them.

"I've always known that I wanted to work in the environmental field," says Kathy Sferra, planner for the Cape Cod Commission. "I've always loved the outdoors and been particularly passionate about land protection." It is this passion that brings her to her current post. After obtaining her B.S. in environmental education from Cornell University, Kathy worked as an environmental advocate in Washington, D.C. Although she found her work there exciting, Kathy decided that she "wanted to do something that would bring [her] more in touch with people and the out-of-doors." Kathy returned to school, and while serving on the local conservation commission, earned her master's of regional planning from the University of Massachusetts.

Cape Cod is among the most rapidly growing regions in New England. It is also among the most cherished, both for its charm and its natural beauty. The growing population, coupled with the crush of summer tourists, places great demands on available open space and other natural resources. Planning is a key element in preserving the beauty of the Cape, while at the same time accommodating the needs of the residents and visitors.

With the creation of the Cape Cod National Seashore in the early 1960s, the area avoided succumbing to the rampant overdevelopment that is so characteristic of the eastern seaboard. Ms. Sferra hopes to continue this trend. "My job is a mix of planning and conservation work," she says. Among her on-the-job activities, she lists, "reviewing proposed development projects for their impact on natural resources, providing technical assistance to town boards (planning boards, conservation commissions), conducting various planning studies on natural resource issues, attending meetings—lots of meetings!—site visits, and field work."

Ms. Sferra's current projects include coordinating a regional walking trail/greenway project, developing an open space protection plan for a closing military base, developing a model bylaw for wildlife habitat protection, and reviewing a proposed subdivision on an undeveloped barrier beach.

Overwhelming? Not for Kathy. In fact, these are only a few of the many projects she's involved in. "At any one time, I'm probably juggling about thirty to forty different projects of different sizes," says Kathy. Throw in serving on her town's planning commission, volunteering with the local land trust, and various other local conservation projects, and you've got Ms. Sferra's schedule. "My job isn't 9 to 5," she says, "it spills over into my 'free' time." But the rewards are worth the long hours and heavy workload. Among the benefits, Kathy lists, "working with creative and energetic colleagues, the mix of indoor and outdoor work, and all the people I meet that support the work I'm doing." Above all, though, what drives Kathy Sferra? "The feeling I'm making a difference in my field." Surely something must frustrate Kathy about her job. "Not having enough hours in the day to do all the things I'd like to."

Michael Rios
Spanish Speaking Unity Council
Oakland, California

Among the difficult challenges confronting the next generation of planners will be accommodating equity in plans for parks and open spaces. Understanding the needs and desires of recent immigrants to the United States is crucial to this task.

Michael Rios traces his interest in urban design and planning to a field trip taken during his early college days at Lehigh University in Bethlehem, Pennsylvania. "A local architect showed us some of his work, which had a certain impact on me, and encouraged me to take a class in architecture. I also had an interest in urban studies, and I combined the two, one thing led naturally to another, and eventually to planning."

After Lehigh, Rios took an internship that made a personal impression on him and would have a lasting effect on his career— working with the New York City Planning Department. Rios's job there was to develop a GIS system to help visualize anticipated zoning changes and their affect on pedestrian patterns. However valuable this technical experience was for Rios, there was a more important lesson learned—where and how urban design fits into public policy making.

Rios's focus on the public is illustrated by his current work with the Spanish Speaking Unity Council (SSUC), a nonprofit community redevelopment corporation that works with the primarily Latino Fruitvale district of Oakland, California. Founded in the mid-1970s, SSUC is "unique in that it looks at community development from a very 'holistic' perspective. We look at not only issues of housing or social support services, but we also think about quality of life issues and try to encourage initiatives that are comprehensive, initiatives that look at the long term when improving neighborhoods, particularly inner-city neighborhoods." In this spirit, SSUC recruited Rios to work on a project that he hopes will have a lasting positive impact on the Fruitvale District—a new waterfront park.

The Fruitvale Recreation and Open Space Initiative, described by Rios as a "partnership project with other local nonprofit groups," focuses on two park projects—improvements and maintenance of an existing urban park, and a campaign urging the Port of Oakland to donate land for a harborfront park. Statistics explain the need for additional open space in the Fruitvale district— the area has one of the densest populations of youth living in Oakland, and has the least amount of open space.

For Rios this is an "equity-of-resources" issue. In developing new recreation areas for Fruitvale, he sees himself narrowing the gap between the working class residents of Fruitvale and more fortunate Oaklanders. Rios describes open spaces as a "key component in the overall improvement of a neighborhood, a crucial piece both in providing alternative activities for youth and as a way to create assets to attract a variety of people into a neighborhood."

Listening to Michael Rios talk about his career in planning, one hears certain phrases echoed: "quality-of-life issues," "equity of resources," and "community-planning process." These are the words of a planner who sees in his work a calling, namely, a desire to improve people's lives by improving their physical environment. Indeed, Rios says, "I don't think you can really get away from that when you're doing planning. After all, the clients are the users, the people who will have to live with the decisions made by the politicians, developers, and planners."

Steven Elkinton
Outdoor Recreation Planner
National Park Service
Washington, D.C.

Planners are called on to perform a wide variety of functions within agencies whose means are sometimes limited. This gives practicing planners an opportunity to use many different skills derived from a diverse personal and educational background.

Even as a fine arts major at Kalamazoo College in Michigan, Steven Elkinton was interested in planning. During the last few months of his senior year, Elkinton worked on a thesis in city and regional planning, "wading" through the works of giants of the planning movement (e.g., Olmstead, Mumford, and Jacobs), an exercise that left him with a great respect for the history of the planning movement, as well as wondering where his own career was heading. An extended postgraduation journey helped him to find some of the answers.

"I went out for a couple of years and wandered around, hitchhiking about, and one of the things I did was to hike for two weeks on the Pacific Crest Trail in Oregon. I said to myself, 'This is a real experience. Why is this trail here? Who built this trail? How did it get here?' It was a profoundly moving experience."

His experiences in Oregon led Elkinton to enroll in graduate school at the University of Pennsylvania, where he studied "landscape architecture with a strong dose of planning." While at UPenn, Elkinton submitted his résumé to the federal government, specifically to the National Park Service, which was, at the time, the largest employer of landscape architects in the nation. Shortly after finishing his graduate work, the Park Service called, and Elkinton left Pittsburgh for Washington, D.C.

At first, Elkinton's work with the Park Service focused on the parks of the metropolitan D.C. area, where he performed a variety of tasks: planning transportation systems and parking lots, cultural landscape projects, studies for the U.S. Park Police, and general management/development concept plans. Elkinton's early planning work would teach him to be a "generalist," to develop an ability to work on a variety of planning and design projects, a skill that would benefit him greatly in his next project—the creation of the Cuyahoga Valley Recreation Area in Ohio.

As project supervisor, Elkinton wore many hats: parkwide planner, site-specific planner, trail planner, sign planner, and even public relations planner. "We ran like crazy for four years to get that park up to speed," says Elkinton, during which time he developed a sensitivity for land-use planning that guides his decisions even today. "You can't just freeze the landscape, you've got to honor its dynamics. You've got to honor the fact that its been disturbed and managed. If you're looking at battlefields or old trail ruts or Indian petroglyphs or a recreation area, realize that they are all cultural landscapes, that they've been impacted by the hand of humanity. You can't just let them go, you've got to figure out how to manage them in an appropriate way. These kinds of planning questions have really been the focus of the second half of my career."

Elkinton tries to apply his philosophy to his current work overseeing the twenty long-distance trails that make up the National Trail System. Although his work with trails is similar in many respects to his work at Cuyahoga, there are differences. "The trails are odd because unlike traditional park landscape projects, trails don't have easily defined boundaries. They're very complicated. There are a lot of jurisdictions involved and a lot of issues involved. Also, trails are way underfunded and widely misunderstood."

Despite these challenges, Elkinton is excited by his work, which he likens to the genesis of the Park Service itself. "This is like starting something new. There's never been a National Trails System in this country. My work is pulling together the people who love it, and making it credible to the people who don't." This public interaction suits Elkinton just fine. "A lot of my work is people-oriented. One of the things I like about my job versus some of the other work I've done is that here I deal mainly with people. I try to inspire them to do miracles." Then, with a chuckle, Elkinton adds, "And sometimes it works."

RESOURCES

Although the list below is small, visiting the websites listed will lead to dozens of valuable leads. In addition to the resources here, also use the resources listed in chapter 11. Land and water conservation issues involve large numbers of planners.

American Planning Association. With more than 29,000 members, the nation's foremost professional planning organization. Maintains the American Institute of

Certified Planners. Organizes the annual APA National Planning Conference. Publishes *Planning* magazine. Website includes job listings, recent articles from *Planning*, discussions of current trends in planning, and a subscription answer service for planners. Student membership available. 122 South Michigan Avenue, Suite 1600 Chicago, IL 60603. (312) 431-9100. Http://www.planning.org.

American Society of Landscape Architects. Association with more than 12,000 members. Interested in site planning, historic preservation, garden design, town and urban planning, and park and recreation planning. Organizes annual meeting and EXPO. Publishes *Landscape Architecture* magazine and *Landscape Architecture News Digest*. Accredits educational programs of landscape architecture. 636 Eye St., NW, Washington, DC 20001. (202) 898-2444. Http://www.asla.org.

Association of American Geographers. Scientific and educational society whose members share an interest in the theory, methods, and practice of geography. Environmental planning, land-use planning, and land-use law are of interest to both planners and geographers. Publishes *The Annals of the Association of American Geographers* and *The Professional Geographer*. 1710 16th St., NW, Washington, DC 20009. (202) 234-1450. Http://www.aag.org.

Association of Collegiate Schools of Planning. Organization of university departments and schools that teach urban and regional planning. Conducts annual conferences. Publishes *Journal of Planning Education and Research* and *UPDATE*, a newsletter. Prepares guides to graduate and undergraduate planning schools, including the comprehensive *Guide to Graduate Education in Urban and Regional Planning* (available from the APA bookstore at 1313 E. 60th St, Chicago, IL 30637). Visit ACSP's Guide to City and Regional Planning and Planning Education website at http://www.plannersweb.com to view the *Planning Commissioners' Journal*. The *PCJ* is a quarterly journal designed for planners, but strives to be clear and understandable for nonprofessionals. Provides relevant, up-to-date reporting on current issues in planning. Website features recent articles from the journal, as well as a look inside the world of planning. P.O. Box 4295, Burlington, VT 05046. (802) 864-9083.

Cyburbia—The Planning and Architecture Internet Resource Center. Directory of Internet resources relevant to planning, architecture, urbanism, and the built environment. Also features mailing lists, newsgroups, and interactive message areas. Http://www.arch.buffalo.edu/pairc_.

Growth Management Institute. A nonprofit institute dedicated to effective and equitable management of growth and changes in human habitats. 5406 Trent St., Chevy Chase, MD 20815. (301) 656-9560. Http://www.gmionline.org_.

Partners for Livable Communities. A nonprofit organization that works with community development institutions, foundations, and city governments to initiate changes designed to increase the livability of communities. Dedicated to increasing and maintaining open spaces in urban areas, and ensuring access to them for people of all backgrounds. 1429 21st St., NW, Washington, DC 20036. (202) 887-5990. Http://www.livable.com.

Planner's Network. An association of professionals, activists, academics, and students involved in various planning efforts in urban and rural areas. Uses planning in an attempt to eliminate the inequalities of wealth and power in our society. Website includes an online newsletter, membership opportunities, and case studies. Http://www.picced.org/resource/pn.

Planning Resources on the Internet. Maintained by the Environmental Design Library at the University of California, Berkeley. Contains links to more than eighty sites or site directories, including schools, organizations, local planning sites, and others of interest to planners. Includes an alphabetized listing of American universities and colleges that grant bachelor's or advanced planning degrees. Environmental Design

Library, UCal, Berkeley, CA 94720. Http://www.lib.berkeley.edu/ENVI/citydir. html.

Urban Land Institute. A nonprofit organization that works toward improving land-use and real estate development. Publishes *Urban Land* magazine and maintains *Land Use Digest*, an online periodical. 1025 Thomas Jefferson St., Suite 500W, Washington, DC 20007. (202) 624-7000. Http://www.uli.org.

5 Environmental Education and Communication

AT A GLANCE

Employment:

Over 300,000 environmental educators and communicators nationwide (includes K–12 and college teachers)

Demand:

5 percent annual growth from 1997 to 2007

Breakdown:

Public sector, 60 percent
Private sector, 15 percent
Nonprofit sector, 25 percent

Key Job Titles:

Camp counselor
College professor
Communication specialist
Community affairs manager
Community relations specialist
Corporate trainer
Environmental advocate
Environmental education specialist
Environmental journalist
Internal communications specialist
Interpretive naturalist
Media relations specialist
Museum educational staff member
Nature writer

Outdoor trip leader
Photographer
Public information specialist
Regulatory affairs coordinator
Right-to-know coordinators
Science teacher
Teacher in-service trainer
Videographer

Influential Organizations:

Council for Environmental Education
Environmental Protection Agency, Office of Environmental Education
National Association for Interpretation
North American Association of Environmental Education
Society of Environmental Journalists

Salary:

Entry-level salaries average $18,000 to $25,000 and sometimes lower. Salaries for experienced personnel fall into the $28,000 to $45,000 range. Upper-end salaries are in the $60,000 to $75,000 range, with some fields paying lower and some higher. Keep in mind, however, that the field also runs on thousands of relatively low-paid seasonal workers, volunteers, and interns.

WHAT IS ENVIRONMENTAL EDUCATION AND COMMUNICATION?

A naturalist explains the effects of wildfire on the ecosystem of Acadia National Park. A reporter writes an article about toxic contamination of local groundwater. A sixth grade biology teacher measures soil moisture with students and puts the data on the World Wide Web. A college professor prepares for a class on forest hydrology. All of these activities are examples of environmental education.

We live in an age of information, communication, and education. The sheer number of schools (110,000), colleges (2,400), community colleges (1,400), nature centers (1,450), training programs, parks, wildlife refuges, newspapers, and magazines that do *some* environmentally related work assures that the field of environmental education and communication will continue to be important.

The Environmental Communication Resource Center at Northern Arizona University defines environmental communication as the "communication of environmental messages to audiences by all means and through all channels . . . and is achieved through effective message delivery, interactive listening, and public discussion and debate." Teaching people how to think critically and creatively to solve environmental problems is the common goal of all environmental education (EE) programs. Essentially, environmental communicators and educators provide their audiences with the knowledge and skills to look at an environmental issue critically and make informed, balanced decisions about the environment that result in taking responsible actions. This requires an interdisciplinary approach that makes connections between environmental issues and the associated social, economic, political, scientific, and technological concerns.

In this chapter, environmental education is defined as including the following:

- Classroom teaching in the schools at all levels.
- Education at museums, zoos, nature centers, parks, and aquaria.
- Print, broadcast, and electronic environmental journalism.
- Public information efforts by corporate and government organizations.
- Education for advocacy.

Although environmental educators work in a wide range of settings, they all share one objective—to help people appreciate and understand the natural world around them.

HISTORY AND BACKGROUND

In the early 1800s, the United States was still overwhelmingly a rural culture, and "environmental education" was the learning one received from agriculture, hunting, fishing, and other daily activities. Already, however, urban areas were growing dramatically, and writers and naturalists such as Henry David Thoreau perceived the need for an education that would incorporate an understanding of nature and raise awareness of ecological degradation. In 1864, with the publication of George Perkins Marsh's *Man and Nature*, people began to realize that human activities could do irreversible damage to the Earth.

By 1891, Cornell University was encouraging schools to teach nature study as part of the core curriculum. Early conservation groups, such as the Sierra Club, formed and undertook education projects among their first tasks. Visitors to newly formed national parks sought some form of "interpretation" for both education and entertainment.

The modern era of environmentalism is often traced to the publication of Rachel Carson's *Silent Spring* in 1962. The various professions trace their emergence as a definable career to different points in time, but all within the last 40 years. Tim Merriman, executive director of the National Association for Interpretation, says that Freeman Tilden's book, *Interpreting Our Heritage*, "really made the identity of the field [of interpretation] more definite." Environmental journalism became an established field in the late 1960s and early 1970s as many newspapers established environmental beats. Environmental education, according to the Presidential Council for Sustainable Development's *Public Linkage, Dialogue and Education Task Force Report* (1997), "dates back at least to the 1972 Stockholm conference on the environment. Two subsequent United Nations' conferences defined the new field."

A dramatic increase in environmental education careers can be traced to the first Earth Day and the first Environmental Education Act in 1970. Earth Day itself was a massive "teach-in," bringing information about pollution and its effects to hundreds of thousands and spotlighting the low level of environmental literacy in our nation. A survey in that year by the National Education Association showed that 78 percent of surveyed teachers felt there was a lack of curriculum for environmental education.

Other important events in the 1970s were the United Nations conferences on the environment: the 1972 Conference on the Human Environment in Stockholm; the Belgrade Conference in 1975, which defined the goal of environmental education; and the Tbilisi conference in 1978, which built on the Belgrade charter and laid out five objectives for environmental education—awareness, knowledge, attitudes, skills, and participation. The issues raised at these conferences provided a framework for the field.

In 1990, Congress passed a new Environmental Education Act designed to coordinate educational efforts at federal, state, and local levels, as well as to promote the exchange of information and publicize model programs to encourage their emulation around the country. Also in the 1990s, the *Brundtland Commission Report* and *Agenda 21* of the United Nations Conference on Environment and Development (UNCED) laid the groundwork for moving environmental education into the 21st century. Those who want to make a difference through environmental education should become familiar with the issues raised during all of the above-mentioned conferences.

ISSUES AND TRENDS

The following sections discuss broad issues that affect employment of environmental educators and communicators.

INTEGRATING ENVIRONMENTAL LEARNING INTO K–12 CURRICULUM

Environmental content in the schools is increasing. It may not be happening as quickly as we would like, or as uniformly, but the general trend is upward. More children are doing projects about energy conservation, destruction of the rain forest, water pollution, recycling, and global climate change. Environmental learning is spread throughout the curriculum, although science class remains the most likely place for learning about how natural systems work and how human activities affect them. That's the good news. The growth of environmental learning, however, does not necessarily translate into increased employment of "environmental educators." Instead, more generally trained teachers are looking for help in the form of nature centers and museums that offer field trips, curriculum guides, materials that can be incorporated into class activities, videos that summarize important issues, and continuing education seminars to help "teach the teachers." Persistent financial pressures on school districts contribute to the problem. Creativity and inexpensive purchases, not a wave of new hiring, are the preferred answers for most schools.

USE OF VOLUNTEERS, INTERNS, AND SEASONAL WORKERS

Here's an interesting statistic. Tim Merriman of the National Association for Interpretation reports that there are over 10,000 full-time interpreters in the United States, and there are more than 250,000 docents active at parks, museums, nature centers, zoos, and aquariums. Most of these are volunteers or hourly, part-time workers. A look through the help wanted ads in *Earth Work* magazine shows the same pattern—many environmental education jobs are available. Most of them are seasonal or intern-level positions.

CABLE TELEVISION AND THE ENVIRONMENT

The number of cable networks continues to expand, and this is good news for environmental educators who create videos and television programs. There is even a whole network dedicated to animals. Although the field is extremely competitive, there are more opportunities here than ever before. You may find environmental and "nature" programming coupled with general science education on television.

CONTINUING CHANGES IN DEMOGRAPHICS

If you aren't familiar with the term *environmental justice*, start familiarizing yourself with it. *Environmental justice* refers to equal protection from environmental hazards for all people regardless of age, ethnicity, gender, social class, or race and came about to address the inequitable distribution of environmental risks to low-income neighborhoods and communities of color. The need to structure education in a way that reaches a diverse audience is a pressing issue for all formal and nonformal education and communication. According to *Education for Sustainability: An Agenda for Action,* classrooms and society in general are increasingly more diverse racially, culturally, and linguistically. Environmental communicators and educators will need to have skills in conflict resolution, intercultural communication, languages, and teaching approaches that are sensitive to cultural values and practices. This points to the need for the development of curricula that is relevant to multicultural audiences and for teacher training so that these ideas can be passed on to students. More obviously, the field needs greater diversity among practitioners. Hispanic, African, Native, and Asian Americans with environmental training are in demand.

ADVOCACY OR EDUCATION?

Rows of school children watch a video about old-growth forests in the Pacific Northwest. Later, the class talks about issues such as habitat destruction, forest practices, endangered species, and the ethics of cutting the last remnants of our ancient forests. Environmental education, right? Suppose you found out later that the video was produced and paid for by Weyerhaeuser Company, the large forest products company? Or, conversely, the teacher ordered it from the Sierra

Club. It's pretty clear that either side would produce "education" with a decided point of view.

There is a concerted effort by environmental education groups such as the North American Association for Environmental Education (NAAEE) to set standards by which EE materials can be developed and evaluated. The goal is to present unbiased, factual information based on scientific evidence, and to include all perspectives where there are different scientific explanations and opinions. The common refrain of EE programs is that they endeavor to teach children *how* to think rather than *what* to think, thereby giving them critical thinking skills that enhance performance in all subject areas. Good EE programs should explore social, political, and economic aspects, in *addition* to the scientific aspects, of environmental problems and solutions.

Lea Parker, assistant professor of environmental communication and journalism at Northern Arizona University says: "Rather than alarmist types of communication, the trend is to inform people of how they can make a difference in working toward environmental sustainability in their respective communities." This indicates a need for skilled education and communication professionals who can completely integrate everything from scientific studies to propaganda, and deliver a concise, complete message about the environmental implications of our way of life to millions of people.

Calls for objectivity have not solved the problem. Many educators continue

Students at Garrett Morgan School of Science in Cleveland ask questions of an environmental professional at career day.

to believe that a major goal of environmental education must be to rouse the public to political and personal action. This is a source of endless controversy in the field.

BABY BOOM ECHO

The "baby boom echo" is a tidal wave of teenagers flooding our nation's high schools. Their parents are baby boomers who set the school enrollment record in 1971. In 1996, that record was broken. The last ten years saw a sharp rise at the elementary level, however, in 1997 that pattern shifted to secondary schools. According to the 1997 *Back to School* report by U.S. Secretary of Education Richard W. Riley, "unlike the previous baby boom (1947–1961) there will be no sharp decline in enrollments" after this boom; rather the student population will level out at a much higher number.

The baby boom echo will also affect higher education in the coming years as the number of full-time college students in the next ten years (1997–2007) is projected to increase by 21 percent. Riley's report says that: "While the number of elementary school teachers is expected to increase 5 percent between 1997 and 2007 . . . the number of secondary school teachers is projected to increase by 14 percent." The report goes on to say that in New York City public schools, for example, there is a shortage of state-certified science teachers. A 1996 survey by Recruiting New Teachers, Inc., reported that 69 percent of urban school districts reported an immediate need for science teachers.

THE REVOLUTIONARY IMPACT OF COMPUTERS AND THE INTERNET

Take a minute to do an on-line search for information on wetlands loss. Within seconds, you will have more information available to you than the most diligent graduate student could have gathered ten years ago. Moreover, you are now instantly linked with scholars, activists, companies, government agencies, journalists, and educators from around the world. You can ask questions, locate the best sources of information, review raw data, and view sophisticated maps prepared by the world's most advanced geographic information specialists. This is all in a day's work for you . . . a high school senior.

The personal computer and high-speed communications have changed the pace and face of education *and* communication. In the next few years the TV, computer, and telephone will become one instrument and the primary source of information. A 1997 survey by Nielsen Media Research reports that about 37 million people in the U.S. and Canada have Internet access. *Education for Sustainability: An Agenda for Action* reports that: "Computer-aided environmental education that takes advantage of new interactive multimedia approaches will grow dramatically in the coming decade."

In 1993, approximately 25 percent of U.S. schools had modems. One year later 64 percent had them, including 77 percent of all high schools. From 1987 to 1997 the number of computers in schools grew from one computer for every 125 children to one for every 12 children.

A whole chapter could be written about how the World Wide Web and the growth of educational CD-ROMs is changing environmental education. For a look at what's happening, read the Case Study toward the end of this chapter.

Robert Braile, an environmental correspondent for the *Boston Globe* who teaches environmental writing at Dartmouth College, says that technology has "radically changed the way journalism is done, from the speed with which a story is produced to the range and depth of that story. It's easier to get expert opinion, for one thing. Some would argue that technology has made things too fast, especially when it comes to environmental journalism. It's more complex than general reporting. Sometimes it just takes time to write."

Another trend in high-tech journalism is the growth of "webzines," magazines that are published (sometimes exclusively) on the World Wide Web. Those that are the on-line companion to print magazines often have an entirely different content. Writing for the Web requires an additional set of skills, as the language is more informal than print journalism, and employs sidebars, photos, humor, and "hot-links" to other sources. David Tenenbaum, feature writer at *The Why Files*, a biweekly electronic science magazine, and freelancer and science correspondent for ABCNEWS.com, says: "To write on the Web, you must keep up with the market—study what else is being done out there. Also, humor is a hallmark of writing on the Web."

Keep in mind that the information on the Internet doesn't get there by magic. People with expertise in website design and management are in demand.

THE SQUEEZE ON ENVIRONMENTAL JOURNALISM

There is a general public awareness that we have immense problems with our planet and atmosphere. However, the 1990s has actually seen a drop in the amount of coverage and a narrow range of coverage in most mass media. A study by the Center for Media and Public Affairs found that the percentage of environmental stories on network evening broadcasts dropped from 2.74 percent in 1990 to 0.86 percent in 1996.

The University of Michigan Environmental Journalism Program conducted a survey in 1996 of 506 environmental journalists representing all media. The survey found that a majority of TV, newspaper, and newsletter writers said that they spent less time reporting about the environment in 1996 than they had in the previous year. A "lack of resources" was cited as the most serious problem facing environmental journalists by 38 percent of those surveyed. Other "major" problems cited were lack of time, low salaries, lack of space, and lack of interest by editors. Only one-third of journalists surveyed said they spent more than 75 percent of their time on their beat.

Orna Izakson, environment beat reporter for the *Bangor Daily News* (see the Profiles section toward the end of this chapter) says part of the problem is that editors who don't have an interest in or understand environmental issues tend not to give them air-time unless pushed to do so. Issues such as crime are being seen as more important, especially in major urban areas. Another reason for decreased coverage is perhaps a sense that the environment is getting better and we have to worry less about it. Izakson says: "We've addressed some of the worst pollution problems. Rivers don't catch fire anymore. L.A.'s air quality is the best it's been in twenty or thirty years . . . [but] it doesn't seem to me that the issues are lessening. . . . We are in a serious state with our fisheries on the east and west coasts. We've got some real problems, and mostly people don't know about it."

Environmental journalists are being asked to deal with ever-evolving complexity at a time when the trend in news communication is to simplify. But many of the complex and interrelated problems plaguing our planet cannot be adequately explained in a newspaper article or a two-minute segment on the evening news. Izakson and other environmental journalists agree that you have to be creative in finding the time and space to more fully report the complexities of environmental issues. You have to be able to make a compelling argument to an editor to get space to write about environmental issues, and you must be willing to work on those stories in addition to assigned stories.

Despite the decline of environmental journalism in the 1990s most environmental journalists feel that the outlook for future employment is good. In *SEJournal*'s 1997 summer issue, Chris Bowman interviews Peter Bhatia, managing editor of the Portland *Oregonian*, with no less than seven environment beat reporters. Bhatia says: "The children who grew up with Earth Day and recycling are going to be caring adults, wanting to know about the world in which they live. The environmental ethic (of youth) is going to produce an appetite for reporting that explains things for them."

RAPID GROWTH IN COLLEGE ENVIRONMENTAL PROGRAMS

Environmental studies programs across the country are experiencing significant growth demand. Classes that a few years ago drew a handful of students are now oversubscribed. Bob Robitaille, director of programs at the Environmental Careers Organization says: "On the university level we're seeing an explosion of interest by undergraduates in the environment. Environmental studies programs are busting at the seams. It's one of the fastest growth areas in American academia—so fast that it's creating problems." Colleges and community colleges are responding by improving environmental courses in traditional disciplines and creating majors in environmental journalism, environmental communications, and environmental education. This, along with the impending increase in general enrollment, suggests that colleges and community colleges will hire additional faculty members in the near term. Dartmouth's Robert Braile says that, "interdisciplinary education, which has always been the hallmark of environmental studies programs, is in a sense becoming a kind of expertise. It's making the generalist an expert. . . . we're producing people who can think across many disciplines. I think that's needed."

REGULATORS AS EDUCATORS

We've seen that environmental regulation is moving away from "command and control" to less adversarial "partnerships" with regulated businesses and the general public. In addition, businesses are working harder to communicate with (and listen to) the public about environmental concerns. This creates opportunities for "environmental communicators" in every sector.

CAREER OPPORTUNITIES

As we have seen, environmental educators and communicators are at work in every part of the environmental community. Each sector, however, requires somewhat different kinds of people and skills.

PUBLIC SECTOR

Environmental education in the public sector ranges from working as a park interpretive ranger at Yellowstone, to directing environmental education programs for state and local agencies, to teaching at a local school.

Federal Government. The U.S. Department of the Interior, with its many agencies, including the National Park Service, the U.S. Fish and Wildlife Service, and the Bureau of Land Management, is one of the largest employers of environmental educators. For many people, in fact, pursuing a career in environmental education is synonymous with becoming an interpretive naturalist at a national park.

If you are one of these people, be aware that these jobs are among the most sought after positions in the environmental field, despite low pay, poor housing conditions, and limited career paths. Literally thousands of people compete for a handful of positions at the major parks, and some work for years as seasonal or volunteer workers without becoming permanent employees. EE programs are conducted on nearly all of the 191 refuges administered by the U.S. Fish and Wildlife Service. These positions are less competitive but still attract large numbers of applicants. However, if you are not dissuaded by this litany, the Advice section later in this chapter will help.

Competition at agencies that more recently began incorporating environmental recreation and education into their agendas is less daunting. These include the Bureau of Land Management (BLM) and the USDA Forest Service (USFS).

The BLM conducts an environmental education program called Wonderful Outdoor World (WOW), which provides neighborhood-based urban camping experiences for inner city youth. BLM also has a website that lists EE and volunteer programs (http://www.blm.gov/education/education.html). The USFS developed a program called Natural Resource Conservation Education, which provides structured educational experiences and activities that are targeted to age groups and populations and that enable people to realize how natural resources and ecosystems affect each other and how resources can be used wisely. These agencies employ professionals to develop and implement these programs.

Other possibilities are the Environmental Protection Agency's Office of Environmental Education, which offers positions for curriculum developers, trainers, and similar educators; the Department of Energy, with its many laboratories; and the Department of Defense; and the U.S. Geological Survey.

State Government. State governments are a rising star in the environmental education profession. Almost every state has a full-time or part-time environmental education specialist position. States play a key role in setting and reviewing curriculum requirements for local schools, creating funding priorities, running grant programs, training teachers, and implementing federal programs and policies. State departments of education are often the focal point for preparation and implementation of environmental education plans under the Environmental Education Act. In addition, each state has a collection of environmental and conservation agencies with growing needs for the skills of educators and communicators. These agencies include departments of fish and wildlife, forestry, environmental protection, natural resources, parks and recreation, cooperative extension, and public health.

The National Environmental Education Advancement Project (NEEAP, see

Field identification is an important part of a good environmental education.

the Resources section at the end of this chapter) manages a program in partnership with the EPA, the National Wildlife Federation, the North American Association of Environmental Education, and the National Fish and Wildlife Foundation called EE 2000. EE 2000 provides seed funding, leadership train-·ing, consulting services, a clearinghouse and a quarterly newsletter to those interested in strengthening state-level EE programs. The idea is to assist states in their efforts to develop "comprehensive" EE programs.

As defined by NEEAP, components of state-level EE programs include: a state EE coordinator and staff; state and regional EE centers; preservice and inservice teacher training; and K–12 curriculum and instruction requirements, among others. Since only four states (Maryland, Minnesota, Pennsylvania, and Wisconsin) have a majority of these components in place and since the plan calls for helping twenty states build comprehensive plans by the year 2000, positions are being created for environmental education specialists in state departments of education.

Local Government. Public schools, from kindergarten to graduate school, hire many times more environmental educators than any other sector. Consider that there are more than 110,000 public and private elementary and secondary schools, more than 2,400 four-year colleges and universities, and more than 1,400 two-year colleges in the United States. All of these schools employ environmental educators. They may be called librarians, science teachers, biology professors, or wastewater certification instructors, but they are all environmental educators.

Career opportunities in teaching vary wildly depending on the economic and population growth of an area. Almost every state in the country has some sort of EE program. Few, however, are comprehensive enough that they attempt to integrate EE into most or all subject areas. States that have a stronger commitment to EE will obviously offer more opportunities than those that have a lesser one. Wisconsin is often cited as having the best teacher-training programs for environmental education nationwide. Other states with good EE teacher-training programs are Florida, Arizona, Colorado, Hawaii, Illinois, Minnesota, Missouri, and North Carolina.

A word about elementary and secondary teaching is in order. Why do it? It requires long training, with usually a master's degree for better positions. Pay is relatively low. Budgets are usually tight. Facilities are poor. Success is often frustratingly slow. And yet, in spite of all of this, no single environmental profession needs talented, creative, and enthusiastic people more than teaching. No career will produce higher rewards in personal satisfaction, and none will create a higher environmental quality return on society's investment. If we are truly serious about environmental change, we must start with the education of our children.

At the community college, undergraduate, graduate, and doctoral levels, the prominence of environmental specialties is increasing in schools of science, health, and public policy. There is a growing demand for professors and instructors in environmental areas, as noted in the Issues and Trends section earlier in this chapter.

In addition to schools, consider other environmental education and communication positions with local government agencies. Solid waste and recycling programs, storm water management agencies, household hazardous waste initiatives, land-use planning agencies, staff offices for elected officials, neighborhood programs, public works departments, water and air pollution agencies, and other local environmental functions have needs for education and communication professionals and their skills. Look particularly for departments that depend on widespread changes in individual behavior, such as curbside recycling efforts. Education and communication efforts in the form of classes, speeches, brochures, community events, school presentations, public meetings, and so forth are usually a large part of these initiatives.

A final arena for environmental educators in local government is the parks and recreation departments. Many cities, towns, and counties operate zoos, museums, summer education programs, arboretums, botanical gardens, large parks, youth camps, cleanup programs, conservation corps efforts, nature centers, and other places where environmental education is the key service. For the aspiring educator, a significant advantage of the local sector is its willingness to accept, train, and use volunteers and interns.

Tim Merriman, executive director of the National Association for Interpretation, says that overall demand for interpreters is growing due to the rapid growth in travel and tourism. "Private tour companies, nonprofit nature centers, and city- or county-based programs are growing the most rapidly," Merriman says. However, he cautions that "there may be fewer line interpretation jobs, but more for docent coordinators" due to the increased usage of volunteer/docent interpreters.

Skills essential to any environmental education position, whether it's in a primary or secondary school, with a private nature center, or with one of the federal land management agencies, include: good leadership skills; group interaction skills; the ability to inspire people to action; and the ability to work with diverse populations. A second or even a third language can also enhance your chances of being hired and a dose of equal parts enthusiasm, creativity, and dedication goes a long way toward a successful career.

PRIVATE SECTOR

Private sector jobs in environmental education include community involvement coordinators for private companies, environmental training services, and the environmental media. This is a small but growing area in total employment.

Corporations. Have you received any "environmental education and communication" recently? Your utility company sent you a colorful brochure highlighting ways you can conserve energy and cut your energy bill. The place mat at the fast-food restaurant where you had lunch was covered with the environmental accomplishments of the company. "Printed on Recycled Paper" was prominently noted. The newsweekly you read on the bus carried a two-page ad touting the pollution prevention record of the chemical industry. When you got home, there was a message on your doorknob from the private recycling firm that collects your trash, inviting you to a neighborhood meeting to discuss changes in the system. The notice is signed by the "recycling education staff." Finally, in the evening newspaper, you discover that environmental activists and the area's largest polluter are sitting down together for talks about reducing the use of toxic materials at the firm. The company's representative is referred to a as "community involvement coordinator."

"It used to be that environmental communicators worked mostly for government organizations or nonprofits. Increasingly however . . . the corporate world is hiring environmental communicators to communicate issues both internally and externally," says Lea Parker, assistant professor of environmental communication at Northern Arizona University. These professionals generally don't have a technical background and so are better able to understand the information needs of the general public or company employees.

Federal regulation has helped inspire this kind of need. One example is the "community right-to-know" requirement under the Superfund Amendment and Reauthorization Act (SARA). Under right-to-know laws, reams of data about corporations' use of toxic chemicals are available to the public. It is in a firm's best interest to provide some assistance to the public in interpreting these data. Without such help (and sometimes with it), the likely response is fear of the unknown.

Corporations in the oil, chemical, waste management, manufacturing, and other industries are employing a broad range of environmental communicators with training in public relations, media coordination, graphic arts, government relations, environmental journalism, compliance, law, and technical fields.

Advertising agencies who have "green" clients are also in the business of environmental communication, enticing people to purchase products and services that are safer for the environment.

Consulting Firms. As mentioned earlier, many environmental laws require that workers be certified or receive specialized training before they are allowed to work. A growing number of private firms have sprung up to provide this service. These firms hire instructors, trainers, and workshop leaders to deliver educational services to corporations and agencies. Career opportunities in this field may not require a great deal of specialized training. If you are a quick study and have a winning classroom presence, training firms may be willing to help you learn the material you will teach.

Environmental training specialists will also be needed to work directly for companies employing significant numbers of seasonal or temporary workers.

The Media. Print and electronic media outlets such as newspaper, book, magazine, and World Wide Web publishers; television and radio stations; audiotape and videotape production companies; and others make up "the media." Since much of what the public knows about environmental issues is learned through the media, environmental stories, insight, news, and information are needed. However, as mentioned in the Issues and Trends section earlier in the chapter, coverage of environmental issues dropped in the 1990s.

According to the survey of 506 environmental journalists done by Michigan State University's Environmental Journalism Program, the only medium in which journalists say they spend more time on environmental coverage is radio. Forty-one percent of radio journalists surveyed said they spent more time reporting on environmental issues in 1996 than in 1995. Six percent said they spent less.

Environmental book publishing is another field where hiring is taking place. Most major book stores have added entire "nature/environment" sections, and large publishing companies are expanding to create departments specializing in environmental books.

"Video technology is one of the fastest growing and most innovative fields in the job market. It's so new that some research projects might not even know they need someone in this position until you suggest and create it. Research institutes and universities may hire these professionals," according to *100 Jobs in the Environment* (Quintana 1997). This is true of many jobs in this field. Who ever thought there was a need for a live picture of the Earth on the World Wide Web until someone creative came up with the idea?

Beth Parke, executive director of the Society of Environmental Journalists (SEJ), says that environmental magazines, "have not had such a great fate," and in television, "there are very few dedicated environmental reporters, or even science/health/environment reporters, but there are some."

On the upside, however, Parke reports that "specialized newsletters is a strong market center for environmental reporting." She cites such publications as *Environment Daily, Oil Spill News, Defense Cleanup*, and *Oil Spill Technology* as examples. Parke continues by stating that "the on-line information services seem to be expanding their hiring [and] a number of news organizations have defined a 'growth beat' [population issues] which is extremely environmental in its underpinnings."

Other areas to consider for jobs are universities and research organizations, which, though they are not considered "news organizations," publish a lot of environmentally related material.

NONPROFIT SECTOR

Nonprofit organizations are a major player in the environmental education field, serving as information resources to the media and education resources to the public at large. Almost all nonprofit environmental organizations engage in education, from small neighborhood groups with one staff person to large international organizations such as Greenpeace and the World Wildlife Fund. Both the writers and the publishers of this book, for instance, are nonprofit organizations.

In *The Environmental Career Guide*, Nicholas Basta suggests: "perhaps the most dynamic form of environmental communication occurs at nonprofit organizations. . . . These organizations try to present a compelling message to the public that will help them form opinions on environmental issues and hopefully act on their belief through writing letters, volunteering for the organization, or changing their daily behaviors to make a difference."

Career opportunities in nonprofit organizations for people skilled in education and communication are greatest with groups in which education is the main activity, such as nature centers that offer field trips for schoolchildren, or with large, well-known groups, such as The Nature Conservancy or the National Wildlife Federation. Environmental education may also be incorporated into the job descriptions of lobbyists, program and research staff members, administrators, and fund-raisers. Much of this work is seasonal, depending on the school year or summer vacation activities to provide "customers." Skills in demand include outdoor skills; the ability to teach environmental fieldwork techniques; knowledge of biology, botany, ornithology, and wildlife science; strong oral communication and teaching abilities; and innovative ideas for curriculum design. Schoolteachers seeking summer work, take note!

SALARY

Salaries in this field vary widely depending on which sector you work in and what particular job you do in that sector. In general, however, entry- to mid-level salaries are low and the rewards come from job satisfaction.

Interpreters may be the most poorly paid in the group. Owen Winters at the Natural Sciences for Youth Foundation (see Resources section), reports that some nature centers provide room and board and hire entry-level people for as low as $12,000 annually. Winters says: "It really puts a lump in my stomach when I see that. We're taking some of our best and most enthusiastic people and just economically abusing them." Nature centers that don't provide room and board pay between $17,000 and $20,000, and "probably with no benefits" according to Winters. The mid-level for interpreters is in the range of $25,000 to $32,000 annually.

Private school teachers fall just below interpreters on the poorly paid list, starting around $16,500 and rising to around $27,500. Public school district salaries are a little higher, with smaller school districts paying less.

Entry-level environmental journalists working for small-town papers start in the mid-teens. This is where the majority of journalism jobs are found. Entry-level journalists at larger, urban daily or weekly newspapers earn about $23,000 annually. A senior editor earns from $28,000 to $45,000. Also, note the following:

- An editor at an environmental newsletter or book publisher can expect to start at between $18,000 and $25,000. Five years' experience increases that range to between $25,000 and $35,000.

- Aquarium instructors start in the low $20s. Experienced instructors can earn up to $30,000.
- A public affairs officer at a nonprofit organization can start as low as $17,000, but increases quickly to around $25,000 or more.
- An interpreter at a federal agency starts at around $20,000. With five years' experience salaries rise to the high $20s or low $30s.

In all sectors except the private, administrators and directors are the only ones who can expect predictable salaries higher than $40,000. Educators, writers, and other communicators in government agencies and nonprofit groups often level off in the $35,000 to $40,000 range. Salaries for "environmental" positions with magazines, newspapers, television and radio stations, and other media outlets are so varied that an attempt to characterize them would be meaningless.

A bright spot in the salary picture is the pay of college professors in environmental fields. Depending on their institution and field, it is not unusual to find professors earning $40,000 to $75,000, after weathering low-paying positions as graduate assistants and instructors.

Environmental educators and communicators like what they are doing for the world. However, choosing a career in environmental education or communication requires that an individual face squarely the fact that some emotionally rewarding jobs are often poorly compensated. If money is a prime motivator, think carefully before choosing this field, and consider educational opportunities and experiences that will maximize your value in the job market.

GETTING STARTED

Even for people who have known since reading *Ranger Rick* at age six that they would grow up to become environmental educators, getting started takes careful planning.

EDUCATION

Educators and journalists often fall into one of two groups. One group emphasizes scientific and technical knowledge, placing secondary importance on teaching and communications. The other group develops teaching and communication skills first and leaves scientific understanding to graduate school or on-the-job training. Today, however, professional advice seems less polarized, calling for interdisciplinary study that combines significant pieces of both academic worlds. According to the Society of Environmental Journalists (SEJ), covering environmental issues requires sophisticated knowledge about science, law, politics, history, ethics, economics, and international relations and assumes a high level of journalistic skills to explain how all these disciplines come to bear on the environment. Chris Rigel, at SEJ says, "The one thing I keep hearing over and over is that just getting a journalism degree isn't enough. It's very important to have a strong science background."

Robert Braile goes even further, saying: "I've never been a fan of the undergraduate journalism major. . . . journalism is best learned by doing it . . . [and] undergraduate journalism majors are seen in the profession as people who are trained to be journalists but don't have anything to write about because they haven't really had any substantive academic experience." As an undergraduate, Braile recommends building journalism experience by writing for student publications or small daily or weekly publications or newsletters, infusing your major with environmental writing, and combining that background with a graduate degree in journalism.

Lea Parker, assistant professor of environmental communication and journalism, sees both science and communications as equally important: "I don't think an environmental communicator can successfully do the job without some background in the sciences. Communication skills needed include critical and analytical reporting, public affairs reporting, and some kind of environmental research and reporting class. Also needed are skills in public relations, interpersonal communication, public speaking and organizational communication."

Jim Detjen, Knight Chair of journalism at Michigan State University's Environmental Journalism Program, weighs in with: "As we move into an increasingly international and increasingly computerized world, I believe it will be vital for journalists to become better educated. I'd like to see more environmental journalists trained in several specialties. A reporter educated in environmental issues and economic theory would be able to provide valuable insights about how business and the environment interact."

It is important to note that many environmental writers who are currently employed do not have formal education in the sciences. But Orna Izakson, environment beat reporter at the *Bangor Daily News*, says that if (like her) you don't have a science background, you should at least have an affinity for biology and chemistry. Izakson says, "the bottom line is that, especially in the beginning, you're not going to be so specialized that any kind of science education will give you all the background you need."

For environmental educators in public and private schools, there will be obvious teacher certification requirements for elementary or secondary opportunities. The vast majority of teachers who consider themselves environmental education specialists have science teaching certifications. *Education for Sustainability: An Agenda for Action* states: "The need for preservice teacher training in environmental curricula can hardly be overemphasized. . . . Most teachers feel that they are not prepared for conveying the broad spectrum of issues and content related to the environment."

For those who wish to pursue a formal degree in environmental education, there are a growing number of college programs of varying quality. In an article titled "Environmental Literacy and the College Curriculum" in the *EPA Journal* (Spring 1995), Richard Wilke says: "While many institutions offer environmentally related minors and majors, they do not require even basic

> The key traits of an environmentally literate citizen are: an awareness and appreciation of their natural and built environment; knowledge of natural systems and ecological concepts; understanding of the range of current environmental issues; and the ability to use investigative, critical-thinking, and problem-solving skills toward the resolution of environmental issues. This then would encompass the key objectives of environmental education.
>
> —Abby Ruskey, "State Profiles in Environmental Education,"
> *EPA Journal*, Spring 1995

instruction in environmental literacy." The North American Association for Environmental Education is a good resource for more information about the quality of environmental studies programs (see the Resources section at the end of this chapter).

Academic preparation for interpretation careers has become more formalized in the past decade and certification adds another layer of formality. Tim Merriman, executive director of the National Association for Interpretation (NAI), says: "Interpreters with multiple skill sets will have an advantage. If you have a strong background in interpretation or communication, it also helps to have a major in zoology, botany, biology, history, or anthropology." Both the National Park Service and NAI have certification programs, and interpreters who want an advantage should pursue certifications in multiple competencies.

ADVICE

Here is a collection of advice from educators and communications professionals on the keys to entering their fields.

Inspire curiosity. "The most important thing for a nature center educator is to be able to answer the question of a visitor so that you give them enough of an answer and a question back so they want to learn and dig for more. You have to understand how to take that spark of curiosity and fan it into a flame that will last a lifetime." Owen Winters, Natural Science for Youth Foundation

Write for newsletters. "When a student asks me where to start I always suggest specialized newsletters and on-line information services. I think a lot of really great daily newspaper reporters got their start or did some time in specialized venues like that." Beth Parke, executive director, Society of Environmental Journalists.

Use professional associations. "Get involved in your profession early. Students who already belong to their professional association have the advantage to the best jobs, promotions, and more interesting venues. Networking has become an essential part of any profession. At a national or regional meeting you can sit down and chat with the director of a major program. Building that personal network can add to your ability to achieve your personal goals for success." Tim Merriman, executive director, National Association of Interpretation.

Be clear. "Journalists have to fight for the space and airtime to explain complex but important environmental issues. They need to work to clearly explain complex subjects in understandable and compelling ways." Jim Detjen, Knight Chair of Journalism, Michigan State University's Environmental Journalism Program.

Develop some experience. "Before you graduate, complete internships to make sure this is what you want. You can never have too much experience." Michelle Jansen, interpretive naturalist and intern coordinator, Carpenter St. Croix Valley Nature Center.

SUMMARY

Environmental education and communication professionals have an influence on environmental results that far exceeds the wages and recognition we give them. The ultimate success of the environmental movement depends on an educated and caring citizenry, who have both the ability and the desire to understand the threats and opportunities before us and to act with wisdom in their personal and political lives. Ecological literacy will be crucial to progress in the 21st century.

Environmental education opportunities are everywhere—in the classroom, on television, and in radio; in newspapers, magazines, and books; at conferences and other gatherings; and through the Internet. Job opportunities in environmental education and communications are growing, not only in the form of specific positions, but in the revisioning of science, management, and regulation positions to include education as an integral responsibility.

CASE STUDY

A Case for Global Environmental Education on the World Wide Web

To get an idea of what Web-based environmental education is all about, consider the following two representative scenes:

At a high school in upstate New York, Becky arrives at school and quickly makes her way toward the computer to check her electronic mail in hopes that a university scientist 100 miles away has received her query and can advise her group (which is composed of students at her school and a neighboring high school) in their study of the causes of pollution in their watershed. Upon confirmation of help from the scientist, she sets up an on-line meeting between all the parties involved to discuss the project.

In Germany, two fourth graders meet on a spring morning at the site of selected native trees to take their turn at observing and recording "budburst." After budburst occurs, approximately one month of daily observation data will be entered into a form on the World Wide Web. This information, along with temperature and precipitation data also gathered by students, will be used by scientists to determine a number of things, including how climate affects vegetation patterns.

The advent of email, the Internet, and the World Wide Web (WWW) has rapidly transformed public access to information and communication, allowing students, teachers, and scientists to work collaboratively in ways never before possible. Today many of the world's best minds on any subject are instantly accessible and willing to share their knowledge (http://www.askanexpert. com). Scenarios such as those described above are taking place worldwide every day. They are facilitated by a number of Internet-based programs and projects such as Global Rivers Environmental Education Network (GREEN, a watershed education network) and Global Learning and Observations to Benefit the Environment (GLOBE, a network for the study of the global environment). These, and other programs like them, help students reach higher levels of achievement in science and math by "doing science," motivate student interaction, experimentation and collaborative learning, and increase scientific understanding of the Earth. Through these programs, millions of students gain a real-world understanding of their roles in the world ecosystem by studying issues that affect their lives and homes. Most web-based EE programs send students into the natural environment for hands-on investigations of their local environmental problems. The phrase "think globally, act locally" is brought to bear in the very nature of such programs. With this understanding, students are inspired and empowered to take responsibility for the environment. The broader educational benefits of using the Web for environmental education include the following:

- Increased literacy where students become mindful of spelling when trying to search for a topic and where students write to a responsive audience of peers, mentors, and strangers, which makes them more conscious of word choice, grammar, and syntax.
- Environmental literacy where students become informed citizens, gain problem solving skills, and are motivated to take action.
- Computer literacy where citizens are not afraid of computers. Indeed, they wouldn't want to try to get along without one.
- Interdisciplinary learning where students explore the ecological, social, political, and economic aspects of environmental problems.
- Critical thinking learned through weighing and comparing diverse viewpoints, and analyzing and synthesizing the information to construct personal understanding.
- Geographic and cultural diversity.
- The ability to work collaboratively through project-based learning, where different strengths and talents are used and appreciated.
- Respect for thinking "outside the box."

- Skills in fieldwork and application of science concepts.
- Increased interest in science careers.

This is not to say that web-based learning should be used as a substitute for face-to-face collaboration, lectures, textbooks, and field-based learning. Rather, it should be viewed as a tool that enhances these activities with a global perspective, bigger data sets to study, expert advice and answers to problems, geographic and cultural diversity, and much more.

Though computers with WWW access aren't yet as common in schools as the chalk and blackboard, they soon will be. Consider that in 1994 just over 3,000 schools in the United States had access to the Web. In 1998, over 12,000 elementary and secondary schools in 80 countries, including over 8,000 in the United States, not only have access, but have constructed their own websites. However, if web-based EE is to be effective, it must be affordable and accessible to all.

Initiatives are being created all over the country, from the federal down to the grassroots level, to bring adequate phone lines, modems, and computers to public and private K–12 schools, public libraries, and even public housing projects. Why? It's very simple—those who have on-line skills have immense advantages over those who don't. The challenges of a new global economy require schools to graduate a new kind of student, one who can think critically, has experience with problem solving, can communicate in writing to diverse audiences, and has the ability to work collaboratively. Every job mentioned in this book relies on communication and partners for success. Web-based learning is thought to engender all these skills and more. But there is no doubt that computers, and the use of them for worldwide communication on any topic imaginable, are here to stay.

One can access thousands of collaborative environmental education projects by cruising the global information superhighway. However this "superhighway" can feel more like gridlock due to frustration caused by the overwhelming volume of information. In an attempt to answer this problem there are now a number of websites that are designed to provide "one-stop-shopping" for various resources, including EE.

You will still need a great deal of patience and persistence, however, to find the right project or partner.

The University of Minnesota's College of Education maintains an "International Registry of Schools on the Web" at their virtual Route 66 homepage at http://web66.coled.umn.edu. In addition, several websites maintain a registry of projects, such as Global SchoolNet at http://www.gsn.org, EnviroLink's Environmental Education Network at http://www.envirolink.org/enviroed, International Education and Resource Network (iEARN) at http://www.iearn.org, and the Community Learning Network at http://www.cln.org.

Another site is Education World ("where educators go to learn") at http://www.education-world.com. A recent database query of "environmental education" on that site yielded over 5,000 links to lesson plans and whole curricula spanning K–12 grade levels that incorporate EE across all disciplines—writing/language arts, math, life and earth science, social studies/government, and even art. For example, a government class in Sweden sought a partner school in the U.S. Midwest to compare legislative processes and collaborate on ideas for how each class might go about influencing environmental lawmaking.

Students and teachers alike are enthusiastic about EE on the Web. A grade school teacher in Florida comments, "any time you put a child in front of a computer they're excited about learning." In an article that appeared in *Educational Researcher* (vol. 25, no. 2, March 1997, pp. 27–33), Ronald D. Owston notes that students "thrive on interacting with the (computer)" and have been raised in a world where computers are an integral part of daily life. In the article, Owston examines whether WWW increases access to education, promotes improved learning, and contains the costs of education to justify widespread use in classrooms. He finds positively for all three questions but qualifies this by saying that the promise of the technology is rooted in how educators use it.

One challenge of EE via the WWW is to give teachers the skills they need to implement EE on the WWW. Initial training doesn't go very far with the rapid rate of technological advances, and EE projects are still new and constantly evolving to work out the bugs. For instance, the GLOBE program, initiated in 1995, evolved considerably between the first and second school years. An evaluation of the second year of GLOBE program operations by SRI International says that, "Although the pace of change has left nearly all program participants with the sense that they are constantly straining to catch up with the latest developments, few doubt that the effort has been worth it."

All Internet users have the ability to collaborate on-line, taking part in experiments, presentations, and interactive lessons and sharing their work with the world. Along the way, all constituencies become students in the education process, challenging traditional ideas about teaching, learning, and schools and fundamentally changing the interactions between students and teachers.

Web-based EE facilitates student-centered learning by allowing them to formulate questions and seek the answers on the Internet, exploring resources that seem promising to them at their own pace. A ten-year-old may well have more capacity for answering computer-related questions about Web-based learning than the teacher. In addition, through the pursuit of environmental investigations and problem solving, students begin to be seen as experts in certain aspects of environmental problems and gain the respect of their communities and professionals in the field.

As students choose to attempt to solve environmental problems that are beyond a teacher's realm of knowledge, teachers must let go of their status as the primary source of knowledge for students and take on the role of facilitator in gathering information and helping the students analyze and understand what they come up with. Clinton Kennedy, a teacher at Cascade High School in Idaho (see profile toward the end of this chapter) says of his advanced biology students: "Never underestimate the power of students—turn them loose on meaningful projects, be ready to give advice, and watch things happen. I learn with the students. . . . I am not the 'sage on the stage,' but the 'guide on the side.' . . . This is a much more rewarding way to run a class."

Finally, schools become only one venue for learning as the WWW allows students, teachers, and scientists to transcend pre-Web obstacles to collaboration, such as the cost of travel and cultural and time zone differences, to form worldwide on-line peer networks. Suddenly "school" is no longer contained in a building in the community but located in a virtual global village. In rural areas where comprehensive libraries are not available, the Web, sometimes referred to as the world's largest library, broadens research capabilities and the whole world is brought within the confines of the classroom.

The Web is a powerful tool for enhancing environmental education. Interactive environmental education encourages thinking and problem solving rather than memorization and regurgitation and increases our knowledge base of our planet through scientific contributions that are shared worldwide. That is how EE projects on the WWW can "make a difference" for the environment.

PROFILES

Clinton A. Kennedy
Science Teacher
Cascade Junior/Senior High School
Cascade, Idaho

The Cascade Reservoir Restoration Project is conducted by advanced biology students at the local high school. The reservoir provides a real-life laboratory in which students must balance scientific, economic, and political aspects in proposing a solution to an environmental problem and implementing their solution. They learn that unless all of these aspects are equally addressed, success is virtually impossible.

Clinton Kennedy, science teacher at Cascade High School, says his desire to teach young people about the environment emerged from his experience as a youth leader for the Boy Scouts: "My greatest satisfaction came from teaching other scouts something new about nature." However, Clint's inclination to teach was side-tracked during his early college years.

After high school, Clint went to the University of Idaho in Moscow, Idaho, where his first major was forestry. However, his "insatiable curiosity" and interest in the "hard sciences" led him to change his major. When he was a senior, Clint became concerned that his biology/botany/zoology major would lead him to a lab job, so he quit college and got a job as a timber faller. This was intended as a stopgap measure to "gel [his] thoughts on [his] career goals." He and his wife decided to start a family and then planned for him to go back to

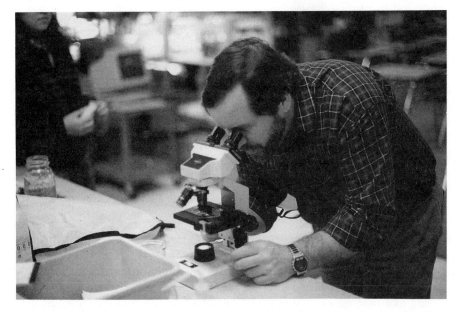

Junior high school science teacher Clinton Kennedy teaches students how to identify lake organisms in his Cascade, Idaho, classroom.

school. However, due to the arrival of identical twins the stopgap turned into a seventeen-year career.

By the late 1980s, Clint was increasingly dissatisfied with his work. He says, "by [then] I was convinced that if our youth were not given the tools to analyze problems and make good decisions as adults, the quality of life in . . . [the] future was in jeopardy. The things I loved so much about Idaho were disappearing for reasons that didn't seem valid or necessary." In order to remain in "small town Idaho" and get back to his first love, science, Clint returned to the University of Idaho to become a science teacher. He earned a B.S. in secondary education with an emphasis in biology.

Today, Clint is a certified teacher in natural science and physical science. The six courses he teaches change from year to year. His school operates on a rotating A/B day schedule consisting of four 95-minute class periods per day—three teaching periods and a preparatory period. In the 1997–1998 school year he teaches seventh grade integrated science, tenth grade standard biology, and tenth grade college prep (CP) biology on A-day schedule. On B-day schedule he teaches seventh grade integrated science, eleventh grade CP chemistry, and a combined eleventh and twelfth grade advanced biology class.

Clint arrives at school at 7:30 A.M. to organize his day. This can include setting up labs or demonstration activities, gathering materials, making copies, and discussing issues with colleagues. Some days students may arrive early to make up labs or get help. At 8:15 the tardy bell rings for first period and announcements are heard over the intercom. Clint takes attendance and lunch count and enters the numbers onto a computer network. He begins each class similarly by taking attendance, and then asks if there are questions on assignments. If students are slow to start the day's discussion, he may ask his own questions—in the form of a quiz! Clint says, "this usually is enough motivation to get them to take the lead and ask questions."

Clint's teaching style relies heavily on discussion that requires students to come to class prepared. He also integrates the hands-on activities of the Project WILD curriculum, an interdisciplinary conservation and environmental education program that emphasizes wildlife. Though each group's needs are different, Clint feels that discussion-oriented classes allow him to focus on areas where students need help and to introduce new material more effectively.

After second period, Clint goes to the teacher's lounge to eat lunch with other teachers. He says, "this is a relaxing and enjoyable time with joking and pleasant discussions." Third period begins after lunch at 12:20. His preparatory fourth period is spent planning, writing, grading assignments, and entering grades onto a computer network. He also supervises independent study classes during that time, and occasionally gets involved in helping other teachers with technology issues.

Cascade High School is strongly committed to technology. Each teacher has a Power Macintosh at his or her disposal and each class may have five or more computers available for student use. Clint has some high-end computers for graphic and World Wide Web work that allow students to do multimedia reports using a variety of sophisticated software.

Clint's advanced biology class is project-oriented with a chemistry prerequisite in which students create their own projects by researching a local environmental problem and proposing a solution. In the first phase of the course, lectures are used to provide a scientific vocabulary and to introduce the fundamentals of limnology. These are complemented by lakeside field work, hands-on labs, and demonstrations.

During the second phase of the course, students begin to identify solutions to environmental problems. They attend water quality meetings, give public testimony, write letters to representatives, and use the Internet to do research and set up cooperative experiments with some of the world's leading experts. Students must build support for their ideas in both the professional and the local communities. If they build enough support, they attempt to raise funds to implement their projects. If the fundraising is successful, students then implement, test, and monitor the success of their work. Finally they write a paper and/or produce a video on their findings. All projects are then put on the class website (http://www.cascadehs.csd.k12.id.us/advbio/home.html) to share with the whole world.

This alternative way of teaching requires that Clint be able to help several groups working on different projects at once. Because of the nature of his advanced biology class, students may need help in the evenings, on weekends, or even during the summer. Clint says: "The rewards from watching the students do real-life, meaningful things with the knowledge I've helped them gain over the years make teaching worthwhile for me. I wouldn't give it up for anything, even though it requires a considerable time commitment." Another thing he likes about his job is that working with large groups of people means no two days are the same.

Besides being on hand to advise students in the summer, Clint runs a youth crew for the USDA Forest Service that does hands-on environmental projects such as Bull Trout habitat improvement, erosion control on trails, and salmon habitat restoration. He also teaches a Project WILD workshop for teachers on environmental issues in Idaho.

On the downside, Clint says: "If you elect to teach a real-life project class, you will have real-life political problems to deal with. Teaching about the environment is very controversial and much political heat can be brought to bear." Clint offers the following advice:

- Respect all opinions
- Identify biases, including your own
- Teach critical thinking—how to think, not what to think
- Honor disagreement
- Stay true to your ideals, but don't be radical
- Listen well
- Be a life-long learner

Clint says: "Teaching . . . can be frustrating, and rewards are not instantaneous. But when students come back a few years after graduating and confide in you about the impact you had in their lives, it makes everything worthwhile."

Michelle Jansen
Interpretive Naturalist/Intern Coordinator
Carpenter St. Croix Valley Nature Center
Hastings, Minnesota

Interpretive naturalists need effective communication skills as well as formal biology or environment-related training. It is essential that they speak and write with confidence while retaining an insatiable curiosity about the natural environment and an eagerness to learn and share new things about it throughout their careers.

Michelle Jansen, interpretive naturalist and intern coordinator at the Carpenter St. Croix Valley Nature Center, didn't consider her current career until midway through college. Though she had been visiting nature centers all her life, it wasn't until she visited her hometown nature center that she realized her education, lifestyle, and hobbies could be integrated into a career as a naturalist.

Initially Michelle thought she wanted to be a doctor and began working toward a biology degree at a small liberal arts college. Along the way she realized that she wasn't cut out to be a doctor and began to take a look at the things she did enjoy, such as being outside and teaching children. She ended up transferring to the University of Minnesota, College of Biological Sciences and graduated with a B.S. in ecology, evolution, and behavior in 1994.

While in college Michelle completed an internship at Wood Lake Nature Center in Richfield, Minnesota. After graduation she interned at the Dodge Nature Center in West St. Paul, Minnesota, and began working as a substitute naturalist at Wood Lake. Over the next two years Michelle sent out résumés for full-time positions while continuing to substitute at Wood Lake, work as a seasonal naturalist at Dodge, and volunteer at several other nature centers and wildlife refuges. In 1996 she was hired by Carpenter St. Croix Valley Nature Center as an interpretive naturalist. Since then she has taken on additional responsibilities as intern coordinator.

"Many times being a naturalist, particularly at a small nature center, is like being a 'Jack of all trades,'" says Michelle. Her primary duties are planning, writing, and teaching one- to two-hour environmental education programs for school children, as well as weekend and evening programs for the general public. However, she gets involved in the operations of the nature center in a variety of other ways.

A recent day for Michelle begins at 8:00 A.M. with cleaning animal cages, weighing the hawk and the owl, and preparing "diets" for all the animals. That done, she prepares for a 9:00 erosion class by gathering supplies and arranging chairs. From 9:00 to 11:00 she teaches fourth graders about erosion. When the students are gone she cleans up and prepares for a class she will teach after lunch. At 11:30 she's back at her desk making a variety of phone calls, including checking references for prospective interns, soliciting donations for a special event, and making inquiries to find a rabbit to add to the program animals. Then she takes a break for lunch and a hikes a portion of the 600-acre property. From 1:00 to 3:00 P.M., Michelle teaches second graders about reptiles and amphibians. Again she cleans up after the class, and then spends a little more time taking care of the animals. By 3:30 she's at her desk again, responding to summer camp requests and researching and writing a newsletter article. At 4:45 she meets briefly with the other four naturalists to discuss an upcoming class. At 5:00 she secures the animals for the night, locks up, and leaves.

In addition to the daily duties just described, Michelle is currently working on special projects, which include: writing a grant to secure funding of the internship program; revising the center's policies for birthday parties; rewriting some of the class curricula; and preparing for a fundraising event called the Apple Blossom Special, a 2K, 5K, 10K, and half-marathon foot race open to the public.

As with many environmental professionals, one of the things Michelle likes most about her job is the variety of skills she calls on to perform her duties and the absence of a "typical day." She says, "I can use skills such as writing, creativity, sense of humor, and organization while at the same time teaching, using natural history and other biology knowledge, and dealing with people." She also enjoys the ability to be outdoors about 80 percent of the time, which allows her to "see the seasons change close up." But Michelle gets the most satisfaction from, "sharing some of [her] deepest values [with] an audience that hopefully will grow with the knowledge and use it in making their decisions."

Michelle admits that there are times when her job "looses the 'spark,'" such as when she's bogged down with paperwork and can't get outdoors; when it starts to pour rain and she has a group out far from cover; or when the program animals make a mess, "always in the wrong place!" But Michelle derives motivation for her job from such things as seeing the look on a child's face when he or she has "gotten it"; noticing a tree bud that has opened; seeing eagles return from migration; and feeling like she's making a difference in the way people view nature.

Michelle advises those who are interested in careers as naturalists to be patient. "It usually takes a while to get a full-time position and when you do, chances are you'll never be a millionaire." But, she adds, "overall it is worth it. The naturalist field is exciting and very rewarding."

Orna Izakson
Reporter, environmental beat
Bangor Daily News
Bangor, Maine

Environmental reporters are often the public's only source of environmental information, yet they often have to fight to cover the environment because of lack of space or lack of understanding and importance in the eyes of editors.

Orna Izakson, a reporter covering the environmental beat at the *Bangor Daily News*, announced to her parents at age fifteen that she was going to be a writer, but her desire to be an environmental writer came after she graduated from college.

During college, Orna gained experience in every aspect of producing and publishing as editor of three student publications and an alumni newsletter. She changed her major often because, she says, "I wanted to have five majors! I wanted to be everything!" Her interest and involvement in filmmaking eventually won out. Orna graduated with a B.A. in film studies from Wesleyan University in Connecticut in 1988.

After college, Orna traveled for a year and a half. Having grown up in Manhattan ("a little island in the lower Hudson estuary" as Orna calls it), traveling provided her first opportunities to hike, camp, and experience the wilderness. It was in New Zealand, where she spent nine months, that she had life-changing hiking and camping experiences. She says: "I found something that made sense to me, like a piece had been missing. Living in cities is fine, but it's not for me, but I had always lived in cities, so I didn't know. This was a big revelation. [That's] how I became interested in environmental issues."

Once back in the states, Orna moved to the west coast to look for a job. She ended up in San Francisco working at *Publish* magazine, a national magazine covering electronic publishing. It was there that Orna's ability to write, her interest in environmental issues, and the opportunity to go to graduate school came together. The impetus came from reading a Gannett Center journal called *Covering the Environment* (Summer 1990), which was subsequently expanded and published as a book called *Media and the Environment* by Craig LeMay and Everett Dennis. She says: "The arguments were intellectually fascinating! (It was) a lot of stuff about objectivity versus advocacy and how to cover the environment . . . and I said yes! I want to do that!"

In 1992, Orna began a master's program at the University of Missouri School of Journalism. There she worked on the *Columbia Missourian*, a daily newspaper. The paper had a health/science/environment beat, but unlike California, environmental issues weren't as "omnipresent." Orna soon realized it would be hard to get the environmental clips she needed to compete successfully for environment beat jobs after graduation.

At the end of her first year, Orna made a proposal to the managing editor of the paper to create a separate environment beat, and when she returned to campus in the fall of 1993, there was one. Orna knows several reporters who have successfully argued for an environment beat.

That summer, Orna interned at *High Country News* in Colorado, a "fortnightly paper covering regional environmental issues in the western United States." The internship was unpaid, but the experience was invaluable. She clipped environmental stories from weekly and daily papers from twelve western states, wrote assigned stories that were closely edited, and left with some good clips of her own.

Orna spent her last semester in Portland, Oregon, where she interned at *Willamette Week*, wrote a "scholarly" paper on objectivity and advocacy in environmental reporting, and looked for a job. After turning down a couple of offers, she accepted a job with the *News-Times*, a twice-weekly paper in Newport, Oregon. She was hired to cover the city government beat, but quickly began reporting on environmental issues as well, writing as many as twenty-four stories in a week and paying her dues. She secured the environment beat after covering it and the city government beat for nine months. In addition, she obtained clips as correspondent to the *Cascadia Times* in Portland, Oregon. In 1997, after three years at the *News-Times*, Orna left to take her current job at the *Bangor Daily News*.

On a recent Monday, Orna writes a follow-up story on a mercury spill that she covered the previous Friday. She arrives at the office and reads a story on the spill written by another reporter over the weekend. She talks to the reporter, then reads a story about the spill from another paper. She learns that environmentalists are protesting near the plant and goes out to cover it. She talks to protesters, takes notes, and keeps her eyes open. After two hours she thinks she knows the protesters' concerns. The story seems straightforward. She leaves the protest and goes to lunch, thinking about how to write the story.

Once back in the newsroom she begins writing. Then the phone rings: "Orna, it's Ned. We're taking them to court." Ned is the commissioner of environmental protection. With that, the pace of her day, as well as the story she is writing, changes completely. She tracks down the spokesperson for the chemical company to get his reaction, makes other calls, and reorganizes the story she was writing, as the deadline nears.

Orna says tight deadlines can be frustrating and some days, "writing feels like pulling teeth." Sometimes figuring out the scientific part and then trying to translate it into English is "like beating your head against a brick wall." Also, people sometimes call and yell at her about letters or editorials they think she wrote, but didn't.

Some things that Orna likes about her job are: getting outdoors to cover natural resource stories; getting past the rhetoric of those she interviews to what is really going on, then putting that into a story; and being able to work outside socially imposed hierarchies in a venue where all people are on par. She says: "It's just as important what the fisher thinks . . . as it is to talk to the governor." She also likes the feeling that her work is important to the public: "My feeling is that underneath it all are fundamental questions about science, about what it means [when mercury is spilled in a river] . . . I could write what it means politically, but for the people to make an informed decision about how much fish they want to eat or whether to support the mercury-reduction law, I've got to say what it means [for the environment]."

RESOURCES

Amazing Environmental Organization Webdirectory. "Earth's biggest environmental search engine." Includes information on environmental education and communication and professional associations. Also don't miss the employment section on the Webdirectory homepage, which provides links to job listings, descriptions, and agencies specifically concerned with environmental employment. Http://www. webdirectory.com.

Association for the Study of Literature & Environment (ASLE, pronounced "az-lee"). An allied organization of the Modern Language Association founded to promote the exchange of ideas and information pertaining to literature that considers the relationship between human beings and the natural world. ASLE encourages and seeks to facilitate new nature writing, traditional and innovative scholarly approaches to environmental literature, and interdisciplinary environmental research. Publications include *Interdisciplinary Studies in Literature and Environment* (quarterly). Website has hundreds of links related to literature and environment. Http://www.people.virginia.edu/~djp2n/asle.html.

Bureau of National Affairs (BNA). Founded in 1950, the first publisher to cover the Environment and Safety field regularly and in depth. Excellent resource for up-to-date comprehensive information on major environmental issues. Also consider BNA as possible employer, as it was rated one of the best companies in America to work for by *Fortune* magazine. Has over 20 different publications related to specific issues. 9435 Key West Ave., Rockville, MD 20850. (800) 372-1033. Http://www.bna.com.

Center for Environmental Communication (CEC, formerly the Environmental Communication Research Program). A research, training, and public service organization that brings together university investigators to provide a social science perspective to environmental problem solving. Rutgers University, Cook College, 31 Pine Street, Brunswick, NJ 08901-2883. (732) 932-8795. Http://aesop.rutgers.edu/~cec.

Council for Environmental Education (CEE). A nonprofit educational organization dedicated to providing environmental education programs that promote stewardship of the environment and further the capacity of learners to make informed decisions. CEE is a national leader in the field of environmental education. They administer Project WILD at the national level, and cosponsor Project Learning Tree and Project WET (Water Education for Teachers). These are the most widely used conservation and environmental education programs among K–12 educators. (CEE) 5555 Morningside Drive, Suite 212, Houston, TX 77005, (713) 520-1936. (WILD) 707 Conservation Ln., Gaithersburg, MD 20818, (301) 527-8900, http://eelink.umich.edu/wild/index.html. (Tree) 1111 19th Street NW, Suite 780, Washington, DC 20036, (202) 463-2462. Http://www.plt.org.

ECONET. ECONET is one of five networks operated through the Institute for Global Communications (IGC) Network. Provides access to a variety of environmentally related homepages, numerous conferences, and resource centers on-line. (IGC) Presidio Bldg 1012, 1st Floor, Tourney Ave., San Francisco, CA 94129-0904, (415) 561-6100. (ECONET) 2051 Parton Lane, Arcata, CA 95521, (707) 822-7947. Http://www.igc.org/econet.

Educational Resources Information Center (ERIC). Sponsored by the U.S. Department of Education, ERIC provides access to education-related literature. Searches can be done on such topics as careers in environmental education. ERIC also develops special publications. ERIC/CSMEE (Clearinghouse for Science, Mathematics, and Environmental Education), Ohio State University, 1200 Chambers Rd., Rm 310, Columbus, OH 43212-1792. (614) 292-6714. Http://www.ericse.org/eric/csmee/environment/environment.html.

EE-Link: Environmental Education on the Internet. Funded and administered by the U.S. EPA in partnership with NAAEE and NCEET as part of EETAP (see separate listing for all three in this section) and housed at the University of Michigan. An on-line source of information about environmental education. Provides access to teaching resources on the Internet, including articles, databases, grant information, and instructional materials. Http://www.nceet.snre.umich.edu.

Eisenhower National Clearinghouse for Mathematics, Science, and Environmental Education (ENC). Identifies effective curriculum resources, creates high-quality professional development materials, and disseminates useful information and products to improve K–12 mathematics and science teaching and learning. 1929 Kenny Road, Columbus, OH 43210-1079. (800) 621-5785. Http://www.enc.org.

Envirolink. "The largest on-line environmental information resource on the planet." Two Envirolink projects that are useful for education and communication are Envirolink News Service, a daily international wire service of the environment, and the Environmental Education Network, a clearinghouse of environmental education materials. Http://www.envirolink.org.

Environment Writer. Published ten times a year by the Environmental Health Center, a division of the nonprofit, nongovernmental National Safety council. Available on request to accredited print and broadcast journalists covering environmental issues. Website lists environmental journalism resources. Environmental Health Center, 1025 Connecticut Ave., NW, Suite 1200, Washington, DC 20036. (202) 293-2270 ext. 469. Http://www.nsc.org/ehc/ewtoppg.htm.

Environmental Communication Resource Center (ECRC). Established in 1996 for information, research, and discussion concerning environmental communication. Mission is to promote scholarship, pedagogy, and public service in all aspects of environmental communication. P.O. Box 5619, School of Communication, Northern Arizona University, Flagstaff, AZ 86011. (520) 523-4661. Http://www.nau.edu/soc/ecrc.

Environmental Education and Training Partnership (EETAP). Funded by the U.S. EPA and managed and coordinated by the NAAEE (see separate listings in this section), EETAP provides training for teachers and other education professionals, improves existing databases of environmental education materials, and develops standards for those materials as well as training on the evaluation of them. 1255 23rd Street NW, Suite 400, Washington, DC 20037. (202) 884-8828. Http://www.eetap.org.

Environmental News Network (ENN). An on-line company that provides daily reports on environmental news stories from around the world. ENN editors filter and moderate all content. Also offers radio broadcasts, special reports, multimedia presentations, television previews, feature articles, on-line forums, website reviews, and website design and hosting services. P.O. Box 1996, Sun Valley, ID 83353. (208) 726-3649. Http://www.enn.com.

Environmental Protection Agency's Office of Environmental Education (EPA OEE). Mandated by the National Environmental Education Act of 1990, the mission of the OEE is to advance and support national education efforts to develop an environmentally responsible public, and to inspire in all individuals a sense of personal responsibility for the care of the environment. Programs of the OEE include two scholarship programs: National Network for Environmental Management Studies, which is a fellowship program that provides stipends to college students for completing research projects based on EPA priorities; and Tribal Lands Environmental Science Scholarship Program, which provides funding for undergraduate and graduate degrees in the environmental sciences to Native Americans. 401 M Street SW, #1707, Washington, DC 20460. (202) 260-4951. Http://www.epa.gov/enviroed.

E2: Environment & Education. Nonprofit organization formed in 1994 that grew out of a project called Earth Time. Dedicated to helping young people develop an awareness of environmental issues and the understanding and skill to take informed and effective action through education. E2 has developed an activity-based supplementary curriculum called Environmental ACTION and offers follow-up support, workshops, and in-service support for schools and organizations to ensure the success of the program. Website has great links. P.O. Box 20515, Boulder, CO 80308. (303) 442-3339. Http://www.enviroaction.org.

Global Rivers Environmental Education Network (GREEN). Action-oriented approach to education based on an interdisciplinary watershed education model. GREEN's mission is to improve education through a global network that promotes watershed sustainability by incorporating all areas of the curriculum into an integrated watershed education program through partnerships with a variety of organizations and individuals. Website has good links to other environmental education projects on the WWW. 721 East Huron St., Ann Arbor, MI 48104. (313) 761-8142. Http://ipc.apc.org/GREEN.

GLOBE Program (Global Learning and Observation to Benefit the Environment). The program works through partnerships, effectively joining together the minds and hands of thousands of young people, school teachers, scientists, and others around the world. Participating agencies include the National Oceanographic and Atmospheric Administration, the National Aeronautic and Space Administration, the Departments of State and Education, the National Science Foundation, and the Environmental Protection Agency. 744 Jackson Place, NW, Washington, DC 20503. (202) 395-6500. Http://www.globe.gov/.

Greenwire. On-line environmental news service published by the National Journal Group, which provides daily briefings on news and events that shape the environmental debate at the state, national, and international levels. Synthesizes coverage of over 200 newspapers and broadcast networks. This is an expensive service, so try to access it through your local university or library. National Journal Group, 1501 M Street, NW, #300, Washington, DC 20055. (202) 739-8400. Http://www.nationaljournal.com/aboutgreenwire.htm.

The Journal of Environmental Education. Published quarterly by Heldref Publications. "A vital research journal for everyone teaching about the environment. Includes case studies of projects, evaluation of new research, and discussion of public policy and philosophy of environmental education. Contact Heldref Publications, 1319, Eighteenth Street, NW Washington, DC 20036-1802. (202) 296-6267.

Journalism Job-Links. Sites compiled by the University of Michigan's Environmental Journalism Program that list journalism internships, awards, fellowships, and/or jobs. The Mighty Internship Review, http://www.daily.umn.edu/~mckinney/; News Mait Writers' Cooperative, http://newsmait.com/jobs.htm; Society of Professional Journalists, http://www.spj.org/awdfell/awards.htm; Investigative Reporters and Editors, http://www.ire.org/jobs/index.html.

National Association for Interpretation (NAI). Two organizations formed in the 1950s, Association of Interpretive Naturalists and the Western Interpreters Association, merged in 1988 to become NAI, a networking organization dedicated to the advancement of the profession of interpretation. Products and Services include: National Interpreters' Workshop, an annual conference held in the fall; Regional workshops in the spring; *Legacy*, bimonthly membership magazine; *Journal of Interpretation Research*, peer-reviewed research journal; *NAInews*, quarterly newsletter; *Jobs in Interpretation*, biweekly job-listing service; and a scholarship program. Website lists books for further reading. P.O. Box 1892, Fort Collins, CO 80522. (888) 900-8283. Http://www.interpnet.com.

National Association of Science Writers (NASW). Professional association founded to "foster the dissemination of accurate information regarding science through all media normally devoted to informing the public. Publishes *Science Writers* (quarterly). Sister organization is the Council for the Advancement of Science Writing (CASW), nonprofit educational corporation that works to improve the public's understanding of science and technology. Some CASW programs are designed for experienced journalists, such as seminars, workshops, and continuing education. Other programs are designed for those still in school or recently out of school, such as fellowships, internships, and on-site training. Publishes a free booklet, *A Guide to Careers in Science Writing.* Obtain a copy by sending a #10 SASE to Diane McGurgan at the NASW address: P.O. Box 404, Greenlawn, NY 11740. (516) 757-5664. Http://www.nasw.org.

National Consortium for Environmental Education and Training (NCEET). Coordinates a national effort to improve the efficiency and effectiveness of environmental education, especially in K–12 settings. Sponsors EE-Link, a gopher and website for environmental education. Located at the University of Michigan, School of Natural Resources and Environment, 430 East University Avenue, Dana Building, Ann Arbor, MI 48109. (313) 998-6726. Http://www.nceet.snre.umich.edu.

National Environmental Education Advancement Project (NEEAP). Established in 1991 at the University of Wisconsin–Stevens Point to assist states and communities in their efforts to fully incorporate quality environmental education programs into K–12 schools. Through its programs NEEAP has gained knowledge of the status of environmental education in all states. 1016 Buckholt Ave., Stevens Point, WI 54481. (715) 346-4179. Http://www.uwsp.edu/acad/cnr/neeap/.

National Environmental Education and Training Foundation (NEETF). Chartered by Congress in 1990, NEETF works to create a national and international environmentally literate citizenry and workforce; facilitate partnerships among federal, state, and local government business, industry, academia, environmental, and international organizations; leverage public and private resources for environmental education, training, and research; and foster an environmentally conscious and committed public. 734 15th St NW, Suite 420, Washington, DC 20005. (202) 628-8200. Http://www.neetf.org.

National Environmental Information Resources Center (NEIRC). A public service provided by The George Washington University and the U.S. EPA that provides links to more than 1,000 websites globally. Designed to provide one-stop access to diverse environmental, educational, and sustainability-related information on the WWW.

National Environmental Training Association. Nonprofit education and professional association dedicated to promoting excellence and standards in environmental, occupational safety, and health training. 3020 E. Camelback Rd., Suite 399, Phoenix, AZ 85016-4421. (602) 956-6099. Http://ehs-training.org.

National Environmental Trust (NET). A nonprofit, nonpartisan organization dedicated to educating the American public on contemporary environmental issues. Its public education campaigns combine research and analysis with effective grassroots organizing and media outreach to provide accurate, up-to-date information on environmental issues and the related public policy debates. Has internship opportunities throughout the year. 1200 18th Street NW, 5th Floor Washington, DC 20036. (202) 887-8800. Http://www.envirotrust.com.

National Sciences Teachers Association. Professional association that promotes excellence and innovation in science teaching and learning for all. Advocates for science educators by keeping members and the general public informed about national issues and trends in science education. Publishes five journals aimed at elementary, middle school, high school, and college science teachers. Other publications include a newspaper, books, and a children's magazine called *Dragonfly*. 1840 Wilson Blvd., Arlington, VA 22201-3000. (703) 243-7100. Http://www. nsta.org.

National Wildlife Federation (NWF). For sixty years, NWF has been one of the nation's most respected providers of environmental education. Offers environmental education programs in communities, outdoors, and in the classroom. 8925 Leesburg Pike Vienna, VA 22184. (703) 790-4000. Http://www.nwf.org/nwf/.

Natural Resources Conservation Education (NRCE). A program of the USDA Forest Service that provides structured educational experiences and activities targeted to varying age groups and populations to enable people to realize how natural resources and ecosystems affect each other and how resources can be used wisely. Publishes a newsletter, *Catalyst* (quarterly). Website has curricular resources and contacts for NRCE in each state. Http://www.fs.fed.us/outdoors/nrce/welcome.htm.

Natural Sciences for Youth Foundation. Works to help localities establish and maintain nature centers by instructing them in organization, fundraising, and education programs. Also the professional organization for personnel of nature centers and small nature museums. Former print publications will be integrated into the website, which is under construction in 1998. Among other things, it will include monthly articles relevant to nature centers; *Opportunities*, a jobs listing; names and addresses of other nature centers to facilitate networking; and a place to present and evaluate nature center curricula. 130 Azalea Dr., Roswell, GA 30075. (770) 594-9367. Website under construction in 1998.

North American Association for Environmental Education (NAAEE). Professional association for individuals active in, and concerned with, environmental education. Membership sections include elementary and secondary education, university environmental education, conservation education, and government and private sector personnel involved in environmental education and communications. Programs and activities include: annual conferences; extensive publications program; the Environmental Education Training Institute; Volunteer-led Investigations of Neighborhood Ecology Network (VINE network), the Environmental Education and Training Partnership (EETAP, see separate listing that appeared earlier), and a National Project for Excellence in Environmental Education. P.O. Box 400, Troy, OH 45373. (937) 676-2514. Http://www.naaee.org.

The Orion Society. A nonprofit membership organization that is also an award-winning publisher, an environmental education organization, and a communications and support network for grassroots environmental and community organizations across the country. Work includes teacher training, model classroom programs, reading tours, and a variety of publications, including *Orion* and *Orion Afield* (both quarterly). Orion magazine has been described as "the literary, artistic, and philosophic voice of the environmental movement." 195 Main Street, Great Barrington, MA 01230. (413) 528-4422. Http://www.orionsociety.org.

Outdoor Writers Association of America. A nonprofit, international professional organization of professional writers, editors, lecturers, photographers, artists, filmmakers, and radio and television broadcasters who communicate the outdoor experience to the public through unbiased coverage of outdoor recreation, natural history subjects, environmental issues, and outdoor ethics. Publishes *Outdoors Unlimited* (monthly) in addition to other publications, provides grants for undergraduate and graduate students pursuing degrees in outdoor communication fields, and sponsors an annual conference. 2155 E. College Ave., State College, PA 16801. (814) 234-1011. No website.

Society of Environmental Journalists (SEJ). Membership organization that includes journalists working for newspapers, television and radio stations, broadcast and cable networks, magazines, newsletters, wire services and photo agencies, as well as educators and students. Works to raise awareness among editors and other key decision makers in the media on the importance of environmental reporting. Offers national and regional conferences, on-line resources, minority fellowships and research projects. Publishes *SEJournal* (quarterly) and *TipSheet*, (biweekly). *TipSheet* provides story ideas for journalists in the areas of environment, science, and health. Also has an international branch, the International Federation of Environmental Journalists. Website has job links page. P.O. Box 27280, Philadelphia, PA 19118. (215) 836-9970. Http://www.seg.org/index.html.

USDA Department of Agriculture—Cooperative State Research, Education and Extension Service (CSREES). International research and education network. CSREES expands the research and higher education functions of the former Cooperative State Research Service and the education and outreach functions of the former Extension Service. Links USDA research and education programs with higher education institutions. Focus is on improving the economic, environmental, and social conditions in the U.S. and globally. Competitive research grants are available. Website has links to related university webpages Agbox 2210, 820 Aerospace Bldg., Washington DC 20250-2210. (202) 401-4141. Http://www.reeusda.gov.

U.S. Fish and Wildlife Service National Conservation Training Center (NCTC). Provides training and education services to the natural resource management community from a variety of agencies and organizations. Has state-of-the-art distance learning capability, including live satellite broadcast and interactive video. Offers such courses as Introduction to Desktop GIS, Public Outreach Planning, Effective Meeting Facilitation, and Environmental Negotiations. Also serves as a good source for other training and academic programs. Rt. 1, Box 166, Shepherdstown, WV 25443. (304) 876-7468. Http://www.fws.gov/r9nctc/nctc.html.

U.S. Geological Survey Learning Web. Website designed to provide teachers with on-line activities to help teach earth science. Developed to meet national earth science curriculum standards. USGS 12201 Sunrise Valley Drive, Mailstop 801, Reston, VA 20192. Http://www.usgs.gov/education/learnweb/About.html.

World Resources Institute (WRI). A policy research and capacity-building institute that works internationally on environment and development issues, WRI's Environmental Education Project works with other organizations to promote quality environmental education in the U.S. and worldwide. Produces secondary school and university-level educational material on a variety of environmental issues. 1709 New York Ave., NW, Washington, DC 20006. (202) 662-2573. Http://www.wri.org/wri/enved.

Part III

ENVIRONMENTAL
PROTECTION
AND ENERGY

6 Water Quality Management

AT A GLANCE

Employment:
Over 300,000 nationwide

Demand:
3 to 4 percent overall with greater growth in the private sector

Breakdown:
Public sector, 40 percent (5 percent federal, 35 percent state and local)
Private sector, 55 percent
Nonprofit sector, 5 percent

Key Job Titles:
Aquatic environmental scientist
Aquatic toxicologist
Attorney
Biologist
Chemist
Civil engineer
Drinking water quality control scientist
Environmental communicator
Environmental economist
Environmental engineer
Hydrogeologist
Hydrologist
Public health officer
Risk analyst
Wastewater engineer

Wastewater treatment plant operators and superintendents
Water conservation specialist
Water quality inspector
Water quality technician
Watershed planner

Influential Organizations:

American Water Resources Association
American Water Works Association
Association of Metropolitan Sewerage Agencies
Association of Metropolitan Water Agencies
Association of State and Interstate Water Pollution
  Control Administrators
Clean Water Network
Clean Water Action
National Marine Fisheries Service
River Network
U.S. Army Corps of Engineers
U.S. Department of Agriculture
U.S. Environmental Protection Agency
U.S. Fish and Wildlife Service
U.S. Geological Survey
Water Environment Federation

Salary:

Entry-level salaries range from $18,000 to $35,000 annually. The lower end of the range represents operators at smaller wastewater systems and the higher end includes scientists and engineers at larger consulting firms. Maximum salaries range widely ($50,000 to 100,000 and higher) for managers and directors in government and industry, senior scientists and engineers, consultants, and academics.

Water quality management employs more environmental professionals than any other field, and it's easy to see why. Water is the lifeblood of our planet. *Everyone* uses water and is concerned about its quality and availability. Most of us agree about the need to protect our lakes, rivers, streams, underwater aquifers, wetlands, bays, and oceans. Wastewater treatment plants and stormwater systems are everywhere. Complex systems for the treatment and delivery of drinking water must be managed throughout the nation. Water is managed for agriculture, industry, power production, recreation, and many other uses. In addition, the millions of species of plants and animals we share the planet with require healthy water for productive habitats.

To meet this ubiquitous demand, a large infrastructure of scientists, engineers, technicians, policy makers, educators, businesspeople, and laborers has arisen, offering thousands of opportunities for environmental workers.

WHAT IS WATER QUALITY MANAGEMENT?

There is no single definition of the water quality management profession. The field is often divided according to the type of water resource being managed, and what water is being managed for. Some of the larger categories, employing most water quality professionals, are described in the sections that follow.

DRINKING WATER SUPPLY AND TREATMENT

Management and treatment of drinking water includes identification of surface water and groundwater supplies, removal and transport of water, regulation of drinking water standards, operation of treatment facilities, promotion of water conservation efforts, and maintenance of the drinking water supply infrastructure. There are more than 55,000 drinking water systems in the United States.

WASTEWATER TREATMENT

Professionals in this area include the thousands of scientists and technicians working at industrial and municipal wastewater treatment plants; the people who design, build, and equip the plants; the chemists who collect and test water samples; and many others. Over 16,000 wastewater treatment plants employ professionals throughout the nation.

GROUNDWATER PROTECTION

Groundwater protection professionals identify pollutants in groundwater; assess levels of risk to human, plant, and animal health; design computer models to predict the dispersal of pollutants; carry out remediation activities where resources are polluted; and design protection strategies to prevent groundwater contamination.

SURFACE WATER MANAGEMENT

Management of surface water resources goes beyond wastewater treatment to identify sources of pollution to lakes, ponds, streams, and rivers and finds ways to reduce or eliminate them. Surface water managers often work with other environmental professionals in comprehensive watershed management efforts to protect water resources for fish and wildlife habitat, as well as for human use.

ESTUARY MANAGEMENT

Coastal waters and estuaries (the meeting grounds between oceans and rivers) are crucial to breeding stocks of fish and wildlife, as well as many plant species. Estuarine managers help protect estuaries from the negative effects of development, industry, and agriculture.

WETLANDS PROTECTION

Inland and coastal wetlands moderate the effects of floods and droughts while serving as natural water treatment areas by removing silt and chemicals from the water. Wetlands are also important habitats for fish and wildlife. This part of the water quality management field includes wetlands ecologists, surveyors, botanists, fish and wildlife scientists, planners, chemists, and water quality specialists.

HISTORY AND BACKGROUND

Water quality issues have been at the heart of the modern environmental movement since its beginning. Dead fish, oil slicks, and polluted rivers provided much of the stimulus for the first Earth Day and the subsequent growth of environmental legislation in the early 1970s. The issue of declining water quality seemed relatively straightforward and was highly visual and emotional—our waters were dying. Congress responded to the public outcry by passing legislation that set a broad goal to "restore and maintain the chemical, physical, and biological integrity of the nation's waters."

In many respects, progress has been remarkable. In announcing his new Clean Water Initiative in 1998, President Clinton noted that since 1972 (when the Clean Water Act was passed) the number of waterways considered safe for fishing and swimming has doubled, industrial discharges have been reduced by billions of pounds a year, the number of Americans served by adequate sewage treatment has more than doubled, annual wetlands losses have been reduced by about 75 percent, and soil erosion on croplands has been cut by more than a third.

Further evidence of improvement comes from the Environmental Protection Agency (EPA). The EPA reported in 1995 that only 8 percent of municipal wastewater dischargers and 6 percent of nonmunicipal dischargers were in "significant" noncompliance with federal requirements.

In our efforts to alleviate the most evident water quality offenses, however, we have discovered new pollution problems that are less visible but no less serious. Forty percent of the nation's surveyed waterways are still too polluted for fishing and swimming. Nearly 2,200 health advisories were issued in 1996 warning against the consumption of contaminated fish. Beaches were closed or warnings were issued more than 2,500 times that year because of contaminated waters. Excess runoff of pollutants such as nitrogen and phosphorous contributed to algal blooms, the outbreak of harmful organisms such as *Pfiesteria*, and a 6,000-square-mile dead zone in the Gulf of Mexico.

In addition to the new problems, we are paying closer attention to our ever more complex understanding of how these problems are caused and perpetuated across media—how, for instance, the air pollution problem of the atmospheric transport of mercury emitted by trash incinerators is causing the water pollution problem of mercury contaminated fish.

"We're taking a much more holistic approach now, involving everyone from soil scientists to microbiologists to facilitators, which is going to require a whole different skill basket in the job candidates that employers will be looking for," said Linda Eichmiller, deputy director of the Association of State and Interstate Water Pollution Control Administrators.

That skill basket will still rest on the laws that have defined water quality problems and directed water quality solutions from the 1972 Clean Water Act through the 1996 Safe Drinking Water Act Amendments.

CLEAN WATER ACT OF 1972

Federal involvement in water quality issues goes back to 1948, when Congress began to provide minimal funding for states to build wastewater treatment facilities. It was not until the Water Pollution Control Act was passed in 1972, however, that the federal government took charge of regulating the quality of the nation's water supplies.

Two major strategies were embodied in the act. First, it required the federal government to provide financial assistance for the construction of local sewage treatment plants so that wastewater is treated before it is released into waterways. Second, it set minimum standards for all industrial and municipal wastewater discharged directly into waterways, and required such discharges to receive a permit through the National Pollution Discharge Elimination System (NPDES).

The need for field sampling helps make water quality management one of the largest employers of environmental workers.

NPDES permitting, together with the minimum standards, has probably created more positions in water quality management than any other single action. The 1972 act also set up regulations on dredging and filling (known as Section 404 regulations), which have since become the government's key tool for protection of wetlands.

CLEAN WATER ACT AMENDMENTS OF 1987

Responding to renewed public concern for water quality issues, Congress was unusually united in overriding a presidential veto and passing the Clean Water Act Amendments in 1987. The new act focused on four main areas.

Water toxins. A key element was a shift of attention to toxic contaminants. These are substances such as heavy metals and organic chemicals that even in low concentrations may have severe effects on human health and the environment. They enter water systems in many different ways, including industrial discharge, urban and rural runoff, and airborne deposition. Acid rain also increases the tendency for certain toxic elements to leach out of the soil and into groundwater. Many of these toxics were emitted through historic industrial practices dating back a century or more, and have persisted to this day.

Nonpoint sources. Another significant change in regulatory emphasis was an increasing attention to "nonpoint" sources of water pollutants. A "point source" can be an outfall pipe that dumps factory pollutants from a manufacturing plant, whereas a common "nonpoint source" is fertilizer and pesticide residue from agricultural lands. Other nonpoint sources include runoff from construction sites, mining areas, and city streets. In each case, the pollutants cannot be traced to any single identifiable (point) source. The EPA estimated in 1995 that nonpoint sources alone impaired 15 percent of America's lakes. Nonpoint source pollutants include heavy metals, damaging nutrients, sediments, and pesticides. Remedies are more complicated than those for point source pollution because of the large number of nonpoint sources and the different types of treatment technologies required. As a result, nonpoint source pollution presents a formidable challenge to policy makers. The 1998 Clean Water Initiative proposed $120 million (21 percent of the total budget) to controlling polluted runoff alone.

Increased state and local responsibility. The biggest change was a shift of requirements and responsibilities to the states. The bill requires states to identify bodies of water that do not meet water quality standards, create programs to control nonpoint sources of pollution, and identify and regulate sources of toxic contaminants. This approach focuses on specific bodies of water and supplements existing industry-by-industry discharge regulations.

Reduced municipal aid and changes in aid from grants to revolving loan programs. The amendments phased out federal assistance for construction of municipal wastewater treatment plants, a large part of the nation's water quality cost. Instead, the federal government is required to provide seed money for loans. Other job-generating responsibilities under the Clean Water Act amendments include a program for improving water quality in estuaries, aid for lakes damaged by acid rain, tightening of implementation procedures for industrial discharge regulations, and an increased commitment to comply with the Great Lakes Water Quality Agreement.

SAFE DRINKING WATER ACT AMENDMENTS OF 1986

Whereas the Clean Water Act focuses on the quality of waterways, the Safe Drinking Water Act (SDWA) regulates the water we consume. The 1986 amendments to the SDWA provide for control of at least eighty-three trace substances, many of which were unknown when the act was first passed in 1974. Congress also inserted provisions to establish a groundwater protection program, particularly for areas surrounding drinking water wells.

SAFE DRINKING WATER ACT AMENDMENTS OF 1996

These amendments furthered Congress's desire to crack down on newly emerging water quality problems, protect water sources, and shift regulatory authorities and responsibilities to the state and local governments. The EPA must assess five new contaminants every five years to determine whether they should be regulated, as well as conduct cost-benefit analyses for each. The EPA must also set new standards for disinfectants and their by-products (surface water treatment, radon, and arsenic) as well as begin a study on sulfates. The amendments require states to identify and assess areas that may threaten drinking water sources, but they may be allowed to design their own protection plans that reflect local conditions. States must also devise water capacity development strategies, and set minimum standards for the certification of water system operators. Public drinking water system operators must inform consumers of their water sources, what contaminants are in their water supplies, and the potential health effects of those contaminants that exceed EPA standards. Finally, the amendments establish a new drinking water state revolving loan fund, with $1 billion authorized annually until 2003. A third of the money can be transferred between Clean Water Act and Safe Drinking Water Act activities through 2001.

ISSUES AND TRENDS

Water quality professionals face a number of daunting challenges as we begin the 21st century. Today's issues go far beyond the need to treat water and wastewater to take in a new world of ecosystems protection.

THE 1998 CLEAN WATER INITIATIVE

In February of 1998, President Clinton proposed the Clean Water Initiative, a $568 million effort to integrate the nation's water quality efforts around a few key concepts. Regardless of how it fares in the budget wars, the ideas behind the Initiative reveal a lot about the future of water quality career opportunities.

Look for information about the Initiative's components throughout this chapter.

WATERSHED PROTECTION APPROACHES AND SOURCE MAPPING

Throughout the environmental professions, pollution prevention, ecosystems protection, and sustainable development are three "megatrends" (see chapter 1). This focus on an integrated approach to environmental and conservation problems is particularly true in the water quality world, where "whole watershed" approaches to water management are rapidly becoming the norm.

The growth of the watershed "movement" has been phenomenal. Watershed approaches have been embraced by the U.S. EPA, and some regional offices are literally restructuring around watersheds as the key unit for protection. A vigorous nonprofit movement, involving hundreds of grassroots watershed organizations, has grown remarkably in recent years, as documented by the Portland, Oregon-based group River Network. Finally, watershed planning is bringing together state, regional, and local agencies in creative and exciting ways.

The 1998 Clean Water Initiative proposes watershed planning as perhaps the core foundation for federal water policy. The initiative proposes an array of land stewardship efforts, including millions of dollars to help farmers control runoff, the creation of two million miles of buffer zones adjacent to waterways, and the development of pollution prevention plans covering more than thirty-five acres of land by 2002. Under the plan, for instance, the U.S. Department of Agriculture will provide Minnesota with over $200 million to promote buffer strips, easements, and other conservation measures on agricultural lands. Maryland has already entered into such an agreement, and proposals from other states are pending.

A key part of all watershed protection is good data about where water comes from, and how healthy it is "at the source." Toward that end, "source mapping" is required throughout the nation. Look for employment opportunities in that area.

Watershed planning will not put water and wastewater treatment professionals out of business. It does represent a big step forward, however, in our efforts to take a pollution prevention approach to all water pollution issues.

GREATER ATTENTION TO TOXICS

The Clean Water Network, relying largely on EPA data, reported in 1997 that toxic pollution from industrial sources and toxic runoff from rural, suburban, and urban areas continue to pollute America's waters, often legally. Point sources discharged over 1.5 billion pounds of toxic chemicals into our waters from 1990 to 1995. Industries emit 8.8 billion pounds of toxics into the air each year. The effects are evident: fish consumption advisories rose by 26 percent from 1995 to 1996 for a total of 2,193, while since 1993, there has been

a 72 percent increase in the advisories. A full 100 percent of the Great Lakes and their connecting waters are under advisories.

One reason for our increased focus on toxins is the remarkable improvement in analytical technologies that enable such toxins to be found, as well as dramatic increases in the monitoring for, and reporting of, selected toxins. "It seems like each month we find out about a new one in drinking water, and so I think we'll see a lot more emphasis in the future on them," said Jack Hoffbuhr, executive director of the American Water Works Association.

"Cross-Media" Solutions

Research suggests a strong link between air, land, and water pollutants, adding dramatic new complexities to the water quality arena. Airborne mercury emissions that find their way into wildlife such as trout and loons are but one example. Nitrogen and phosphorous runoff from poor land-use practices that enters rivers and lakes is another. "Increasingly, there's a multimedia approach to pollution problems depending on the issue, and so from a water quality perspective, all the land and air policies are being better integrated into the water policies," said Paul Schwartz, national campaigns director of Clean Water Action, an environmental group. Watershed planning approaches, mentioned earlier, are part of the cross-media pollution solution.

Interns with the U.S. Bureau of Land Management gather streambed gravel samples in the Koyukuk mining district of Alaska.

CONTINUED WETLANDS LOSS

The EPA reported in 1995, its most recent estimate, that America continues to lose wetlands "at a significant rate, but the net rate of wetlands loss appears to have slowed from the 458,000 acres lost per year during the mid-1950s through the mid-1970s, to between 70,000 and 90,000 acres per year between 1982 and 1992 on nonfederal lands." The losses are a result of commercial and residential development, road construction, agriculture, and industrial development. Wetlands are also being degraded by pollutants. Expect a steady increase in local, state, and nonprofit innovations to purchase, protect, and reconstruct wetlands, including the construction of partially artificial wetlands for use as "natural" waste water treatment facilities. Also expect a continued push to strengthen wetlands regulations through reauthorization of the Clean Water Act.

The 1998 Clean Water Initiative calls for a net increase of 100,000 acres of wetlands by 2005, including a 50 percent increase in the number of wetlands to be restored and enhanced by the U.S. Army Corps of Engineers. The federal government will also increase its emphasis on wetland restoration as a remedy for Clean Water Act violations, as well as create an interagency system to more accurately track wetlands loss, restoration, and creation.

GROUNDWATER PROTECTION WORK CONTINUES

More than half of the United States depends on groundwater resources for its drinking water supply, and contamination rates are much higher than previously believed. Once contaminated, groundwater is more difficult and expensive to purify than surface water. Throughout the 1990s, state governments put groundwater monitoring programs into place as a step toward greater protection. By 1995, the EPA reported that thirty-three states had such programs, and the need for accurate information about groundwater contamination continues to grow. Computer-aided systems to monitor groundwater and project future patterns of contamination will be in high demand. Also expect hazardous waste cleanup projects around Superfund sites, landfills, military bases, and former dumps to focus on groundwater contamination. Cleaning up the nation's 139,000 leaking underground fuel storage tanks will continue to be a priority. There will be an increasing interface between the Safe Drinking Water Act and Clean Water Act requirements as they pertain to groundwater, which will create new job opportunities.

UPGRADING THE NATIONAL CLEAN WATER INFRASTRUCTURE

Following the passage of the Clean Water Act in 1972, America spent roughly $1 trillion building new wastewater and drinking water treatment plants, as well as other projects. These facilities are aging and need repairs and upgrades estimated to run between $3 and $4 trillion over the next fifty years.

States will be spending $200 billion over the next twenty years on "pipes, plumbing, and prevention" alone to begin to address infrastructure problems estimated at $280 billion, says Clean Water Action's Schwartz. "Just looking at that piece of the puzzle, there's an $80 billion funding gap," he says. The AWWA's Hoffbuhr agrees, noting an area of emphasis will be replacing America's water distribution system, the pipes that take water from plants to taps, especially as concern mounts over such exotic microbiological organisms as cryptosporidium and pfiesteria. "We do know that microorganisms live in the water system, and so I think we'll see some emphasis on this," he says.

PROTECTING COASTAL WATERS

From the "dead zones" in the Gulf of Mexico and Long Island Sound, to the decline of coastal and ocean fisheries off New England and the Pacific Northwest, America's coastal waters continue to face ecological stresses that are drawing more attention. The U.N. declared 1998 the International Year of the Ocean, while the Center for Marine Conservation reported in 1997 that during its annual coastal cleanup the year before, it collected 3,757,123 items of debris—from sofas to sleeping bags. An entire house was found by Louisiana volunteers in Shreveport's Cross Lake.

The 1998 Clean Water Initiative calls for a coordinated federal response system to support state and local efforts during major events such as algal blooms and pfiesteria outbreaks. Amendments to fisheries management plans will identify essential fish habitats and ways to minimize harm done by state and federal agencies. The federal government will push for enforceable state plans by December 1999 to cut polluted runoff to coastal areas. "There's going to be increased attention to this issue, and it's going to require everyone from new enforcement attorneys to more certified nutrient experts in the field," says Jessica Landman, senior attorney at the Natural Resources Defense Council, an environmental group. The effect of urban and agricultural runoff will be especially targeted, she adds.

CAREER OPPORTUNITIES

Water quality management is big business. The *Environmental Business Journal* reported in its 1997 Annual Industry Overview that while the $181 billion environmental industry has experienced only limited growth over the previous decade, the $76 billion water sector has grown steadily. This growth rate elevates water issues "to the forefront of the industry, supplanting air pollution, hazardous waste management, and remediation, which took turns in the sun as the industry's best growth prospects between 1975–1995."

All good news for environmental professionals, right? Well, yes and no. As you will see, federal and state government agencies are expecting increased demands within limited budgets (translation: not a lot of new jobs), while local governments and the private sector will experience better job growth.

Public Sector

Lines are blurring between "public" and "private" sector water careers, as government agencies increase the "privatization" of water management. Still, the public sector remains a large employer of water professionals.

Federal Government. Jobs are tough to come by at federal agencies, as efforts continue to shrink the size of the federal bureaucracy. "We're not seeing any new positions, but we are seeing existing jobs change," says Deborah Lebow, the air/water coordinator in the EPA's Office of Water.

Several trends are at work in the EPA and other federal agencies that will set the course for job descriptions in the coming years. The agencies are moving away from the "command-and-control" relationship with states and localities that existed for decades, and toward a stewardship and partnership relationship. The federal government hopes to work with, rather than against, states and localities to solve water quality problems.

Agencies are moving toward a watershed approach, as we have seen, and some EPA regional offices have actually been reorganized by geography rather than issue (e.g., air and water). Finally, the agencies are relying more heavily on their regional offices, rather than on their Washington headquarters, to address those problems.

All three trends, federal officials say, point to a continued need for scientific and engineering expertise. Scientific understanding, however, must be coupled with a keen sense of the interdisciplinary relationships between, and provincial nature of, water quality problems. Agencies are seeking people who combine the best qualities of the scientific expert and the public policy analyst.

Two of the more significant recent developments in water quality—the Safe Drinking Water Act Amendments of 1996 and President Clinton's 1998 Clean Water Initiative—illustrate the trend. Under the amendments, for instance, states must identify and assess areas that threaten drinking water supplies, but may then design their own protection programs, reflecting an understanding that local conditions may vary. Many of the elements of the Clean Water Initiative have been discussed earlier under Issues and Trends. The watershed approaches in the Initiative will impact federal (and all government) employment in some very specific ways, says the EPA's Lebow.

"The watershed approach has meant that you have to broaden your knowledge," Lebow says. "All of a sudden, you have to know the entire statute and not just a piece of it. All of a sudden, you have to know several different statutes and not just one. All of a sudden, you can't know just hydrology, but have to know physics, chemistry, and biology, as well. All of a sudden, you have to know both health risks and ecological risks. You can't just say you're a biologist and shut out chemistry, or a hydrologist and shut out ecology. We're looking for people who have a broader perspective."

So are a lot of other federal agencies with a stake in water quality. The U.S. Fish and Wildlife Service is responsible for ensuring water quality for plants and animals, especially rare, threatened, and endangered species. The U.S. Army

Corps of Engineers is responsible for, among other things, ensuring that projects are sufficiently mitigated to protect water supplies before they are awarded Section 404 permits to develop wetlands. Protecting water quality from timber cuts and ski area developments on public lands is an issue for the U.S. Forest Service, while the National Park Service must deal with the impact of hordes of tourists on lakes and rivers. Finally, the U.S. Department of Agriculture has the considerable job of ensuring that farm practices do not damage our water.

State Government. The shift in responsibility from the federal government to the states that got underway with the 1987 Clean Water Act Amendments has only gained steam since. The 1996 Safe Drinking Water Act Amendments and Clinton's 1998 Clean Water Initiative are driving the action. "Most of the regulatory action is on the state level," said Clean Water Action's Schwartz. "The states are the ones allocating most of the money and making most of the decisions."

The question is, How much of that shift in responsibility is resulting in new jobs at the state level? Linda Eichmiller of the Association of State and Interstate Water Pollution Control Administrators (ASIWPCA) notes that state budgets and staff are static, and there is limited growth to report. Schwartz sees it much the same way, despite the "huge increase in actual dollar flow" over the last twelve years from the federal government to the states. "In many states they've put freezes and caps on hiring. From Congress, they receive additional money for state programs, but from the state legislature they are told not to hire new people," he says. "We've been trying to find agreement with the states to do additional hiring."

That a wide array of new people is needed is clear, Schwartz and others say. The 1996 Safe Drinking Water Act Amendments amount to three new, and significant, responsibilities for the states: assess and deal with threats to drinking water, better involve and inform the public on water quality issues, and administer the $1 billion annually in federal aid to the states to improve drinking water facilities, especially small systems.

"This is going to force all sorts of investments in monitoring equipment and in people who know how to use it," Schwartz says. "Billions of dollars will be spent on the new physical infrastructure, and so technicians will be needed who can run new filtration and disinfection infrastructure, as well as do the lab work." And with the surge in new concerns from children's health to environmental justice through White House executive orders and other initiatives, "there will need to be a lot more research on the variable affects of contaminants, and so for the research community, there should be a lot more work out there," says Schwartz.

With the new emphasis on watersheds, "there will be a lot more money going into best management practices, land conservation, watershed management, and source water protection, and so we should see a lot of programs, probably voluntary at first, on point and nonpoint source controls in watersheds. This will generate jobs for the attendant people who can do modeling

Groundwater scientists gather samples in the field. The samples will be analyzed on site in a mobile laboratory.

for biological and chemical loads, as well as for people who can take engineering approaches to cleaning up watersheds," Schwartz says.

With over $200 billion in needs over the next 20 years, and with state revolving loan funds growing, the job picture could be very bright if states go ahead and spend the money, Schwartz adds. "It's been estimated that 22,000 to 50,000 new jobs are generated by each billion dollars in water quality investment."

Local Government. Ensuring adequate water quality is largely carried out on the local level. Water and wastewater treatment plant employees dominate the water field. A few numbers tell the story.

According to 1996 EPA data cited by the Association of Metropolitan Sewerage Agencies, there are 16,024 wastewater treatment plants and 55,000 community drinking water systems in the country. Many tiny drinking water systems need few, if any, employees. A typical, medium-sized plant or system, however, employs about fifty people, including superintendents, operators, engineers, inspectors, laboratory personnel, and (in the case of wastewater plants) pretreatment technicians who deal with industrial and commercial waste coming to the facilities. Larger plants will have attorneys and regulatory affairs professionals, as well.

As we will see in the discussion that follows, many of these jobs are becoming "privatized," as local governments turn over water and wastewater operations to the rapidly expanding water industry.

Local water-related employment outside of treatment plants is also increasing, as the trends toward watershed management, cross-media analysis, and local land-use control take hold.

"I don't expect growth in the environmental programs at the state level, but I think there will be significant growth on the local level, because they will be responsible for dealing with this new generation of problems dealing with local land use and other local concerns," says the ASIWPCA's Eichmiller.

With the billions of dollars already spent over the last few decades to build wastewater and drinking water treatment plants, the infrastructure emphasis will continue to shift toward maintaining and upgrading those facilities, but also taking on new infrastructure concerns, such as the pipe delivery systems, especially as concern over the harmful effects of everything from metals to microorganisms continues to rise. There will be continuing needs on the local level for everyone, from technicians who monitor and analyze water quality, to engineers who design and build new delivery systems.

But the emphasis on watershed management, cross-media analysis, and local land-use controls will require an entirely new generation of professionals who might not have previously thought of their work as water related. Toxicologists will continue to be needed to identify and assess contaminants, but so will land-use planners (to develop zoning measures that better protect waters from runoff) and civil engineers (to upgrade wastewater treatment plants so that discharges to downstream rivers are cleaner). Agricultural engineers must educate downstream farmers to use fewer pesticides and herbicides so that rivers can better disperse wastewater. Source water mappers and modelers, especially those experienced in GIS modeling, will continue to be needed to identify water sources. Finally, public outreach communicators must convince landowners to place conservation easements on tracts sitting near or atop those sources.

"It's going to be the sort of situation where, for instance, cities won't be able to grow unless local agricultural practices are brought under control," says the ASIWPCA's Eichmiller.

PRIVATE SECTOR

One source of steady job growth for water professionals is in the private sector, where the $76 billion water business dominates the $181 billion environmental industry, and is expected to continue to do so. As the *Environmental Business Journal* (*EBJ*) put it in its 1997 analysis of the water and wastewater markets, "Steady demand for water/wastewater treatment and the steady revenues it generates function like a herbivore in the environmental industry food chain, providing a stable foundation for the rest of the environmental industry ecosystem. In short, water delivers a steady, dependable source of business: Where water flows, so does cash."

Table 6.1 shows water industry revenues, as tracked and projected by *EBJ*. Overall, the water business will experience 6 percent annual growth between

Table 6.1 Water Industry Revenues 1996–2000

Business Type	1996 Revenues (in billions)	Year 2000 (in billions)	% Growth
"Full solution" companies	1.38	5.09	269.0
Wastewater equipment and chemicals	16.14	18.11	12.2
Consulting and engineering	5.26	7.32	39.2
Instruments	.57	.69	21.0
Analytical services	.41	.45	9.8
Wastewater treatment works	24.02	27.80	15.7
Water utilities	26.36	29.90	13.4
TOTAL	74.14	89.36	29.2

Source: Environmental Business International.

1996 and 2000, with revenues nearing $90 billion by the end of the decade, *EBJ* reports.

The AWWA's Hoffbuhr says that with $2 to $3 billion in water quality needs over the next few years, "we can predict growth in all aspects of the field. The manufacturers are predicting growth for their products, from pipes to treatment products. And consultants had a heck of a good year last year, which they think will continue, not just because it's a good time, but because of the growth in international business."

As municipalities and local governments face rising responsibilities, one of the hottest growth areas for industry is in "contract out" services, where towns and cities effectively hire private companies to deal with their water quality needs, Hoffbuhr says. Indeed, *EBJ* noted in its 1997 Annual Industry Overview that the U.S. contract operations market exceeded $1 billion in revenues in 1996, with growth estimated at an astounding 20 to 30 percent annually over the next few years. Some estimate that the market could top $3 billion by 2000. "Some of the municipalities believe they cannot maintain the expertise to operate a system, and so we're seeing the advent of contract operations companies emerging all across America, with a great need for people who can operate these systems," Hoffbuhr says. "In some cases, municipalities are selling their assets outright and privatizing, but that won't be the big trend. The big trend will be in contracting out."

Besides systems operators, everyone from microbiologists who can identify microbiological contaminants, to communicators who can explain to customers why higher rates are necessary to finance system improvements, will be needed, says Hoffbuhr.

NONPROFIT SECTOR

When an enterprising young man recently knocked on the door of Doug Bogen, Clean Water Action's Northern New England coordinator based in

Portsmouth, New Hampshire, Bogen had to deliver the hard news: "Things are so tight, I'm trying just to keep my own job."

The nonprofit sector is indeed struggling, and in a high profile way. Greenpeace's decision in 1997 to significantly trim its staff and resources made national, page-one news. "For the drinking water utilities and wastewater utilities, there are expanding opportunities, as well as to some degree for the federal and state agencies, but for the activist, nonprofit sector remains fairly moribund," says Bogen's boss, Clean Water Action's Schwartz.

Water quality remains a top priority among environmental groups, especially with the push for a strong reauthorization of the Clean Water Act. But with budgets ever tightening, hiring remains a luxury. And environmental groups are getting more clever about how to maintain their agenda within tight fiscal constraints.

For instance, many top groups came together in 1992 to form the Clean Water Network, a Washington-based umbrella organization focusing efforts on reauthorization of the Clean Water Act. The organization has a broad agenda reflective of its now 900 members nationwide, including an act that better protects wetlands, ends toxic pollution, ensures enforcement, curtails runoff, allows communities to protect their own waters, and spends the money necessary to ensure clean supplies. Its members include some of America's top environmental groups—the Natural Resources Defense Council, Earthjustice Legal Defense Fund, American Oceans Campaign, Center for Marine Conservation, U.S. PIRG, and others—drawing on the resources of each. But its actual full-time staff consists of just four people—a national coordinator, outreach coordinator, Southeast field coordinator, and government/business outreach coordinator.

"In all of the Washington-based environmental groups, there are a total of only three full-time people working on drinking water, and that's stretching it," says Clean Water Action's Schwartz.

Growth is better at the local and state levels, as evidenced by the dozens of watershed protection groups listed in River Network's "River and Conservation Directory," which noted literally hundreds of local organizations. Leaders at many of those groups had a staff of one to five people, however, and depended on volunteers and interns for much of their work.

Still, for those who want a career in environmental nonprofit advocacy, there is room for everyone from chemists and biologists to economists and communicators, if you are willing to work for less pay. "There are certainly jobs in the grassroots groups, and salaries have gotten better," says Clean Water Action's Bogen. "In our organization, we're paying between $15,000 and $25,000 a year, and sort of work on the Ben and Jerry's model, where no one in the organization gets paid more than five times what the lowest paid person gets."

SALARY

Salaries in water quality vary widely depending on your field and where you work. Wastewater engineers start at around $30,000 annually and climb to

$70,000 and higher. Six-figure salaries are not uncommon. Wastewater treatment plant operators can start at wages as low as $18,000 in a small system to $27,000 at larger ones. Expect nominal annual increases and cramped upward mobility. Water pollution inspectors earn $27,000 to $34,000 at the entry-level and rise to the mid-40s and above. Consultants in water conservation and other water issues can earn significant money. Scientists and engineers start at around $29,000 and climb quickly with quality work to $50,000 after a few years. Senior consultants earn from $65,000 to $85,000 or more. Entry-level hydrologists start at $30,000 annually and rise to $45,000 with quality work. Aquatic environmental scientists and wetlands ecologists generally are paid in the low to mid-30s to start. A senior position might mean a salary in the low 60s, and supervising scientists can earn $70,000.

For other information on salaries, check out the trade association websites mentioned in the Resources section of this chapter.

GETTING STARTED

New opportunities in the water quality management field are being driven mostly by the need to:

- Reduce toxic and nonpoint source pollutants
- Protect groundwater and source water
- Protect coasts
- Manage watersheds
- Stop wetlands destruction
- Improve water quality standards
- Deal with cross-media issues
- Upgrade and rebuild the water quality infrastructure
- Manage the transfer of authority to state and local governments
- Manage the "privatization" of local water works

Also prominent among the emerging opportunities is communications, especially with the cross-media complexities of watershed management, and with increased attention on the public's right to know. Training in these areas will make you competitive, but everything starts with a solid education.

EDUCATION

If your goal is to join the thousands of water professionals who work at a private or public water or wastewater treatment plant, your best bet may be a two-year technician's degree at a community college. Water and wastewater plant operations involve training on the latest equipment, coupled with on-the-job experience through apprenticeships or internships. In addition, states require that operators meet rigid certification requirements and pass tests to prove competency. Quality two-year programs are designed to prepare applicants well, with curriculums that combine academic, practical, and test prep classes.

Many of the nation's wastewater engineers, plant superintendents, and public water system managers began their careers at water and wastewater treatment plants. Ask the professionals who run systems in your area to recommend quality programs, or check with your state department of environmental quality.

Concern over toxic and microbiological contaminants in effluent, runoff, and groundwater is creating positions for people with the scientific and technical backgrounds to detect trace contaminants, analyze their public health and environmental impacts, and design methods of removing them from water supplies, or preventing them from entering the supplies to begin with. Strong backgrounds for this work include analytical and organic chemistry; toxicology; chemical, industrial, and environmental engineering; mathematics; and risk assessment. An advanced degree is advisable.

As in many other fields, environmental and civil engineers are required throughout the water quality management field. Wastewater is an established specialty in the engineering profession and many colleges have excellent programs. Further advances in pollution prevention approaches will require more process and industrial engineers, as well.

Groundwater scientists remain in demand, although less so than in the late 1980s and early 1990s, when schools could not turn out graduates quickly enough. These professionals monitor groundwater quantity and quality, develop computer modeling of groundwater flow, and engage in treatment of polluted groundwater. Hydrogeologists with advanced degrees are required on the staffs of any full-service consulting firm, and at all state environmental agencies. The most common undergraduate degrees in this field are geology, civil engineering, and chemistry. Most of those with undergraduate degrees find jobs doing on-site sampling and measurement. Undergraduate course work should include geology, groundwater engineering, water chemistry, inorganic chemistry, engineering hydrology, and calculus.

People with both undergraduate and advanced degrees in biology and chemistry are still needed in the water quality field, especially those who have taken strong laboratory and fieldwork classes in college.

With the emerging emphasis on watershed management and cross-media analysis, an education in policy and communication is also needed, either exclusively or, better yet, in combination with a technical, engineering, or science degree.

"What would make a good career path?" asked Ronald Poltak, executive director of the New England Interstate Water Pollution Control Commission. "We need people who have—to be very precise—undergraduate training in the sciences, in chemistry, or biology. If we can find that sort of person coming right out of school, get them two to three years of working experience with us, and then get them to go to graduate school in policy with a commitment to come back to us afterwards, then we have a helluva person."

ADVICE

Here is a collection of advice from water quality professionals on the keys to getting into their fields.

Choose science, or management, if you do not excel at both. "What I tell people is that they've got two major things to think about, and make a decision about," says the AWWA's Hoffbuhr. "One is, Do you want to be involved in the science of the profession? The other is, Do you want to be involved in the management of the profession? In the latter case, it helps to have a science background, but also some communications and policy skills. Many times in the profession, companies or agencies take their best scientist or engineer and promote him or her to manager, and then find out it doesn't work too well. There are two tracks—science and management. People can excel in both. But it's better to choose one track or the other. It may take a few years in the field to decide, but it's a critical decision to make."

Become bilingual. "Water quality management is becoming very international these days, and so it's very important to be bilingual," says the ASIWPCA's Eichmiller. "The only way firms are going to survive is by balancing national and international work, and you're dealing with a lot of students in the United States who are bilingual from the get go. So if a firm has the choice between an engineering student who's bilingual and one who's not, they'll choose the bilingual one."

Don't be afraid to be a generalist. Welcome advice for many undergraduates. "It's better not to specialize *too* much anymore, because at places like EPA, you kind of learn by osmosis. You learn on-the-job, and so getting a general degree better prepares you for that," says Deborah Lebow, the EPA's air/water coordinator in the Office of Water.

Get into geographic information systems. With all of the emerging emphasis on watersheds and cross-media analysis, "somebody who really wants a career in this field should be looking at GIS watershed modelling." says Jessica Landman, senior attorney at the Natural Resources Defense Council and cochair of the Clean Water Network.

SUMMARY

Water quality management is the largest employer of environmental professionals, and is likely to remain so. The first generation of water quality pollution remedies has created a large infrastructure of water-related regulations, water and wastewater treatment plants, and monitoring stations. This infrastructure must be managed, maintained, and (in many cases) rebuilt, resulting in many employment opportunities.

The next generation of water quality professionals will work on watershed planning, nonpoint source control, toxics use reduction, and other innovative solutions to our water problems.

Opportunities exist for an exceptionally wide range of scientists, engineers, social scientists, communicators, educators, and managers at thousands of public and private employers.

CASE STUDY

Nation's first interstate water pollution control agency is well prepared for the "new" water protection approaches

Some water quality professionals have been working on watershed planning, nonpoint source pollution, and other problems of the late 1990s for years, as this case study of the New England Interstate Water Pollution Control Commission illustrates.

In 1947, Congress passed legislation more prescient than it could have known. The legislation allowed states to form interstate water pollution control commissions, so they could better deal with pollution that, as the cliché goes, knows no boundaries.

Civil and environmental engineers are a large part of the workforce at water and wastewater treatment agencies, such as Seattle's "Metro."

The prescience came in anticipating what environmentalism, and especially water quality management, was to become a half century later. The emerging emphasis on watershed and cross-media approaches to water quality suits perfectly the "transboundary" thinking of the commissions, says Ronald Poltak, executive director of the New England Interstate Water Pollution Control Commission (NEIWPCC), the first such commission to form in the nation.

"Eventually, in the business of environmental protection, comes the necessity transcending boundaries, whether they be town, county, or state," Poltak says. "And so this new approach, dealing with water on a watershed basis, is actually not new to us at all. It's what the commission is about, and has always been about."

Connecticut, Rhode Island, and Massachusetts were the original members of New England's commission, followed soon by Vermont, Maine, New Hampshire, and New York. There are thirty-five individual members, five from each state, who generally represent the water quality agencies within each state. The initial charge was to come up with stream classifications and uses, which remains the charge today, as 40 percent of America's waters are still not fishable or swimmable. But there is also a lot more, Poltak says.

There is a growing concern over the relationship between water quality and public health, especially with regard to the threats of toxic metals and microbiological organisms, all of which are becoming more evident as analytical technology continues to be refined, Poltak says. "We have the sophistication and scientific capability to detect contaminants to such a degree that we can now see their impacts on public health," he says.

As point-source pollution continues to wane, nonpoint source pollution continues to become evident and is considered to be responsible for 76 percent of lake impairment and 45 percent of estuary impairment nationwide. This too remains a challenge in New England, where runoff comes from farms and cities alike, which requires the commission to now begin addressing land-use issues. "Environmental protection starts with what we do on the land," Poltak says. "We can beat ourselves to death coming up with uses and classifications, but in the end, we have to deal with what we do on the land. It comes down to that."

And as the cross-media relationships become sharper and more apparent, the commission is crossing boundaries that may not even be local. "With 25 percent of the nitrogen entering Long Island Sound coming from air deposition, you have to consider overlapping media issues," Poltak says. His deputy director, Susan Sullivan, agrees. "Air deposition is a big factor for us now, even though we're a water commission," she says.

Reflecting these broader concerns, NEIWPCC has been involved in an array of projects across the Northeast. A sampling of the commission's work reads like a review of the entire water quality management field as we prepare to enter a new century. Just a *small* list of the agency's current work includes:

- Developing a source protection guidance manual for water suppliers.
- Creating a groundwater education resource book for K–6 school teachers.

- Launching an interstate regulatory cooperation project with the U.S. EPA and the New England Governor's Conference to evaluate emerging environmental technologies.
- Bringing state-of-the-art wastewater technologies to northern New England.
- Coordinating interstate work groups on nonpoint source protection, wetlands preservation, "biocriteria," financial management, underground tanks, and more.
- Reviewing research on mercury in the environment, including questioning the widely held assumption that mercury found in the Northeast comes from the Midwest.
- Joining initiatives to protect major New England rivers and bays, including Long Island Sound, Lake Champlain, and Lake Ontario.
- Training professionals and academics through an array of courses and seminars.

All of these efforts make a transboundary commission conceptualized a full quarter century before passage of the 1972 Clean Water Act perfectly poised for water quality management into the next century. "We're 'in-the-stream' oriented. We're 'in-the-wetland' oriented. We're 'in-the-groundwater' oriented. We're 'in-the-air' oriented. We're 'in-everything' oriented, as we see more and more how things are intertwined," Poltak says.

PROFILES

Doug Bogen
Northern New England Program Coordinator
Clean Water Action
Portsmouth, New Hampshire

Citizen support for water protection is critical. Nothing happens at the public or private levels unless people demand it, as voters and consumers. Mobilizing people at the grassroots, however, is a difficult task, with long hours and modest pay. The rewards, however, can be immeasurable.

It is not unusual to find Doug Bogen out on dark, cold winter nights, trudging through the snows of New Hampshire, knocking on doors at dinnertime in search of dollars for his local chapter of Clean Water Action, the national grassroots environmental group. The ordeal is so demanding that one can only ask, Why?

"I'm a progeny of activists," Bogen says. The thirty-nine-year-old grew up in New York's Westchester County as the son of Quaker activists, attending peace vigils and breathing in the ethos of Vietnam-era social activism. His father was the local coordinator for the SANE/FREEZE campaign, and his mother was a psychiatric social worker. "I had a good upbringing, and was taught to be concerned about the problems in our society."

That concern began to be focused on the environment when Bogen attended Colorado College, graduating in 1980 with a bachelor's degree in biology, and Cornell University, graduating in 1985 with a master's degree in science and environmental education. At Cornell especially, "there was a pretty large progressive community, and so I got involved with a lot of community efforts, organized conferences on campus, and led the 'Dump-Watt' campaign," he says, referring to the controversial Reagan administration interior secretary James Watt.

After a three-year stint with the New Hampshire chapter of the League of Conservation Voters where he mostly canvassed, and after a couple of years "bouncing around, doing some landscaping [and] some substitute teaching," Bogen found a home in 1991 at Clean Water Action's New Hampshire chapter, first as a canvasser and then working his way up through various program positions.

The group suited Bogen, as it is directed toward local organizing, and it is at the local level where the power to effect environmental change lies, he says. "If you talk with the national environmental groups, they'll admit the power lies at the local level. I've had opportunities to go to D.C. and work at that level, but I prefer to be in touch with what's out in the field." That work has recently been focused on toxics, where Bogen and others are fighting for a moratorium on sludge spreading in New Hampshire, and for tougher state and federal action to combat acid rain and mercury deposition across the Northeast.

It has not been easy, Bogen admits. Clean Water Action went through a downsizing in 1994. There has been a shortage of volunteers. Industry has devised its own brand of what Bogen considers phony grassroots activism— "We sometimes call it astroturf," he says. And salaries, while not bad, are not great.

"Most people working in this movement are not in it for the money," Bogen says. "I'm in it because of my upbringing. I've always had a very strong concern for the future, I've always taken the long view, reading up on environmental ethics, philosophy, spirituality, and I still believe that we still need some people to work for the betterment of the planet."

But enduring that requires commitment, Bogen adds. "I've been an environmentalist since way back," he says. "I've been hugging trees since I was a little kid. And I think, to do this work, you have to have that. You have to have a deep appreciation for nature. You have to have a sense of grounding in your environment."

David Evers
Research Biologist
BioDiversity, Inc.
Freeport, Maine

Although the bulk of water quality professionals are primarily concerned with human uses of water, polluted or reduced water supplies can have devastating impacts on wildlife and plants. Where does "wildlife protection" end and "water quality" management begin?

As one might expect from someone trained as a conservation biologist, David Evers sees the world in terms of interrelationships. He sees linkages not just between species that form the biodiversity he seeks to preserve, but between the scientific community that researches problems and the policy community that addresses them.

That view compelled Evers in 1994 to create BioDiversity, Inc., a nonprofit consulting and research group dedicated to making sense of those linkages, and especially the science underlying them, so that problems may be solved. "Our interest is in taking issues and filling in the science, interpreting the work, and then getting the results out to the public and policy makers," Evers said. "So it's sort of full circle."

His group, which now has four full-time staffers, including himself and a dozen seasonal part-timers, is "very mission oriented, very cause oriented," says Evers, who received a bachelor's degree in wildlife management from Michigan State University in 1984, a master's degree in zoology from Western Michigan University in 1991, and hopes to defend in late 1998 his doctoral dissertation in conservation biology from the University of Minnesota. Much of his time these days is spent studying mercury in the environment for various federal and state agencies, as well as private companies.

Evers's group is part of an ongoing research team that includes the U.S. Fish and Wildlife Service and Tufts University School of Veterinary Medicine, which found in 1997 that loons in the Northeast had the highest levels of mercury in their blood and feathers in the country, levels so dangerously high that the loons are at risk. Evers's group is also conducting research for a private client, Central Maine Power, to determine the availability of mercury in the electric utility's reservoirs as part of Central Maine's bid for new licenses from the Federal Energy Regulatory Commission.

But again, to Evers, linkages are what matters most. "We see ourselves as a group that can bring together a lot of different stakeholders—federal and state agencies, [nongovernmental organizations], industry—and it really works well, because the issues nowadays are so complicated in so many different arenas that using the skills from each of these stakeholders provides a stronger product."

He says it is also important that the scientific community, generally monastic in their inclination to get involved in policy issues, begin stepping outside of itself and contributing what it knows, as long as it retains its scientific credibility by being objective. Here too, BioDiversity can pave the way, not by becoming advocates, but by informing them, he says.

"It's tough, because it's kind of a new approach," Evers says. "I'm sure we'll have conflicts with a few people, like university or academic types who believe science should be separate from policy. But we think there can be a good marriage of the two by objectively offering our findings to advocacy groups. That way we can still maintain our scientific credibility without conflict of interest."

Given the new emphasis in water quality management on watersheds and cross-media analysis especially, BioDiversity's approach represents "a growing field. I see a lot of different people coming together to find answers, and the way we do things is to bring as many of them together as possible so they can feel comfortable with what we come up with," Evers says.

Deborah Lebow
Air/Water Coordinator
Office of Water
United States Environmental
Protection Agency
Washington, D.C.

An integrated approach to water quality management—across political bound-aries and media—is increasingly important to manage today's most difficult problems. Professionals with a diverse background and grasp of many different policy dimensions, including the ability to work with stakeholder groups, are most likely to succeed.

After working at the EPA for eleven years, her dream job ever since she was in law school at Albany in the late 1970s, Deborah Lebow did something unusu-al—she left the agency to work for two years at a nonprofit group, the Renewable Natural Resources Foundation. "I wanted to see what a nonprofit was like," she says.

"It was the best thing I could have ever done," says Lebow, who earned her bachelor's degree in international relations in 1976 from Johns Hopkins University, and after earning her law degree in 1979—"taking all the environ-mental courses I could find"—went straight to the EPA. Until she left the agency in 1990, "I was very EPA. But the group I went to worked with Interior, Agriculture, Parks, Fisheries," she says, referring to other agencies, "and I got a much broader sense of environmental issues. I felt like I came out of the trenches and saw the sunlight."

Lebow's eclectic awakening prepared her well for the new EPA of the 1990s, one in which cross-media analysis is de rigueur. Prior to 1990, she had several positions—"the beauty of the EPA is that you can move around," she says. However, she generally worked on waste issues, first solid waste and then haz-ardous waste.

But to illustrate how diverse Lebow's life at EPA has become, a simple description of her current position says it all. It was created two years ago out of the recognition that "there are a lot of water quality problems coming from the air, and we've basically ignored that for a long time," she says. "But all of a sudden we realized that we can't meet our water quality goals until we under-stand what comes from the air and how to stop it."

Lebow deals with the interface of air and water pollution from her position with EPA's Oceans and Coastal Protection Division of the Office of Water.

"I'm working specifically on how air pollution contributes to water pollution," she says. Her position was originally conceived by Congress not in water legislation, but air legislation, specifically the 1990 Clean Air Act Amendments. "It just took us a few years in Water to realize we had to look at this problem too," she says.

As the EPA continues to evolve, not just by embracing watersheds and cross-media analysis but also by addressing concerns ranging from environmental justice to children's health, policy development is becoming more complex and challenging. And for Lebow, who not only always wanted to work for the EPA but craft policy for the agency, she finds herself in the right place at the right time.

"What you think you're going to do may not be what you end up doing, but I still think that this is the place to be if you want to do environmental policy," Lebow said. "My sense is that environmental groups are still on one side of the issues, industry is on the other, and it's our job at EPA to find solutions that make sense. We take information from all sides—we have more information than anyone else—and we then set policy, which I like. You can't do this anywhere else."

RESOURCES

Resources on water-related careers are remarkably abundant. Use the list here to find links to other sources. The resource lists in chapters 4 and 11 are also useful.

Amazing Environmental Organization WebDirectory. "Earth's biggest environmental search engine." Includes information on water quality and professional associations. Also, don't miss the employment section on the WebDirectory homepage, which provides links to job listings, descriptions, and agencies specifically concerned with environmental employment. Http://www.webdirectory.com.

American Rivers. National nonprofit river-conservation organization dedicated to protecting and restoring America's river systems and to fostering a river stewardship ethic. Programs address flood control and hydropower policy reform, endangered aquatic and riparian species protection, western instream flow, clean water, and urban rivers. Offers four- and three-month internships each quarter. Website includes links to relevant environmental laws, as well as an extensive list of other river- and water-related organizations. 1025 Vermont Ave., NW, Suite 720, Washington, DC 20005. (202) 547-6900. Http://www.amrivers.org.

American Water Resources Association. Membership organization whose mission is to promote the understanding of water resources and related issues by providing a multidisciplinary forum for education, professional development, and information exchange. Offers conferences and symposia and has a student chapter. Publications include *Journal of the American Water Resources Association*, which publishes original papers with a broad approach to water resources issues. Website has job listings and an excellent guide titled *Searching for Water Resources Jobs on the Internet*, by Bryan R. Swistock. Also has links to related sites. 950 Herndon Pkwy, Suite 300, Herndon, VA 20170-5531. (703) 904-1225. Http://www.uwin.siu.edu/~awra/index.html.

American Water Works Association. International nonprofit scientific and educational society dedicated to the improvement of drinking water quality and supply. Members represent the full spectrum of the drinking water community: treatment plant operators and managers, scientists, environmentalists, manufacturers, academicians, regulators, and others. Publications include *Journal AWWA* (monthly) and *WaterWeek* (weekly), as well as manuals, standards, textbooks, software, videos, and more. Website lists water industry jobs, educational programs, and events, as well as links to related organizations. 6666 West Quincy Ave., Denver, CO 80235. (303) 794-7711. Http://www.awwa.org.

Association of Metropolitan Sewerage Agencies. National organization involved in all facets of water quality protection. Represents the interests of wastewater treatment agencies. A nationally recognized leader in environmental policy and technical resource on water quality and ecosystem protection issues. Offers conferences, a number of publications, and networking opportunities to members. 1000 Connecticut Ave., Suite 410, Washington, DC 20036. (202) 833-2672. Http://www.amsa-cleanwater.org.

Association of Metropolitan Water Agencies (AMWA). Represents the interests and concerns of the nation's larger metropolitan water supply agencies. Brings together water utility agencies with a common need to develop, guide, and influence public water policy to assure uninterrupted delivery of safe drinking water to the public at a reasonable cost. Holds an annual meeting each fall and a Legislative and Regulatory conference in late winter. Publishes a newsletter, *Federal Water Review*. Does periodic surveys on such subjects as trends in water usage. Website has a utility job listings. 1717 K St., NW, Suite 801, Washington, DC 20036. (202) 331-2820. Http://www.amwa-water.org.

Association of State and Interstate Water Pollution Control Administrators (ASIWPCA). Professional organization of state water program managers who implement surface and groundwater quality management programs on a daily basis. Provides for coordination and communication between and among states, as well as with the federal government and the public and private sectors. Also has a public education program that includes youth education programs and technical assistance to state executives and members of Congress. Offers a number of publications ranging from nonpoint source pollution to children's education. ASIWPCA publications are available to the public for a fee. Website has links to related organizations. 750 First St, NE, Suite 910, Washington, DC 20002. (202) 898-0905. Http://www. asiwpca.org.

Association of State Drinking Water Administrators (ASDWA). Professional association providing national representation to state drinking water program administrators. Other state and local drinking water regulatory personnel participate as associate members. Publishes a quarterly newsletter, *ASDWA Update*, as well as a number of other publications. Website has links to related sites. 1120 Connecticut Ave., NW, Suite 1060, Washington, DC 20036. (202) 293-7655. Http://www.asdwa.org.

National Ground Water Association. Nonprofit professional association whose mission is to provide professional and technical leadership in the advancement of the ground water industry and to protect, promote, and responsibly develop and use ground water resources. Offers annual trade shows, short courses, and workshops nationwide, as well as a catalog of books and other educational materials. Operates the National Ground Water Information Center. Publications include a monthly trade journal, *Water Well Journal*, a bimonthly academic journal, *Ground Water*, and a quarterly technical journal, *Ground Water Monitoring and Remediation*. Offers two kinds of scholarships—one limited to undergraduate women and the other open to everyone. Website has job listings and links to related sites broken down by category. 601 Dempsey Rd., Westerville, OH 43081. (614) 898-7791. Http://www.ngwa.org.

Natural Resources Defense Council. National environmental organization whose programs include a water program under which they work to protect and restore water quality, fisheries, wetlands, the Everglades, and ocean life, as well as an urban program that focuses on water quality and water supply in major urban centers. 40 West 20th St., New York, NY 10011. (212) 727-1773. Http://www.nrdc.org.

River Network. Nonprofit organization dedicated to helping people organize to protect and restore rivers and watersheds at the local level. Publications include the quarterly journal *River Voices*. Website has links to related sites and a searchable directory of river and watershed organizations. P.O. Box 8787, Portland, OR 97207. (503) 241-3506. Http://www.rivernetwork.org.

Universities Water Information Network (UWIN). Disseminates information of interest to all concerned with water resources. UWIN is housed at the headquarters of the Universities Council on Water Resources at Southern Illinois University and funded through a grant from the U.S. Geological Survey. Website lists employment opportunities, has a calendar of water events, publishes calls for papers, has links to water databases, and provides lists of annotated websites broken down by category. 4543 Faner Hall, Southern Illinois University, Carbondale, IL 62901-4526. Http://www.uwin.siu.edu.

U.S. Department of Agriculture's (USDA) National Agricultural Library (NAL) Water Quality Information Center. Part of the Agricultural Research Service. As the focal point of NAL's water quality efforts, the center collects, organizes, and communicates the scientific findings, educational methodologies, and public policy issues related to water quality and agriculture. Website has searchable lists, such as educational resources, expertise, and general water resource information. Also has links to water-related databases. NAL, Water Quality Information Center, 4th Floor, 10301 Baltimore Blvd., Beltsville, MD 20705-2351. Http://www.nal.usda. gov/wqic/.

U.S. Environmental Protection Agency (EPA), Office of Water. The EPA is the primary federal agency responsible for the regulation, protection, and improvement of water resources and supplies of the U.S. USEPA, Water Resource Center, RC-4100, 401 M Street SW, Washington, DC 20460. Http://www.epa.gov/ow.

U.S. Geological Survey (USGS) Office of Water Quality. Federal agency that provides leadership and coordination in the development of programs to address issues concerning the quality of the nation's surface water and ground water resources. Also provides support in the application of techniques for the collection, analysis, and interpretation of water quality data. Operates the National Water Quality Laboratory for the preparation and analysis of water and biological samples. Scientists and technicians of the USGS develop, document, and implement field procedures, laboratory methods, and interpretive techniques for water quality data. Information about water quality is available through USGS publications such as *Selected Water-Resources Abstracts*, *USGS Fact Sheets*, and other USGS water resources publications. Website has links to related sites. (703) 648-6861. Http:// water.usgs.gov.

U.S. Water News. Monthly publication that offers the latest news concerning water issues. Coverage includes water supply, water quality, policy and legislation, litigation and water rights, conservation, climate, international water news, and more. Classified ad section has job postings. Print and on-line versions have different articles. 230 Main Street, Halstead, KS 67056. (316) 835-2222. Http://www.uswaternews.com/homepage.html.

Water Environment Federation (WEF). International nonprofit technical and educational organization whose goal is to preserve and enhance the global water environment. Members are water quality professionals and specialists, including engineers, scientists, government officials, utility and industrial managers and operators, academicians, students, equipment manufacturers, and others. Their mission is to promote and advance the water quality industry by providing high quality products and services to members and by protecting and enhancing the global water environment. Publishes *WEF Reporter* each Wednesday. Offers conferences, workshops, and professional development courses. Website has a job bank and provides links to related sites. 601 Wythe St., Alexandria, VA 22314-1994. (703) 684-2400. Http://www.wef.org.

Water On-line. A website with loads of news and information about water quality management. Offers discussion forums, an events calendar, and, most importantly, a "career corner" in which you can post a resume and/or search for a job. Http://www.wateronline.com.

Water Quality Association (WQA). International trade association representing the household, commercial, and industrial water quality improvement industry. 4151 Naperville Rd., Lisle, IL 60532. (630) 505-0160. Http://www.wqa.org.

7 Air Quality Management

AT A GLANCE

Employment:
80,000 air quality professionals nationwide

Demand:
1 to 4 percent annually

Breakdown:
Public sector, 20 percent
Private sector, 75 percent
Nonprofit, 5 percent

Key Job Titles:
Air Quality Engineer
Air Quality Modeler
Air Quality Planner
Atmospheric Chemist
Environmental Attorney
Environmental Auditor
Environmental Economist
Environmental Manager
Environmental Policy Specialist
Environmental Quality Analyst
Environmental Scientist
Environmental Writer
Inspector, Field Staffer
Meteorologist

Public Information Specialist
Toxicologist

Influential Organizations:

Air and Waste Management Association
Association of Local Air Pollution Control Officials
Center for Clean Air Policy
Clean Air Task Force
Environmental Defense Fund
National Oceanic and Atmospheric Administration
National Park Service
Natural Resources Defense Council
Northeast States for Coordinated Air Use Management
State and Territorial Air Pollution Program Administrators
U.S. Department of Transportation, Federal Highway
    Administration
U.S. Environmental Protection Agency

Salary:

Air quality engineers and inspectors with engineering backgrounds start at
around $33,000, which can rise quickly. Entry-level scientists start in the
high 20s. Average salaries for more experienced professionals are from
$50,000 to $65,000 annually. Managers and successful consultants can earn
$75,000 to $90,000 or more.

WHAT IS AIR QUALITY MANAGEMENT?

It's been decades since drivers crossing the Verrazano-Narrows Bridge from
New York could smell New Jersey before they could see it, pumping lead into
the air as they motored through the acrid stench of stack emissions along the
shore. It's been half a century since a bizarre, five-day temperature inversion
trapped dense, dark clouds of coal plant emissions in Donora, Pennsylvania,
near the ground, killing twenty people in what has become America's most
infamous air quality disaster.

Nowadays, the air is much cleaner—but not by accident. Fueled by mounting environmental concern in the 1960s, Congress passed the Clean Air Act
Amendments of 1970, one of the country's landmark environmental laws. In
many ways, it reflected the air quality management thinking of the time—crack
down on gas-guzzling cars, massive industrial plants, and other specific, local-
ized, visible emitters with tough regulations backed up by stiff penalties, and
watch the air grow cleaner with each passing day. Jobs in air quality at the time
followed suit, concentrated mostly in engineering.

By most accounts, the thinking worked. In 1971, the EPA identified and set
standards for six "criteria pollutants"—carbon monoxide, lead, nitrogen diox-

ide, ozone, particulate matter, and sulfur dioxide—to monitor America's progress in cleaning the air. And in a January 1998 EPA report on those National Ambient Air Quality Standards (NAAQS), (the agency's most recent) concentrations of all six pollutants were found to have dropped considerably from 1977 to 1996, mirroring as significant an emissions cut in five of the six pollutants.

But as anyone at EPA will tell you nowadays, there is more to air pollution than the criteria pollutants. So much more, that air quality managment in 1970 and 1998 have about as much in common as the visibility in each of those years from the Verrazano-Narrows. The differences extend as well to jobs in air quality management.

New concerns have emerged, from stratospheric ozone depletion and the greenhouse effect on the global level, to toxic air emissions such as mercury on the regional level, to naturally occuring indoor air pollutants such as radon in your own home. New understandings of old concerns have emerged, resulting in tougher standards such as the ones the EPA set in July 1997 for ozone and particulate matter, and more complex challenges such as the transport of ozone precursors from the Midwest to the Northeast.

And new realities have occurred. The old "command and control" approach toward polluters that worked so well through the 1970s and much of the 1980s, and to a certain extent still works today, has gradually given way to "partnering" with those polluters. Mandatory compliance has given way to voluntary compliance. Regulatory penalties have given way to market-based incentives. Dictated authorities have given way to delegated authorities. Confrontation has given way to consensus.

The result is that working in air quality management nowadays requires more than an engineering degree and the presumption that no matter how you say what you say, you will be understood. Candidates most sought after in every sector have as wide a spectrum of talents and training as the new complexity of air quality itself. They are also willing to adapt their talents and training to the needs of their employers. They may still be engineers, but engineers versed in economics, science, policy, law, communications, trade, and perhaps above all, diplomacy.

HISTORY AND BACKGROUND

If there is one law that has driven air quality management more than any other in recent decades, it's the Clean Air Act. First passed in 1955, replaced in 1967, and amended in 1970, 1977, and 1990, the law has defined the air quality management landscape for much of its existence.

And as the EPA's 1998 National Air Quality and Emissions Trends Report makes clear, air quality in America has generally improved over the more than forty year history of the Clean Air Act. Problems remain, and some problems are being redefined as more serious as standards under the Act evolve to become more stringent. But by and large, America's air is cleaner now than it was before the Act was passed, the measurements for which are themselves a record of the history and background of air quality management. Key findings of the report are as follows:

- Air quality has improved in terms of the NAAQS standards, but not entirely, the EPA says. Between 1977 and 1996, concentrations of carbon monoxide dropped 61 percent, lead 97 percent, nitrogen dioxide 27 percent, ozone 30 percent, and sulfur dioxide 58 percent. No information was available on particulate matter. The concentration drops reflect emissions drops of 31 percent for carbon monoxide, 98 percent for lead, 38 percent for ozone, 73 percent for particulate matter, and 39 percent for sulfur dioxide. But emissions of nitrogen oxide have actually increased by 8 percent. And the report is working off of the weaker, pre-1997 particulate matter standard.
- Visibility in twenty-nine national parks and wilderness areas, measured in the form of average aerosol light extinction, improved 10 percent in the eastern United States and 20 percent in the western United States between 1988 and 1995, the EPA reports. However, when the haziest days are considered, visibility worsened in the East by 6 percent.
- For a second consecutive year, most of the EPA's monitoring sites for ozone precursors showed significant declines in nitrogen oxide, volatile organic compounds (VOG), and other precursors, the EPA reports. But the reductions for benzene and other mobile-related VOCs in 1995 and 1996 were not as large as those for 1994 and 1995.
- As stated, the EPA reports that 3.7 million tons of toxics are still emitted annually. However, after using a new approach (National Toxics Inventory) over the last two years for measuring air toxics, the EPA found that mobile and area sources account for 75 percent of the emissions.
- When the 1990 amendments were passed, 274 areas around the country were found to be out of compliance with at least one ambient standard. By 1997, that number was down to 158. But the analysis does not account for the tougher, 1997 ozone and particulate matter standards set by the EPA, which are expected to significantly increase the number of areas out of compliance.
- Locally, in what are known as Metropolitan Statistical Areas (MSAs), there has been some improvement, but also some decline, in air quality over the last decade, the EPA reports. Some 217 MSAs showed a statistically significant downward trend in at least one criteria pollutant, while the number of "unhealthful" days between 1987 and 1996 dropped 51 percent in the Los Angeles basin and 75 percent in the remaining cities across the country. But 13 MSAs showed a statistically significant increase in ambient concentrations for at least one criteria pollutant.

Meanwhile, the times have diminished the influence of the Clean Air Act, and especially the influence of the 1990 Amendments. The air quality management landscape has broadened in recent years to include global problems such as climate change, to consider previously unrelated concerns such as land use planning, transportation, and utility deregulation, and to take up new strategies such as emissions trading (for which the 1990 Amendments set the stage, but never fully developed). As relationships between pollutants and their sources are becoming increasingly evident, the Amendments' discrete approach to pollutants and their sources is becoming increasingly obsolete.

Politics, economics, and ideology are also factors. Government downsizing, especially on the federal level, has been a hard reality ever since the temporary shutdown of the federal government in 1995. And with both major political parties seeking to ease the federal regulatory burden on Americans, to indeed ease the federal presence generally, federal laws such as the Clean Air Act are seen more as defining the ground rules on issues, leaving the game to be played by state and local governments and the private sector.

KEY LEGISLATION

Although they are declining as an influence in air quality management, an understanding of the 1990 Amendments is still considered valuable. So, too, is an understanding of the Kyoto Protocol signed by America and over 150 other nations in 1997.

The 1990 Clean Air Act Amendments. The Amendments, signed by President Bush, were considered progressive by environmental and industry groups at the time, although not everyone was pleased. They established seven titles, each dealing with a specific issue.

Title I: Improving Air Quality Standards took aim at ozone, carbon monoxide, and particulate matter. With the EPA's tough new standards for ozone and particulate matter, which was issued in 1997, many areas now in compliance would no longer be.

Title II: Reducing Motor Vehicle Emissions targeted "mobile sources" of pollution, which account for the majority of urban pollution. Emissions of these pollutants continue to decline, although the rate of decline for some of them is slowing, the EPA found in its 1998 report.

Title III: Controlling Airborne Toxic Emissions dealt with dioxins, cadmium, mercury, and numerous other pollutants—189 in all—that threaten public health. It gives the EPA to the year 2000 to come up with maximum achievable control technology standards that polluters will have to meet. The goal is to cut air toxics by 75 percent. The EPA says in its 1998 report that 3.7 million tons of air toxics are emitted annually.

Title IV: Preventing Acid Rain sought to cut in half by the year 2000 the 20 million tons of sulfur dioxide emitted annually by electric utilities and other sources. That goal has already been met, thanks to a market-based emissions trading program established in response to the title that started in 1995, and has served as a model for other emissions trading programs in development.

Title V: Creating Incentives required polluters seeking operating permits to pay a specified amount per ton emitted, providing an economic incentive to reducing pollution while generating revenues to fund abatement programs on the state and local levels. Job growth as a result of those revenues has leveled.

Title VI: Closing the Ozone Hole sought to phase out ozone-depleting chloroflourocar-
bons, halons, and carbon tetrachloride by the year 2000, as required by the
Montreal Protocol.

Title VII: Increasing Enforcement stepped up fines for environmental violations, providing teeth to EPA regulations.

The Kyoto Protocol. The Kyoto Protocol, which was signed in December 1997
by over 150 nations, including the U.S, and widely believed to be at best a
good first step, but not a solution, toward solving the climate change problem,
calls on 38 industrial nations to reduce the emissions of six major greenhouse
gases below 1990 levels between 2008 and 2012. It further calls for a global
emissions trading program by which countries that fail to meet their targets
may strike deals with other countries that have, to acquire the excess "quota."
Developing countries, where emissions are rising the fastest, are asked to make
voluntary cuts. The Protocol will take effect once it is ratified by at least 55
nations that represent 55 percent of the 1990 carbon emissions.

Since the U.S. emissions in 1990 represent 37 percent of the total, with
Germany representing another 8 percent, the Protocol will sink or swim based
on whether the U.S. Senate ratifies it in the next year or so, says C.V. Maphai,
principal scientist at the Arizona Public Service Company, a member of the Air
and Waste Management Association and one of the largest investor-owned utilities in the Southwest. "It is crucial that the U.S. Senate ratify the Protocol if
it is to go into effect," he says. While the Senate's approval is unlikely, should
it occur, it would spur the only anticipated growth in air quality jobs in the federal government and private sector, Maphai says.

ISSUES AND TRENDS

There are jobs to be found in the air quality management arena, ranging from
field staff monitors who need no more than an associate degree to environmental scientists with doctorates in atmospheric chemistry. In addition to having a far more eclectic background than candidates of the past, today's candidates must keep a watchful eye on air quality issues and trends, as they will
define the job front in the near future.

DECLINING INFLUENCE OF THE 1990 CLEAN AIR ACT AMENDMENTS

For reasons stated earlier—a growing awareness of global air quality problems
such as climate change, and of the air quality role of transportation, planning,
and other previously unrelated concerns; the rise of new tactics for improving
air quality such as emissions trading; our improving understanding of the syn-
ergistic relationships between air pollutants; government downsizing; and the
desire politically to ease the federal regulatory burden—the 1990 Clean Air Act
Amendments are waning in influence. "Are the 1990 amendments still relevant?" asks Susan Gander, senior policy analyst at the Center for Clean Air
Policy. "I think the aspect of them that related to promoting trade and eco-

nomic incentive programs is still relevant. But in terms of their influence in shaping the whole environmental management universe, I think they've kind of played out."

MOUNTING CONCERN OVER CLIMATE CHANGE

Global carbon emissions—which in the atmosphere form carbon dioxide (CO_2), the key greenhouse gas—hit a record 6.2 billion tons in 1996, four times the 1950 emissions, according to the Worldwatch Institute's 1998 *State of the World* report. The atmospheric CO_2 concentration is now 29 percent above the preindustrial level, higher than at any time in the last 160,000 years. Industrial countries are responsible for 76 percent of the world's carbon emissions, which is why they voluntarily agreed at the 1992 Earth Summit to hold their emissions to 1990 levels by the year 2000. But three key countries—the U.S., Australia, and Japan—actually *increased* their emissions 8.8 percent, 9.6 percent, and 12.5 percent, respectively, by 1996. Developing countries are experiencing the fastest growth in emissions, as industrialization takes hold. Emissions in 1996 were 44 percent higher over 1990 levels, and 71 percent higher over 1986 levels, with rapid economic growth in East Asia and Latin America leading the way, Worldwatch reports. The Kyoto Protocol is considered inadequate to stabilize the climate, given these increases.

MEETING EPA'S NEW OZONE AND PARTICULATE STANDARDS

The EPA concluded in 1997 that its ozone and particulate matter standards did not adequately protect public health. Ozone was causing problems under the old standard from aggravated asthma to loss of lung function. Particulate matter under the old "PM10" standard was causing even worse problems, from respiratory illness to death. The EPA expects its new standards to annually prevent about 15,000 premature deaths, 350,000 cases of aggravated asthma, and 1 million cases of significantly decreased lung function in children. The new "PM2.5" standard especially, as it applies to particulate matter whose aerodynamic size is less than or equal to 2.5 micrometers, is considered very rigorous. The EPA has set a long time frame for compliance, all the way to 2012. And the first step is a three-year nationwide monitoring program to see just how severe the problem is, and to decide which areas of the country are out of compliance. Some 1,500 monitors will be set up across the country, with $35 million in EPA funding in fiscal year 1998 alone.

MARKET-BASED AIR QUALITY STRATEGIES

Many air quality players are not waiting for the Senate to decide on the Kyoto Protocol and are pursuing "joint implementation" and emissions trading projects, which are market-based strategies called for in the 1992 Rio treaty, Energy Policy Act of 1992, and the Protocol itself. Emissions trading allows companies to buy or sell pollution credits within a broader emissions reduction program. Joint implementation takes the idea a step further—a company emitting greenhouse gases invests in a domestic or foreign project to reduce emissions there, (e.g., by converting that project to cleaner fuels) and then gains credits to offset its own emissions. For example, Maphai's APSC has been involved in such a project with New York's Niagara Mohawk, another utility, giving SO_2 credits to Niagara Mohawk in exchange for CO_2 credits from Niagara Mohawk. APSC also obtains credit through its involvement in a project on Mexico's Baja Peninsula to electrify a small fishing village with solar and wind power, backed up by diesel. It has even given CO_2 credits to the Environmental Defense Fund, which EDF then retired, providing APSC again with credits, Maphai says.

TRANSPORTATION AND LAND-USE PLANNING AS AIR QUALITY CONCERNS

For years, transportation and air quality were seen as having little in common, even though cars and trucks contribute greatly to smog. But the 1991 Intermodal Surface Transportation Efficiency Act (and its 1998 update) shifted the country away from a reliance on motor vehicles and toward an ecologically healthier transport mix ranging from public transit to telecommuting, making the link between how people move and what they breathe more evident. The link with where people live has also become more evident, right down to how better to design cities so that commuting is not so much of a difficulty. "It's the next place to tackle," said the Center for Clean Air Policy's Gander. "We've done a lot with utilities and other stationary sources, but industry has not done everything it can with motor vehicles. More can be done on the technology and fuel ends. But the bigger issue is land use. The demand for transportation is largely, although not entirely, a function of how we utilize our land space, with the fact that people are forced to commute 30 miles to get to their jobs because there isn't a strong public transportation system."

AIR QUALITY CONCERNS OF ELECTRIC UTILITY RESTRUCTURING

Utility restructuring is about competition—break up monopolizing utilities into generation, transmission, and distribution companies, and bring competition to energy production, and rates should drop. However, it's not going that smoothly. Utilities abide by varying regulations. Some utilities have an easier time of it than others. As they reposition themselves in a competitive market, the concern is that the less regulated ones that are cheaper to operate will thrive, thereby increasing pollution. Combine that with industry downsizing, and the pressure is even greater to cut costs through dirty power generation. In a January 1998 report, the Northeast States for Coordinated Air Use Management found that several large Midwestern power companies, which are among the less regulated, boosted their short-term wholesale power sales between 1995 and 1996 with deregulation. The increased sales were accompanied by boosted generation at several of the companies' highest polluting, coal-fired power plants during the same period.

CAREER OPPORTUNITIES

Although career growth in the air quality management field is not robust, there are pockets of growth in all sectors built around new trends and technological innovation.

PUBLIC SECTOR

If you're interested in working for the federal government, this might not be the best time. "In the latter part of the '90s, the federal government projects little or no growth, a stable work force at best," says Dale Evarts, program manager at the EPA's Office of Air Quality Planning and Standards. The drive to shrink the federal bureaucracy has taken its toll. "The air program at EPA has not been immune to the other restraints placed on the federal government by reduced budgets, and therefore the steady job growth projected in the early 1990s after the passage of the Clean Air Act Amendments in 1990 has not been sustained—it has basically stopped. We've had to strategize on how to shift our resources to the highest priority issues," Evarts says.

Again, should the U.S. Senate ratify the Kyoto Protocol, there is some possibility for growth in that area of the federal bureaucracy that deals with climate change. To the extent that jobs are available, they are emerging on the policy front, especially in developing pollution prevention, market-based, or voluntary air quality programs.

But regardless of the Protocol or downsizing, the federal government is expected to continue playing the same air quality management role—and requiring the same air quality management professionals—it has played in recent years. The EPA especially will continue setting national standards, and will need researchers, scientists, and other experts to develop them. It will continue to provide technical support to states and localities, and will need policy experts, government liaisons, and others who can translate often complex federal standards, policies, and regulations to the states and localities, as well as help them access federal resources to comply with them. And it will continue to play an oversight and enforcement role, and will need everyone from field staff monitors to determine on-the-ground compliance, to environmental attorneys to deal with violations.

Key existing federal air quality management work includes:

- Basic research and laboratory work carried out by both engineers and environmental scientists (e.g., chemists, biologists, physicists, mathematicians, and microbiologists), and including engineering analysis, development, and design of technologies to meet certain standards.
- Risk assessment work, determining what pollutant levels pose a risk to

human health and the environment, including comparative risk assessment work, or the relative risks of one pollutant versus another.

- Crop, forest, and other ecosystem damage assessment work.
- Mathematical modeling of air pollutant dispersion and the effect of pollution control strategies. Professionals with backgrounds in meteorology and climatology are examining how pollutants combine and disperse in the atmosphere, providing information to computer science and data management specialists to interpret.

The job prospects in the state and local governments are brighter, but only a bit. The states, like the federal government, are downsizing, even though one key way in which the federal agencies are downsizing is by delegating regulatory authorities to the states, increasing the importance of state agencies. Nonetheless, one of the largest local air agencies in the country, California's South Coast Air Quality Management District, cut its staff by 40 percent late in 1997.

"From 1995 to 1997, the Congressional appropriation to the states declined by 25 percent, yet the responsibilities increased greatly for the states," says William Becker, executive director of the State and Territorial Air Pollution Administrator (STAPPA) and the Association of Local Air Pollution Control Officials (ALAPCO). Congress increased the appropriation in 1998, "but that money is not going to people, but rather infrastructure, like air quality monitors," he says. The states are reluctant to increase taxes and fees, as they themselves are in a fiscal pinch, he adds.

Still, Becker predicts "expanded efforts on both the state and local levels," if only because "without expanded growth on those levels, air pollution programs will suffer, and we will not be able to provide the kind of health and welfare protection that the public demands."

However, as a result, the brightest prospects for job candidates (in state government especially) are for those who are "the most well-rounded, most thoughtful, whether they are engineers or not," Becker says. Most valuable are those whose diverse talents and training make them flexible in their responsibilities, he says. "The analogy in sports is that the New England Patriots may be looking for a defensive back, but the best athlete available in the draft may be a quarterback. So they take him, because that quarterback can be trained to be a defensive back," Becker says. The sorts of professionals who will be working in the state air quality agency of the next few years will include not just engineers, but policy specialists, atmospheric scientists, mathematical modelers, attorneys, communicators, economists, and risk analysts.

Locally, the best job prospects lie in the work that must be done to comply with the EPA's new ozone and particulate matter standards, says Bruce Anderson, president of ALAPCO and division director of permitting in the Wyandotte County Department of Air Quality in Kansas. The money that the Title V program under the 1990 Amendments generated to expand state and local air quality programs has not been enough to offset the cuts in other fed-

U.S. Environmental Protection Agency scientists carry out long-term studies to understand the effects of air pollution on plants and trees.

eral funding sources, making budgets tight. But three years of monitoring for ozone and particulate matter is about to begin, "and agencies will be hiring folks to do that," Anderson says.

Local air agencies typically have staffs that include air quality engineers, modelers, and inspectors. Chemical, mechanical, and environmental engineers are also employed on the local level, to evaluate sources of air pollution, design and set up networks to monitor ambient pollutants and emissions, conduct laboratory analyses, and analyze computer-generated data. Also employed are environmental scientists to analyze data and identify pollutant sources, public health specialists to do risk assessments, inspectors to check for compliance with regulations, and occasionally in the larger local agencies, attorneys, microbiologists, toxicologists, epidemiologists, and meteorologists.

PRIVATE SECTOR

"The magic words are deregulation, competition, and downsizing, especially in the electric industry," says Maphai, of APSC. "Everyone is trying to cut costs to stay in business. There's tremendous pressure to cut costs all across the board." Technology advances enabling companies to replace employees with machines have altered the work picture, he adds.

The consulting and engineering (C&E) business, which thrived in the heyday of the 1980s, is also in decline. The *Environmental Business Journal* reported in May 1997 that 1996 was the first year on record of an aggregate market

Environmental staff at Chrysler Motors perform regular tests to reduce emissions and confirm compliance with environmental regulations.

decline. The $1.39 billion C&E market in air quality declined 6 percent in 1995 through 1996.

"My personal opinion is that consulting will go down even further," Maphai said. "It's been in decline for the last couple of years. The whole environmental field has. And it will continue to be in decline. Of course, it all depends on whether the Senate does something on climate change. If it does, then all the rules will change."

Still, most of America's air quality management professionals work in the private sector, with estimates running as high as four out of every five jobs. Those jobs, many of which are in utilities, technology development and marketing, and consulting, are far-ranging—everyone from entry-level monitors and samplers to engineers, special project developers, and managers. With the onslaught of deregulation, economists, marketers, and financial specialists of every stripe will increasingly play a major role as companies seek to compete while maintaining their bottom lines. Also likely to increasingly play a major role are environmental affairs specialists, everyone from government and legislative liaisons to regulatory compliance experts, as companies try to adapt to a rapidly changing relationship between government and industry in air quality. While consulting is on the decline, agencies such as EPA as well as major utilities and other companies will continue to seek them out for expertise across the board, from engineering, to research, to compliance.

NONPROFIT SECTOR

Nonprofit organizations, ranging from grassroots citizen action groups and regional and national environmental groups, to industry and public health associations, have perennially occupied a small slice of the air quality management pie. And little growth is expected. But two areas hold some promise for growth, not just in air quality, but across a wide array of environmental issues. Groups are themselves consensus builders and problem solvers, says Ruth Hennig, administrator of the John Merck Fund, a foundation based in Boston that provides about $1.5 million annually to environmental groups.

"The two growth areas I see, where projects are being developed or there are positions that CEOs are seeking to fill, are for people who can develop and implement strategic campaigns in a political sense, and people with communications skills," Hennig says.

"The other area, and this is not overly glamorous, is for grassroots organizers who can do the old-style organizing of a constituency to force action on an issue," Hennig adds. "These people are in very high demand. Every group I know of is looking for organizers. These are usually entry-level positions, not well paid, that tend to attract young people, and so there's a lot of turnover. But almost every organization I know of wants organizers."

SALARY

Annual salaries for entry-level positions at the EPA range from about $26,000 to $32,000 for all positions except engineers, who are paid slightly more, says the EPA's Evarts. Other federal agencies are comparable. Nonprofits vary widely, depending on their size and resources, paying literally nothing at all to salaries similar to government positions.

State agency salaries fall within a similar range as federal agency salaries. A STAPPA/ALAPCO survey completed in January 1998 found that state agencies pay salaries ranged from about $36,000 to $49,000 for engineers; $27,000 to $42,000 for environmental scientists, inspectors, and field staffers; $31,000 to $42,000 for modelers and meteorologists; and $40,000 to $54,000 for planners and rule writers.

At Andersen's Wyandotte County Department of Air Quality, located in Kansas, where the cost of living is "relatively inexpensive compared to the coasts," environmental scientists start at $25,000 a year and environmental engineers at $30,000, Andersen said. An employer on either coast would have to pay more, he added. And most local and state agencies still have to fight to keep employees from leaving for higher paying jobs in consulting and private industry, even if consulting is on the decline and industry is downsizing.

GETTING STARTED

Entry-level jobs in air quality management appear to be available the most in state and local governments and going to candidates with diverse backgrounds combining expertise in a particular area with fluency in many others. Those who can see linkages between areas—engineering and economics, science and policy, for instance—appear especially desirable. Those who can also communicate eloquently and relate diplomatically are even more in demand.

EDUCATION

Engineering remains an important degree, although again not so much in the classic sense of a discretely trained civil or chemical engineer, but in a broader sense, perhaps best reflected in the steadily maturing environmental engineering degree. Planning degrees are also relevant, especially in land-use and transportation planning. Degrees in the sciences, economics, marketing, business administration, communications, international affairs, government, political science, computer science, and law can serve as a base, especially when they have some relationship to the environment.

Environmental specialties, such as environmental engineering, are maturing as rigorous degrees, and may be best suited to the eclectic nature of the new air quality management arena, as well as to the environmental arena itself. Again, there are jobs across the degree spectrum—from A.A. to B.S. to M.A. to Ph.D. Pursue the degree that best suits your job goals, and be prepared to accept one beneath it, at least initially. However, regardless of the job, you need to be able to communicate well, especially in writing.

And keep an eye on air quality management issues and trends, as they will shape job opportunities in the coming years. For instance, the relationship between transportation planning, land-use planning, and air quality promises to offer opportunities, but likely only for those who recognize that relationship and prepare for it with the appropriate planning degrees. As the APSC's Maphai says, "Growth, especially in the West, is occurring on isolated patches, and so we need people doing land-use planning and transportation planning to look at air quality impacts, which also have an impact on climate change." Such planning "is becoming a key issue" in air quality management, he says.

The same may be said for joint implementation (JI) and emissions trading ventures, which are only just starting to get off the ground, but are the future when it comes to air quality management and, again, require the appropriate degrees, which in this case are focused more on finance, marketing, and business. "There's a big opportunity for development of international emissions reductions, and so for folks interested in working abroad in developing countries to find greenhouse gas reduction projects," says Susan Gander, whose Center for Clean Air Policy started one of the first "JI" projects in the city of Decin in the former Czech Republic. There have been 878 projects across all sectors—electricity, transportation, and others—since 1995, she says.

Such work "probably requires a combination of things—a business degree like an M.B.A., an environmental engineering degree, maybe others," Gander says. "You need to be able to go in and analyze a project, to see how it works. Probably people with all sorts of backgrounds will be doing it."

ADVICE

Air quality professionals working in the field say you need to do the following if you want to work with them.

Know the economics of environmental issues. "The importance of having a grasp of the economic elements of environmental issues, having some exposure and experience with that, just can't be ignored," says Gander of the Center for Clean Air Policy. "You will be much more marketable with that, whether working for government or industry."

Plug in to renewables. "People in college need to start looking more into renewable technologies—solar, wind, fuel cells, power distribution, and permitting in remote areas," says Maphai of Arizona Public Service Company. "Again, it's a matter of looking at technologies for reducing emissions, and how those technologies can be put in the field. There's a tremendous need for people with such training."

Consider environmental engineering. "If I was speaking to young kids today who are interested in this field, I'd recommend going to a school with an environmental engineering program," says Hendersen, of ALAPCO. "We happen to hire a lot of chemical engineers, because chemical engineering is a good basis for air quality work, but also because there are not many environmental engineers out there. But there's getting to be more."

Communication skills are key. "There's a different kind of skill set that is becoming a demand in regulatory agencies—the ability to communicate," says Jason Grumet, executive director of NESCAUM. "You've got to be able to write. Engineers can no longer wander out of [Rensselaer Polytechnic Institute], or wherever they went to school, and expect to do well if they can't construct a tight memo and a coherent regulation."

Pound the pavement. "There's no substitute for arranging as many interviews with people as you can, even if they don't have openings, and just sitting down and talking with them," says Becker of STAPPA and ALAPCO. "Pound the pavement. Walk down the street ripping off resumes to government agencies, businesses, public interest groups, and then be willing to accept a job that may not be the ultimate one, but that will provide valuable experience. It's so much easier to get your second job, once you get your first."

SUMMARY

The last edition of this book, published in 1993, noted that "You could not ask for a better time to launch a career in air quality management than the mid- to late 1990s. The relative doldrums experienced in this field during the 1980s clearly came to a halt with the 1990 Clean Air Act amendments."

What a difference a few years make. Rising environmental concerns are converging with rising economic constraints resulting in considerably more jobs needed than provided. A successful job candidate today will have to be as creative and innovative as the air quality solutions he or she must craft.

CASE STUDY

Northeast States for Coordinated
Air Use Management
Boston, Massachusetts

Air pollution problems aren't confined within state boundaries, and so dealing with them adequately requires interstate cooperation. Such coordination is complicated, requiring flexibility and general competence as much as expertise in a specific technical area. Today's air quality professionals can come from a variety of educational backgrounds, so long as they understand how to work with people of contrasting backgrounds and viewpoints.

Jason Grumet, a 1989 graduate of Brown University with a degree in environmental studies and the executive director of the Northeast States for Coordinated Air Use Management (NESCAUM), is having a tough time remembering the areas of expertise in his staff of fifteen people.

He's pretty sure there's a core policy staff of six—one with a doctorate in chemistry; another with a law degree; four with a master's in environmental studies, energy studies, air quality meteorology, and public policy, respectively; and one with a bachelor's in toxicology. The senior staff includes a couple of doctorates, one in toxicology. There are four administrative staffers, some with college degrees. Grumet himself is a semester away from a law degree.

Some executive directors might be a touch flushed, not knowing the backgrounds of their staff. And Grumet is, but in a way he says is revealing about NESCAUM (an interstate association comprised of the eight state air quality programs in the Northeast) and the world of air quality management in the 1990s.

"My chagrin in not knowing the particular backgrounds of some of my staff is actually instructive. As a quasi-governmental entity, flexibility, general competence, and creativity are far more valued than any particular expertise," Grumet says. "This is part of NESCAUM, of air quality management, of environmentalism these days."

Everything about NESCAUM would suggest the group really is the "organizational chamelion" Grumet says it is, diverse and evolving through its history to reflect changing issues. It was formed in 1967 among the six New England states "ostensibly to put an end to the unfortunate practice of states siting their most obnoxious pollution sources 100 yards from their downwind borders," and with "a strong sense" that collaborating on air quality problems made sense, he says. New York joined in 1970, and New Jersey in 1979.

After a decade of exchanging information and another developing policy, NESCAUM hit its stride in the late 1980s when it pushed through a regulation to reduce the evaporative rate of gasoline sold in the region. "This effort, which was highly successful, launched the modern era of NESCAUM," Grumet says. It has since been deeply involved in pollution transport issues, most recently completing a two-year study showing that as deregulation of the electric industry has proceeded, weakly regulated, dirty power plants in the Midwest have actually stepped up power generation, threatening the Northeast with more ozone problems. It plans to complete a sweeping study of mercury pollution in 1998.

Grumet says one of NESCAUM's challenges "is to bridge the scientific and political communities that constitute environmental protection. That's one of our main roles. Far too often, the technical experts who know fundamental things about the world are too constrained by their training and job titles to express them to anybody. And far too often, the people who are responsible for rendering policy judgments are too distracted and confused to know who to ask. The number one cause of bad environmental policy is the failure to connect these two communities."

The communities are also made up of people, and here, too, NESCAUM plays a role. "It can be somewhat lonely, working in a state agency," Grumet says. "Many people whose responsibility it is to, say, calculate the emissions inventory for small industrial boilers can feel somewhat like the last white rhinoceros. And so getting someone like that together with seven other people calculating the emissions inventory for small industrial boilers is important to both building the expertise of our state agencies and maintaining the energy and morale of the state staff."

In that sense, Grumet says, "we're a little bit like a Cheers bar for air pollution control programs."

PROFILES

C.V. Maphai
Principal Scientist
Arizona Public Service Company

Professionals trained in pure science are well equipped to deal with technical problems, but frequently find that it's the political problems that are most vexing. Consensus is needed (and is attainable) if you learn how to go about it.

From his days over thirty years ago as an undergraduate and graduate student in his native India, to lobbying on Capitol Hill more recently on air toxics and visibility regulations, it's been a long, strange trip for C.V. Maphai, principal scientist at Arizona Public Service Company, one of the largest investor-owned utilities in the Southwest.

But it's also been an instructive trip, not just for Maphai, but for anyone interested in a career in air quality management in the 1990s, when scientific solutions are not enough. "If I've learned anything in my career, it's that you have to meld technical knowledge with the realities of the world, and come up with common denominators," he says.

After earning undergraduate and graduate degrees in physics and mathematics in India, Maphai came to the U.S. in 1969 to do graduate work at the University of Minnesota, earning a master's degree in physics and mathematics. After earning a doctorate in atmospheric physics from the University of Oklahoma, he spent three years doing post-doctoral work at the University of Calgery on urban air quality issues, "particulate matter in particular—no pun intended," he says.

Maphai then joined a Los Angeles air quality consulting company, Aerovironment, as a senior scientist for five years. He then landed a job with APSC, working initially as a technical staffer, but gradually, through promotion after promotion, Maphai "got more and more involved on the policy side." APSC itself became increasingly involved with the 1990 Clean Air Act amendments, advising other companies on what positions to take as the law was being drafted, and Maphai found himself making weekly jaunts to Washington to lobby Congress on the law.

Once the law was enacted, Maphai then began work on the issues that now take up his time—climate change and visibility. And it's here that his belief in bridging science and reality in policy through broad consensus was put to the test, and he learned a hard lesson about environmentalism in America.

Maphai said he spent five arduous years working with many interest groups in nine western states, including five Native American tribes, on a large commission to develop recommendations to the EPA for regulations to protect visibility in 158 "class one" areas in national parks. The commission presented those recommendations in a June 1996 report. However, the EPA "totally ignored them," opting for "more onerous" requirements, Maphai says.

When it comes to bridging science and reality in consensus based policy, Maphai says, "it's a little like making sausage—the process is kind of ugly."

Still, ugly as it may be, it's a process Maphai believes is the future of air quality management. "It's definitely a trend, moving to consensus," he says. "Some environmental groups have realized that they have to work with industry, and some businesses have realized that they have to cooperate, too. Businesses have amended their positions from ten or twenty years ago, and are more willing to work with environmentalists now because it is for the common good."

Bruce Hill
Senior Scientist
Appalachian Mountain Club
Pinkham Notch, New Hampshire

The discipline in which an air quality professional is trained may not be the one in which some or even the majority of his or her work is done. Air quality professionals learn to adapt their skills to different problems, ranging from public health to visibility. The more flexible you are, the wider the field, and the more exciting the opportunities available to you.

By training, Bruce Hill is a geologist. He earned a bachelor's degree in geology from the University of Vermont in 1980, and a doctorate in hardrock geology and geochemistry from Stanford University in 1984.

But by profession, Hill is anything but a geologist. He has worked for the last seven years on air quality issues for the Appalachian Mountain Club (AMC) an old, prestigious conservation and recreation group based in Boston. Hill's office is in the group's North Country lodge at Pinkham Notch in New Hampshire's White Mountain National Forest.

At AMC, he has monitored air quality, visibility, alpine plants, climate change, and hiker health as it is affected by air quality in "the Whites," gradually moving from a New England focus to a national one, especially with the onset of pollution transport issues in the last few years. He's expanded AMC's air quality work by recently launching two new projects, one to monitor stream chemistry in the Whites for acid deposition, and the other to assess how people respond to haze, a "visibility perception study," he says.

But what's a geologist doing in air quality? "The overarching answer is that when you go to college, you learn skills—scientific methods, technical writing, analytic thinking—and when you come out of school, undergraduate or graduate, you may be trained in a specific area, but more often than not, you adapt your skills to another area," says Hill, who worked for a while in the oil industry in Utah before joining AMC, and who nowadays also teaches environmental science and earth science at the University of New Hampshire's College of Lifelong Learning.

"And so I may have spent four years studying geology as an undergraduate, and another four in graduate school, but I've spent the last seven years on air quality, and I know more about air quality than geology," Hill continued. "It's a matter of adapting your skills."

That adaptation, which forced Hill to think "out of the box," has prepared him for what he considers "a marvelous opportunity . . . translating the research" in air quality management specifically and environmentalism generally. "There has to be a link between science and policy. If you become an atmospheric chemist, you can do that or do applied research, but you won't be the person out there translating the research to people. My job is not just doing the research, but understanding it and translating it to people and in policy."

It's a job that's just starting to get noticed, Hill says. "I do think the need to translate is being given greater attention. There's a great body of knowledge that has yet to be translated into policy. I don't see much competition in the field yet, and so I think it's a real opportunity. I can't tell you how many times people have said to me it's great to have a scientist talk with us, because lawyers can tell us what's in the law, but scientists can tell us what the problem is, and how to solve it."

Hill says he occasionally runs up against institutional bias within the scientific community, those for instance who feel the only people qualified to speak about atmospheric chemistry are atmospheric chemists. But as far as he's concerned, Hill is where he needs and wants to be. "I'm a hybrid, and I don't try to sell myself as anything else," he says. "Besides, you always have the capacity to learn."

Robin Dunkins
Senior Environmental Engineer
EPA Office of Air Quality Planning
and Standards
Research Triangle Park, North Carolina

Very often in environmental professions new legislation or federal rules create instant opportunities for people with the right qualifications. It's important to keep an eye out for campus recruiters, if only to find out what they're looking for. You may find that you're looking for them too.

As a child growing up in Washington in the early 1970s, Robin Dunkins spent her summers learning about the environment at camps sponsored by the Smithsonian Institution, just a few years after the EPA was created. "I was always aware of the EPA, had a fascination with it, and to a certain degree, always thought I'd work there," she says.

And for the last ten years, Dunkins has worked at the EPA, serving as team leader on the particulate matter program at the agency's Office of Air Quality Planning and Standards. The "PM" program is arguably the most popular in air quality, thanks to a new PM standard announced last year.

But while Dunkins may have sensed she'd end up at America's premier federal environmental agency, it did not always seem that way. On her way to a bachelor's degree in chemical engineering from Howard University in 1983, she did two summer internships at Exxon in New Jersey.

"When I was in the chemical engineering program, I became interested in Exxon, because at the time the oil companies were the leading companies for chemical engineering and they were recruiting on campus, so I thought I'd try it," Dunkins says. After one summer scaling towering oil tanks, she had some misgivings. But the next summer working in research convinced her that research was her future.

After completing her undergraduate degree, Dunkins headed off to a master's program in chemical engineering at North Carolina State University. "I thought that if I wanted to go into research, I should go to graduate school," which she did, finishing her course work. But when she was a thesis short of a degree, the EPA passed its first PM standard, and came to campus recruiting chemical engineers to work on the PM program.

"So I went over, thinking I'd just hear about the job," Dunkins says. "The position was in environmental engineering, but they were looking for chemical engineers to fill it. After listening to what the job entailed, I thought it sounded interesting. The next day, they called and offered it to me. So I took it, thought I'd work for a year and figure out what I wanted to do. I've been here 10 years and I am still trying to figure that out," she laughs.

But when it comes to working at the agency, "I've enjoyed it," Dunkins says. "Every job has its ups and downs, but the last couple of years have been fast paced, working on the new standards." She has spent over two and a half years leading a group of government, academic, industry, and environmental representatives in developing an implementation strategy for the new ozone and PM standards. She has also spent the last four years serving as the federal women's program manager for the EPA's Research Triangle Park, helping to identify and overcome barriers to women at the agency, an effort parallel to other such programs for Pacific Islanders and Hispanic, African, Asian, and Native Americans at the EPA. "I believe in what I'm doing," Dunkins says.

Is the EPA what she thought it would be, back at those summer camps? "It's more than what I wanted it to be," Dunkins says. Especially in air quality. She had once considered working in water quality or waste management, "but if I had to start all over at EPA, air quality is what I'd pick now."

RESOURCES

Air and Waste Management Association (A&WMA). One Gateway Center, Third Floor, Pittsburgh, PA 15222. (412) 232-3444. Http://www.awma.prg. Purpose is to enhance environmental knowledge by providing quality information on which to base environmental decisions. Website hosts "EM Online," which features articles on key environmental issues.

American Lung Association (ALA). 1740 Broadway, New York, NY 10019-4347. (212) 315-8700. Http://www.lungusa.org. ALA fights for improved government standards for air quality, including laws to protect nonsmokers from secondhand smoke. It is a resource for air quality information on a variety of hazards.

Center for Clean Air Policy (CCAP). 750 First Street, NE, Suite 1140, Washington DC 20002. (202) 408-9260. Http://www.ccap.org. Nonprofit group focused on market-based approaches to environmental problems. Through efforts at the state, federal, and international levels, the center emphasizes the need for cost-effective, pragmatic, and comprehensive long-term solutions.

Environmental Defense Fund (EDF). 257 Park Avenue South, New York, NY 10010. (800) 684-3322. Http://www.edf.org. EDF is dedicated to protecting the environmental rights of all people, including future generations. Website is an excellent resource for information about environmental issues and contains a section on global warming and the ability to search for air quality-related items.

National Park Service, Protected Areas Air Resources Web. Http://www.aqd.nps.gov/ard. Two organizations, the Air Resources Division of the National Park Service and the Air Quality Branch of the U.S. Fish and Wildlife Service, work side-by-side to protect and improve air quality in federally protected wilderness areas. A part of NatureNet, this site is a collection of pages on air pollution in the U.S. national parks and national wildlife refuges. Resources section includes links to air quality sites and atmospheric sciences sites.

Natural Resources Defense Council (NRDC). 40 West 20th Street, New York, NY 10011. (212) 727-1773. Http://www.nrdc.org. NRDC uses law, science, and the support of more than 40,000 members nationwide to protect the environment. Impressive website covers many topics, and information is accessible in many ways, including articles by topic, bulletins, guides, background information (sorted alphabetically by subject), frequently asked questions, facts, scrapbooks, and the journal *e-Amicus*. Their Air/Energy Program focuses on clean air standards, global warming, transportation, energy efficiency, renewable energy, and electric-industry restructuring.

Northeast States for Coordinated Air Use Management (NESCAUM). 129 Portland Street, Suite 501, Boston MA 02114. (617) 367-8540. Http://www.Nescaum. org. A quasi-governmental regional leader in air quality management involving eight northeastern states. Sponsors air quality training programs, participates in national debates, assists in exchange of information, and promotes research initiatives. Discusses recent activities in state agencies, reviews new policies, and explores recent developments in control technologies. Air report library has many articles, and maps and data section has helpful ozone information.

South Coast Air Quality Management District (AQMD). 21865 E. Copley Drive, Diamond Bar, CA 91765. (909) 396-2000. Http://www.aqmd.gov. AQMD is the air pollution control agency for the four-county region that includes Los Angeles and Orange counties and parts of Riverside and San Bernardino counties in California and is responsible for controlling emissions from stationary sources of air pollution. Although a regional organization, its website has a lot of information that addresses air quality issues.

State and Territorial Air Pollution Program Administrators (STAPPA)/Association of Local Air Pollution Control Officials (ALAPCO). 444 N. Capitol Street, NW, Suite 307, Washington, DC 20001. (202) 408-9260. Http://www.4cleanair.org. These two national associations representing air pollution control agencies encourage the exchange of information among air pollution control officials, enhance communication and cooperation among federal, state, and local regulatory agencies, and promote good management of air resources. Website includes links sorted by air-related agencies/organizations or air pollution topics.

U.S. Environmental Protection Agency (EPA), Office of Air Quality Planning & Standards (OAQPS). Mail Drop 10, Research Triangle Park, NC 27711. (919) 541-5616. Http://www.epa.gov/oar/oaqps. The hub of EPA's air pollution programs under the Clean Air Act. Directs national efforts to meet air quality goals, particularly for smog, air toxics, carbon monoxide, lead, particulate matter (soot and dust), sulfur dioxide, and nitrogen dioxide. Responsible for more than half of the guidance documents, regulations, and regulatory activities required by the Clean Air Act Amendments of 1990. Website has a plethora of information on air quality, and it links directly to and shares some of the same air quality information with the EPA Office of Air and Radiation website.

Washington State Department of Ecology Air Quality Program. PO Box 47600, Olympia, WA 98504-7600. (360) 407-7169. Http://www.wa.gov/ECOLOGY/air/airhome.html. Good example of a state air quality agency. Thorough website includes information on agricultural burning, wood stoves, and vehicle emissions checks.

See also the Resources sections in other chapters for publications on environmental advocacy, education, and business. Many of these publications cover air quality along with other environmental issues.

8 Solid Waste Management

AT A GLANCE

Employment:

More than 250,000 positions nationwide

Demand:

2 to 5 percent annual average

Breakdown:

Public sector, 40 percent

Private sector, 50 percent

Nonprofit sector, 10 percent

Key Job Titles:

Chemist

Civil engineer

Community relations specialist

Economist

Environmental engineer

Environmental technician

Hydrogeologist

Hydrologist

Landfill manager

Logistics/Operations manager

Market developer

Mechanical engineer

Planner

Product designer

Recycling coordinator

Solid waste department manager
Transportation planner

Influential Organizations:
Air and Waste Management Association
Association of State and Territorial Solid Waste
  Management Officials
Environmental Defense Fund
Environmental Industry Associations
Institute of Scrap Recycling
National Recycling Coalition
National Solid Wastes Management Association
Natural Resources Defense Council
Solid Waste Association of North America
U.S. Environmental Protection Agency
U.S. Occupational Safety and Health
  Administration
Waste Equipment Technology Association

Salary:
Entry-level salaries are as low as $22,000 to over $40,000 annually. A 1997 salary survey of engineers, scientists, and managers in *Environmental Protection* magazine revealed average salaries across all sectors of $50,000 for people with six to ten years of experience. The director of a major metropolitan solid waste utility earns between $80,000 and $100,000 annually. There are also many hourly wage positions in the $10 to $12 range.

Solid waste management is the second-largest employer of environmental workers, after water quality. After rapid growth in the 1980s, the field has undergone fundamental change in the 1990s, creating uncertain employment trends. Solid waste concerns in government and industry are being consolidated into overall hazardous, solid, and waste emission programs. The nation's concern over dwindling landfill areas has given way to a glut of new space, driven largely by new federal landfill regulations and economies of scale. A flurry of new waste-to-energy incinerator construction has subsided, largely because of public opposition to the facilities and the inability of incineration companies to produce consistent waste flows for economic viability. Finally, recycling has taken off, diverting nearly a third of America's waste from landfills and incinerators.

WHAT IS SOLID WASTE MANAGEMENT?

Solid waste management, as defined by Allen Blakey of the Environmental Industry Associations, is the use of proven, effective tools to reduce the volume and toxicity of solid wastes and manage the recycling and disposal of what remains, in an environmentally sound fashion. The field has a waste disposal hierarchy that favors source reduction over recycling, and recycling over land-filling or incinerating garbage.

Each method creates different kinds of environmental employment oppor-tunities.

SOURCE REDUCTION

The best way to manage waste is to prevent its creation in the first place. For example, packaging can be reduced or eliminated. Products can be designed to be taken apart and reused instead of trashed. Source reduction also refers to reducing the toxicity of materials before they enter the waste stream. Source reduction is becoming an employment growth area as entrepreneurs and designers focus on how to redesign products and processes to reduce the need for solid waste disposal.

RECYCLING

The growth of recycling is a great American success story, and a great en-vironmental employment generator. In 1970, there were only two curbside recycling programs in the country. Today, there are more than 7,000. Paper, glass, plastics, and metals are the materials most often recycled.

Americans are now recycling 27 percent of our wastes, and that amount is expected to grow by 1 percent a year, according to the U.S. Environmental Protection Agency (EPA). Recycling also includes the growing practice of composting, one of the most popular areas in the waste management picture.

Recycling is not without its problems, however. The practice is growing more difficult to sustain as fewer wastes remain that have great potential as recyclables. In addition, American desire to purchase items made from recy-cled wastes has not kept pace with our willingness to recycle.

Finally, it's interesting to note that, while recycling is growing, the United States lags far behind other nations. We are fifteenth in paper recycling among the twenty most industrialized nations and nineteenth in glass recycling. Ninety-six percent of U.S. plastics goes into landfills, and 50 percent of our paper.

COMBUSTION

Combustion of wastes for energy production, also called waste-to-energy incineration or resource recovery, is an offspring of the age-old practice of simply burning wastes. This newer form of incineration now manages about 16 percent of America's wastes, but the EPA does not expect it to grow.

LANDFILLS

Landfills are still the eventual end point for most solid wastes, handling 57 percent of our garbage. The nature of those landfills is changing. Hundreds of older, smaller "dumps" are being shut down and wastes are being sent to newer, larger landfills that are more rigorously designed to protect the environment.

Siting landfills remains difficult, however. (See Issues and Trends, later in this chapter) and the combination of remaining older landfills with newer ones has resulted in a glut of space. This drives down "tipping" fees and makes investments riskier. Ironically, as the cost of landfilling drops and technology reduces negative environmental impacts, sending garbage to the landfill once again becomes an attractive option.

HISTORY AND BACKGROUND

As long as human beings have been around, we have been dealing with solid waste. Archaeological digs show lots of bones, stone tool chips, pottery shards, and other debris, sometimes in concentrated points around early human settlements. The first written records of a dump date back to at least 500 B.C. in ancient Greece, and dumps have been springing up across the landscape ever since.

Open-air dumps, coupled with trash burning, were the preferred methods of waste disposal for centuries. As cities grew, crude incineration became a larger part of waste management efforts, converting mounds of wastes into clouds of smoke. These methods came to a halt in this country with the enforcement of new federal clean air regulations in the late 1960s. Chicago, for example, was forced to close three of its four incinerators, requiring the city to reorganize its disposal methods.

Landfills were the next answer, and the shift was rapid. In 1960, when crude incinerators were still used, landfills received 62 percent of all municipal solid waste. By 1980, the drop in incineration drove the total to 81 percent. In 1988, development of cleaner waste-to-energy incinerators brought the landfill portion of the total waste stream back down to 73 percent. Now, it's 57 percent and still dropping.

Landfills have had serious problems. Many landfills built before 1970 did little but shift pollutants from the air to the water table. Leaking landfills became hazardous waste disasters, with dangerous chemicals leaching into wells, lakes, streams, and rivers. Staten Island's ominously named Fresh Kills landfill once leaked as much as four million gallons a day. Of the over 30,000 most serious hazardous waste sites in the nation, many are former landfills.

The landfills were also overflowing. This problem was graphically illustrated in 1987, when the infamous *Mobroi*, a barge laden with trash from Islip, New York, set sail in search of a port in which to dump its load and generate methane gas to sell to power companies. The barge was turned away at every port—it was eventually even chased away by the Mexican Navy—and it became a symbol for environmentalists seeking to drive home the point that the "out-of-sight, out-of-mind" approach to waste disposal was history.

Meanwhile, the new waste-to-energy incinerators that came on the scene in the late 1980s, and that were thought to be the answer to those leaking land-fills, ran into trouble of their own. Their high cost—often in the hundreds of millions of dollars each—required incinerator companies to strike deals with neighboring towns and cities to guarantee that their wastes would go to the incinerators and nowhere else. These "flow-control" deals were barred by the U.S. Supreme Court in 1994.

Incinerators were facing mounting public opposition anyway, as fears of dioxins, heavy metals (such as mercury, cadmium, and lead), and other conta-minants in the stack emissions and ash residues caused concern. Siting ash land-fills grew difficult. As popular support for recycling grew, wastes were being diverted from the incinerators to "materials recovery facilities" (MRFs), threat-ening the financial survival of incinerators.

Virtually no waste-to-energy incinerators are being built in America today, Blakey and others say. Over the last few years, since the EPA established new regulations for landfill design in 1991, the nation has settled into a less con-tentious, but still problematic, mix of solutions to manage waste.

Looking back at the history of solid waste management over the last decade, "the messages have changed a bit," says Blakey, who sees career opportunities opening up for everyone from innovative design specialists who can devise new ways of manufacturing products so they are easier to recycle, to efficiency experts who can come up with new ways of collecting those recyclables.

The bleak crisis of the late 1980s and early 1990s has given way to a calmer, brighter period, during which the basic methods of "integrated waste manage-ment"—landfilling, recycling, and incineration—are settling into established patterns, revealing some good news to report.

In the EPA's most recent overview of the nation's solid waste management picture, ("Characterization of Municipal Solid Waste in the United States," 1996), the agency found that the generation of solid wastes dropped from 209 million tons in 1994 to 208 million tons in 1995. Americans were also indi-vidually generating less wastes—4.3 pounds per person per day in 1995, down from 4.4 pounds per person per day in 1994. We are also throwing away less—only 3.2 pounds per person per day in 1995, down from 3.3 pounds per per-son per day in 1994.

Recycling had grown to recover 27 percent of the waste in 1995 (56 million tons, up from 25 percent in 1994), with over 7,000 curbside recycling pro-grams, 9,000 drop-off centers, and 300 materials recovery facilities up and run-ning in 1995.

While paper and paperboard recovery hit 40 percent in 1995, accounting for over half of all the wastes recovered, recovery of yard trimmings soared to 9 million tons, accounting for 30 percent of the wastes recovered, the second-largest fraction of all wastes recovered. The percentage of yard trimmings com-posted has doubled since 1992.

The 57 percent of our nation's waste managed by landfills in 1995 was down from 60 percent in 1994, while the total sent to incinerators (16 percent in 1995) was up 1 percent over the previous year.

In terms of the immediate future, the EPA projected that per capita generation of wastes should hold steady through 2000, as any increases in generation will be offset by source reduction. The agency also projected that yard trimmings will continue to be diverted from the waste stream, as backyard composting spreads, and as more municipalities ban trimmings from landfills. Generation rates for paper, paperboard, plastics, and wood are expected to increase faster than population growth through 2010, while rates for glass, metals, and food wastes are expected to grow at about the same rate as population, the agency believes.

Americans are expected to produce more wastes overall—222 million tons by 2000 and 253 million tons by 2010, the EPA projects, with containers and packaging expected to account for more than a third of the wastes. But recycling is also expected to grow to perhaps as high as 35 percent of the wastes in 2000 and 40 percent in 2010, the agency believes. Incineration should hold steady at 16 percent by 2000 and 15 percent by 2010. And landfilling is expected to remain the majority disposal option through 2010, says the EPA.

"Right now what's going on is that incineration has stayed relatively constant for the last decade, and the percentage of materials being landfilled has gone down commensurate with the increase in materials being recycled," says Bob Dellinger, director of the EPA's Municipal and Industrial Waste Division.

"Recycling continues to rise," Dellinger adds. "We've set a goal to establish markets that will maintain that trend, so we can reach 35 percent by 2005. We haven't seen anything yet to make us feel that this trend line will not continue."

The federal law that governs solid waste management in America is the *Resource Conservation and Recovery Act* (RCRA). Enacted by Congress in 1976, and most recently reauthorized in 1984, the law's goals are to protect human health and the environment from the potential threats of waste disposal, to conserve energy and natural resources, to reduce how much waste is generated, and to ensure that wastes are managed in an environmentally sound fashion.

Rules that established more stringent landfill design requirements under RCRA were issued in 1991 and became effective in 1993.

ISSUES AND TRENDS

Rapid, and sometimes revolutionary, change has been a familiar part of the solid waste scene for the last few years. Professionals and entrepreneurs must stay on top of shifting issues and trends, such as those described below.

DESIGN FOR THE ENVIRONMENT

Although there are many issues and trends facing the professionals who deal with solid waste once it is generated (see the discussion that follows), it's generally agreed that the real action lies on the source reduction side. Within that broad category, "design for the environment" is popular.

Just about any product or service can be redesigned with the goal of reducing waste or environmental impact. Computers and other machines, office products, consumer goods, automobiles, homes, and construction materials are just a few of the more obvious examples.

"Design for the environment" is nothing less than the unmaking of the "throwaway" culture and offers well-paid opportunities for a wide variety of engineering and design professionals. Look for more information about this field on the EPA website (see the Resources section toward the end of this chapter).

SITING NEW LANDFILLS

There were roughly 6,000 U.S. landfills in 1990. As smaller, older, more polluting landfills have been closed and/or replaced, the total number of landfills has nearly been cut in half to 3,100. This is great progress.

Continuing this trend may prove difficult in the coming years, as siting landfills faces stiff opposition. No one wants to live next to a landfill. Old methods, such as placing dumps in poorer neighborhoods, are out of the question. The growing environmental justice movement has provided powerful evidence that people of color and low income communities are disproportionately burdened in the siting of these facilities. Grassroots organizations have sprung up to stop what are suspected as racist practices.

People with legal, planning, transportation, management, community relations, mediation, and related skills are needed to create agreements on siting facilities when they are necessary. Such professionals work on all sides of the siting question, at activist groups, government agencies, consulting firms, and private companies.

INTEGRATED WASTE MANAGEMENT

Thirty years ago, "waste management" meant getting garbage to the dump and the incinerator. Sophisticated management was not needed. Today's professionals face a much more difficult task. Leaders at solid waste utilities are asked to simultaneously reduce overall waste production at thousands of businesses and households; collect, sort, separate, and sell an ever-growing number of recyclables; assure that toxic materials are kept out of the waste stream; and bury or burn the rest without damage to our land, air, and water. If the organization performing this task is a private business, two crucial jobs are added. You must make a tidy profit, and stay ahead of your competitors.

To meet the task, the solid waste field has developed a need for sophisticated business planning and operations professionals to integrate reduction, recycling, and disposal operations into a unified system. Today's professionals are constantly assessing how dozens of variables affect one another. What does a reduction in tipping fees at the landfill mean for recycling efforts of marginally priced materials? Should we invest in new environmental improvements at the existing landfill? Shut it down? Start a new one elsewhere? Can we cut costs in the garbage collection department by making the routes more efficient? Should we merge with a firm offering resource recovery services? What about the new state mandate that raises our recycling goal to 40 percent?

More importantly, the solid waste management field continues to merge with hazardous waste management to create a single field with a unified profession. As waste volumes decline and both fields mature, the workforces will grow together. This has already happened at many corporations and municipalities. Be prepared to manage a complete waste stream.

Landfill Technology and Operations

As we have seen, landfills continue to handle 57 percent of our waste. We have also seen that strict regulation requires landfills to handle thousands of tons of garbage without polluting air, land, or water. These requirements create employment opportunities for people who can design, build, and operate high-technology systems. Professionals must create cost-effective designs and technologies that seal landfills top and bottom, gather and treat leachates and air emissions, and carefully monitor an array of variables. The trend is for still greater environmental control within tight budgets.

Toxic Materials

Chapter 9 discusses professionals who deal with hazardous materials and wastes. Clearly, however, there is a large amount of integration with solid waste management work. Simply put, solid waste professionals look for ways to keep regulated and/or toxic materials out of the solid waste stream.

Look for continued growth in community hazardous waste days and other segregated collection methods, strict regulation on toxic materials used by business and government, pollution prevention services to help users find non-toxic substitutes for the worst offenders, and other innovations. Solid waste professionals must keep toxic materials out of the system because of the high financial and regulatory cost of dealing with them.

Sludge Management

When municipal and industrial sewage plants have done their work, the water they produce is clean enough to discharge into rivers, bays, and lakes. Left behind, however, is a new solid waste—sludge. If heavy metals, toxic chemicals, and other hazardous materials exist in high enough concentrations, sludge can become an official hazardous waste. Where should we dispose of it, and how? Water quality planners are working with solid waste professionals to find solutions. In a sign of how complex these problems can be, one of the proposed solutions—processing sludge into fertilizer for sale to farmers and others—has created immense controversies, with heavy metals turning up on lands "fertilized" by the sludge, generating lawsuits and citizen action.

COMPOSTING

Nearly a quarter of all solid waste is organic matter, such as yard clippings and food waste. Rather than dumping this material in landfills or burning it, innovative solid waste managers are developing community composting programs. In many states and municipalities, laws are being passed that actually prevent or limit yard waste from being landfilled or incinerated, creating a whole new population of backyard composters. These programs are becoming a bigger part of solid waste strategies, and successful professionals will devise systems to make them even more effective.

RECYCLING

As we have seen, recycling has been a national solid waste success story, soaring from a fledgling start to account for 27 percent of the nation's waste stream. The EPA thinks it can go as high as 40 percent by 2010. There is *a lot* of work to be done, however, and many of the easy tasks are completed. In terms of job creation, recycling creates far more jobs per ton of waste than any other option.

What are the trends here? New markets for recyclables must be developed, which will depend on new uses not just for materials now being recycled, but materials not yet being recycled. Products must be completely redesigned, so that they will be easier to recycle at the end of their useful lives. New, more efficient ways of collecting recyclables must be devised to make it easier for people to participate. Continued improvements in separation technologies are needed to reduce recycling costs. And people must continue to be educated about the value and integrity of recycled products, so those products are purchased.

Government policy makes all the difference in pushing recycling forward. Recycling advocates such as Allen Hershkowitz at the Natural Resources Defense Council point to several ways that government can help, including:

- Pass a national recycling act. Germany and Japan have such laws, and it's no accident that they are world leaders in recycling.
- Remove subsidies for using virgin materials. Hershkowitz notes that the petroleum industry, for example, receives government tax breaks and subsidies, creating de facto support for using virgin plastic instead of recycling.
- Force manufacturers to accept responsibility for the disposal cost of their products. Germany and other nations have experimented with "polluter pays" regulation, which has increased the number of products sold with minimum packaging and the number of products that are designed to be taken apart and recycled instead of trashed.

• Require that government agencies buy products made from recycled stock.
  Anything that helps spur the marketplace is for the good.

Market developers, product designers, process engineers, efficiency experts,
materials scientists, outreach coordinators, and others will need to join forces
with the civil engineers, government regulators, and others traditionally
involved in recycling to make recommendations such as Hershkowitz's become
a reality.

CAREER OPPORTUNITIES

Although growth rates have slowed due to reduced waste streams, corporate
mergers, and a maturing profession, the solid waste field remains large and
diverse, with thousands of career opportunities.

PUBLIC SECTOR

Public sector jobs in waste management account for 40 percent of total jobs in
the field. The majority of government positions are at the local and state level.
Although a small employer, the federal government plays an important role in
agenda setting, as discussed in the section that follows.

Federal Government. Although there has been some hiring in the last few years
at the EPA's Office of Solid Waste and Emergency Response (the federal government's principal office for solid waste management), a significant number of
new hires is unlikely, says Bob Dellinger of the U.S. EPA.

"I don't think this is a growth area at the EPA, because we're finishing up
most of the work Congress asked us to do," Dellinger explains. "It's not like
we've been given a new statute and have 100 new regulations to get out. It's
more a case now of tweaking the system."

The agency is overseeing the transition from smaller, older, more polluting
landfills to larger, newer, safer ones, as prescribed by design criteria issued
under RCRA in 1991. It is also adopting more of a research role, possibly creating more job opportunities on that front. "We're positioned to do research
once at the federal level, as opposed to seeing it done fifty times at the state
level, and so we're working with state and local governments to find out what
their information needs are, and then deliver those needs to them at [a] considerably lower cost than if they had to do it on their own," Dellinger says.

The most promising career opportunity at the EPA may be more economic
than environmental. "The major thrust in our agency and our division is in the
area of market development," Dellinger says. "We're trying to create markets
for recycled materials, and are working with state economic development agencies to make them aware that recycling businesses and companies are a viable
industry. In essence, we're trying to marry the environment with business
development, and we've been fairly successful."

One example of this effort is an EPA program called Jobs Through Recycling, which was launched four years ago. The program offers $1.5 million in matching grants to help spur markets. Expect federal government opportunities at EPA and elsewhere to focus on programs such as these.

State Government. States are extremely active in legislation and planning for solid waste management and offer some of the most exciting opportunities for environmental professionals.

Many state governments are engaged in some form of statewide solid waste planning, including mandated levels of recycling and requirements for local solid waste management plans, usually with a mandated focus on recycling. The number of curbside programs would be much smaller if not for state action. Many states also operate regional siting authorities, require recycling of beverage containers through bottle deposit laws, restrict wastes coming into the state, and work to stimulate new markets for recyclables.

Municipal landfills are often a state concern. Many states set environmental criteria for landfills, specifying what materials can and cannot be placed in them. Fully half of the states have special regulations on the disposal of incinerator ash. With the 1991 EPA minimum standards for landfill siting, design, construction, and closure now well underway, states are aggressively pushing the transition to safer landfills. This will generate new state needs for sanitary landfill experts who can work with stringent requirements.

The Association of State and Territorial Solid Waste Management Officials, one of the country's top groups of state solid waste officials, is working on many fronts to help state agencies, illustrating the challenges those agencies currently face. The group has formed five task forces focusing on managing nonhazardous industrial waste, dealing with lead-based paints and other "municipal D" waste issues, developing "beneficial uses" for wastes, reducing the toxicity and volume of such "special" wastes as incinerator ash, and providing greater opportunities for training and technology transfers.

As evident in those challenges, state positions in solid waste management will continue to include planners, communications and education specialists, lobbyists, program managers, recycling experts, enforcement personnel, hydrologists, geologists, materials specialists, engineers, planners, and generalists.

Local Government. Solid waste management is inherently local. "Trash service is mostly dealt with by local governments, as in essence they make the decisions on how trash services will be provided," says the EPA's Dellinger. "So in terms of trend lines, that's really the cutting edge," he says.

To get an idea of how many local solid waste positions there are, remember that there are over 19,000 municipal governments, 3,000 county governments, and 16,656 towns and townships in the United States. Thousands of them have responsibility for solid waste and those that don't have farmed out the duty to a private company or created one of the country's 31,000 "special districts."

It is in the residential subdivisions, shopping malls, and industrial parks that waste is collected and separated, and then either recycled, landfilled, or incinerated. However, for many municipalities, contracting these services out to private firms is the preferred way to go because it holds down local government employment and related long-term costs.

Local government is usually the home of the recycling coordinator, a rapidly changing position. Eileen Zubrowski, recycling coordinator for the city of Waltham, Massachusetts, notes that many small towns are served by regional recycling coordinators who serve a collection of townships. She knows of one coordinator who serves twenty-five communities. This career is particularly appealing to environmental generalists because it can be entered from many different educational backgrounds. There is still a need for people who design and manage recycling programs, find markets for collected goods, educate the public, and push to keep ever higher levels of waste out of the landfills.

Finally, local government bears the brunt of most landfill and incinerator siting battles and must handle landfill closures as well. These activities may be handled as much by the planning and legal departments as by the solid waste department.

Depending on the size of the population served and whether privatized contracting is done, the solid waste department may be very small or quite large. In many municipalities, there may be no solid waste department at all. Solid waste may be incorporated into public utilities departments with other duties. In any city, however, professional planners, coordinators, educators, and managers *and* waste pickup, landfill management, and combustion operation staff can be found at some combination of public agencies and private firms.

Local government is an excellent place to start your environmental career in general, and this is even more true when it comes to solid waste management.

PRIVATE SECTOR

The solid waste business occupies a huge portion of the national environmental industry. According to the 1997 Annual Industry Overview of the *Environmental Business Journal,* solid waste activities collectively dominate the $181-billion environmental industry, with $33.9 billion spent on solid waste management services, $12 billion on waste management equipment, and $14.3 billion on resource recovery activities.

The business has traditionally hired a wide range of people, from plant operators, laborers, truck drivers, technicians, and others, to engineers, regulatory compliance specialists, lawyers, environmental scientists, and community relations staff members.

But the face of the business is changing. Amid the glut in landfill space, declining tipping fees, growth in recycling, and a "dead" waste-to-energy incineration industry (as the *Environmental Business Journal* [*EBJ*] put it) major companies are consolidating.

"There's definitely a huge wave of consolidation in the waste industry right now," says Blakey of the Environmental Industry Associations. "What's driving this is that the industry has experienced flat growth, the amount of garbage has declined, and expansions internationally have not worked out as well as expected. As a result, acquisitions and takeovers are growing."

There are other reasons, as well, for the consolidation of the solid waste business around fewer and fewer companies, although financial pressures are part of all of them. Environmental regulations place the cost of a modern, environmentally safe landfill beyond the means of the small family businesses that once dominated waste disposal. Small businesses are being replaced by companies that can make the investments in plant and equipment now required by law. Insurance liabilities for hazardous wastes in landfills have created financial and legal barriers that only a well-heeled company can overcome. Finally, communities are requiring comprehensive services from their solid waste vendors, and the cost in staff, benefits, and financing is more than many smaller outfits can afford.

The consolidation of the solid waste industry has resulted in the creation of a few giant companies, led by Waste Management, Browning-Ferris Industries, Republic, Allied Waste, and Norcal. Together, these five companies employ over 100,000 people and operate a large percentage of the nation's landfills, incinerators, waste-to-energy plants, materials recovery facilities, transfer stations, and recycling operations. Industry leader Waste Management, Inc. (with Waste Management International, and Wheelabrator Technology) employs over 50,000 people at hundreds of sites on earnings of $9.2 billion annually and continues to merge with others at a rapid pace. In 1998, the firm completed a merger with former third-largest company USA Waste ($2.6 billion in 1997 revenues), to create an even larger industry giant at the top of the heap.

The September 1998 edition of *Waste Age* magazine carries a listing of the top 100 companies in the waste business and is a valuable resource for aspiring solid waste professionals.

"I don't want to say we're a shrinking industry," Blakey says. "The future will still require more specialists in landfill design, leachate control, and other areas. [The Occupational Safety and Health Administration] has just come out with new standards for MRFs, and they will change operations in a lot of places, because now you have to consider what sort of dangers are presented by conveyor belts, that sort of thing, so there will be a need for more safety engineers."

Jim Keefe, group publisher of *Recycling Today*, agrees that new jobs are still on the horizon. Waste industry giants that traditionally collected and dumped waste, and then ventured a few years ago into recycling as well, are now going back to their roots, seeking to sell off their recycling investments because of the ever fluctuating recycling markets, and the difficulty of actually manufacturing a new product, rather than simply hauling and dumping wastes. For innovative entrepreneurs, the split between the haulers and recyclers may mean opportunities to access the recycling industry, he says.

"There are definitely jobs," Keefe says. "I see them in these growth companies, these MRF operating companies, for instance. These companies will continue to grow and produce opportunities on the operations side for low and no skill labor, basically picking stations jobs, but also for plant managers."

Keefe also believes there will be opportunities in "progressive companies finding new uses for recycled materials." One company he cites, FCR, Inc., of Charlotte, North Carolina, has invested in cellulose insulation made from recycled paper. Another company, American Tire Recyclers, Inc., of Jacksonville, Florida, shreds tires and mixes them with soil, resulting in a product that can be used in sports facilities to better cushion impacts, Keefe says. A third company, KirkWorks of Durham, North Carolina, coordinates regional recycling investment forums, bringing together recycling start-up companies with venture capitalists.

Even consolidation holds some promise, Keefe says, as many of the smaller companies being acquired are family businesses going back generations, "and in a family owned business, if you were not in the family, you could not get a job." As corporations typically have no such restriction, "that's changing," says Keefe.

Private-sector waste management also includes consulting firms that design and build landfills and incinerators, assist communities in the design of waste strategies, and help private companies run their own waste management programs. This sector of the environmental industry has generally declined since the early 1990s, but a slight surge is expected by 2000, by which time the current $15.2 billion sector is expected to grow to $15.8 billion, according to *EBJ*. Of that sector, consulting and engineering services in solid waste in 1997 totaled $1.1 billion, *EBJ* says.

Nonprofit Sector

Nonprofit groups employ the fewest solid waste management workers of the three sectors, accounting for less than 15 percent, if that. These groups are involved in solid waste management in three ways: as providers of recycling services, as advocates for new legislation to reduce waste and improve recycling, and as activists to restrict the siting of landfills and incinerators or ensure their safety. A steadily emerging involvement is focused on environmental justice, working to ensure that poor and minority communities do not fall victim to a disproportionate number of waste facilities.

Small, nonprofit, community recycling programs have been a mainstay in recycling until recently, when local governments and private industry began to take over the field. In many communities, recycling remains a community initiative, however, often run by volunteers or activists who have provided the service because government would not.

Local, state, and national advocacy groups have pushed government at all levels into bottle deposit legislation, statewide solid waste planning, packaging limitations, community composting programs, mandatory recycling goals, and other innovations. Through lobbying, initiative petitions, and public education, organizations such as the public interest research groups have helped raise the standard of success each time a new benchmark is achieved.

Finally, nearly every proposed siting of a landfill or incinerator has sparked the creation of a local group to fight back. Often working with more established state and national groups, these groups (often unstaffed and unincorporated) have been successful in many cases.

Solid waste management professionals in the nonprofit sector include lobbyists, planners, environmental scientists, lawyers, fund-raisers, public education specialists, and recycling service providers, such as truck drivers and collection and separation technicians.

SALARY

Recycling coordinators start at around $30,000 annually in medium-sized cities and go up to $40,000. Salaries for the position title that includes recycling coordinators at the city of Seattle start at $40,000 and top out at $46,760. A 1997 salary survey of scientists, engineers, and managers in *Environmental Protection* magazine showed that average salaries in solid waste management were highest at municipal landfills ($66,250) and lowest at other related government agencies ($47,232). Consultant pay averaged $55,000 annually and those in manufacturing and at utility companies averaged $55,000 and $62,000, respectively. One particular bright spot of the solid waste field is that there were many high school graduates earning up to $50,000 per year. Finally, keep in mind that laborers at recycling facilities are often hourly workers. Wages can start in the low to mid-20s.

GETTING STARTED

The field of solid waste management is still evolving, and so entrance requirements are not clear cut. Although specific fields of study will lend credibility to the newcomer and ease the pathway to a new job, failure to have the "right" degree will not prevent an interested person from getting into solid waste management. Hands-on experience, enthusiasm, and an ability to get things done are just as important.

EDUCATION

Degree programs in integrated waste management, with classes in source reduction, recycling, hazardous waste issues, composting, "waste-to-energy" incineration, sanitary landfill design and operations, operations, and transportation, and regulatory issues do exist at some colleges. Some people we talked with suggested that future professionals seek out such specialized training.

Most, however, were happy to report that people come to the field of solid waste management from every conceivable background, and that practical experience and a desire to succeed were the main criteria.

Still, some fields are more in demand than others. Civil, environmental, mechanical, and electrical engineers are needed, as are environmental scientists in hydrology, hydrogeology, earth science, chemistry, and toxicology.

Because private-sector solid waste management is an extremely competitive business with tight profit margins, people with business administration, operations, logistics, marketing, sales, and finance backgrounds are all in demand. Good planning and scheduling skills, supplemented by high-tech tools, are crucial.

Experience, however, continues to drive professional success. Summer jobs, internships, or even taking a leave from school to put in some serious job time are recommended. This is a profession that is learned in the field.

ADVICE

Additional advice and tips to those starting careers in solid waste management include the following:

Be a realist. "Young people tend to be idealistic environmentalists, which is fine," says *Recycling Today's* Jim Keefe. "Remember, however that this is primarily a business. That's why postconsumer recycling ran into trouble. It's great to be in the field for environmental reasons, but it has to be economically viable."

Look to high tech opportunities. "There's a lot of garbage, and it still needs to be picked up and properly managed," says Allen Blakey of the Environmental Industry Associations. "Yes it's still a pretty low tech industry. But there are a lot of interesting high tech things we're doing with solid waste, particularly in the area of consumer product responsibility, where products are designed so they're easier to recycle."

Think creatively about solid waste management. "In the area of resource conservation and new businesses, there are a lot of entrepreneurs out there thinking about how to reuse materials to make products," said the EPA's Bob Dellinger. "That's going to be a trend. There will be more and more expertise needed in the area of reutilizing materials, and there will be a lot of technology innovation going on."

Learn from the more advanced, help the less advanced. As in any field, solid waste management has a few superstar agencies and companies where people are lining up to apply for jobs. Instead of seeking work at already successful places, consider mastering the principles of their success and offering your services to help less successful employers catch up. There are still thousands of towns that would love to improve recycling rates, launch a household hazardous waste day, or decrease landfill pollution. There's a lot of work to be done below the cutting edge.

Keep pushing recycling rates up. "I believe that if there isn't a continual effort to promote recycling, it will decline," says Eileen Zubrowski. "People need that push."

SUMMARY

After a decade of change and uncertainty, solid waste management is stabilizing somewhat into a predictable mix of disposal solutions, with state-of-the-art landfills and innovative recycling programs leading the way. As the roller coaster of change has subsided, complex challenges are beginning to emerge that will require the most creative, innovative work yet done in this field.

The next decade will require work as scientific as it is political, as technological as it is economic. The need for further innovation is everywhere, from building better landfills, to collecting recyclables, to designing products, to changing consumer lifestyles and perceptions. The days of the dump are long gone. Those hoping to succeed in this arena will have to be more diversely talented than ever before.

CASE STUDY

Reducing waste through voluntary action in New Hampshire

Reducing solid waste doesn't have to involve lots of regulation, loads of professionals, and high costs. Good ideas, a lot of passion, and a willingness to volunteer can accomplish a lot, as this case study of WasteCap in New Hampshire demonstrates. A time comes, however, when low-cost volunteer solutions reach their limits.

Barbara Bernstein has spent a lot of time thinking about waste—where it comes from, where it goes, and how to reduce, reuse, and recycle more of it. Her story goes back to her days at the University of Massachusetts at Amherst, where she earned a bachelor's degree in environmental design in 1983 and master's degrees in business administration and regional planning in 1987.

"I did my master's project on ways that government could help small generators of hazardous waste. One of my professors thought it was going to be the dullest project he ever read. That was my first introduction to this."

By "this," Bernstein was referring to WasteCap of New Hampshire, a program created in 1991 to help New Hampshire's business community reduce, reuse, and recycle its waste, and help the state achieve its goal of diverting 40 percent of its waste stream in those ways by the year 2000. Similar programs are up and running in Vermont, Maine, Massachusetts, Missouri, Wisconsin, and Pennsylvania, but New Hampshire's was among the first.

For Bernstein, who came to WasteCap of New Hampshire in 1995 after working in various waste management positions in Florida and Vermont, her experience has been an education in just what companies are willing to do, and not willing to do, to save money and the environment by cleaning up their acts.

By most measures, WasteCap has been a success, capitalizing on New Hampshire's strong sense of volunteerism and aversion to government involvement. In 1997 alone, WasteCap worked with nearly 400 businesses in the state to divert four tons of trash a day from the waste stream. Those businesses include some of the state's largest companies, colleges and universities, hospitals, and others. All this, with only two full-time staff members (Bernstein is one of them) and twenty volunteers.

Now that a basic "reduce, reuse, and recycle" infrastructure is in place with little cash needed, the question is whether WasteCap can take New Hampshire's business community to another level by persuading it to make the capital investments necessary to further divert wastes, Bernstein says.

"In many cases, the resistance of upper-level managers has always been there, but until recently, waste reduction, reuse, and recycling have been really easy. We have done a lot without capital commitment," Bernstein says. "I mean, what does it take to put out a dumpster for cardboard? If that cuts your waste disposal bill by 50 percent, why not support it? When it comes to making capital investments that will truly make a difference, they don't seem as interested."

At this point, Bernstein says, "what we feel we need to do, first and foremost, is support our environmental managers out there and help them develop the kinds of programs that will get the attention of upper-level managers, so we don't just have reduction, reuse, and recycling programs, but others, as well."

WasteCap is actually a program of programs, nine to be exact, that offer diverse assistance to the business community. Those programs include: conducting site visits; providing hot-line technical assistance; operating a materials exchange; publishing a newsletter; developing new waste tracking software; recognizing outstanding WasteCap members; producing an annual report; coordinating business recycling consortia; and holding workshops and conferences on waste reduction. Based on its 1997 WasteWatch 2000 report, Bernstein and her twenty-one colleagues have been very busy people. They have:

- Made twenty-one site visits to companies across the state, advising them on how to expand existing recycling programs and reduce packaging. One success story is Cirtronics, Inc., of Milford, which devised a new packaging system relying on corrugated plastic boxes. Customers return them when they are empty, thus eliminating a lot of shipping waste. After a short payback period, the company expects to cut its packaging costs in half.
- Handled 161 hot-line technical assistance calls since April alone.
- Signed up 88 new companies for materials exchange, and tracked at least 26 exchanges, in one case generating $30,000. The program went on-line in 1996, thanks to a $10,000 grant from the American Plastics Council, better enabling WasteCap to publicize materials exchange opportunities.
- Put *WasteNotes* onto its website, http://www.wastecapnh.org, and created links to other waste exchanges and recycling organizations.
- Launched a Waste (NOT!) Challenge program in June 1996, to recognize significant waste reduction efforts among companies based on content, policy, and communication.
- Developed two business recycling consortium projects across the state, one in Londonderry and the other in Manchester, two of the state's largest cities. Developed as well a plastics packaging business recycling consortium,

which was created to specifically recycle plastics produced in manufacturing circuit boards and involves four manufacturers who are recycling thirteen tons of plastics a month. Ongoing programs in two other large cities, Nashua and Keene, continued to expand and evolve.

- Helped coordinate waste reduction conferences and workshops across the state.

"Since the start of WasteCap in 1991, our program has grown in many different directions," Bernstein says. "But the crux of it is still there, that sense of volunteerism, that sense that we don't need government to tell us what to do. We can do this without government, and if it's the right thing to do, we'll do it."

Some of the bottom line corporate savings are especially impressive. For instance, HADCO Corp., a circuit board manufacturer with facilities in three New Hampshire cities and others in New York and California, has been saving $23,000 a year on disposal costs by recycling and reducing waste, WasteCap reports. The savings have also been innovative. For instance, when K.W. Thompson Tool Company decided it needed a new roof at its facility, it recycled its old one, made of aluminum, for $2,000, offsetting the cost of the new roof.

Reducing, reusing, and recycling wastes works for New Hampshire companies "because it's good business," Bernstein says.

It also works because WasteCap provides its assistance with a good dose of confidentiality, putting at ease companies that may fear they will get into trouble with government agencies if legal or regulatory violations turn up, Bernstein says. "It's a huge benefit to our program, not being a government agency. Even programs within government agencies that grant confidentiality still have that stigma. They're just too close to government. And so a lot of businesses still call me to get assistance." If a WasteCap site visit does turn up a violation, Bernstein says she advises the company "off the record" to deal with it. It has not happened often—only three times in the last three years, she says—and the companies have generally dealt with the problems.

The challenges to continued success are predictable. Markets for recyclables remain scarce and unsteady, frustrating companies that were initially making money in diverting their wastes, but may now be paying to do the same. Many companies also produce small quantities of recyclables, leaving them with the choice of paying a lot more to have them transported for recycling than they would pay if they had more to recycle, or storing the wastes on-site until they amass in quantities large enough to make transport profitable. And on-site storage can be a problem for small companies strained on space.

Many companies lack the staff and resources to develop and run recycling programs, especially at the initial stages, when start-up costs and time can be steep. Also, some wastes such as circuit boards and plastic-lined paper bags are difficult to recycle because they are made with two or more materials, each of which may be recyclable, but taken together, are not. And separating those materials can be tough. Hazardous wastes remain difficult to recycle.

But perhaps the biggest obstacle to WasteCap's continued success is "the green wall"—resistance from upper-level corporate managers who are willing to reduce, reuse, and recycle wastes as long as they can profit by it, or at least break even or not pay out much, but who are less willing when major investments are needed, Bernstein says.

"We have all these environmental managers with all these great things they want to do, but those things may not be what upper management wants to do. We once did a survey of companies where we had done site visits, and we found that a number of companies did nothing with the information we gave them. In 100 percent of those cases, they did nothing not because the information was not good, but because there wasn't any upper-level support," Berstein says.

Yet while Bernstein believes WasteCap, and business community recycling generally in New Hampshire, are at a "pivotal" point, it is also clear to her that "businesses are working in broader ways to be environmental. For me, one of the tremendous things about doing this job is that I have yet to find someone who has put in some sort of system to protect the environment who has not benefited by it. And so I've seen the philosophy grow that if you run your company in a way that cares for the environment, you will have a better company. WasteCap planted the first seeds for this in New Hampshire, and they have grown since."

PROFILES

Paul Koziar
Former Manager of the Waste Tire Program
State of Wisconsin Department of Natural Resources
Madison, Wisconsin

Managing difficult solid waste problems offers an opportunity for creativity, both in policy design and in technical solutions. But beware of the urge for perfect solutions. They are not always possible, and it is the role of managers to find that work.

Paul Koziar is very proud of the fact that after more than a decade of working in an innovative position at the Wisconsin Department of Natural Resources (WDNR), he is out of a job. He is still with WDNR, "but I really don't know what my current position is," he jokes.

That is because Koziar and his staff accomplished the unusual in American environmentalism; government, industry, or nonprofit. They actually solved the problem they were assigned to solve. As director of WDNR's waste tire program since 1987, Koziar oversaw a bold, unusual—and yes, controversial—effort to get rid of the twenty million used tires that had been stockpiled around the state, creating an enormous fire and pest hazard.

Tire piles abound nationwide. While sitting there, they create remarkably abundant habitats for mosquitoes and other insects, some of which may transport diseases. Once engulfed in flames, they pose a serious toxic threat, as heavy metals such as cadmium and lead, as well as other dangerous components of the tires, are released into the air. The fires are also virtually impossible to extinguish.

Faced with a crisis, the Wisconsin state legislature passed a law in 1987 that gave the WDNR the authority and money to deal with the state's tire problem, which was only worsening. Besides the stockpiled twenty million tires, some five million more were being generated each year, roughly one tire per state resident.

No state, then or now, wants to enact new taxes, and Wisconsin was no different. So instead, it did what a lot of states do—impose a fee. In this case, anyone who bought a new car in the state between 1988 and 1997 was assessed a one-time-only fee of $2.00 for every tire on the vehicle, or $10.00 total per car (including the spare). The state generated $2.75 million a year to deal with its tire problem in a way that was virtually unnoticeable to tax-paying residents.

Since the state's car registration process was already in place, "it was easy creating another line on the registration form for the fee, and it was easy from a political standpoint," Koziar says. "Paying ten more dollars when you're buying a new car for $15,000 or $20,000 is not huge."

The legislature did not tell the WDNR exactly how to spend the money. It only told the WDNR to solve the problem. But it did set up a direct rebate program for the money, mirrored on a program developed in Oregon in 1985. Basically, if you used waste tires for an environmentally sound purpose, you could be directly rebated with money from the $2.75 million generated each year.

"It wasn't a case where government was deciding to give a grant to a specific company or individual for a specific disposal process or idea," says Koziar. "It was simply the case where government said if you do what we've asked you to do—use the tires for an environmentally sound purpose—the state will provide a direct rebate to you." The rebate was spread over six years. Once the money was in place in the first year, it was up to those companies and individuals to step up with those "environmentally sound purposes."

"We leveled the playing field, and told everyone—Okay, the state will provide the money, now go out there and do the best you can," Koziar says.

Here is where controversy set in. The tires got burned, not in raging uncontrolled fires, but in waste-to-energy incinerators. The WDNR did everything it could to cultivate many different disposal solutions, but in the end, incineration rose to the fore as the sole one. Others, from rubberized asphalt to tire recycling, were not feasible, says Koziar.

"Because of the volume of the tires we had and the disposal problem it posed, as well as the lack of markets for tire recycling, I had to accept the fact that the way we had to deal with this problem was not the preferred alternative," Koziar says. But it did work. As of June 30, 1997, only a few thousand of the twenty million tires remained, and all of the newly generated tires were being dealt with, thanks to incineration, which remains Wisconsin's tire disposal method of choice.

The problem? To some environmentalists, burning tires in an incinerator results in roughly the same threats as burning them in an open field. And so the state had its critics, and still does. But to Koziar, an imperfect solution is better than no solution at all. "We certainly dealt with the question of environmental harm these stockpiled tires around the state raised. And we've created the infrastructure to collect and process additional tires," he says.

"But somewhere along the line you have to look at the reality of what you can do, and make progress along that line," Koziar adds. "I think a lot of states don't do that. They want to recycle it all, for instance. It's great to try to achieve perfection. But if perfection sidetracks you, and you don't deal with the problem, then that's not what you're in government for."

James Warner
Director of the Groundwater and Solid
Waste Division
State of Minnesota Pollution Control Agency
Minneapolis, Minnesota

There are initiatives afoot that will change the face of environmental management. Agencies are reorganizing and consolidating to deal with multimedia approaches in a multidisciplinary way. The outlines of future environmental protection agencies are beginning to emerge.

While James Warner has been a state environmental official for more than two decades, his last two years have been especially interesting, as he has participated in a sweeping, innovative effort to restructure the Minnesota Pollution Control Agency (MPCA) to reflect a new age of environmental protection.

When that restructuring takes hold, the result will be one "that you probably won't find anywhere else in the country," Warner says.

Like many state environmental agencies, MPCA has been structured along the lines of environmental "media," with separate divisions to regulate air, water, and waste. MPCA took an innovative step in the late 1980s, when it combined groundwater and solid waste regulation into one division, reflecting "a conscious decision that groundwater was most closely related to, and impacted by, solid waste and hazardous waste, and so that threat was what we needed to address," Warner says. Still, the agency was pretty much like those in other states.

But GOAL 21, the MPCA's restructuring plan launched in 1996 and expected to be fully implemented by late 1998, has made that innovation look traditional by comparison. It mirrors restructuring efforts underway in other state agencies, as well as at federal agencies such as the EPA, in the end dictating not just a new way of thinking about environmental regulation and protection, but a new array of environmental career opportunities in government.

MPCA is being overhauled top to bottom. The media divisions will be replaced by six new divisions, reflecting a shift from media-based regulation to geographic and multimedia-based regulation. Three of the new divisions will be geographically based in the state's northern, southern, and Minneapolis/St. Paul metropolitan regions, better enabling the agency to localize its efforts. The three other divisions will be more multimedia, focused on administrative services, policy and planning, and "environmental outcomes," says Warner.

"I think it's a precursor for state environmental agencies nationwide. When I talk with the EPA and other states, they see what we're doing as a test ground for moving out of a programmatic approach, and into a multimedia approach," Warner says.

Underlying the restructuring is the concept of GOAL 21, an acronym whose terms signify a new, "systems thinking" approach to environmental regulation that is about as far removed from the traditional "command and control" model as can be imagined.

"G" stands for "shared goals," the notion that environmental problems are now so complex that agencies can no longer simply impose expectations on the regulated community, but must instead build a consensus with that community on what those expectations must be. For instance, with problems such as nonpoint source pollution involving so wide an array of sources and contaminants, "clearly the sort of command and control regulatory approach will not be successful in so nontraditional an area," Warner says.

"O" stands for "environmental outcomes," stressing the idea that actual, measurable improvements in the environment should be the barometer of an agency's effectiveness and not bureaucratic processes toward such improvements. "We've been measuring our success in outputs—fines we collect, permits we issue—but the bottom line should instead be what is the environment doing, how are our efforts having a positive effect on the environment? We want to shift from being an output-based agency to an outcome-based agency," says Warner.

"A" stands for "situational alliances," the view that any agency can only do so much, and that taking environmental regulation to a higher level requires reaching out to the regulated community for its support. "For us, it means we don't always have to be in the lead," Warner says. "I think, viewed from the outside of the agency, we've developed a certain arrogance. But what we've really come to understand is that we have to leverage more people, we have to get to 4.5 million Minnesotans if we want to protect the environment."

"L" stands for "learning organization," the idea that the agency must continue to "expand its capacity to seek and embrace new ideas and change for the future," as the GOAL 21 plan states. Doing so will only enhance its ability to achieve its three other objectives—shared goals, environmental outcomes, and situational alliances. "It's a definite move to establish a culture of learning, where you don't blame others for mistakes or errors, where you learn how to take risks, and where you make decisions," says Warner.

Environmental protection in state government is a different world from the one Warner came to in the 1970s, fresh with a 1971 undergraduate degree in civil engineering from Long Beach State College, a few years of experience at the National Oceanic and Atmospheric Administration, and a 1976 master's degree in environmental engineering from the University of Minnesota. But that was then, and this is now, a time when he and the MPCA "are looking to how we can do environmental protection in the future," he says.

Eileen O. Zubrowski
Recycling Coordinator
City of Waltham Department of Public Works
Waltham, Massachusetts

Managing trash may not be the sexiest environmental career, but it is one where the results of your efforts are quantifiable in tons and one that clearly makes a difference for the earth.

Eileen Zubrowski began her environmental career with the city of Waltham nearly thirty years after she received her bachelor's degree in English literature. She had several different careers, but after twenty years as a psychotherapist in private practice she felt a strong urge to do environmental work. She was already involved with the education and outreach programs of MassRecycle (a statewide membership organization) and was on the recycling committee in her town. But Eileen wanted to do more than just work for the environment in her spare time.

She applied for environmental jobs that appealed to her, but this approach to changing careers wasn't working. So in 1990 she began a master's degree in environmental studies at Antioch New England College while continuing her therapy practice. She focused her studies on solid waste management, but gained a broad perspective of environmental challenges.

Upon graduation in 1993, Eileen was hired almost immediately by the city of Waltham. The position was created through the efforts of a citizen's group called the Waltham Recycling Committee, but the city only funded a part-time salary when Eileen was hired. She says: "I did pretty much what I do now except I did it faster. I nearly killed myself trying to get everything done in half the time."

Eileen worked part time for three years, still counseling to make up the rest of her income before she was able to get full-time funding for her position. She did this by developing a position paper. Once she developed a good argument, she presented her case to the mayor and City Council and in 1996 became a full-time recycling coordinator. Eileen says that creating your own opportunities is a big part of working in the environmental field.

Eileen is responsible for all public education and outreach efforts and says: "That's a big part of this job, to get the word out and encourage participation . . . [I also try to] develop the program by increasing [recycled] tonnage, [tracking] the economics of it, and [making] a case to the city for existing programs and new programs. . . . [O]ver and over I have to make the case for the city that not only is recycling environmentally safer but it's good economics as well. Being a recycling coordinator is selling, selling, selling to the community and city government." In addition, Eileen goes to conferences and seminars around the state where she learns about criteria for grant programs and connects with other recycling coordinators to share ideas about programs that are working as well as ones that aren't. She also spends a portion of her time pursuing federal and state grants to fund recycling programs.

To meet state grant requirements, Eileen implemented a "buy recycled" policy for all municipal building purchasing. She is currently working on two major projects: Waltham's annual Earth Day celebration and a regional residential Hazardous Waste Collection program, which Waltham is undertaking along with eight other communities. The details of a recent day provide a taste of Eileen's work.

Eileen begins work at 8:30 A.M. with a call to the Waltham Conservation Commission agent, who she is working with to produce Earth Day. Next she goes over a bill from Browning Ferris Industries (BFI), who the city contracts to pick up trash, yard waste, and recyclable materials at curbside. This bill is the first one for a new program to recycle fluorescent light bulbs and other hazardous waste from municipal buildings. The next order of business is to call a school nurse who requested information about how to make schools more responsible in the safe handling of hazardous wastes. Then she calls the Building Department to reserve the Government Center building for a Saturday meeting for the Hazardous Waste Committee. Next she calls the person in the Engineering Department responsible for the city's annual report. They worked on a report contrasting the profit from the recycling program with the "staggering costs of trash disposal." Then she talks to the public works assistant to secure funding for bins needed for the municipal building paper recycling program. Finally, she prepares for the Hazardous Waste Committee meeting, calls the coordinator to submit some agenda items, and talks about the latest setback—a change in siting of the storage center for hazardous waste.

Clearly the job of a recycling coordinator involves a lot of administrative detail. Eileen says: "Sometimes I really get weary with it, but I try to remind myself that implementing any kind of environmental program comes down to sticking with it. . . . [I]f I don't address the details, the programs don't happen." The weariness doesn't last long. Eileen is endlessly intrigued by the workings of municipal government and seeing, up close, how the whole democratic process works. Another thing she likes about her job is initiating new programs: "I also try to keep in mind the ultimate goal, which is environmental protection. I'm a rabid environmentalist in disguise. I try to keep a cool profile around here, but that's mainly what motivates me."

RESOURCES

Most of the resources below have extensive Internet links to other organizations, companies, and information on recycling and solid waste management. Major companies such as Waste Management, Browning Ferris, Republic,

Allied Waste, and Norcal provide current job listings. For more resources, see chapter 9, which includes some references that intersect with this chapter.

Air and Waste Management Association. Nonprofit international professional organization that aims to strengthen the environmental profession, expand scientific and technological responses to environmental concerns, and assist professionals in critical environmental decision making. Provides training, information, and networking opportunities through a series of conferences, workshops, and courses to help keep members up to date on new developments in the profession. Website has section on employment. Publications include *Journal of the Air & Waste Management Association* and *EM, a Magazine for Environmental Managers* (both monthly). One Gateway Center, Third Floor, Pittsburgh, PA 15222. (412) 232-3444. Http://www.awma.org.

Amazing Environmental Organization WebDirectory. "Earth's biggest environmental search engine." Includes information on solid waste management (click on pollution, then waste management). Also don't miss the employment section on the WebDirectory homepage that provides links to job listings, descriptions, and agencies specifically concerned with environmental employment. Http://www. webdirectory.com.

American Waste Digest. National monthly magazine for the solid waste and recycling industries. 226 King Street, Pottstown, PA 19464. (800) 442-4215. Http://www. americanwastedigest.com.

Association of State and Territorial Solid Waste Management Officials. Membership organization whose mission is to enhance and promote effective waste management programs and effect national waste management policies. Focuses on the needs of state hazardous waste programs; nonhazardous municipal solid waste and industrial waste programs; recycling, waste minimization, and reduction programs; Superfund and state cleanup programs; waste management and cleanup activities at federal facilities; and underground storage tank and leaking underground storage tank programs. Website has useful links to state and federal solid waste agency websites. 444 North Capitol St., NW, Suite 315, Washington, DC 20001. (202) 624-5828. Http://www.astswmo.org.

Biocycle: The Journal of Composting & Recycling. Leading magazine on composting and recycling. Shows how to launch and expand composting and organics recycling programs and offers cost-cutting ideas. Gives timely reports, accurate data, project results, and analyses of emerging trends for waste management professionals. (800) 661-4905. Http://www.jgpress.com.

CCHW Center for Health, Environment, and Justice (formerly Citizens Clearinghouse for Hazardous Wastes). National environmental organization whose mission is to give people the technical information and training they need to fight for their right to a clean and healthy environment, to hold industry and government accountable, and to work toward a healthy and environmentally sustainable future. Works with grassroots community groups on environmental issues such as toxic waste, solid waste, air pollution, incinerators, medical waste, radioactive waste, pesticides, sewage, and industrial pollution. Has over 100 guidebooks and information packages on topics from hazardous waste to environmental racism. Publishes *Everyone's Backyard* (quarterly). 150 S. Washington, Suite 300, Falls Church, VA 22040. (703) 237-2249. Http://www.essential.org/cchw.

The Journal of Solid Waste Technology and Management. An international peer-reviewed quarterly journal. Covers municipal solid waste management and technology subjects. Published by the National Center for Resource Management and Technology at the University of Pennsylvania and the Widener University School of Engineering. Sponsors the International Conference on Solid Waste and Technology Management. Dept. of Civil Engineering, Widener University, One University Place, Chester, PA 19013-5792. (610) 499-4042. Http://www.widener.edu.

National Pollution Prevention Center for Higher Education (NPPC). Created by the U.S. Environmental Protection Agency to collect, develop, and disseminate educational materials on pollution prevention (P2) for university professors. The NPPC is housed at the University of Michigan. NPPC offers an internship program, professional education and training, and conferences. It also publishes the *Directory of Pollution Prevention in Higher Education: Faculty and Programs* ($20). Website has good links to other P2 sites. Dana Building, University of Michigan, 430 E. University, Ann Arbor, MI 48109-1115. (734) 764-1412. Http://www.umich. edu/~nppcpub/.

National Pollution Prevention Roundtable. Membership organization devoted solely to pollution prevention (P2). Their mission is to provide a national forum for promoting the development, implementation, and evaluation of efforts to avoid, eliminate, or reduce waste generated to air, land, and water. Website has job listings, provides access to industry experts via the Internet, publishes a list of listservers related to P2, information about conferences, and access to legislation concerning P2. 2000 P Street, NW, Suite 708, Washington, DC 20036. (202) 466-P2P2. Http://www.p2.org.

National Solid Wastes Management Association. Membership organization representing 1,700 businesses in all 50 states that seeks to advance the safe and environmentally protective management of nonhazardous and hazardous wastes through the private waste services industry. Member services include state lobbying, federal representation, industry information, research and analysis, education and training, networking opportunities, and more. Part of the Environmental Industry Associations (EIA). The EIA Research and Education Foundation provides grants for research and educational projects in waste management trends and environmental protection. EIA sponsors the WasteExpo conference annually. 4301 Connecticut Avenue, NW, Suite 300, Washington, DC 20008. (202) 244-4700. Http://www.envasns.org/nswma.

Natural Resources Defense Council. National environmental organization whose programs include an urban program that focuses on garbage and recycling in major urban centers. 40 West 20th St., New York, NY 10011. (212) 727-1773. Http://www.nrdc.org.

Occupational Health and Safety Administration (OSHA). A key federal agency regulating health and safety standards for those whose work brings them in contact with solid waste. Part of the U.S. Department of Labor. 200 Constitution Ave., NW, Washington, DC 20210. (202) 219-8151. Http://www.osha.gov.

Solid Waste Association of North America. Nonprofit education organization dedicated to providing municipal solid waste professionals with the most current information and training materials on issues impacting the municipal solid waste management field. 1100 Wayne Avenue, Suite 200, Silver Spring, MD 20910. (301) 585-2898. Http://www.swana.org.

Solid Waste On-line. Website with loads of information about solid waste management. Offers case studies, the latest news and analysis with articles on issues such as brownfields cleanup, job listings, and much more. Http://www.solidwasteonline.com.

U.S. Environmental Protection Agency (EPA), Office of Solid Waste and Emergency Response. Federal agency that develops guidelines and standards for the land disposal of hazardous wastes and for underground storage tanks. Offers technical assistance in the development, management, and operation of solid waste activities and analyzes the recovery of useful energy from solid waste. The EPA has a comprehensive website with a wealth of searchable articles. Check out their Office of Pollution Prevention and Toxics site at http://www.epa.gov/p2/home. USEPA Waterside Mall (5101), Washington, DC 20460. (703) 308-8254. Http://www.epa.gov/oswer.

9 Hazardous Waste Management

AT A GLANCE

Employment:
Over 150,000 employed, including remediation projects

Demand:
2 to 5 percent annual growth

Breakdown:
Public sector, 22 percent
Private sector, 77 percent
Nonprofit sector, 1 percent

Key Job Titles:
Biologist
Chemical engineer
Chemist
Civil engineer
Emergency response staff
Environmental attorney
Environmental economist
Environmental engineer
Environmental health specialist
Environmental planner
Environmental policy specialist
Geologist
Geophysicist
Geotechnical engineer
Hazardous materials specialist

Hazardous waste engineer
Hazardous waste technician
Hydrogeologist
Industrial hygienist
Pollution prevention coordinator
Process engineer
Project manager
Radioactive waste engineer
Risk analyst

Influential Organizations:

Air and Waste Management Association
American Chemical Society
Association of State and Territorial Solid Waste
    Management Officials
Center for Health, Environment, and Justice
Earthjustice Legal Defense Fund
Environmental Defense Fund
Environmental Industry Associations
National Pollution Prevention Center for Higher
    Education
National Pollution Prevention Roundtable
Natural Resources Defense Council
U.S. Environmental Protection Agency, Office of Solid
    Waste and Emergency Response

Salary:

Starting salaries vary widely. Hazardous waste engineers start from $28,000
to $35,000 and can rise quickly. Technicians are paid $19,000 to $25,000,
and can become chemists ($25,000 to $35,000) and supervisors ($32,000
to 42,000). Compliance specialists might earn $30,000 to $40,000.
Government pollution prevention specialists providing technical assistance
start at around $30,000 and rise to around $45,000 or higher. For experienced technical personnel, expect salaries of $45,000 to $70,000. For more
senior managers, companies pay over $75,000 to $100,000 and higher.

A few years ago, hazardous waste management was touted as the fastest-growing career field in the environmental world. And why not? Citizen concern
about toxic waste was clear, pushing the issue to the top of the environmental
agenda. More and more chemicals were being labeled as hazardous, requiring
special monitoring, storage, and disposal. In addition, thousands of toxic waste
sites were identified as needing expensive clean-up, including over 1,200 on the
national Superfund "priority" list. Billions were allocated to do the job. Finally,
the United States was far and away the world leader in the production of hazardous waste, generating *60 times* more hazardous waste in 1990 than we did
twenty years before.

More regulation, thousands of costly clean-ups, rising waste generation—all the traditional drivers were in place. The job creation potential seemed enormous. Estimates of the need for hazardous waste management professionals ranged as high as 18 percent annually and salaries were high.

Today, things are different. Only 300 Superfund sites have been cleaned up since 1980, although $40 billion has been spent, much of it in court. Efforts to change the Superfund law continue to be hotly debated and everyone agrees that major changes are needed. Important questions have been raised about the environmental benefit of toxic waste clean-ups relative to the cost, and not only from industry.

While we argued about *yesterday's* waste, a quiet decrease was happening in the use of toxics *today*. America is producing less hazardous waste than it used to. The EPA reports that hazardous waste generators produced 214 million tons in 1995, down from 258 millions tons in 1993. The number of treatment, storage, and disposal facilities (popular employment spots for hazardous waste professionals) actually declined. Regulation and pollution prevention was starting to work.

The combination of maturing management, legislative and funding indecision, and reduced generation completely altered the picture for hazardous waste employment. Firms consolidated or got out of the business. Technicians chose other specialties.

And then . . . brownfields redevelopment entered the picture. Brownfields are abandoned and contaminated industrial sites that are polluted enough to make them public health concerns (and liability risks for investors), but not serious enough to qualify for Superfund status. There are as many as 450,000 such sites in the nation.

The brownfields movement has quickly picked up steam, linking economic development with environmental restoration. Congress appropriated $200,000 for pilot projects in 1995 and a $2 billion tax incentive program in 1996 and approved a $300 million effort in 1997. Prominent investors and city governments have jumped in with multimillion dollar efforts.

Will brownfields projects result in a new boom for hazardous waste professionals? Will the generation of hazardous waste continue to drop, with or without pollution prevention efforts? Will politicians finally agree on a new Superfund law, creating demand for new clean-ups? These are important questions for the year 2000 and beyond.

WHAT IS HAZARDOUS WASTE MANAGEMENT?

We might start by asking, What are hazardous wastes? Hazardous wastes can range from the most toxic manufacturing by-products to used battery acid and household cleaning materials. The EPA defines a hazardous waste as any substance that is ignitable, corrosive, reactive, or toxic. This broad definition covers the hundreds of millions of tons of material produced annually.

Although hazardous wastes are produced everywhere, a few sources account for high percentages of the problem. The chemical industry accounts for roughly 60 percent of all industrial hazardous wastes, while metals and related industries such as electroplating and metal finishing contribute another 20 percent. Other sources include the military, especially on its own facilities, as well as the cumulative waste of millions of households and small businesses. Hazardous waste managers must find ways to deal with it all.

The following are key hazardous waste management activities. Together, these duties make up the bulk of all hazardous waste management work. Look at the list carefully. Eleven out of the thirteen involve careful management of today's hazardous wastes. Only two concern the clean-up and redevelopment of past sites.

- Finding alternatives to materials that will become hazardous wastes.
- Identifying and characterizing hazardous wastes.
- Permitting (requiring and issuing permits) to control production, transportation, treatment, and storage.
- Tracking to ensure safe waste handling.
- Disposing of hazardous wastes according to strict regulations.
- Monitoring disposal sites to ensure their safety.
- Reducing the use and toxicity of hazardous materials.
- Cleaning up hazardous spills and contaminated sites.
- Developing innovative treatment technologies.
- Assessing public health and ecological risks and impacts.
- Assessing waste disposal liability.
- Communicating with the public about the problem.
- Redeveloping waste sites.

HISTORY AND BACKGROUND

The concept of handling hazardous wastes carefully and disposing of them properly sounds like common sense today, but it is markedly at odds with our history. For decades, we were ignorant of the threats posed by our more dangerous wastes. Until recently, most industrial wastes were simply dumped where they were generated, often into a stream, pond, or lake or simply onto the ground. New England's waters are still recovering from hazardous wastes thoughtlessly dumped over two centuries. Individuals have followed suit, pouring motor oil, paint thinner, pesticides, and other wastes onto the ground and into storm drains.

Although hazardous wastes are now subject to legal disposal requirements that differentiate them from solid, or nonhazardous, wastes, these materials were commonly mixed with municipal solid wastes until just recently. Most older landfills contain large amounts of hazardous wastes along with plain old garbage. In some communities across the country, household products that qualify as hazardous wastes are *still* being disposed of with more innocuous trash.

Early environmental legislation may have contributed to the problem. Muc waste was diverted to landfills to avoid releasing it into the air or water becau: of pollution control requirements in the Clean Water and Clean Air Act Technologies developed to clean air and water produced unexpected new ha: ardous wastes: air pollution abatement devices such as scrubbers capture larg amounts of wastes; wastewater treatment plants produce hazardous sludge and municipal waste-to-energy incinerators produce significant volumes of as containing heavy metals, considered by some federal and state regulations to b hazardous. For years, these products of environmental protection went straigh to the landfill.

These dumps can leak hazardous wastes into groundwater and generat toxic airborne emissions, as well. And so the history of hazardous waste man agement until just a few years ago is a perfect example of the ecological she game of changing regulations that shift pollutants from one place to anothe without eliminating them. Dealing with the legacy of these dumps is a crucia task for hazardous waste professionals, and will remain so until they ar restored to ecological health.

Making today's disposal sites safe and reducing the generation of hazardou waste at the source, however, is where the action is in hazardous waste man agement. A massive effort is being made in the areas of waste minimization pollution prevention, technology innovation, toxicity reduction, waste reuse and others, which are all aimed at a simple goal—if the waste is not generatec in the first place, then there will be nothing to clean up. This has changed the career landscape dramatically.

"We've basically modified behavior," says Jim Berlow, director of the EPA's Hazardous Waste Minimization and Management Division.

"We're not given the authority to tell people what to do in their industrial processes," Berlow says. "But the more prudent businesses have realized that the best way to compliance is not just by putting a gizmo on the end of the pipe, but by not generating the waste to begin with."

Pollution prevention may be the best method of dealing with our hazardous waste problems, but as long as waste is generated, professionals must deal with it according to the law. Three major federal laws constitute the core of federal hazardous waste regulation.

RESOURCE CONSERVATION AND RECOVERY ACT (RCRA)

RCRA applies to current operations of private businesses and other hazardous waste generators. Passage of RCRA in 1976 signaled the federal government's entry into the business of regulating solid and hazardous wastes. RCRA estab- lishes a "cradle-to-grave" system for tracking and permitting hazardous wastes from their point of origin to their disposal time and location—and thirty years beyond.

The Hazardous and Solid Waste amendments of 1984 greatly amended RCRA. Changes include the following:

- A several-fold increase in the number of hazardous waste generators under regulation.
- A schedule to ban land disposal of hazardous chemicals.
- Encouragement of source reduction efforts.
- Development of a process for classifying wastes.
- Formulation of regulations involving underground storage tanks.

If a contest were held for the most controversial of all federal environmental laws, RCRA would likely win. Its sweeping provisions labeled more than 360 million tons of wastes hazardous and brought anyone who produced more than 100 pounds of such wastes a month under regulation. Dry cleaners, photo development shops, auto repair outfits, and other small businesses are examples.

More important, RCRA has proven difficult to comply with, even for environmental professionals who want to if only to avoid fines or imprisonment. The catch is that under RCRA, hazardous wastes must be properly treated and disposed of. That means treatment, storage, and disposal facilities—or TSDs—must be available on site or close enough so the waste can be safely transported. But these facilities can be difficult to develop, and no one wants a hazardous waste disposal facility anywhere near his or her neighborhood.

The EPA reported in its 1997 National Biennial RCRA Hazardous Waste Report that in 1995, 1,983 TSDs managed 208 million tons of hazardous waste. That represented a decrease on two fronts since 1993—yes, 27 million tons less waste, but also 601 fewer TSDs.

The EPA and state leaders have recognized the problem, and have been working hard in the last four years to "streamline" RCRA permitting, making it faster and more efficient, flexible, and effective in meeting the bottom line: safely managing wastes. "Folks are doing whatever they can to lower the regulatory barriers to getting things done as soon as possible," says the EPA's Berlow.

Still, the need to comply with and enforce RCRA virtually created the hazardous waste profession. Anyone interested in this field will need to get acquainted with its provisions as the very first step.

COMPREHENSIVE ENVIRONMENTAL RESPONSE, COMPENSATION, AND LIABILITY ACT (CERCLA)

Hardly anyone calls this law by its full name. Most know it by the large amount of money it authorized to fulfill its mission—Superfund. While RCRA regulates the ways in which existing businesses dispose of hazardous waste, Superfund is aimed at cleaning up abandoned, inoperative, contaminated sites.

Most agree that the original CERCLA legislation of 1980 was woefully inadequate, considering the scope of the contamination problem. In response, Congress passed the Superfund Amendments and Reauthorization Act of 1986

(SARA), reauthorizing Superfund for another five years, as well as including provisions for the following:

- Expanding and strengthening the clean-up program.
- Increasing the Superfund Trust Fund from $1.6 billion for the first five years to $8.5 billion for the second.
- Establishing a new trust fund to clean up leaking underground petroleum storage tanks.
- Requiring disclosure of hazardous waste sites under community and worker "right-to-know" regulations.

By general agreement, Superfund has not yet been particularly effective in cleaning up contaminated sites. As of February 1998, there were 1,191 sites on the National Priority List. Thousands more were on their way to being listed until many of them were reclassified as "brownfield" sites by the Clinton administration.

But only a handful of sites, Superfund and brownfield, have actually been cleaned up. Congress has been working to reauthorize CERCLA for years, and under pressure from Republicans especially, Clinton has sought to make dramatic changes in the law that may speed up cleanups while lowering costs. The EPA and the Clinton administration have already adopted some of the changes into existing regulations, but oppose others, arguing those changes will gut Superfund at the expense of public health and the environment.

Regardless of what happens to it, Superfund remains a promising career venue. For instance, as more of an effort is placed on cleaning sites with their potential use in mind, so that a site to be used as an industrial park need not be as clean as one for a day care center—a strategy endorsed by both sides in the Superfund debate—there will be an increasing need for experts in risk assessment. As efforts are made at some sites to contain contaminants rather than clean them up, there will be a need for more hydrogeologists and geophysicists. As less expensive, "passive" clean-up remedies are explored (like bioremediation and phytoremediation), plant physiologists and biologists will be needed.

Toxic Substances Control Act of 1976 (TOSCA)

TOSCA was designed to give regulators and the general public advance warning that manufacturers are considering commercial production of a substance that may be toxic. Manufacturers submit a notification to the government along with detailed data and must win approval before proceeding.

ISSUES AND TRENDS

Issues and trends in the hazardous waste management field are divided between those that engage the attention of remediation workers on old sites, and those that involve the prevention, treatment, and disposal of today's wastes.

SITE REMEDIATION ISSUES AND TRENDS

Site remediation projects employ engineers, chemists, biologists, laborers, industrial hygienists, attorneys, planners, and more. Trends such as those discussed next are carefully watched by the consultants, engineering firms, and government agencies involved in clean-up projects.

Debate over Clean-up Standards and Liability. It is clear that there are hundreds of thousands of contaminated sites in the United States. They are abandoned factories, military bases, gas stations, landfills, and so forth. To restore them to full ecological health would cost hundreds of billions of dollars and guarantee employment for hazardous waste professionals throughout the next century. We've seen, however, that progress (and job creation) is slower than expected. Why? The answer is complex, but two issues are clear. First, there is disagreement over "how clean is clean?" Should a site that will be used for a new factory meet the same standards that a residential subdivision would require? The issue is an important one for generating employment. The standard selected can reduce (or increase) the price of a remediation job by millions of dollars. Failure to agree on a standard practically assures that no work will begin.

Second, there is disagreement over who bears future liability for a "cleaned-up" site. The discussion that follows illustrates how this issue affects the brownfields movement.

The Brownfields Movement. We have seen that there are as many as 450,000 brownfields (abandoned and contaminated properties that keep investment out of inner cities, but that are not polluted enough for Superfund status) in the United States. The Clinton administration has launched the Brownfields Partnership Initiative to redevelop these sites—a $300 million effort involving fifteen federal agencies and twenty-five other organizations. The effort represents a new direction for contaminated site clean-up, but is not without critics.

"EPA Administrator Browner has described this as an environmental victory, and we just don't see it that way," argues Stephen Lester, the science director at the Virginia-based Center for Health, Environment, and Justice, the group formerly known as the Citizens Clearinghouse for Hazardous Wastes.

Lester, and other activists, argue that efforts that release new property owners from long-term liability threaten future ecological and human health. Investors won't put up money without being released from liability. Communities won't allow redevelopment and new ownership without promises that contamination from the site won't cause problems in the future. Clearly, nothing will happen without political compromise.

Federal Sites. As the federal government moves to force hazardous waste clean-ups around the country, it is finding that some of the toughest clean-ups are on its own land. The Office of Technology Assessment estimates that 5,000 to 10,000 federal military bases and other sites need clean-ups that may cost as much as $250 billion. And the wastes continue to accumulate. It's been estimated that the military produces more hazardous waste than the top five U.S. chemical companies combined.

Military base clean-ups have also become vital to the economic well-being of many states. With the Cold War over, the military is downsizing. Communities see the bases as having extraordinary development potential as airports and industrial parks, but contamination is preventing such development.

Federal clean-up sites require professionals in all of the key job titles listed at the beginning of this chapter, and the need is growing.

Streamlining the Process. As noted earlier, the EPA and states are trying to speed up the process of cleaning Superfund sites, a process that now averages seven to ten years per site from listing to clean-up. The professionals required to achieve this goal must be as diverse as the complexities involved—engineers, biologists, chemists, risk assessment experts, attorneys, geologists, regulators, and others all play a role.

But it is not just Superfund that is being streamlined. All hazardous waste regulatory processes these days are being reviewed to see if there are faster, simpler ways of getting the job done while protecting public health and the environment.

One example is the "performance partnership agreement" effort underway between the EPA and states for the last three years. That effort spans all environmental issues, including hazardous waste. Rather than work independently of one another, EPA and state officials meet regularly to coordinate on the issues, avoiding duplicative actions that can slow clean-ups and other activities.

"We sit down and decide what we'll do, and what EPA will do, and so we're more efficient and oriented about the achievement of goals, rather than about points to check off on a list," says Philip O'Brien, a board member of the Northeast Waste Management Officials Association and Waste Management Division director at the New Hampshire state Department of Environmental Services.

New Technologies in Remediation. In spite of all the issues we've discussed, many sites do get cleaned up! To do the job, environmental professionals are constantly inventing new methods of removing toxics from the land. Some of the most exciting technologies involve phytoremediation—the use of plants to take up contaminants. Engineers and scientists will find opportunities at the EPA, in research labs, at major consulting firms, in industries with heavily contaminated sites (such as the petroleum business), and in academia.

WASTE MANAGEMENT ISSUES AND TRENDS

Although clean-ups are an important part of the hazardous waste management world, the lion's share of professionals are involved in the day-to-day work of preventing and processing today's wastes. Here are some of the trends facing these workers.

Strategic Environmental Management Approaches. We saw in solid waste management (chapter 8) that firms and municipalities are looking for greater levels of integration in their approach to waste, including hazardous waste. The trend is toward inclusive strategies that combine prevention, reuse, recycling, treatment, storage, and disposal of *all* waste and *all* emissions. Often called "strategic environmental management," the idea is to solve a wide variety of environmental problems through a carefully integrated set of actions. To position yourself for a management or consulting future in hazardous waste management, you will need to go well beyond *just* a focus on hazardous waste.

Fewer Treatment, Storage, and Disposal (TSD) Facilities—Industry Consolidation. We've seen that there were 601 fewer TSD facilities in 1995 than in 1993 (a total of 1,983) to handle 214 million tons of hazardous waste. Prevention, reuse, and recycling (as well as plant closures and operations that move overseas) are reducing total tonnage and the pressure is on for TSDs to survive in a market that is consolidating around a few large companies.

Still, there is a lot of hazardous waste out there and the industry has a solid core market. Hazardous waste companies are continually seeking new, more competitive methods of treating wastes, especially ones that can turn waste into useful products that can be sold.

Impact of "Right to Know" Laws. Tucked away in the Superfund Amendments and Reauthorization Act (SARA) of 1986 were provisions requiring users of hazardous materials and generators of hazardous waste to make information available to the public. The "right-to-know" law led to the creation of the national Toxics Release Inventory (TRI) and provides details of toxic use to emergency service providers such as fire departments.

The effect of these laws has been amazing. The act of providing detailed information on toxic emissions to activists, academics, the professional community, government officials, and the general public has arguably led to more pollution prevention efforts than anything else. The TRI makes possible "worst polluter" lists, beloved by activists and journalists, and despised by industry. More than one toxics reduction effort has begun so that a business can get off the list. More seriously, TRI data are used by activists to communicate the existence of toxic emissions to neighborhood residents, creating an urgency that can open dialogues with industry. The result of this dialogue can be "good neighbor" agreements to reduce toxic emissions. It can also be a heightened awareness of the complexities surrounding toxicity and public health. For the scientific community, the existence of annual data from the same sources about the same chemicals is essential.

Finally, the need to accurately track, record, and disseminate information about toxics has created employment for environmental professionals, database designers, and public affairs coordinators.

Pollution Prevention (P2) and Toxics Use Reduction. Pollution prevention is at the heart of hazardous waste management. The federal Pollution Prevention Act of 1990 mandates a focus on prevention first, and the U.S. EPA has set up a wide array of programs, including:

- *The Common Sense Initiative.* Seeks "cleaner, cheaper, smarter" production in six industries (printing, electronics, auto assembly, metal finishing, iron and steel, and petroleum refining).
- *Design for the Environment.* Promotes safer products and processes in dry cleaning, screen printing, and electronics.

State governments are also pursuing pollution prevention as a key approach to reducing hazardous waste. Over half of the states have passed pollution prevention legislation and budgeted funds. At least forty states have set up confidential, on-site technical centers for small and large businesses. Over thirty operate information clearinghouses and have some form of "facility planning" program to facilitate P2.

Most really big generators aren't waiting for government help, however. They are pursuing P2 on their own. Corporations such as 3M, Xerox, Ford, DuPont, and Monsanto are large polluters, but, they are also pursuing P2, and saving money.

Pollution prevention takes many forms, but the main ones are: toxics use reduction, raw material substitution, industrial process/equipment modification, product redesign, training for less wasteful operations, improved inventory control, production planning, and sequencing. Every one of these activities creates employment opportunities, mostly for engineers and scientists, but also for trainers, planners, and educators.

You can stay abreast of trends in P2, which change rapidly, through the website of the National Pollution Prevention Roundtable and the EPA Office of Pollution Prevention (see the Resources at the end of this chapter).

On a negative note, some argue that P2 is happening more in policy papers than it is in the field. Writing in the EPA report *Pollution Prevention 1997: A National Progress Report,* consultant Warren Muir contends that pollution prevention is far from a mainstream concept and is neither at the center of environmental regulatory reform nor a top priority for industrial decision makers. He goes so far as to say that P2 "has had no discernible impact on aggregate toxic chemical waste generation" and that the number of source reduction activities reported by industry has actually declined.

Household Hazardous Wastes. Every household uses hazardous wastes in quantities large enough to be a problem if the wastes are not disposed of properly. Local governments across the nation employ household hazardous waste coordinators to deal with the problem through education, disposal networks, collection days, and promotion of nontoxic household products. Household hazardous waste programs have become some of the most successful nationwide in dealing with everyday wastes that may not in any one home amount to much, but taken together pose significant threats.

Cross-Media Pollution. Efforts to eliminate hazardous waste are required to address the problems of "cross-over" pollutants. Incineration methods that avoid creating airborne toxic emissions, and land disposal methods that protect groundwater and surface water supplies, need further development. This will stimulate research in the private sector, at universities, and in federal agencies by toxicologists, chemists, hydrologists, and air pollution scientists. One of the hottest areas within this trend is dealing with mercury as an airborne toxic. The heavy metal is emitted through various industrial processes, including waste incineration. And it has become a pervasive threat to public health and the environment—as many as forty-three states have issued advisories warning people to limit their consumption of freshwater fish, because they contain elevated levels of mercury, which can cause an array of neurological and other health problems.

Abandoned mines throughout the West have left a trail of dumps, many with hazardous wastes that contaminate land and water.

Cooperation between the Sectors. The trend toward cooperation among diverse interests may be more a wish by practitioners than a social reality. However, many professionals in the field believe that the relatively ineffective and cumbersome system of hazardous waste management will become so infuriating that all parties will work together to create better solutions within the law. "The trend is toward compliance and assistance, and that certainly has implications for careers," says the New Hampshire DES's O'Brien.

Exporting Expertise. America is well ahead of most of the rest of the world in hazardous waste management. Consulting and engineering services and hazardous waste disposal companies are looking to expand their markets outside the country, and with good reason. Billions of dollars in the construction of new waste-to-energy incinerators, state-of-the-art landfills, and other facilities are now available in Third World and Eastern European countries, among others. As "joint implementation projects" grow (allowing companies to offset their environmental impacts here by improving the environment elsewhere), exporting expertise will only increase.

CAREER OPPORTUNITIES

The demand across all sectors of the hazardous waste management field is low to moderate. Current employment remains largely focused on the daily management of waste and clean up of approved sites. Brownfields redevelopment, pollution prevention, and innovations in technology represent rapidly emerging fields. A few types of professionals are common in the field. These include:

- Hazardous waste enforcement agents—Carry out inspections and review reports to assure that our hazardous materials regulations are being complied with.
- Hazardous materials and waste management technicians—Found at private companies and responsible for characterizing waste, preparing it for shipment, assuring regulatory compliance needs are met, and carrying out treatment, storage, and disposal procedures. Often have undergraduate training in chemistry, and may be called "chemist" or "environmental technician."
- Quality control and assurance professionals—Usually have chemistry backgrounds. They assure the accuracy of data and of overall waste management results.
- Chief chemist—Oversees waste management procedures and supervises people such as those listed above.
- Field samplers and field sampling supervisors—Gather water, soil, and air samples at identified/potential hazardous waste sites and at regulated businesses.
- Hazardous waste remediation engineers—Supervise field teams, prepare remediation strategies, manage remediation projects—Come from a variety of engineering backgrounds.
- Spill response scientists—Characterize the type and extent of spill problems and design workable solutions.

- Pollution prevention specialists—Work for government agencies and consultants providing information and advice to industry and government on P2 options.
- Toxicologists—Essential to the hazardous waste field. Provide expertise on the toxicity to humans and the environment of waste products at various concentrations.
- Process and industrial design engineers—Crucial for pollution prevention projects involving materials substitution, process changes, toxics use reduction, and so forth.
- Environmental attorneys and policy makers with experience in hazardous waste issues.
- Innovative technology experts—Design, evaluate, and implement emerging technologies.
- Economists and accountants—Determine the economic feasibility of clean-up and treatment options.
- Environmental activists—Assure that business and government are protecting the public interest and obeying the law and to promote innovative solutions to hazardous waste problems through legislation, education, research, and legal action.
- Trainer—Often provide required health and safety courses to hazardous waste workers.
- Information systems managers—Deal with the incredible volume of record keeping involved in purchasing, storing, using, transporting, treating, and monitoring hazardous waste under "right-to-know" laws and for other purposes.

PUBLIC SECTOR

Although the growth of hazardous waste management employment in the public sector has declined, a strong core of professionals is needed at all levels. The type of work performed, however, varies greatly from the policy makers at the federal level to the on-the-ground work performed by local governments.

Federal Government. Although the private sector dominates employment in the hazardous waste management field, federal legislation is the impetus behind regulation and clean-up activity. Each of the EPA's ten regional divisions administers and enforces Superfund, RCRA, and TOSCA regulations. As these three programs have expanded, so has the EPA staff charged with executing them. And after a brief hiring hiatus from 1995 to 1997, the EPA is once again expanding its staff.

"Right now we're going through a wave of hiring unlike anything we've had in ten years," says the EPA's Berlow. He notes that Congressional debate over the agency's budget froze hiring for several years, but that support for the EPA's work now seems strong. In addition, Berlow sees increases in new areas such as the common sense initiative, children's health initiatives, and brownfields.

Another current that is likely to open employment doors at the federal level is a surge in retirements already underway and likely to continue, Berlow says. "Retirement parties around here are a lot more common now than they were five or ten years ago."

While the EPA is the primary federal agency in the hazardous waste arena, it is not the only one. The Department of Energy (DOE) and the Department of Defense (DOD) are big players. DOE is spending billions to clean up sites contaminated by forty years of nuclear weapons production during the Cold War. The agency is also charged with finding a long-term repository for radioactive waste from both military and electric utility sources. The end of the Cold War has also produced the closure of dozens of military bases, many of them contaminated (see the discussion earlier under Issues and Trends).

The Brownfields Partnership Initiative brings in a new range of agencies, including the Department of Housing and Urban Development, Department of Transportation, Department of Interior, and others.

State Government. As regulatory responsibilities in hazardous waste management continue to "devolve" from the federal to the state governments, states are finding themselves in a tough spot. On the one hand, they want those responsibilities so they can better tailor clean-up remedies to local conditions and generally have more control over their implementation and completion. On the other hand, they lack the money to meet those responsibilities, many of which are legally binding. And so the need for new staffers is greater than the positions available to offer them.

"Generally speaking, states do not have the money to accept devolved responsibilities, and so there has to be a devolution of resources, too, not just responsibilities," said New Hampshire DES's O'Brien, who is familiar especially with the bind in the Northeast as a board member of the Northeast Waste Management Officials Association.

The states have plenty of hazardous waste work to do, and that work load is increasing. Under most scenarios of Superfund reform, for instance, responsibilities dramatically increase for the states. And the states already have many responsibilities, not the least of which are hazardous wastes sites of their own, listed as state hazardous waste sites rather than federal. For example, New Hampshire has 18 federal Superfund sites, but more than 100 state hazardous waste sites over and above the 18 federal ones. In urban states with industrial histories, the number will be several times higher.

"State hiring varies over time and is hard to predict," O'Brien says. "It's more a matter of replacing rather than adding staff here, and from what I've heard in discussions with other states around the country, our situation here is pretty much like the others. We're not expanding rapidly at the moment in hazardous waste management."

One area that might be bucking the trend is pollution prevention, as we saw in the P2 trend section earlier.

Local Government. All hazardous waste is generated and disposed of in some municipality or county. Thus, despite a complicated web of federal and state regulations, hazardous waste ultimately is a local issue. The result of this is increasing amounts of local activity and local awareness of hazardous waste issues.

Hazardous waste management jobs in local governments are located in many places. Fire departments, police and emergency response sections, planning departments, public health divisions, sewer and water outfits, and solid waste departments all can house hazardous waste professionals.

County governments are involved as well. Dozens of counties have supplemented the "right-to-know" provision of the Superfund Amendments and Reauthorization Act (SARA) with community right-to-know ordinances of their own that force the disclosure of hazardous waste locations. Counties have also created household hazardous waste collection programs, groundwater mapping projects, waste reduction assistance for area businesses, and emergency response teams to protect the community in the event of a hazardous waste accident.

In fact, handling spills and accidents is a major concern for hazardous waste professionals, with oil and chemical spills being by far the most common. There were 25,693 oil and chemical spills reported in 1997, 1,451 railroad-related spills, 170 "continuous releases," and 113 "generic incidents." These,

An intern working on environmental contamination projects at Department of Defense installations in Raleigh, North Carolina.

of course, were only those that were reported and responded to by industry or government professionals. Although this is an unacceptably large number, nearly all of these statistics represent a significant decline from previous years. Oil and chemical spills, for example, have fallen dramatically. In 1994, there were 31,378 spills, over 5,000 more than the 1997 total.

Hazardous waste professionals in local government tend to have health and safety backgrounds. Safety engineers, hazardous materials specialists, industrial hygienists, and those with similar backgrounds are in demand. And as local governments have tended to follow the lead of the states and federal government in pursuing pollution prevention programs, opportunities have emerged, from household hazardous waste clean-up coordinators to health department communicators who tour local schools speaking about the need to better manage everyday wastes.

PRIVATE SECTOR

Hazardous waste management is overwhelmingly a private sector affair. Industries either hire employees to manage company waste, or employ contractors from the hazardous waste management industry to do it for them. Likewise, the clean-up of toxic waste sites, and the development of brownfields, is generally carried out by private business. When we talk about the hazardous waste industry declining (as we will below), it's good to keep in mind that it still employs over 70 percent of a 150,000-person industry.

Hazardous waste professionals within regulated companies are usually found in the "EHS" (Environment, Health, and Safety) department. In the private environmental industry, some firms provide "full service," while others specialize in consulting, removal and disposal, small quantity or specialty waste, training programs, transportation of waste, operation of TSD facilities, emergency response, or site remediation.

The field has been hit hard. Declining quantities of waste to treat, intense competition among companies, overcapacity of treatment facilities, and a rash of consolidations have put many companies out of business. The *Environmental Business Journal* (*EBJ*) reported in its 1997 Annual Industry Overview that hazardous waste management has been in decline since 1993, fading from $6.6 billion in revenues in 1992 to $6.0 billion in 1996. The hardest hit sector was in the management of industrial hazardous waste, which had $3.8 billion in revenues in 1996, a drop from the $4.1 billion in 1995, *EBJ* reports.

One of the industry leaders in the hazardous waste field is certainly Laidlaw Environmental Services, which merged with Safety-Kleen Corporation in 1998, and now goes under the latter name. Even before the merger, the company was billed as "the world's largest hazardous waste management company," with more than 100 locations, 4,400 employees, and $850 million in revenues. The company operates eight of the nation's twenty-three permitted hazardous waste landfills, and ten of the twenty-three permitted incinerators for hazardous waste. Overall waste industry leader Waste Management, Inc.

(with services in both solid and hazardous waste) operates seven hazardous waste landfills and two incinerators.

For a ranking of the top hazardous waste management companies in the nation, consult *Waste Age* magazine from the Environmental Industries Association, which publishes an annual list. (See the Resources section at the end of the chapter for contact information.)

Hazardous waste consulting and engineering, the largest in environmental consulting and engineering, has experienced similarly hard times, *EBJ* reports. The $4.18 billion industry in 1996 declined 6 percent over the previous year, and it is expected to decline another 3 percent by 2000, *EBJ* reported in May 1997. But one of the growth areas in consulting and engineering is pollution prevention, *EBJ* reports. It had $570 million in 1996 revenues, an increase of 2 percent over 1995, and is expected to grow 6 percent by 2000. This was coupled with $800 million in pollution prevention and process technology in 1996, a number that was also rising.

Finally, expenditures on remediation and "industrial services" hit $8.6 billion in 1996 and has leveled off.

"Within the hazardous waste industry there seems to be an incredible amount of consolidation going on, and that has to do in no small part with companies taking pollution prevention action rather than contracting for large amounts of treatment capacity," says the EPA's Berlow.

The numbers support that, but they tell another story as well. Adding the 1996 figures—$6 billion for hazardous waste management, $4 billion for engineering and consulting, and nearly $9 billion for remediation—shows that $19 billion was spent on hazardous waste the old way and less than $1.4 billion on prevention. The *trends* are toward prevention, but most of the jobs are still in treatment, storage, disposal, and site remediation.

That's not surprising. One of the things about the hazardous waste management and remediation business is that it is a much more labor-intensive method of dealing with waste. Prevention will never create an industry the size of hazardous waste management. How many people does it take to *eliminate* waste? In many cases, it doesn't take any *new* people. Existing process engineers, chemists, toxicologists and others can be put to work on the task, or a consultant can be hired. That's one of the reasons business likes pollution prevention approaches.

In the hazardous waste management business, there are few new kinds of employment opportunities. Turnover in many entry-level positions is relatively high, and only so many of these technicians can be promoted to supervisory positions. This creates opportunities for people to gain valuable experience.

Clean-ups will produce some new careers. One of the better opportunities will be in conceiving, designing, implementing, and monitoring more "passive" clean-up technologies such as bioremediation and phytoremediation, as government at every level seeks to cut the costs of clean-ups while still protecting public health and the environment.

Brownfield clean-ups will intensify the need for diversely talented profes-

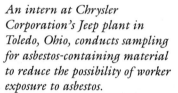

An intern at Chrysler Corporation's Jeep plant in Toledo, Ohio, conducts sampling for asbestos-containing material to reduce the possibility of worker exposure to asbestos.

sionals. Companies are looking for people who can handle the complex financial and legal negotiations, and community relations professionals who can work with citizens' groups and local government to develop contaminated properties with fewer law suits.

Walter Kovalick, Jr., director of the EPA's Technology Innovation Office, expects private business to tackle the problem with teams of people, from traditional engineers to innovative scientists trained in the emerging discipline of "green chemistry."

"As the world of hazardous waste remediation evolves, this appreciation for, and understanding of, the need to connect these disciplines—civil engineering, chemistry, chemical engineering, microbiology, environmental engineering, and others—will be vital," Kovalick says.

Nonprofit Sector

Unlike advocacy on other environmental issues, which tends to be sustained either by large, national groups or small, grassroots groups, advocacy on hazardous waste issues embraces both.

Grassroots and environmental justice groups have grown, as the linkages between toxicity and public health have become clearer, and as ecological concerns have fused with those of class and race. Success at this level is measured not by incremental changes in sweeping federal environmental laws, but by cleaning up the dump down the street.

"When we got involved in this work in the early 1980s, no one was doing what we were doing," says Lester of the Center for Health, Environment, and Justice, which focuses on grassroots coalition building. Formerly known as the Citizen's Clearinghouse for Hazardous Wastes, the Center was founded by Love Canal activist Lois Gibbs.

"Today, there are many groups on the state and local levels," Lester says. "Many are environmental justice groups. It's certainly a changing landscape."

Local clean-up and brownfields groups are part of the changing face of environmentalisms. They are not just opposing projects and fighting for clean-ups. They are also looking for solutions, the kind that clean sites, restore neighborhoods, and create jobs. Total nonprofit employment in the field is small, but effective groups are influential far beyond their numbers.

Succeeding in today's nonprofit group requires more than passion. Training in chemistry, biology, planning, economics, technology, toxicology, and law is important. An interdisciplinary sense of those areas is even more so. Finally, fundraising, membership, organization, and management skills are in demand.

"Someone stopped me on 125th Street the other day to shake my hand and thank me just for getting the information out on environmental issues," says Peggy Shepard, executive director of West Harlem Environmental Action, which is based in New York and is one of America's best-known urban grassroots groups.

"The ultimate accomplishment is the regular man on the street complaining," Shepard says. "That's when you know you've changed something—when it hits the grassroots level."

See the Profiles section toward the end of this chapter for more about careers in community activism.

SALARY

Salaries in hazardous waste management tend to fall in the $25,000 to $60,000 range across a wide array of position titles and academic disciplines in both the private and the public sectors.

PRIVATE SECTOR

Salaries at well-known hazardous waste firms such as CWM, Philips, and General Chemical are roughly similar. Field technicians start at $9 to $12 an hour, and foreman positions pay $13 to $17 an hour. "Chemists" (who may have other environmental science backgrounds) earn $25,000 to $35,000 annually. The next step up is "supervisors," who earn $32,000 to $42,000. Operations supervisors start at around $40,000 and rise to $60,000. Lab managers are in the same range. Compliance and health/safety specialists earn around $30,000 to $40,000 at major companies, and most pollution prevention staff will be found in this range. Managers in these departments earn $50,000 to $60,000. Finally, plant managers at TSD facilities are paid $60,000 to $75,000 and senior managers earn over $100,000 annually.

Similar salary structures are found at corporations that operate their own hazardous waste management programs, usually under the direction of a vice president for Environment, Health, and Safety

GOVERNMENT

At the EPA, hazardous waste management salaries reflect those throughout the agency. Starting salaries are determined by education level, grade point average, and location in the country. For instance, a staffer with a B.S. and a 3.4 grade point average can expect a base salary of around $25,000. But if the position is in New York, Boston, San Francisco, or Los Angeles, add 16 percent to that salary range.

Also, promotions at the EPA come quickly with hard work and strong performance, "so it's not hard after five or six years to be in the $50,000 range," says the EPA's Berlow.

State agency salaries are similar. The starting salary for a hazardous waste management specialist with a bachelor's degree and three years of experience is $28,000 to $31,000.

NONPROFITS

Nonprofit sector salaries are lower. Executive directors at the grassroots levels earn $28,000 to $35,000. Program staff and organizers are in the low and mid-20s. Salaries vary wildly with grant writing and fundraising success, so predictions are difficult.

GETTING STARTED

Technical, scientific, and engineering fields dominate the educational needs of hazardous waste professionals, although pollution prevention and brownfields redevelopment approaches broaden the field.

EDUCATION

"Definitely come in with a strong chemistry background, maybe a little bio-chemistry, and absolutely some knowledge of statistics," says the EPA's Berlow. "Everyone comes in with computer skills. We tend to have a big supply of folks who come with general environmental sciences backgrounds, so what we really snap up are the ones with more detailed, technical skills, like chemical engineers, environmental engineers, and environmental economists. Those are the ones who are really attractive."

What's true at the EPA is even more true in the private hazardous waste management industry. Chemists, chemical and environmental engineers, toxicologists, and hazardous waste technicians with associate degrees are in demand. Clearly, undergraduate training in chemistry is a good choice, although firms report that people with other types of science backgrounds (biology and environmental science, for instance) can do much of the daily work.

On the remediation side, a similar range of fields is needed. In addition to engineers of all types (e.g., civil, environmental, chemical, and hydrogeological), there is a strong need for people with education in real estate development, finance and economics, biology, communications, hydrogeology, botany, environmental health, environmental law, and more.

Finally, anyone working in the hazardous waste management field will require training in health and safety procedures, including a forty-hour course mandated by the Occupational Health and Safety Administration (OSHA), and other courses that certify that you can work safely in a "moon suit." Refresher courses are also required. Employers love to find qualified people who already have these trainings, to save money. If you feel the need to boost your competitiveness, you should consider adding this training to your education. If you are a strong candidate, however, your employer will pay to have you trained.

Educational opportunities for people with an interest in pollution prevention have expanded dramatically. The National Pollution Prevention Center for Higher Education at the University of Michigan has published the *Directory of Pollution Prevention in Higher Education: Faculty and Programs* since 1991. The 1997 edition had 402 entries (up from 100 six years earlier) and found courses or programs at 113 colleges in the United States and internationally. The majority of the classes are associated with engineering programs, but pollution prevention is also part of environmental science, environmental studies, architecture, chemistry, toxiciology, business administration, and environmental policy.

The emergence of brownfields redevelopment in the hazardous waste world calls for a new group of additional professionals, with education that is quite different from the traditional remediation professionals. Because brownfields projects aim to develop properties for new commercial, industrial, and recreational uses, instead of simply cleaning them up, companies need people with degrees in architecture, landscape architecture, finance, community relations, and more.

ADVICE

Advice for the aspiring hazardous waste professional from current workers in government, industry, and the nonprofit world is remarkably similar. Some suggestions include:

Study specific industries. Pollution prevention specialists, particularly, should understand the specific toxic use patterns of industries they want to work in. Consider plastics, electronics, electric utilities, auto manufacturing, paper products, metals, and so forth.

Get some experience. Internships are a crucial element in your educational preparation. Also, consider working in the field between your undergraduate and graduate educations. Doing so will sharpen your sense of exactly what you want to study in graduate school. "Get some practical exposure before going into an advanced degree," says New Hampshire DES's O'Brien. "Find out what it's like. Be willing to work at less than the going rate for a year, and then go back to school to become excellent in that area."

Consider community work. "There's a future in nonprofit advocacy on hazardous waste issues, but it will definitely not be on the model of the large national groups, because if you're going to be involved in clean-ups, you have to have a stake in them, and that usually means redevelopment and reuse of the sites. So in terms of career opportunities, organizations invested in communities very much have a need for folks in hazardous waste management and related fields," says Shutkin, of Alternatives for Community and Environment.

Learn project management skills. Whether you opt for a career in pollution prevention, site remediation, treatment and disposal, or brownfields redevelopment, your ability to plan and manage complex projects that involve many stages will be tested often as your career progresses.

Develop a comprehensive waste management career. The fields of hazardous waste management, solid waste management, pollution control, and pollution prevention are coming together. Where one begins and another ends is more and more unclear. Even if you consider yourself a "hazardous waste" professional, keep your eyes on broader environmental management goals. (See the profile on CH2M Hill's Starr Dehn later in this chapter.)

SUMMARY

The hazardous waste field involves four major activities:

- Monitoring, and reporting on, the use of hazardous materials under the law.
- Transport, treatment, storage, and disposal of hazardous wastes.
- Pollution prevention and toxics-use reduction activities.
- Clean-up of contaminated areas, including Superfund sites and "brownfields."

The field is undergoing rapid changes and rethinking many basic assumptions. America's grand experiment in hazardous waste clean-up, Superfund, has proved a multibillion dollar disappointment, and the public wants better answers that will clean more sites at a faster pace and for less money. Waste sites are not just dumps to clean. They are development, employment, race and class equity opportunities. They are the future as much as the past.

In addition, the public is taking action on its own, from properly disposing of household hazardous wastes to mobilizing to clean up neighborhood dumps. Companies that produce hazardous waste are following suit, generating less of it and moving the waste disposal industry to explore innovative technologies that will reduce, and even eliminate, much of our hazardous waste.

Working in hazardous waste management will require imagination, vision, and creativity to resolve problems that rank among the most complicated in all of environmentalism.

Site remediation is a major environmental task, employing a wide variety of different professionals. There are thousands of contaminated properties throughout the United States.

CASE STUDY

Alternatives for Community and Environment Roxbury, Massachusetts

Throughout the nation, the effort to redevelop the nation's 450,000 brownfields and address other urban environmental issues has been met with creativity and imagination by community groups and activists. Bill Shutkin and Alternatives for Community and Environment (ACE) are among the leaders in this grassroots movement.

When Bill Shutkin was an undergraduate at Brown University in the 1980s, he studied history, earning a degree from the Ivy League school in 1987. But he also kept a watchful eye on what was going on currently just beyond the Providence, Rhode Island, campus—in the poorer neighborhoods on the south side of the city.

Compelled to act on interests that had begun growing through his life, Shutkin found the time while still a student to develop an environmental program for the inner city children living on that side of the city, the first of several opportunities he had to meld his concerns for environmental protection, economic development, and social justice.

He followed that up after graduation with another program, the Green Guerillas, an initiative based in New York City and aimed at training homeless men to maintain trees and plants, better enabling them to get jobs with the city's parks department. "The program still serves people today," he says.

Shutkin went on to earn graduate degrees in law and history from the University of Virginia. But by the late 1980s and with the nationwide emergence of environmental justice as an issue, his course was set—to start a nonprofit group that would take American environmentalism in a new direction.

The group would put in action environmentalism infused with a drive to create clean development and jobs and to eradicate unfairness, environmentalism that was ultimately "a function of democracy—to the extent democracy works, environmental protection works. To the extent democracy fails, environmental protection fails," Shutkin says.

The result was Alternatives for Community and Environment (ACE), a Roxbury-based group Shutkin cofounded with his fellow senior attorney Charles Lord in 1993. It has three goals: educating citizens on their rights and opportunities in environmental and public health decision making; developing the capacity of neighborhoods to take control of problems affecting their health and environment; and creating systematic solutions to address the unequal distribution of environmental burdens, as well as to promote safe, sustainable economic development.

And while only five years old, ACE has made great strides. Working with other local groups, it helped defeat a proposed asphalt plant that would have exacerbated local traffic and smog. In nearby New Bedford, it helped develop a more expeditious mediation process with the EPA and state to clean up a Superfund site. In nearby Lawrence, it helped a local group persuade the city to drop a plan to burn sludge at an incinerator. In Boston's Chinatown, it worked with residents to stop the city's plan to build an off-ramp from the Central Artery that would have funneled 25,000 cars a day into the neighborhood. And in Vermont, ACE worked with the Abenaki tribe to stop a proposed gas station development on wetlands that are valued by the tribe.

Those accomplishments—for which ACE has received awards from the EPA, city of Boston, American Bar Association, Massachusetts Audubon Society, and others—reflect ACE's premise that the best environmentalism is driven by those with a direct stake in its outcome, who need only to be empowered with expertise and information.

The battle against the asphalt plant was a case in point, especially in the collaborative way ACE brought together concerns of environmental protection, economic development, and social justice. In fighting the plant, ACE worked with residents to argue that the plant would further burden an area of the city that is already overburdened, threatening public health and the environment.

"We were sick and tired of land-use decisions that brought more pollution and few jobs," Shutkin says. ACE and the residents further argued that in being overburdened, that area of the city was a victim of unfairness. "Why do some neighborhoods get dumped on more than others?" he asks. And along the way, a new group was formed, Neighborhoods United for the South Bay, which was aimed at devising proactive strategies for dealing with such poor land-use decisions, but also at drawing clean "eco-development" and jobs to the area, he says.

"This case, like the others, became an ongoing project for developing neighborhood empowerment and strategies for environmental protection and economic development, with the understanding that if you achieve those two goals, you will achieve at least a small measure of justice," Shutkin says.

ACE currently has the following four major programs underway, all of which offer free services to communities.

Community Representation Project. Through this program, ACE attorneys have worked with eight to twelve neighborhood groups to develop creative strategies for dealing with polluting facilities, unwanted land uses, pollution from auto-related businesses, redevelopment of brownfield sites, indoor environmental quality in public housing, and resident participation in cleanups. ACE relies on the law to ensure residents are empowered to participate in decision making, but litigation is used as a last resort, reflecting Shutkin's belief that creative solutions are preferable in being less expensive, and in casting a wider net on environmental problems than specific laws and regulations can.

Roxbury Environmental Empowerment Project. Through this program, which focuses on developing leadership among youth, ACE works with more than 300 students a year in four Roxbury schools and two summer programs, helping them to identify, understand, and solve environmental and public health problems in their own neighborhoods.

Massachusetts Environmental Justice Network. This program got underway in 1995 with the intent of filling the need for pro bono legal and technical support to underserved communities throughout Massachusetts.

Alternatives Resource Center. The Resource Center will provide technical assistance to communities on GIS software, analyze environmental data, map conditions in neighborhoods, and share the results from ACE's successful legal and educational efforts. ACE will also be developing a resource library and computer workstation, which will enable residents to research and map the conditions in their own neighborhoods.

Shutkin believes that organizations such as ACE must be the future of environmentalism. He sees an environmentalism that reaches beyond resource protection to embrace economic development and social justice and that recognizes the need for local solutions drawn from the residents themselves. He calls for an environmentalism that has a greater place for people.

"Environmentalism has often failed as a social movement because it has not concerned itself enough with the lives of everyday people," Shutkin says. "This is reflected in our obsession with wilderness and parks, places where people don't live. We need to develop new laws and policies that deal with American neighborhoods as environments, not at the expense of protecting our natural resources in the traditional sense, but in a way that ups the ante on protection efforts in the cities, older suburbs, and rural areas. While environmental organizations are protecting piping plovers and redwood stands, as essential and vital as they are, we're sort of missing the forest for the trees (excuse the pun) because our neighborhoods are suffering."

PROFILES

Rita Chow
Environmental Protection Specialist
U.S. Environmental Protection Agency (EPA)
Office of Solid Waste
Washington, D.C.

Most of the nation's hazardous waste regulation begins in the offices of the Environmental Protection Agency. As an environmental protection specialist, Rita Chow participates in the balancing act of science and politics that is the rule-making process.

When Rita Chow wrapped up her chemical engineering degree at the University of Maryland in December of 1996, she assumed she was headed for a job in industry. She had interned with a major company, International Paper, and she had only taken two environmental courses as an undergraduate, both of which focused more on technology than on regulation and law. She wasn't even sure just how acute her environmental interest was.

"I really hadn't thought of working for the EPA to begin with," Chow says. I wasn't sure how a chemical engineer would work for the EPA, how I could get my foot in the door. Basically I wanted to work for industry. But I couldn't find anything interesting to do. I also wanted to work in the D.C. area, and for chemical engineers, that means consulting or government.

She checked out the research and development arena, but like the job offers she got from industry, "there was nothing stimulating enough for me to pick up and move," Chow says. Then in January 1997, the EPA called and asked her to come in for an interview. "So I decided to check it out," she says.

She learned about the government's Quality Scholars Program, which recruits recently graduated students with a grade point average of 3.5 or higher, for which she qualified. She spoke with an EPA official in the waste treatment branch, and learned about what the office does, especially in setting disposal standards. "And it all sounded very interesting to me," Chow says.

And so when the job offer came, Chow accepted, joining the agency in February 1997 even though "I really didn't know what to expect." She has not been disappointed in her decision.

At the EPA, Chow has spent most of her time working with others on rule making, specifically treatment standards for toxicity characteristic metal wastes. "Basically, we were revising the metals standards so that the same standards are applicable to characteristic metals as listed metals," she says. Listed metals have hazardous constituents. Characteristic metals have constituents that may at times exceed toxicity standards. The two groups of metals have been subject to differing standards, creating confusion. "But now, we're reconciling the standards to make them uniform," Chow says.

As that work has drawn to a close, Chow has been assigned other responsibilities, including responding to inquiries from the states or public on land disposal regulations and writing formal agency comments on the issues surrounding manufactured gas plant remediation waste. She has also been working on alternative, soil-specific treatment standards. "Those are the main things," she says.

She enjoys the challenges, be they technical or procedural. "I still don't feel I have my own project," Chow says. "But I do feel like I have my hands in a lot of different things." Upcoming challenges will include new treatment standards for mercury and "reinventing" her office's program as a whole, "to fix things that might not work so well, to make the program more flexible while still protecting human health and the environment."

Chow is looking forward to both challenges because she'll be involved from the inception. With her prior work, "I came in at the middle," she says.

What has struck Chow as especially interesting about the EPA is the difficulty it faces as an agency in balancing competing demands. Going into the agency, Chow says she had an impression its work was more along the line of an outright advocacy group, such as the Environmental Defense Fund (EDF).

"Coming in, I felt first and foremost that the agency would prescribe very stringent treatment standards, which it has," Chow says. "But at the same time, it has to balance that with what industry wants, and so from what I've seen, the agency has a very difficult time getting its work done. I thought it would be more like EDF, but now I see that the EPA is not that extreme. It is trying to balance everyone's concerns, and that is a tremendous burden for the agency."

It is also a burden that Chow is not always comfortable with. "I've seen people here who are very environmentally oriented, more of the EDF mindset," she says. "I've also seen people here who are more of the balanced mindset, but still want to protect the human health and the environment. There is room for both. But sometimes it feels like the balancers are more dominant. Sometimes I have to question how things are done."

Still, Chow is pleased with her decision to join the EPA. "I'd like to stay for a while in the agency, and try and work in the different program areas like the Office of Air, or the Office of Water," she says. "I'd like to get an overview experience of the agency. I think it's a very good place to work for. There is movement within the agency, which was one of the biggest points for me. I knew that coming here, I'd experience different jobs and different programs.

Peggy Shepard
Executive Director, West Harlem
Environmental Action
West Harlem, New York

The environmental justice movement is at the heart of today's environmentalism. People of color and low income individuals in urban neighborhoods, rural areas, and on native lands are struggling to protect their communities from disproportionate environmental contamination and to assure that the country brings social justice to its environmental and community development efforts. Peggy Shepard's work in New York City is complemented by dozens of other groups in St. Louis, Oakland, San Francisco, Atlanta, New Orleans, Albuquerque, and throughout the nation.

Her frustrations as a freelancer had already been building in trying to write the "serious" stories about the African American community, stories about alcoholism, smoking, and other issues that other major African American magazines such as *Essence* and *Ebony* "weren't ready for at the time." At *Verb*, she had finally positioned herself to write those stories.

After only a year, *Verb*'s publisher abandoned the magazine. Shepard was offered a position with the publisher's office of public relations, but she wasn't interested. A speech-writing job opened up at the New York State Division of Housing and Community Renewal, which she accepted instead, sensing she could tell her stories there.

"I was a little disenchanted at that point, thinking I was going to be an editor of a major magazine, and so I decided I wanted to do something more substantive," Shepard says one afternoon in her New York City office of West Harlem Environmental Action, or WE ACT, one of America's most active and progressive urban environmental justice groups. Shepard cofounded the group in 1988 with Vernice Miller, now the director of environmental justice at the Natural Resources Defense Council, and Chuck Sutton.

"I was sort of feeling closed out from writing about the serious issues that impacted our community, and I thought speech writing would be a way to do something more substantive," Shepard says.

That urgency, that sense of having an important story to tell and facing resistance in her attempts to tell it, characterizes much of Shepard's work at WE ACT, and really characterizes WE ACT itself, which has battled over the last decade to improve the health and well-being of the predominantly African American and Latino communities of North Manhattan.

"It is a tactic of the environmental justice community, more so than the mainstream environmental community, to be more willing to confront and use direct access strategies, mostly because we have been kept from the table and have not had an opportunity to have our voices heard," Shepard says.

The issue for which WE ACT is best known is the North River Sewage Treatment Plant, a $2-billion, 170-million-gallon-a-day behemoth of a plant spanning 137th Street to 145th Street in New York that was built by—and poorly managed by—the city. Shepard first heard about it in 1985, when she was running successfully for Assembly District Leader in her community. "I first thought the issue was getting people hired at the plant," she says. "Then when it went on line, people started complaining about the emissions at the plant, and that's how I got involved in environmental issues."

Shepard mobilized the community into action. One morning in 1988, she convinced 100 residents to block traffic on West Side Highway and Riverside Drive, getting arrested in the process. She formed WE ACT that year, recognizing the plant was only one of many threats to the community and that a group was needed to address them all. WE ACT filed suit against the city that year with the Natural Resources Defense Council, charging that the plant was a public nuisance. They even filed suit against then Mayor David Dinkins, a former Manhattan borough president and WE ACT ally who had been supporting their efforts against the plant.

"When we sued [Dinkins] personally as well, he asked us why, and I said it's because we cannot simply count on this political friendship," Shepard says. "Our group needs to hold the city accountable, and he will not be in office forever. It's interesting, what happened to many other advocacy groups that supported Dinkins at the time. They lost a lot of ground because they were uncomfortable holding friends accountable. Even though he was our friend, we had no compunctions about doing that."

WE ACT won a landmark $1.1 million settlement in 1993 from the city. The money went into a fund to address environmental and public health concerns in Harlem. Just as important, the settlement gave WE ACT an opportunity to have its voice heard by granting the group formal authorization to monitor the plant on a daily basis, as well as a mandate to hire consultants to conduct two studies on sewage flow in the North River, track odor problems, and assess the city's efforts to correct the plant's problems. The city undertook a $55 million program to fix the plant in 1993, which is now ongoing.

While the plant occupied much of WE ACT's agenda from the start, it was not the only agenda item in 1988, and is certainly not now. WE ACT has also fought the Metropolitan Transit Authority for building six of the city's seven bus depots north of 99th Street. Hundreds of buses file in and out of each depot every day, spewing potentially toxic diesel fumes into nearby homes and schools, threatening public health in a community that already has an elevated asthma mortality rate and an array of respiratory problems.

WE ACT is also involved in many community programs on issues from diesel particulates to brownfields redevelopment to dry-cleaner emissions to lead poisoning, working with players from the EPA to Columbia University's School of Public Health. And its style remains confrontational. Last year, it ran a $50,000 campaign in Harlem posting ads in bus shelters. The ads depicted a grandfather walking his grandchildren to school. All wore gas masks. The ad read: "If you live uptown, breathe at your own risk."

It's been twenty years since her disappointment over the editing job, but

Shepard says she's finally telling the stories she's sought to tell. Fighting for a seat at the table, for the right to speak unencumbered by obstacles from electoral politics to editorial whim, may not be what every environmental justice group is about, she says. But for WE ACT "experience has taught me that this is the way for us to operate."

Starr Dehn
Vice President
CH2M Hill
Sacramento, California

Starr Dehn was profiled five years ago in The New Complete Guide to Environmental Careers. *Since 1993, the environmental consulting industry has gone through sweeping changes, requiring new responses from industry leaders such as CH2M Hill, as well as altering the career paths of employees and managers.*

"There have been a lot of changes in our industry, and at CH2M Hill, over the past few years," says Starr Dehn. "We have seen tough times in the environmental consulting business, because the political climate has been one in which very few new environmental initiatives were launched. Federal and state budgets have also shrunk, and marketplace pressure has led to the consolidation of many firms."

Dehn has noticed several other important changes. "Environmental consulting used to have a focus on technology delivery to solve client problems. With the impact of total quality management (TQM) approaches, we have a more comprehensive sense of project delivery. We have also reorganized to reduce costs in response to client needs and competition."

A shift to international environmental work is a final change that Dehn has seen. "Many people believe that the largest environmental challenges are located outside the United States, in locations where the standard of living could not support high investment in environmental controls. These areas include the former Soviet Union, eastern European nations, and parts of Asia. At any rate, there is a general migration to a global economy for all of us."

While the environmental world has been changing, Dehn's responsibilities have also been shifting. "When I last talked with the Environmental Careers Organization, I was a division manager for the Hazardous Waste and Industrial Processes Division at CH2M Hill. Now, as a vice president, my duties have expanded."

Those expanded duties include service as project delivery manager for the company's Nevada/California region and chairperson of the Project Management Council. In the first role, he is responsible for selecting project managers for a wide range of jobs, as well as for coaching, auditing, and monitoring the managers as they compete for new assignments and complete existing ones.

As chair of the council, Dehn is a leader in the company's project manager certification program. "Like many organizations, we are working hard to raise the skill levels of all project managers," he explains. "At CH2M Hill, candidates are placed at levels that start at associate project manager, and rise through five additional levels. Senior program manager is the highest level."

These jobs have given Dehn an increased appreciation for the role of project management skills in the consulting world. "I would encourage engineers and scientists currently in college to seek courses in project management," he says. "People need an understanding of critical path scheduling, cost control techniques, and contracting methods."

One part of Dehn's work that has not changed over the years is his role as program manager for environmental services at McClellan Air Force Base. "We do a wide range of environmental work, including Superfund cleanup, pollution prevention, air quality permitting, community relations, and lots more."

In the last three years, McClellan has been selected as one of many military installations to be closed. This has changed the nature of CH2M Hill's work at the base. Activities are now focused on cleaning up the property so that it can be closed and turned over to private or public buyers for other uses. Potential business buyers are naturally concerned that all contamination be remediated (or at least well documented) so that they are not accused later of causing contamination that was the result of Air Force activities.

Cleaning up military installations is one kind of environmental work that Dehn expects to remain at current levels for now. He anticipates a slow decline in this career area after the year 2000. Cleanup of Department of Energy facilities formerly involved with the manufacture of nuclear weapons will likely see an increase in the next ten to twenty years, he predicts.

Dehn's own pathway to environmental engineering and consulting was a natural one. He studied at the University of Washington in Seattle for his B.S. and M.S. degrees in civil engineering. "Most of the courses were very quantitative, like physics and engineering. Then I took a course that dealt with water quality and its impact on lake systems. It was very different from other courses and got me interested in the environmental field." After he had spent some time working with a small consulting firm, an older brother suggested he apply to CH2M Hill, one of the world's largest engineering firms.

As for the future, Starr Dehn is reticent to make too many pronouncements. "It is getting increasingly difficult to predict with much reliability what the future will bring in the environmental field. It does appear that political pressure to reduce spending on environmental regulations is likely to continue. The greatest growth opportunities will continue to be overseas."

The only sure thing is that the work will continue to be interesting. Consulting "is not a mundane type of job where you are doing the same thing every day," Dehn says. "It is extremely challenging and rewarding for people who enjoy solving problems. That is what drives a lot of people in this business. You work with a lot of different people, and get involved with things you've never dreamed of."

RESOURCES

Academy of Certified Hazardous Materials Managers (ACHMM). A membership organization dedicated to fostering professional development through continuing education, peer group interaction, and the exchange of ideas and information relating to hazardous materials management. Hosts an annual national convention. The Institute of Hazardous Materials Management offers a multidisciplinary program for certification and recertification. Publications include *Handbook on Hazardous Materials Management*, which covers such topics as treatment and disposal of hazardous wastes and hazardous waste storage. Website has job postings and links to related sites. 11900 Parklawn Dr., Suite 450, Rockville, MD 20852-2624. (301) 984-8969. Http://www.achmm.org.

Air and Waste Management Association. Nonprofit technical, scientific, and educational organization that aims to strengthen the environmental profession, expand scientific and technological responses to environmental concerns, and assist professionals in critical environmental decision making. Provides training, information, and networking opportunities through a series of conferences, workshops, and courses to help keep members up to date on new developments in the profession. Publications include *Journal of the Air and Waste Management Association* and *EM, a Magazine for Environmental Managers* (both monthly). One Gateway Center, Third Floor, Pittsburgh, PA 15222. (412) 232-3444. Http://www.awma.com.

Amazing Environmental Organization WebDirectory. "Earth's biggest environmental search engine." Includes information on hazardous waste management (click on pollution, then hazardous waste or waste management). Also don't miss the employment section on the WebDirectory homepage, which provides links to job listings, descriptions, and agencies specifically concerned with environmental employment. Http://www.webdirectory.com.

Association of State and Territorial Solid Waste Management Officials. Membership organization whose mission is to enhance and promote effective waste management programs and effect national waste management policies. Focuses on the needs of state hazardous waste programs; nonhazardous municipal solid waste and industrial waste programs; recycling, waste minimization, and reduction programs; Superfund and state cleanup programs; waste management and cleanup activities at federal facilities; and underground storage tank and leaking underground storage tank programs. 444 North Capitol St., NW, Suite 315, Washington, DC. (202) 624-5828. Http://www.astswmo.org.

Brownfields Nonprofits Network. A network of nonprofit organizations helping to promote the redevelopment of brownfield properties throughout the U.S. Website lists these organizations and has links to those that have webpages. Also offers the ability to ask questions of the Network, in-depth analyses of brownfields issues, case studies on successful Brownfields redevelopment, and extensive links to related government and nongovernment websites. Send mail c/o Clean Sites, 901 N. Washington St., Suite 604, Alexandria, VA 22314. Http://www.brownfieldsnet. org.

CCHW Center for Health, Environment, and Justice (formerly Citizens Clearinghouse for Hazardous Wastes). National environmental organization whose mission is to give people the technical information and training they need to fight for their right to a clean and healthy environment, to hold industry and government accountable, and to work toward a healthy and environmentally sustainable future. Works with grassroots community groups on environmental issues such as toxic waste, solid waste, air pollution, incinerators, medical waste, radioactive waste, pesticides, sewage, and industrial pollution. Has over 100 guidebooks and information packages on topics from hazardous waste to environmental racism. Publishes *Everyone's Backyard* (quarterly). 150 S. Washington, Suite 300, Falls Church, VA 22040. (703) 237-2249. Http://www.essential.org/cchw.

CLU-IN, Hazardous Waste Clean-Up Information. Website developed by the U.S. Environmental Protection Agency, but intended as a forum for all waste remediation constituencies. Provides information about innovative treatment technology to the hazardous waste remediation community. It describes programs, organizations, publications, and other tools. Http://www.clu-in.com.

Hazardous Substance Research Centers (HSRC). Consists of five collaborating regional centers that cover all relevant scientific and technological subjects related to hazardous substances except human health effects research. The centers provide short- and long-term research on the manufacture, disposal, clean-up, and management of hazardous substances; dissemination of research information and findings; and training, technology transfer, and technical outreach and support to benefit organizations, communities, and individuals involved with hazardous substances. Established by the U.S. Environmental Protection Agency to develop better, cheaper, faster, and safer methods to assess and clean up hazardous substances. Publishes a newsletter, *On-Site Insights.* Contact the Program Director, U.S. EPA (8703), Washington, DC 20460. (202) 260-7454. Http://www.hsrc.org/.

National Environmental: Training for Hazardous Materials and Asbestos. Fully approved by the U.S. Environmental Protection Agency (EPA) and satisfies Occupational Safety and Health Standards (OSHA). Offers such courses as "Transportation of Hazardous Material," "TSDF Hazardous Waste Handling," and "Hazardous Materials Technician/Specialist." 1019 W. Manchester Blvd., Suite 102, Inglewood, CA 90301. (310) 645-4516.Http://www.natlenviro.com.

National Solid Wastes Management Association. Membership organization representing 1,700 businesses in all 50 states that seeks to advance the safe and environmentally protective management of nonhazardous and hazardous wastes through the private waste services industry. Member services include state lobbying, federal representation, industry information, research and analysis, education and training, networking opportunities, and more. Part of the Environmental Industry Associations (EIA). The EIA Research and Education Foundation provides grants for research and educational projects in waste management trends and environmental protection. EIA sponsors the WasteExpo conference annually. 4301 Connecticut Avenue, NW, Suite 300, Washington, DC 20008. (202) 244-4700. Http://www.envasns. org/nswma.

National Spill Control School. Located in the College of Science and Technology at Texas A&M University, Corpus Christi. Conducts training courses in oil spill management, response and safety, hazardous material/waste management, and spill response and safety. This school is written into the Oil Pollution Act of 1990 as a training and research resource for the National Response Team. Texas A&M University, Corpus Christi, Natural Resources Center, Suite 1100, 6300 Ocean Drive, Corpus Christi, TX 78412. (512) 980-3333. Http://www.sci.tamucc.edu.

Natural Resources Defense Council. National environmental organization that, among other things, has a nuclear program under which they survey and analyze developments on a variety of nuclear weapons issues, including the problems of waste and fissile material disposition. 40 West 20th St., New York, NY 10011. (212) 727-1773. Http://www.nrdc.org.

Occupational Health and Safety Administration (OSHA). A key federal agency regulating health and safety standards for those whose work brings them in contact with hazardous materials. Part of the U.S. Department of Labor. 200 Constitution Ave., NW, Washington, DC 20210. (202) 219-8151. Http://www.osha.gov.

Solid Waste On-line. Website with loads of information about hazardous waste management. Offers case studies, the latest news and analysis with articles on issues such as brownfields cleanup, job listings, and much more. Http://www.solidwaste.com.

Superfund Basic Research Program. Program created and implemented by the National Institute of Environmental Health Sciences (NIEHS). Receives funding from the U.S. Environmental Protection Agency (EPA) and Superfund Trust monies. The NIEHS/EPA Superfund Basic Research Program provides funding to eighteen programs at seventy universities and institutions around the U.S. to study the human health effects of hazardous substances in the environment, especially those found at uncontrolled, leaking waste disposal sites. Develops methods and technologies to detect hazardous substances in the environment; advanced techniques for assessment and evaluation of the risks and effects on human health presented by hazardous substances; and biological, chemical, and physical methods to reduce the amount of toxicity in hazardous substances. Offers grants and research opportunities. Contact the Program Administrator, Superfund Basic Research Program, NIEHS, P.O. Box 12233, Research Triangle Park, NC 27709. (919) 541-4638. Http://www.niehs.nih.gov/sbrp/home.htm.

U.S. Environmental Protection Agency (EPA), Office of Solid Waste and Emergency Response. Federal agency that develops guidelines and standards for the land disposal of hazardous wastes and for underground storage tanks. Offers technical assistance in the development, management, and operation of solid waste activities and analyzes the recovery of useful energy from solid waste. The EPA has a comprehensive website with a wealth of searchable articles. Check out their Office of Pollution Prevention and Toxics site at http://www.epa.gov/opptintr/p2home; their brownfields site, which has a job training program, at http://www.epa.gov/brownfields; and their Superfund site at http://www.epa.gov/superfund. USEPA Waterside Mall (5101), Washington, DC 20460. (703) 308-8254. Http://www.epa.gov/swerrims.

10 Energy

AT A GLANCE

Employment:
180,000 environmentally related professionals nationwide. Energy industries employ an estimated six million Americans.

Demand:
3 to 9 percent annually

Breakdown:
Public sector, 20 percent (mostly federal)
Private sector, 70 percent
Nonprofit sector, 10 percent

Key Job Titles:
Chemist
Climatologist
Communicator
Efficiency designer
Engineer
Forecaster
Modeler
Manager
Marketer
Planner
Policy Specialist
Regulator
Researcher
Statistician

Among many other experts in transportation, national security, meteorology, hydrology, forestry, waste management, sustainable development, trade, diplomacy, advanced technology development, consulting, computer programming, insurance, and others. Support positions as monitors, technicians, construction workers, equipment and plant operators, fuel haulers, and others also exist in energy.

Influential Organizations:
Alliance to Save Energy
American Council for an Energy-Efficient Economy
Association of Home Appliance Manufacturers
Clean Fuels Development Coalition
Edison Electric Institute
Electric Power Research Institute
Environmental Defense Fund
Lawrence Livermore National Laboratory
National Association of State Energy Officials
National Renewable Energy Laboratory
Natural Gas Supply Association
Natural Resources Defense Council
Oak Ridge National Laboratory
Solar Energy Industries Association
Union of Concerned Scientists
U.S. Department of Energy
U.S. Environmental Protection Agency

Salary:
Salaries in the energy field vary widely by sector and position type. Entry-level scientists at Department of Energy research labs earn from $28,000 (B.S.) up to $60,000 (Ph.D.) annually. Consulting engineers and scientists start in the high 20s or low 30s. Energy specialists at public utilities start at around $30,000. Entry-level environmental staff at electric utilities and petroleum companies start in the low 30s, depending on academic and work experience. Career professionals in the public sector can rise to $80,000 annually, and private sector managers and professionals often exceed $100,000.

WHAT IS ENERGY?

Energy is ubiquitous. It so pervasively touches our lives that we don't think about it. We flick a switch and assume the light will go on, without thinking about the coal burning in power plants producing the necessary electricity. We turn a key and assume the car will start, without thinking about the oil that had to be refined into gasoline to power it.

Because energy comes from so many sources, is produced through so many processes, is used in so many ways, has so many ecological consequences, and is ever-evolving, depending on everything from innovative technologies to global politics, it embraces a dizzying array of possible careers.

Not every energy career is "environmental." Indeed, many energy professionals are harming the environment. But for those interested in the environmental end of the energy profession, remarkably numerous and diverse possibilities exist. Some of these possibilities involve finding new ways to produce energy in environmentally safer ways, such as alternative or renewable energy. Several involve making our energy use more efficient, so that we get more out of the energy we use. Many involve conservation, so that we use less energy. Finally, a large number of opportunities can be found in jobs that mitigate the ecological harm done by more environmentally destructive forms of energy use.

Chemists, physicists, engineers, and researchers all work in energy, to name just a few common professions. But so do architects, who devise energy-efficient homes; planners, who map new communities that rely less on transportation; and geneticists, who develop fast-growing trees to feed biomass plants and absorb some of the carbon dioxide that fuels global warming.

Economists, diplomats, statisticians, regulators, national security experts, biologists, entrepreneurs, lobbyists, builders, consultants, advocates, venture capitalists, and countless other professionals work daily in energy, a $500-billion-a-year industry in this country that shows no signs of shrinking as the demand for energy grows, its ecological impacts mount, and natural resources remain finite. Additional challenges spring from the effects of fossil fuel emissions on global climate, deregulation of electric utilities, and the national security threats posed by dependence on foreign oil. Those challenges promise to make energy one of the premier arenas for environmental professionals for years to come. Conquering them will require new technologies, new management strategies, and new ways of thinking.

To get a handle on energy and the careers it offers, it would help to view it the way the U.S. Department of Energy (DOE) does. To the DOE, energy breaks down into consumption, or how we use it, and supply, or where we get it.

Energy is consumed in America in four main sectors, according to the DOE's April 1998 *Comprehensive National Energy Strategy*—transportation, industry, residential, and commercial. Overall energy use is expected to grow, from 94 quadrillion Btus in 1996 to 118.6 quadrillion Btus in 2020, according to the DOE's 1998 *Annual Energy Outlook*. All four uses involve professions that have shaped those uses for decades, everything from electrical engineering to petroleum geology, as well as emerging professions that will shape them for decades to come, from fuel cell researchers to hybrid car designers.

Transportation accounts for 26 percent of energy use, and two-thirds of the petroleum used in the country. As pressure to clean up America's air continues, professionals, from chemists who can develop cleaner fuels, to mass-transit planners who can devise more energy efficient travel modes, will be needed. Some of the most interesting work being done in this area is in reinventing cars.

The work of creative professionals is changing today's aerodynamic designs, fuel types, and body materials to build a vehicle that can get 80 miles per gallon, emit no pollution, and have all the power of a Porsche.

Industry accounts for 37 percent of energy use, and some industry uses are particularly energy intensive. In 1995, environmental writer Gregg Easterbrook reported that "nearly half of U.S. electricity was consumed by process motors in factories." Although industry depends on a mix of energy sources, petroleum and natural gas are the dominant ones. In an effort to improve financial bottom lines, companies seek the expertise of a wide range of energy professionals to help them stay competitive by reducing direct expenses and reducing energy-related emissions that harm the environment and drive up regulatory costs. Professionals help with conservation efforts, which range from installing new light bulbs to eliminating energy intensive process steps to reducing the miles driven by company car fleets.

Residential use accounts for 20 percent of energy consumption. Half is used for heating rooms and water, and most of the rest for appliances such as stoves, refrigerators, and air conditioners. Commercial use accounts for 16 percent of energy use, again largely to heat and light buildings. Some of the most innovative work in the energy field is focused on residential concerns and commercial uses. It includes work by manufacturers who develop and market more energy-efficient modular housing, by electrical engineers who design and install photovoltaic roof panels that generate their own electricity, and by site planners who position homes and buildings so they maximize use of the sun.

America will become more energy efficient even though it will be consuming more energy. The nation became steadily more energy efficient from 1970 to 1986, improving at a rate of 2.3 percent a year. It held steady from 1986 to 1996. But it is expected to improve by 0.9 percent a year from 1996 through 2020. Energy-related careers are growing as the transportation sector, industry, home builders, commercial enterprises, and every-day citizens work to become more energy efficient.

The other side of the energy coin is supply. America gets its energy from oil, natural gas, coal, nuclear power, and renewables such as solar, wind, biomass, geothermal sources, and hydropower. As the DOE noted in its 1998 *Comprehensive National Energy Strategy*, oil accounts for 22 percent of the supply, natural gas for 27 percent, coal for 31 percent, nuclear power for 10 percent, and renewables—mainly hydropower—for 10 percent.

But those numbers will change, depending on everything from energy efficiency to electric utility restructuring, according to the DOE's 1998 *Annual Energy Outlook*. And how those numbers change, taken with America's evolving energy consumption patterns, offers another insight into where jobs may be found in the coming years.

Oil production will decline at an average annual rate of 1.1 percent to a projected level of 4.9 million gallons a day in 2020. Natural gas production will rise from 19 trillion cubic feet in 1996 to 27.4 trillion cubic feet in 2020. Coal production will also rise by 1.1 percent a year, from 1,064 million tons in 1996 to 1,376 million tons in 2020. Nuclear power will decline sharply as many of

America's 100 plants are retired, dropping from the 101 gigawatts available in 1996, to 52 gigawatts in 2020. And despite the intense interest in renewable power production, especially within industry, the DOE does not expect this production to rise between 1996 and 2020.

HISTORY AND BACKGROUND

From the Industrial Revolution through the 1960s, the challenges posed by energy were primarily to find, drill, process, sell, and burn coal and oil. With the exception of a few prophetic voices who viewed smoke-filled skies with alarm, both fossil fuels were seen as boundless in supply and innocuous in use. Add nuclear power, built on development of the atom bomb during World War II and carried through the Cold War years of the 1950s and early 1960s, and America's energy picture appeared complete and, in retrospect, blissful. "See the USA in your Chevrolet" was the theme not only of one of America's leading car manufacturers, but also of the day. Until thirty years ago, talk of "volatile organic compounds" occurred in chemistry class, not Congress.

By the early 1970s, however, America's energy picture was changing rapidly. The 1973 oil embargo shook America's confidence in a limitless supply of inexpensive oil from foreign lands. For drivers of the time, the long lines of cars waiting to fill up became a legendary symbol of an insecure energy future. The 1978 revolution in Iran was another reality check for the nation, forcing Americans to recognize that our energy supplies were global and not wholly under our control. If further proof were needed, the 1991 Gulf War with Iraq proved beyond a doubt that oil was America's lifeblood—so vital that we would go to war to protect our Persian Gulf supplies.

Even before dramatic events such as the 1973 oil embargo, America's attitude toward coal and oil had begun to change, not because of what was happening overseas, but because of air pollution at home. Visible clouds of smog, directly related to energy use, were a rallying cry for the first Earth Day in 1970 and gave birth to the most recent wave of environmentalism. Laws such as the 1970 Clean Air Act ended our century-old notion that we could burn coal and oil as much as we liked and pay no ecological price for it.

The 1970s also saw the beginning of American disillusion with the energy source that was poised to replace fossil fuels—nuclear power. Our largely unquestioned faith in nuclear energy was shattered on March 28, 1979, when radiation leaked from Pennsylvania's Three Mile Island power plant. The blow was underscored seven years later on April 26, 1986, with the meltdown of the Chernobyl plant in the former Soviet Union. The nuclear power industry in this nation has yet to recover from these iconic events and the anti-nuclear protest movement they helped along.

Even without spectacular accidents such as Chernobyl, nuclear power was (and is) under attack. Environmentalists have successfully focused on the problem of radioactive waste to galvanize public opposition. Here is waste so persistently lethal that academics were once commissioned to develop warning signs for nuclear waste disposal sites that people could read 10,000 years from now, presuming those people will no longer speak any known language.

The results are clear. The DOE says that no new nuclear power plants are expected to be built in the next twenty years.

The 1970s are remembered not only as the decade that saw the beginning of an attack on conventional energy sources, but as the period that launched a search for alternative energy options. The development of renewables such as hydroelectricity, geothermal sources, wind, biomass, and solar power was fueled by federal and state laws enacted in the 1970s that provided incentives for investments in alternative energy and required coal and oil utilities to buy power from alternative energy producers.

Renewables also got a boost from our perception that they were a national security necessity. The more we relied on our own resources for energy (it was thought) the less we would be dependent on those in politically shaky foreign nations.

Unfortunately, the burst of enthusiasm for alternative energy supplies that saw a peak during the Carter administration never reached its potential. Today, renewables account for only 10 percent of America's energy mix. Moreover, the dominant renewable source—hydroelectric power—has become an ironic choice. What was once praised by environmentalists as a promising form of alternative energy is now panned by many activists, as negative impacts to river ecosystems by dams and diversions have become well-known. One reason the DOE expects energy generation from renewable sources to remain constant through 2020 is the strict regulation brought to bear on hydroelectric power.

The energy challenge for America as we enter the 21st century is how to meet the nation's growing demand for it when conservation can reduce that demand only so much, energy efficiency can be developed only so quickly, and existing technologies are hampered by pollution, impracticality, or both.

But the challenge is not limited to shifting supply sources and advanced technologies. Energy's reach has become enormous, making the challenge complex. It is an international trade issue, a national security issue, a consumer affairs issue, a lifestyle issue, as well as a political, ideological, ethical, cultural, and justice issue. In the end, it is perhaps like no other environmental issue in that it affects everything, from a gallon of gas to the greenhouse effect.

And so energy offers two promises to aspiring environmental professionals. First, you will be challenged, and for a long time, in resolving issues whose complexities have not yet even been fully understood, from global warming to electricity deregulation. Second, there are nearly as many career opportunities as there are careers, with jobs for attorneys to architects, economists to ecologists, designers to deregulators, marketers to managers.

ENERGY LEGISLATION

Virtually every major federal environmental law can be linked in some way to energy. Air quality laws such as the Clean Air Act bear upon energy by restricting air emissions, for example. Water quality laws such as the Clean Water Act pertain to energy by ensuring stream flows through hydropower projects. Waste laws such as the Resource Conservation and Recovery Act involve energy by regulating waste-to-energy plants. Transportation laws such as the Transportation Equity Act for the 21st Century affect energy by attempting to diversify travel modes and force a decline in motor vehicle use. The National Environmental Policy Act bears upon energy by making sure many new projects face scrutiny for their environmental impacts.

Even the Endangered Species Act concerns energy. Toxic mercury, for instance, gets emitted by incinerators, finds its way through atmospheric deposition into ecosystems, and ends up in federally protected bald eagles.

In addition to broad environmental legislation, presidential initiatives and international treaties play a crucial role in shaping energy policy in relation to the environment. Some of these initiatives, both enacted and proposed, are reviewed below. Environmental professionals with an interest in the energy field follow these debates closely.

The Energy Policy Act of 1992. Signed by President Bush, this law authorized over $1.8 billion in spending in fiscal year 1994 for an array of new initiatives to implement the Bush administration's National Energy Strategy. It is the most recent, major federal law enacted on energy. The law:

- Promoted energy efficiency through tax exemptions for energy conservation investments.
- Supported nuclear power by reforming the nuclear power plant licensing process and encouraging the development of advanced nuclear power plant designs.
- Established a government-owned corporation with a five-member board to take over the DOE's civilian uranium enrichment operation.
- Promoted mass-transit and vanpools by increasing the tax-free limit on employer-provided benefits to $60 per month.
- Streamlined oil pipeline regulations.
- Supported the environmentally sound use of coal through research and development of advanced technologies.
- Provided alternative minimum tax relief worth over $1 billion over five years for independent oil and gas producers.
- Removed obstacles to increased competition in electricity generation by amending the Public Utilities Holding Company Act of 1935 and increasing transmission access.
- Promoted greater use of ethanol by extending tax exemptions for more ethanol blends.
- Promoted the development and use of clean-burning alternative motor fuels by providing tax incentives for alternative fuel vehicles and refueling facilities, establishing an alternative fuel fleet program, setting up electric vehicle demonstration programs, and providing financial support for demonstrations of alternative fuel use by urban mass transit systems.
- Promoted greater use of clean-burning natural gas by providing the natur-

al gas industry with expanded market opportunities in areas such as electricity generation and powered by natural gas vehicles.
- Encouraged increased research and development on a wide range of energy technologies, including high efficiency heat engines and advanced oil recovery.

The Kyoto Protocol on Climate Change. Signed by the parties to the United Nations Framework Convention on Climate Change in December 1997, the protocol seeks to reduce greenhouse gas emissions by setting and enforcing binding emissions targets in industrialized nations and achieving those targets through market-based methods.

Those targets vary, from 8 percent below 1990 baseline emissions levels for the European Union, to 6 percent below for Japan, and 7 percent below for the United States. The deadlines also vary and occur over five-year periods. The United States has the first deadline—we must achieve our 7 percent reduction from 1990 levels between 2008 and 2012. Six principal gases are targeted for reductions.

The protocol calls for an international emissions trading program, through which countries or companies may purchase emissions credits from other countries that have met their targets and have spare credits to sell. The approach is seen as more effective than strict regulation because it harnesses free-market forces to cut emissions, encourages the development of new technologies to achieve those cuts, and provides flexibility in meeting targets.

The protocol also calls for "joint implementation" projects, through which countries with targets may get credits toward meeting them by reducing the emissions in other countries, in ways ranging from financing stronger air pollution controls on industrial stacks, to preserving forests that absorb carbon dioxide, one of the targeted gases. Companies in the developed world may similarly pursue "clean development mechanisms" in the developing world (e.g., building efficient power plants that enable the companies to earn credits while helping the developing nations prosper).

The protocol is subject to ratification by the member nations. To be enacted, 55 percent of the developed nations that produce 55 percent of the targeted gases must sign on. The United States alone produces 25 percent of the controlled gases.

1998 Climate Change Technology Initiative. In his 1998 State of the Union Address, President Clinton proposed to Congress a $6 billion plan to take on climate change through tax cuts and research and development on greenhouse gas emissions. Much of the initiative, which is pending Congressional approval, focuses on an array of energy efficiency measures. According to the DOE, key features of the proposal include:

- $3.6 billion in tax credits over five years for energy efficient purchases and renewable energy. That includes credits of $3,000 to $4,000 for consumers who buy advanced technology and highly fuel efficient vehicles; up to

$2,000 for consumers who buy rooftop solar power systems; and other credits in the areas of energy efficient homes, wind and biomass power, and combined heat and power systems.

- $2.7 billion in research and development over the next five years covering the four major greenhouse gas–emitting sectors of the economy—buildings, industry, transportation, and electricity. The research and development would also cover greenhouse gas removal and sequestration, federal facilities, and "cross-cutting" analyses and research.

1998 Comprehensive Electricity Competition Plan. President Clinton has also proposed to Congress recommendations aimed at shaping new legislation to restructure and introduce competition to the electric utility industry. The recommendations have become part of the broader debate on Capitol Hill over what role, if any, the federal government should play in restructuring the industry. The key goals of the plan are to:

- Reduce America's electricity bill by at least 10 percent or $20 million a year.
- Achieve a significant reduction in greenhouse gas emissions, focused on making a 25 million to 40 million metric ton reduction in carbon dioxide emissions alone by 2010.
- Substantially increase nonhydroelectric renewable energy sources by 2010.

The plan's goals would be met by:

- Establishing clear federal support for wholesale and retail competition in the electricity industry.
- Maintaining flexibility for the states so they may craft their own approaches to competition.
- Helping consumers by ensuring competition actually occurs, and by making it easier for them to make competitive choices.
- Establishing systems benefits charges and renewable portfolio standards to promote energy efficiency, renewable energy, and other public benefits.
- Reducing emissions through competition.
- Requiring key market players to join an organization that would set and enforce reliability standards for the electric system subject to oversight by the Federal Energy Regulatory Commission.
- Clarifying federal and state authorities for governing a restructured, competitive electricity industry.
- Allowing existing public power facilities used in competitive electricity markets to retain tax-exempt financing.
- Providing trading authority for nitrogen oxide (NO_x) emissions to promote cost-effective, market-driven NO_x reductions.

ISSUES AND TRENDS

Opportunities for environmental professionals in the energy field are affected by a wide range of economic, financial, technological, and legal considerations. A few of the major ones are summarized below.

RESTRUCTURING THE ELECTRICITY INDUSTRY

In the tradition of restructuring such industries as coal, natural gas, and long-distance telephone service to introduce competition to regulated monopolies and benefit consumers with lower rates, a move is afoot to restructure the electricity industry. Driven in part by the Energy Policy Act of 1992, the effort is taking shape on a state-by-state basis across the country. The DOE reports that as of April 1998, ten states have enacted restructuring legislation, six have issued comprehensive regulatory orders, twenty have orders or legislation pending, twelve have commissions or legislative investigations ongoing, and only three have taken no significant action. Deregulating the electricity industry is a complex venture that has the potential to give consumers a choice in the source of their power and, with proper incentives such as net metering, renewables portfolio standards, and research and development funds, could make green power available and affordable to the plurality of Americans who consider themselves environmentally conscious. It requires such professionals as energy attorneys, regulators, economists, engineers, marketers, communicators, and others. Competition is expected to decrease employment opportunities in traditional areas, but increase it in newer ones. "What does this mean? It means fewer people will be employed in the old-style utilities, but a lot of opportunity in competitive electricity production and marketing and at companies that produce power from alternative sources that may be more environmentally sound," says Susan Holte, director of the Demand and Integration Division of the DOE's Energy Information Administration.

Environmentalists are not in agreement on the positive benefits of deregulating the electric utility industry. While some see deregulation as a crucial step toward the development of local energy markets that will spur growth in conservation and renewable energy production, others envision a negative scenario in which states compete to release powerful utility companies from environmental and consumer protection restrictions with dire consequences for the public and the environment.

Aspiring energy professionals should study arguments on all sides of the deregulation issue, as well as track local, state, and national debates that will affect employment opportunities.

RESPONDING TO CLIMATE CHANGE

Concern has mounted in the last decade over the build-up of global greenhouse gases that scientists say could raise the planet's temperature and cause widespread upheaval in climate patterns. The concern peaked in December 1997 with the Kyoto Protocol to the United Nations Framework Convention on Climate Change, an agreement signed by over 150 developed nations aimed at reducing greenhouse gas emissions by 6 to 8 percent below 1990 levels by 2012 (see discussion on page 266). Should the nations ratify the protocol, implementing it will require an extraordinary array of professionals, perhaps the most eclectic group ever assembled to solve an environmental problem. It will include experts in international energy trade, law, finance, and diplomacy; in sciences such as chemistry, biology, physics, and geology; in macroeconomics and statistics; in foreign languages and cultural anthropology, among others. Everyone from foreign diplomats who can create international agreements, to city planners and civil engineers who can relocate coastal highways and bridges as global warming induced sea levels rise, is needed. "We're going to have to move things, and so there will be a lot of civil engineering projects, a lot of infrastructure projects," says Daniel Becker, director of the Global Warming and Energy Program at the Sierra Club.

NUCLEAR POWER'S UNCERTAIN FUTURE

The DOE projects that energy generation from America's nuclear power plants will drop from 101 gigawatts generated by 100 plants in 1996, to 52 gigawatts generated by 65 plants in 2020. Decommissioning plants and disposing of years of waste safely will be a critical concern, requiring the expertise of nuclear engineers, transportation safety experts, utility economists, hardrock geologists, toxicologists, and more.

Moreover, nuclear power may not be dead after all. Greenhouse gas emissions are clearly one of the leading environmental issues of our time. Along with its well known problems, nuclear power has one clear benefit—it produces no greenhouse gases at all. Electric utility officials, and some in the DOE, argue that keeping existing plants running could be critical in meeting climate change emission reduction targets.

"Job growth in the areas of decommissioning plants, extending their lives through advanced technologies, and managing their waste safely, could (to some extent) offset the jobs lost through the reduction in operating nuclear power," according to Jim Owens, a spokesman for the Edison Electric Institute.

AN INCREASING ROLE FOR NATURAL GAS

With nuclear power on the wane, coal and oil power continuing to create environmental problems, and renewables far from playing a major role in the energy mix, America's appetite for energy will be filled in the coming years by natural gas. The DOE projects gas consumption will increase from 3.0 quadrillion Btus in 1996 to 10.1 quadrillion Btus in 2020. Jobs are likely to follow in the areas of natural gas production, transport, marketing, and planning. "Clearly there will be a serious decline in the nuclear industry, but the significant trend, what's more striking, is the increase in natural gas, particularly for electricity generation. Depending on how you measure it, it will triple over our forecast to 2020, and so that clearly indicates the possibility of jobs in gas production and marketing," the DOE's Holte says.

ENERGY EFFICIENCY AND ENERGY TECHNOLOGY

Some of the most creative work in the energy world is being done by those finding innovative ways to improve our energy efficiency. Energy efficiency opportunities are literally everywhere, and the savings can be remarkable. Some of the more visible energy efficiency efforts include EPA's "Energy Star" program, which promotes computers that minimize energy use, and the "Green Lights" effort to convert industry to high efficiency lighting. Big progress has also been made in the creation of energy efficient clothes dryers, refrigerators, air conditioners, cars, industrial processes, and much more. Homes and buildings are becoming more efficient through basic design changes and innovations such as "superwindows," which offer insulation as good as that of walls.

Progress in reducing energy use has been astounding, and our progress has consistently outpaced the projections of the energy industry. In 1990, for example, the Edison Electric Institute predicted that the U.S. would require 72,000 megawatts of new capacity by the year 2000. Demand has fallen so much since then that only a tiny fraction of this new capacity is being built. In fact, the Electric Power Research Institute says that the American lifestyle could be maintained with around 70 percent of mid-1990s power use.

Energy conservation advocates such as Amory Lovins believe we could do much better. He has projected that, with proper investments, the U.S. could support itself at a comfortable level with only 30 percent of our current capacity. In addition, the investment needed to bring about the energy efficient economy would more than pay for itself.

Energy efficiency creates employment throughout the economy. Because energy efficiency improvements promise bright financial and social returns when successful, government and industry are pumping money into research and development efforts, creating a hot market for innovators. Among the hottest ventures is work on new fuel cell technologies. Research jobs in academia, think tanks, agencies, and consulting firms are on the rise.

Finally, the work of energy efficiency is not limited to technological improvements. It also requires the daily efforts of millions of citizens who leave the car at home, turn off the lights, turn down the thermostat, open the window on a hot day, and generally use less energy.

A CONTINUING PUSH FOR GREEN POWER

"Green power," or renewable energy, includes wind power, solar energy, methanol from biomass, and state-of-the-art hydroelectric power. Some include natural gas as "green." As we enter the 21st century, green power accounts for a very small portion of America's energy mix. In addition, the DOE expects relatively minimal growth in the overall percentage of energy drawn from renewables. Environmental supporters of renewable energy, however, are working hard to make green power a bigger part of our energy picture.

John Byrne, director of the Center for Energy and Environmental Policy at the University of Delaware, points out that the rise of green power is part of a collection of changes that are altering our energy future. "We're moving away from large scale energy supply systems to more of an energy service model, combining local sources, renewables, and highly efficient technology," Byrne says.

Several factors will determine how quickly green power grows. A big consideration, of course, is the price and availability of other energy sources. For this reason, many suggest that the fastest way to spur the growth of renewable energy is to tax fossil fuels more heavily, so that the price of oil and coal matches its "real" cost. More directly, the growth of green power will depend on technological breakthroughs and the deregulation of the power industry.

Progress has been swift in the first area, but not sufficient. Solar energy developments, for instance, are a mixed bag. Although solar fuel cells can be found in an increasing number of buildings across the country and are being developed for use in hybrid vehicles, solar technologies remain relatively expensive for the efficiency offered. Similarly, commercial production of electricity from solar cell arrays has had limited success without substantial subsidies. Costs are falling rapidly, however, and the conversion efficiency of solar technologies continues to grow. Investors and entrepreneurs are optimistic that the solar industry is poised for rapid growth.

Wind power has already become competitive with other sources in some parts of the country. The Electric Power Research Institute suggests that wind power may produce as much as 50,000 megawatts by the year 2010, and wind advocates believe the number could be much higher. Many parts of the northern plains, Rocky Mountain west, and Sierra Nevadas have the combination of steady wind and broad open space appropriate for wind energy. As the industry moves away from a focus on large windmills to many smaller machines, opportunities are growing.

Electric utility deregulation is expected to push renewable energy forward. As restructuring creates competition in local areas where monopolies once reined, "green power" companies will be able to compete for customers. Some polling suggests that a substantial portion of the populace is willing to pay more for nonpolluting energy from local sources. "We'll all be involved in promoting a green power alternative—energy choices that allow us to get off fossil fuels. We want more local renewable energy use," says Kirk Stone, assistant director for energy policy at the New Hampshire Governor's Office of Energy and Community Services.

For a fascinating overview of the renewable energy movement, read *Charging Ahead: The Business of Renewable Energy and What It Means for America*, by John Berger (University of California Press, http://www.ucpress.edu).

CAREER OPPORTUNITIES

Because energy work is so broad and diverse, opportunities can be found throughout the economy, as seen below.

PUBLIC SECTOR

Government plays a crucial role in shaping our energy future, through regulation, policy, financial subsidies, research, development, and more.

Federal Government. The chief federal agency involved in energy issues is the U.S. Department of Energy, although other federal agencies, including the U.S. Environmental Protection Agency, U.S. Army Corps of Engineers, and U.S. Fish and Wildlife Service, all play roles. Much of the most innovative work is being done in the national laboratories. Prominent national labs such as Argonne near Chicago, Lawrence Livermore in northern California, Oak Ridge in Tennessee, and the National Renewable Energy Laboratory in Colorado are leading research establishments for energy and environmental scientists. Researchers at these facilities are often at the cutting edge of the nation's energy work. Tracking projects at these facilities is a must for aspiring innovators.

Like much of the federal government, however, the DOE is downsizing, making if difficult to get a job, regardless of how numerous and pressing the demands are on the agency. "We're not expanding," says the DOE's Holte. The downsizing began with the temporary shutdown of the federal government in the mid-1990s, which resulted in a long-range plan at the DOE and other agencies to restructure their workforces, "seriously cutting back on employment," Haile says. "So far that plan is still in place, so we are hiring contractors instead of new employees. The last fiscal year for the plan is 2000. Employment in this department is shrinking, and it has been throughout the agency."

The DOE's Energy Information Administration, a policy-neutral arm of the DOE that does integrated analysis and forecasting on energy, had 435 to 450 employees before the downsizing began, Holte says. It was down to about 340 in early 1998, "and our target is 361 by the end of the fiscal year on September 30. There's been some talk of shifting our targets, but right now it's 348 by the end of fiscal year 1999."

Beyond the DOE and its laboratories, the EPA offers interesting opportunities for energy policy and research professionals. Because energy use and efficiency affect air pollution and other concerns regulated by the EPA, the agency has begun programs to help a wide range of industries, from computers and appliances to cars and buildings, use energy more wisely. Hiring, however, is relatively small.

Even in times of limited hiring, a wide array of opportunities can exist. Research positions at federal contractors, for example, remain strong. Moreover, replacement jobs emerge as people retire or move to other opportunities. And, if a major new program arises, such as ratification of the Kyoto Protocol, there will be a dramatic increase in positions.

The University of Delaware, for one, is not worried. Its Center for Energy and Environmental Policy graduates six to eight students a year with Ph.D.s and twenty to twenty-five with master's degrees. "We have no problem finding employment for our students after they graduate," he says. Graduates go to all sectors, but many find research jobs in the federal bureaucracy, Byrne notes. Some have found employment at the DOE and the EPA, while others work at the General Accounting Office and Congressional Research Service.

Prospective energy professionals should monitor the usual employment sources—agency websites, recruitment fairs, help wanted ads, and word-of-mouth networks—to stay in touch.

State Government. State energy offices have differing names, and fall under differing arms of state government, but share common goals that then dictate the sorts of professionals who work for them. Those professionals include engineers, economists, statisticians, forecasters, policy experts, regulators, and communicators.

The energy offices are also facing challenges that affect future career opportunities. Those challenges include getting the DOE (and federal government generally) to streamline federal energy offices in ways that provide better service to states. States also request that any federal action taken to legislate restructuring of the electricity industry not impede the progress already made by states.

Other challenges include reversing the decline in federal aid to the state energy agencies from the DOE, clarifying when the Strategic Petroleum Reserve may be used, increasing federal efforts to ensure constant energy supplies, and promoting alternative fuels. Within states themselves, the agencies work to implement many programs, including weatherization, low-income heating fuel assistance, and retrofitting state office buildings for improved energy efficiency. Among the biggest challenges, of course, is restructuring the electricity industry.

State energy officials perform a wide range of duties, from high-level policy work to "on-the-ground" assistance programs for low-income people for whom available energy is a crucial need. According to the National Association of State Energy Officials, state-level responsibilities include:

- Advising governors and legislators on energy issues.
- Ensuring that the needs and issues of industry, business, and residential and other small energy consumers are considered during energy policy development.
- Helping businesses to use energy effectively, modernizing industry and retaining and creating jobs.
- Bringing together divergent public interests and work to build consensus to

implement energy efficiency and renewable energy projects and programs that benefit the economy and the environment.

- Assisting energy providers during energy emergencies and natural gas disasters to mitigate supply disruptions and coordinate state, local, and regional responses.
- Supporting residential and other small energy consumers in meeting their energy needs with an emphasis on the most cost-effective and energy-efficient solutions possible.
- Demonstrating the application of the most cost-effective, advanced energy efficiency and renewable energy technologies in real world situations.
- Working to deploy cutting-edge technologies that reduce energy costs at publicly supported facilities.
- Working with state agencies to deploy cost-effective, state-of-the-art technologies to reduce energy consumption.
- Communicating to the public the importance of energy to our economy and environment, emphasizing the value of cost-effective energy efficiency measures.

State energy officials are also not provincial to state energy offices. Such officials may work in other state agencies, from state environmental agencies doing air quality modeling, to state transportation agencies improving mass transit options, to state public utilities commissions ensuring that consumers are subject to appropriate rates.

Local Government. On the local level, energy professionals are employed in many ways. Some work for municipalities as energy code inspectors, evaluating residential, commercial, and industrial construction to make sure it is energy efficient. Many of those inspectors are former builders who have become versed in energy efficiency. Professionals also work as municipal or county energy officers, trying to find ways of improving the energy efficiency of public facilities and local transportation. Regional coalitions of local government officials now often include energy committees working on regional energy efficiency.

As restructuring of the electricity industry takes hold, and competition drives rate prices down, more and more communities will be developing, with the help of their state energy offices, new energy supply options that will combine some traditional oil, coal, gas, or nuclear power with local renewable sources, from wind to rivers. Local energy officials will therefore come to play a major role in determining what renewable sources their communities have.

"Communities will be doing what they can to save energy, and to keep the energy supply local and recirculating," says Stone of the New Hampshire Governor's Office of Energy and Community Services, which is working with New Hampshire's 234 communities on energy concerns.

PRIVATE SECTOR

The trends that will dictate the private sector's job needs in the coming years are the same as those that will dictate job needs in the other sectors—restructuring the electricity industry, responding to climate change, dealing with the declining nuclear power industry and growing natural gas industry, developing new energy efficiency technologies, and promoting green power.

The private sector will move aggressively to meet its energy needs, according to John Castagna of the Edison Electric Institute, an organization supported by the electric companies that produce 79 percent of America's electricity. Despite industry consolidation, decommissioning of nuclear power plants, and other developments that will cut into the energy work force, a dazzling array of new opportunities are expected to emerge as businesses work to meet late-20th-century energy challenges.

Energy employment in the private sector depends heavily on the future of electric utility deregulation. A new "energy services" industry is expected to grow out of deregulation, generating an estimated $400 billion annually over the next ten years. "There will be wholly new customer service areas, requiring a whole new class of professionals," says Castagna. "Those who can identify new service areas, and put them in the hands of customers, will be needed. In addition, we'll need people who can explain to today's executives why new services are important, and should be provided."

"Someone will have to envision these technologies and figure out how they will all work," Castagna says. "And so these kids now in high school, or even in elementary school, will become that class of engineers who will get us to very special places not too long from now." Some students need not look far right now to get a glimpse of the future, as entire school districts in Texas and California have converted to photovoltaically generated solar power, he says.

In the same vein, while the DOE believes renewables will remain static over the next few decades, corporate America is thinking differently, says Castagna. "Renewable energy will become increasingly important," he says. "Right now, only a small portion of the nation's power comes from renewables, but anyone who has an interest in, or talent for, science might think about a career in solar, wind, or hydropower, because companies are bullish on renewables. Talk with them instead of the DOE, and you'll hear a different story. Green power may seem a little touchy right now, but you're going to see more and more of it, because competition is forcing companies to distinguish themselves from one another. Companies are realizing that if they can distinguish themselves in the eyes of customers as producing clean power, that will be good for them down the road."

Energy marketing, fueled by competition, "will require energy suppliers who can think outside of the box, energy marketers who can spot consumer needs before consumers themselves know they have those needs, and so be the first on the block," Castagna says. As energy supply shifts to "distributed generation"—power produced by many small, local generators relying in part on locally available renewable sources, rather than by centralized power plants located far from customers—not only will marketers become important, but so will "professionals who know what to do with distributed generation systems, know how to manage them, how to bring them to people, including a new class of community planning professionals," he says.

It doesn't stop there. Becker, of the Sierra Club, says the energy consulting field is growing to meet the nation's ever-evolving energy needs, from figuring out what to do with nuclear waste, to whether all these new technologies will actually work. In transportation, car manufacturers will be looking for engineers to develop fuel cell technologies, designers to develop lightweight vehicles, chemists to develop cleaner fuels, and more.

The private sector opportunities mentioned above are primarily in companies specifically related to energy development, marketing, and generation. A great deal of the nation's energy-related employment, however, is hidden in other job titles. Facilities management and purchasing staff, for example, play a large role in the way business manages energy, through daily decisions about light bulbs, windows, computers, building design, control of the company car fleet, and more. Look for industry "environmental" staff to work more closely with facilities and process-design people for "total environmental quality management," including energy use.

NONPROFIT SECTOR

As is the case on other issues, getting an energy job in an environmental group is tough. In fact, getting any job in an environmental group is tough. "For any given job at the Sierra Club, we have a minimum of 250 resumes if the job is advertised, and so these are very hard jobs to get," says Becker, the Sierra Club's director of the Global Warming and Energy Program.

Many of the major national groups—the Sierra Club, Natural Resources Defense Council, and Environmental Defense Fund, among them—have launched energy programs in recent years. The programs often include global warming and climate change components, but also clean air, transportation, electricity industry restructuring, and advanced technologies components, among others. The programs are typically staffed by policy experts, communicators, attorneys, and atmospheric scientists, among other professionals. But the staffs are small, and while turnover does occur regularly, competition for these jobs can be fierce.

Regional groups have also become more involved in energy issues, focused not so much on Beltway politics and Capitol Hill lobbying aimed at shaping national policy, but on issues in their own backyards. New England's Conservation Law Foundation (CLF), for instance (arguably the region's most influential environmental group) has become increasingly involved in energy. The group has been working to shut down dirty coal and oil plants in the region and have them replaced by natural gas plants. It has also gotten involved in hydroelectric facility relicensing requests to the Federal Energy Regulatory Commission, orchestrating agreements between other conservation groups, utilities, and state governments that result in concessions by the utilities to preserve riverfront land, improve stream flows, or achieve other environmental benefits as part of winning new licenses. And CLF has been involved in the efforts in states across New England to restructure the electricity industry.

Again, jobs at regional groups such as CLF are not plentiful. But they do turn up from time to time, typically for environmental attorneys and environmental scientists. The same is true for statewide environmental groups, although the jobs there are even fewer.

Finally, an array of groups exist that are focused on specific energy alternatives, from electric cars to wind power, offering staff and volunteer opportunities for energy advocates.

SALARY

Like other federal agencies, the DOE employs people according to a grade and step system known as "GS." In 1998, the lowest GS position, GS-1, had a starting salary of $13,902 and a salary after ten years at that GS level of $17,393. The highest position, GS-15, had a starting salary of $77,798 and a salary after ten years of $101,142. A mid-level position, for instance GS-7, had a starting salary of $26,532 and a salary after ten years of $34,487. Salaries are comparable in other federal agencies. Which GS position a job candidate qualifies for depends primarily on his or her academic training and degrees, as well as overall professional experience.

At the state energy agencies, the National Association of State Energy Officials (NASEO) found in a 1995 survey of its members that 12 percent of state energy agency staff earn $25,000 to $40,000, 41 percent earn $41,000 to $60,000, 34 percent earn $61,000 to $80,000, 3 percent earn $81,000 to $100,000, and 3 percent earn more than $100,000.

These state agency staff "would be the lead energy officials in a state, most of whom are specializing in energy efficiency or energy security matters and are not regulators," says David Terry, NASEO's communications director. "They are the people who run energy programs."

For local energy officials working at the municipal level, salaries can vary widely, depending on everything from academic training to job title to location in the country, says Donald Osborn, Manager of the Photovoltaic and Distributed Technologies Department at the Sacramento, California, Municipal Utility District, one of the more progressive utility districts in the country.

"It really depends on the subfield," Osborn says. "A person working as a local government energy officer is probably making somewhere around $15,000. They are generally not well paid. On the other hand, someone who is managing an energy program for a public utility, who is an engineer in an engineering management position, will be making $75,000 to $90,000. So part of it depends on whether it is an engineering position or a program management position that doesn't require an engineering degree, because policy positions tend to pay less than engineering positions."

Private sector salaries are wildly diverse, from the $15,000 earned by technicians, to the $25,000 a year paid to policy specialists, to the $65,000 earned by engineers, to the six-figure annual salaries earned by energy consultants, to the $1 million-plus salaries earned by company CEOs. Much depends on the job one has. Other factors include professional experience, academic training and degrees, location in the country, and of course, employer.

Salaries for entry-level positions in the nonprofits typically range from the mid-teens to the mid-20s. After that, salaries climb slowly and tend to peak in the 50s to 60s in the more established groups, with the exception of presidents and executive directors, whose salaries can climb into six figures and be dramatically higher than even the number two people in their groups. Many of the major nonprofits have been criticized in the media in recent years for paying their executive directors so much, while the vast majority of staff members at those groups get paid considerably less.

"Entry level in the Sierra Club is in the low-20s," says the Sierra Club's Becker. "They're a little higher at the National Resources Defense Council (NRDC), a little lower at Public Interest Research Group (PIRG). The top jobs here are lower than the top jobs in most of our competition. The NRDC and Wilderness Society pay 30 to 40 percent more than we do. But, you know, you don't go into the environment if you want to get rich. The pay you get is psychic pay. And if that's not enough, you won't be happy."

GETTING STARTED

Because the energy field is so vast, getting started requires some front end decison making. Do you want blue-collar or white-collar work? Do you want to work in industry, advocacy, government, academia, or some combination of those?

Do you want to focus on science, economics, statistics, policy, law, business, marketing, trade, communication, regulation, research, planning, development, design, architecture, or another of the many careers involving energy?

Answering such questions is more important in planning an energy career than maybe any other in environmentalism, simply because of the diversity of opportunity energy offers. Energy careers are as far-ranging as energy itself, and so the sooner such front-end, career-orienting questions are answered, the better able you will be to prepare yourself for entry into the field.

EDUCATION

There are literally tens of thousands of jobs in the energy industry that do not require any more academic training than a high school degree, although they might require some vocational or job-specific training that can be acquired at vocational schools, in the military, or elsewhere. There is another tier of energy professionals who typically have associate's or bachelor's degrees, usually in their specific career areas. They include technicians, computer programmers, drafters, inspectors, and monitors.

Yet another tier includes the energy professionals who typically have graduate degrees, sometimes more than one, and whose careers are often the net result of their undergraduate and graduate training.

Engineers of virtually every stripe work in energy, including environmental, chemical, civil, solar, electrical, design, mechanical, and genetic. Chemists, geologists, physicists, earth scientists, biologists, climatologists, meterologists, and foresters work in energy. Mathematicians, architects, and economists do too.

Attorneys, policy makers, statisticians, modelers, policy experts, regulators, communicators, advocates, forecasters, researchers, and marketers also work in energy. And for this tier of energy professionals, those already at work in energy advise once again that you make your career decisions as early as possible, because those decisions will dictate courses of academic study, desired internships and entry-level jobs, as well as movement through your career.

Beyond that, there is one word of advice that continues to turn up among professionals working in energy, be they in the public, private, or nonprofit sectors—regardless of which course of study you pursue, make sure it includes some consideration of the environment and economics relative to energy. Study law or policy, geology or physics, engineering or architecture, because any of those areas of study can be made to work in energy. But complement those areas of study with an understanding of the environment and economics, because in the end, those are energy's bottom lines, whether it be in promoting joint implementation projects overseas, in developing cleaner fuels for cars and trucks, in planning communities that rely on mass transit, or any other work in energy.

"Folks with a knowledge of energy systems and energy's impact on the environment and economy will be key," says Byrne of the Center for Energy and Environmental Policy at the University of Delaware. "We're generally going to see a mixing of environmental, economic, and energy thinking, which means careers are going to be different from the old-styled electrical engineering professions. They're going to have a more interdisciplinary outlook, and so those in them will need to know a bit more about environmental matters, economic matters, and energy matters. That will only increase."

ADVICE

For those interested in working on the environmental end of energy, those in the field suggest that you have what many environmentalists have—a strong sense of the issues and a desire to resolve them.

Think of energy as environmental and economic, and not just energy. "If you're going to get into energy, get into the environmental aspects of energy, and get into the economic aspects of energy. Don't focus on energy strictly as resource technology, because that's too narrow for the future," says John Byrne, director of the Center for Energy and Environmental Policy, University of Delaware.

Be committed. "Volunteer. If you can show an organization that you care enough to volunteer for them, then that's how you will show you're of value to them," says Daniel Becker, director of the Global Warming and Energy Program at Sierra Club.

Stay flexible, but directed. "Be persistent, and realize that it may take a while to get in there. Job hunting in any field these days is not a one-week or one-month process. It takes quite a while, if you're looking for something specific, if you're looking for the right job. But just because there might not be any jobs available right now doesn't mean there won't be later," says Erin Boedecker, operations research analyst at U.S. Department of Energy.

SUMMARY

An environmentalist seeking a career in energy must be willing to take on some daunting, but vital, challenges, if America and the world are to live sustainably. There is the challenge of converting from nonrenewable to renewable power—from coal, oil, and nuclear power to solar, wind, and geothermal power. There is the challenge of getting more out of the power we use, and developing energy efficiency and conservation so that we live well on less. And there is the challenge of rectifying the energy errors of our past, ranging from 50 years of nuclear waste that will remain lethal for 10,000 years more, to a century of greenhouse gas emissions that are bringing the planet to the brink of extraordinary climate change. The challenges are arguably more formidible than any in environmentalism, and the energy professional of the 21st century must be ready for them.

CASE STUDY

Corporation for Solar Technology and Renewable Resources
Las Vegas, Nevada

The enthusiasm that many entrepreneurs share for renewable energy resources is difficult to translate into commercial success. To overcome the technical obstacles and market barriers to solar energy, government support is needed in the form of subsidies, tax breaks, portfolio standards, and other creative policy mechanisms. The intrepid spirit of entrepreneurs willing to brave difficult new terrain will also be required.

At its birth in 1995, the future of the Corporation for Solar Technology and

Renewable Resources (CSTRR) appeared as bright as the sun that beats down on the southern Nevada desert.

CSTRR, a nonprofit corporation created to develop solar and renewable power in Nevada for nationwide transmission, had a market study in hand indicating there was a government and private sector demand in the region alone for 100 megawatts of solar power. The Energy Policy Act of 1992 encouraged greater production of solar and renewable power. Also that year, President Clinton signed an executive order making that boost in solar and renewable power a national goal, and directing the U.S. Department of Energy to lead the effort to make it happen.

If that weren't enough, CSTRR has received a $3 million grant from the U.S. Department of Energy. As one of America's first, on-the-ground ventures to make the rhetoric of renewable power a reality, the organization was funded to play matchmaker between those with a desire for solar power (e.g., agencies, utilities, and Native American tribes), and those willing to provide it by building and operating solar generating facilities and distribution networks.

But three years into the venture, CSTRR "has not generated one kilowatt of power," says CSTRR President Rose McKinney-James. It has been impeded by obstacles such as antiquated federal regulations that work against the development of solar and renewable power. The rush to deregulate the electricity industry is another possible obstacle. Deregulation may drive down rates for electricity generated by nonrenewable sources, and so make more expensive renewable sources even less competitive economically.

"We are the poster child for why these initiatives are having difficulty going forward," McKinney-James says. In that sense, the story of CSTRR's struggle to get solar power off the ground offers a glimpse into the realities of renewables in America, and with it the realities of careers in this arena.

Conceived in part to cope with the downsizing of the Nevada Test Site in the wake of Clinton's imposed moratorium on nuclear testing, CSTRR was the product of a task force formed by U.S. Senator Richard H. Bryan of Nevada in 1994 and cochaired by McKinney-James, then the state's director of the Department of Business and Industry.

According to McKinney-James, the task force identified three niche markets for solar power. Federal facilities were first on the list because of support in the federal government for power generated by alternative sources and because many facilities were paying top-dollar rates for conventionally generated energy. Native American tribes came second because of their desire for energy independence and because many were located in areas with great solar power generating potential. Finally, electric utilities were considered a market because they were experimenting with solar and renewable power already.

The task force determined that the solar market had a potential demand of 1,000 megawatts in the ensuing decade, but it set a short-term goal of developing 100 megawatts by the year 2000 in a "solar enterprise zone" made up of five generating sites in southern Nevada. The task force floated a nationwide request for proposals in 1995 to power providers, received fourteen responses, and announced four finalists in January 1996.

"This is where it became interesting," says McKinney-James.

Two of the power providers soon fell by the wayside, one because of bankruptcy and the other because of a management shift. That left the two others— Amoco Enron Solar Project Development Corporation, based in Houston, and Nevada Power Company, based in Las Vegas. Amoco Enron was ready to take on the full 100 megawatts, creating a "solar farm" to generate electricity that could be delivered at 8 cents a kilowatt hour. This was easily the best offer, says McKinney-James.

But then more problems arose. CSTRR had surveyed federal facilities across the country and found that nine to ten of them were interested in buying its power, totaling 83 megawatts. But federal procurement regulations prohibit federal facilities from entering into energy contracts for more than ten years. The regulations also require facilities to choose the least expensive source of that energy.

The only way Amoco Enron could provide its solar energy at 8 cents a kilowatt hour was through a thirty-year contract that better enabled it to recover its initial capital costs. A ten-year contract would drive up the rate to 25 cents or more. Meanwhile, even 8 cents was more expensive than the rates for non-renewable power, especially as fossil fuel prices had dropped and there was a glut of generating capacity. McKinney-James points out that low rates for conventional energy are deceptive, because they do not consider "externalities," such as the cost of cleaning up pollution caused by fossil fuels, a cost that does not exist with solar. Still, the law is the law.

And so no deals with federal facilities have gone forward. CSTRR got a commitment in 1996 from the Nevada Test Site to buy 10 megawatts, but that is still pending. Further complicating the problem is the fact that regulations require federal facilities to buy power from state certified utilities, most of which do not provide solar power. And CSTRR is not such a utility. Unless the regulations are changed or an exception can be crafted, CSTRR is stalled in selling to federal facilities, McKinney-James says.

Things are not much brighter in the private market. CSTRR did award the Nevada Power Company a 1 megawatt deal in 1996 for whatever market demand developed after the Nevada Test Site project, based on rates agreed to between the two parties. But then as industry deregulation took hold, Nevada Power came under pressure from its largest customers, especially the casinos, to cut its rates. The company went ahead and cut its rates for those largest customers, making the already more expensive solar energy rates even less competitive economically.

And so that deal is also on hold, as are talks generally with utilities, who are reluctant to commit to renewables, given the deep uncertainty that deregulation has created in the energy market.

CSTRR's problems did not stop there. Recognizing that the greatest challenge to getting solar power off the ground was up-front capital costs, CSTRR decided to pursue tax-exempt status with the Internal Revenue Service. Unlike nonrenewables, renewables are virtually free after capital costs are paid, with solar eventually costing customers as little as 2 cents a kilowatt hour. CSTRR earned tax-exempt status in 1996. With it, CSTRR believed it could then float tax-exempt bonds to finance the capital costs for projects such as Amoco Enron.

But just as CSTRR received its tax-exempt status, there was a change in the federal tax code that prevented it from floating bonds, taking away a major funding mechanism for the projects. Floating the bonds "was the whole idea" behind the tax-exempt status, and so losing that "was a huge setback," McKinney-James says.

"And so, candidly, we've been trying to work through all of these issues in the last few months," McKinney-James states in a 1998 interview. Its $3 million grant will run out in the third quarter of 1999, and so it is seeking non-federal and private sector funding. It tried to impose a fee for its services as matchmaker, but imposing such a fee on the DOE would prevent CSTRR from receiving DOE grants. Imposing fees on Amoco Enron, Nevada Power, or any other power provider would only result in higher rates for solar power. There was some thought given to CSTRR itself becoming a power provider, but its tax-exempt status precludes that.

McKinney-James says CSTRR recognized by 1997 that it had to work for legislative changes if it was to achieve its energy goals. And so it pushed through legislation on the state level to establish a "portfolio standard," a provision that requires a percentage of the state's power mix to come from renewables, in this case two-tenths of 1 percent, ratcheted up to a full percent in 2010. It also got legislation passed to establish electricity metering in the state and to create tax incentives for companies considering relocation to the state.

But McKinney-James says legislative changes are needed on the federal level if solar and renewable power are to gain a real toehold in the energy mix, with the best example of what is needed provided by President Clinton himself. The president announced in June 1998 his "Million Solar Roof Initiative," aimed at promoting solar energy by installing solar energy systems on a million rooftops in the next decade. To jump-start the initiative, Clinton committed the rooftops of 20,000 federal facilities. But McKinney-James says the initiative came with no money to make it happen, money especially needed to "buy down" the costs of solar power to the developer and customer. And more to the point of CSTRR's experience, she says "those 20,000 rooftops will face the same procurement obstacles in the federal regulations that CSTRR faces."

The federal regulations need to be amended to allow contracts longer than 10 years, McKinney-James says. The regulations must also recognize the externalities of nonrenewable energy sources, as well as their true costs and subsequent rates, understanding especially the extraordinarily cheap cost of solar power once capital costs are paid off. Regulations must also allow federal facilities to buy power from entities other than state certified utilities. During the years it takes to make such regulatory changes, exceptions should be allowed to enable projects to proceed, she says.

Finally, the federal government's preference for market-driven rather than subsidy-driven development of solar and renewables makes it difficult to admit that with restructuring of the electricity industry, solar energy is not price competitive in the short term, McKinney-James says. Until it is, the solar energy option will remain rhetoric, not reality.

"CSTRR is a target case study of what works and what doesn't in solar and renewables," says McKinney-James. "We've tried to exhaust all our remedies. But it's our view that we need legislative action to make this happen. There have been many pronouncements that have been promising, but when it comes down to actually deploying these technologies, there are economic, market, and procurement obstacles that really prohibit these projects from moving forward."

And so "for our little operation, it's been tough," McKinney-James continues. "It's a prime example of a worthy mission that's been thrust into a reality that precludes the fulfillment of that mission. We have not given up. We've found a few optimists who say it can be done against all odds. But there are occasions when we're so frustrated that we wonder if it's worth it. I've certainly been there."

PROFILE

Gautam Bakthavatsalam
Marketing Specialist
ASE Americas, Inc.
Billerica, Massachusetts

The potential for renewable energy in the developing world is great, both because it does not face entrenched competitors and because renewable energy can be generated at remote locations, independent of an existing unreliable infrastructure. But the obstacles, such as finding suitable partners and capital, are still formidable, and the field is not one for the faint of heart.

Gautam Bakthavatsalam is twenty-four years old, but he can still recall the brownouts and blackouts during his childhood years that would strike on especially hot days in New Delhi and in villages throughout his native India.

"In the big cities, we used to have frequent power shortages in the summer lasting three or four hours, making for a lot of inconvenience," says Bakthavatsalam, who grew up in New Delhi. "You have to understand—power is a luxury in India. Most cities and villages do not have good connections. If they do, it's a luxury. In many cities and villages, people are living in the dark for sixteen hours a day, and so I know the need for continuous power."

And so there is something personal behind Bakthavatsalam's work as a marketing specialist at ASE Americas, Inc., where he is primarily responsible for breaking into India's hot photovoltaic market. ASE develops, produces, and markets photovoltaic modules, cells, and associated components internationally.

Bakthavatsalam's work in India, he says, "is an opportunity to provide power to Indians, and so to change their way of life, to lift their economic status, to help them climb the social ladder."

Bakthavatsalam is well-suited for the task. His resume includes solid academic credentials, as well as professional experience, all in addition to the asset of being a native of the country his company wants to set up shop in. He earned a bachelor of science degree in engineering, specializing in electronics and communication, in 1994 from the Sri Jaychamaranrjendri College of Engineering in Mysore, India.

He then worked from 1994 to 1996 with Marg Securities Ltd., an investment banking firm in Madras, India, where he was a project analyst specializing in renewable energy. "The reason I got into this field is that I had an opportunity during that time to evaluate projects for the renewable energy sector, and that gave me a background in the financial side of the industry," he says.

He then came to the United States in 1996 to enroll in the M.B.A program at the Rochester Institute of Technology, specializing in international finance and business. He has finished his course work, and will be wrapping up his degree shortly. He joined ASE in March 1998 to head the company's division focused on new business and new project development, but initially with an eye toward India.

"ASE has plans of entering India, and I will be in charge eventually of all of our projects there," Bakthavatsalam says. "We want to set up joint ventures with one or two parties, where ASE would provide the cell technology. There's a huge market there, and we think there is potential."

Fueling that market is a planned expenditure by the World Bank of $15 million sometime in 1998, specifically for photovoltaic market development in India, Bakthavatsalam says. The World Bank is also planning to spend $5 million in Kenya and $5 million in Morocco for the same purpose, he said. The investments are part of the larger effort among developed nations to bring sustainable development to developing countries.

Bakthavatsalam's job, simply put, "is to develop a strategy for ASE to be in that initiative," he says. That involves a great deal of research, which takes up much of his normal workday. His research examines current affairs in India, financial sources for development projects, existing power distribution systems, Indian financial markets, and the credibility of potential partners.

"We have to find a local partner to work with ASE when we write a proposal, and because everyone wants to make a quick buck, we have to be careful," Bakthavatsalam says. "We have to make sure they're serious. That's the biggest challenge—the seriousness of the partner." He has not yet traveled all that much, but soon will, and not just to India. ASE has interests all over the world.

ASE has already accomplished much domestically and internationally for a company that was formed only in 1994. Among those accomplishments:

- A multimillion-dollar contract in 1997 for solar cells and technology transfer with Al Jazirah Solar of Saudi Arabia to power cellular sites for Lucent Technologies International in Saudi Arabia.
- Selection by the U.S. Navy to provide 300-watt photovoltaic (PV) modules to produce electricity on Santa Cruz Island off the coast of California for power generation and water pumping.
- Selection in 1996 by Applied Power Corporation to supply modules for the Dangling Rope Marina on Utah's Lake Powell, the largest PV system ever installed in a national park.
- Selection in 1996 by the Arizona Public Service Company to install modules at Arizona's Carol Springs Mountain to power two communications towers, replacing diesel generators there.
- Several high-visibility East Coast projects in 1996, including the lighting system in Martin Luther King Memorial Park in Atlanta, used during the 1996 Summer Olympic Games; an electric vehicle charging station at the Florida State Energy Office and a grid-tiered system at Florida State University's Florida Solar Energy Center; the power needs at various locations at the DOE's Washington headquarters; the power needs for emergency call boxes along New Jersey's Route 55; and the power needs for the 1996 Pageant of Peace Festival in Washington.

But for now, Bakthavatsalam is focused on India. "I'm very passionate about it, because I know the need for this type of technology in India, and I want to work hard to make it work," he says. Passion, he adds, is a quality anyone interested in a career in the field of renewable energy must have.

"You have to believe in this technology, have to really believe in it, because this technology has the potential to be our future," Bakthavatsalam says. "You should not look at this as just another job."

Steve Pedery
Conservation Assistant
Sierra Club Global Warming Team
Sierra Club
Washington, DC

One of the most crucial tasks in creating a safe and clean energy industry is making sure accurate information is available to voters, decision makers, and the media. Nonprofits play the most important role in this exciting area of work. The route may be difficult, but for those who follow it, it can be deeply fulfilling.

In the spring of 1994, Steve Pedery was doing what a lot of college students must do—he was looking for work.

Pedery had had many jobs since entering the University of South Carolina in 1993 to study government and international relations, having earned an associate's degree at Piedmont Technical College in criminal justice in 1992.

He'd worked everywhere from a video store to USC's contract grant accounting office. "I was a very typical college student, making a progression from job, to job, to job," he says.

"But when I was looking that spring, I saw an intriguing ad in the local newspaper, a sort of cryptic ad that simply said 'progressive organization seeks part-time administrative assistant to work on environmental issues,'" Pedery says. "I took a chance on it, because at the time I was part-timing at the school newspaper as a sales rep for ads, and that's not the most pleasant job."

That "progressive organization" turned out to be the Sierra Club, one of America's oldest and most established environmental groups. Pedery was hired in the Club's South Carolina state chapter office to work on grassroots organizing.

"I was an environmentalist and a college student, and so I thought it was a dream job," Pedery says. "And it turned out to be. USC is not exactly a hotbed of environmentalism. When I was there, it had only one environmental organization, and that was essentially a hiking club. I was looking for an outlet to be an advocate, and there really wasn't one. I wanted to make a change, to do something where I could bring about progressive change in society. And this was it."

Pedery is only 26, but has risen through the ranks at the Sierra Club. He paid his dues as a part-timer in South Carolina, mobilizing support for the group's agenda in the state, until he landed a temporary, nearly full-time job with the group's national office in 1996, although he is still based in South Carolina. That job became a permanent, full-time job later that year, only now based in Washington on the group's Global Warming Team, where he has been since. Along the way, he left USC, although he plans to complete his education.

In many ways, Pedery's short career typifies that of the nonprofit advocate. When he first came to the South Carolina state chapter, he found it staffed by only two others. "Originally I worked day to day to free up the director's time to lobby in the state legislature, or hold meetings and press events," he says.

Things changed quickly, Pedery adds. "In the first couple of months, I went from answering phones and clipping articles to actually writing articles for the state newsletter; setting up our phone, email, and fax trees; setting up and speaking at meetings; talking with the press; helping to draft press releases, doing research on environmental issues; drafting flyers; and supporting the various Sierra Club local groups around the state."

The chapter was focused on three issues in the State House, Pedery says. It was his job to bring grassroots pressure to bear on them. The issues, all manifest in legislation, were takings, environmental self-audits, and factory hog farming. The chapter scored a few wins, especially on hog farming. "The governor at the time was courting factory farms, trying to get them to come to the state by offering easy access to permits, tax incentives, and other things that ended up on a right-to-farm bill," he says. "We not only blocked that bill, but got some strong regulations in place."

Then in 1996, the Club launched an environmental public education campaign that involved hiring nearly full-time staffers out of the national office and placing them in state chapters. Pedery got one of the grant-funded positions, and ended up working thirty hours a week in the very same South Carolina state chapter.

In June, when a diesel pipeline operated by a major fuel company burst, sending 1 million gallons of fluorescent green fuel into the nearby Reedy River, Pedery got the attention of the Club's Energy and Global Warming program director, Dan Becker, when Pedery called Becker to ask if the Club had any background information on the company, as well as on similar spills around the country. "That was my first chance to work without a net, as the chapter director was not around," Pedery says. "The press was very interested in the company, and whether there had been other spills, and it turned out the company had spills up and down the Eastern seaboard."

Becker, impressed with Pedery's initiative, came to the obvious conclusion: "How could I *not* hire him?" When a job opened up in Becker's office later in 1996, roughly around the time that Pedery's grant ran out, that's just what Becker did.

As a member of the Club's Global Warming Team, Pedery has spent his time building grassroots support around the country to fight global warming, but also building support within the Club on the issue, as the Club has a long history of involvement with land protection and related issues. He's helped develop the Club's webpage, including his team's own page (http://www.toowarm.org) and more recently has been working on a public service announcement campaign.

He likes the Sierra Club "because it's one of the only organizations in the country that can do what it does—bring grassroots support to bear on national policy issues." He believes he's found a place in which to make the sort of progressive change he's long sought to make, a place that offers him the daily challenge "of working on something so big, with implications so long term." And while it has not been an easy career route, he'd recommend it.

"It's work that allows you to live out your ideals in the real world and actually see the results. You can have a hands-on effect in making things happen," Pedery says. "There are not a lot of careers where you get to do that."

Erin Boedecker
Operations Research Analyst
Energy Information Administration
U.S. Department of Energy
Washington, DC

Workers in the energy field have much to contribute to the environment, even if their work isn't strictly environmental. A more efficient, effective energy distribution network is in the interest of energy users, the government, and the environment. It also makes for rewarding work.

Erin Boedecker is fascinated with the real world, with applying her training in mathematics and engineering to actual problems, from finding oil underground, to shipping U.S. Air Force supplies to their destinations, to what she does now, which is tracking how much energy America's commercial sector uses.

In fact, Boedecker likes what she does so much that she commutes an hour each way in her car and on the subway to get to and from her job as an operations research analyst at the Office of Integrated Analysis and Forecasting in the Energy Information Administration, the independent statistical branch of the U.S. Department of Energy.

On the face of it, Boedecker's job might not seem all that "environmental," perhaps not as environmental as marketing photovoltaics in developing nations or convincing everyday Americans to care about climate change. But when you consider how much energy the commercial sector uses, the ecological impacts of that use, and the need to understand both before you can begin the hard work of making the sector more energy efficient, the environmentalism in Boedecker's job becomes apparent.

At the DOE, Boedecker is the principal analyst for the commercial sector's energy demand, a job she's held ever since she came to the DOE in 1994. She uses a mathematical modeling system to keep tabs on the commercial sector's energy use, analyzing how much energy it has used and is using, and forecasting how much it will use. "I like modeling because of my interest in problem solving, especially the mathematical end of problem solving," Boedecker says.

That interest began during her undergraduate days at Virginia Tech, where she majored in mathematics, but with a specific interest in "any type of applied mathematics where I could use equations to solve real world problems," Boedecker says. She earned a bachelor of science degree in mathematics from the school in 1981.

Come senior year, the two big industries recruiting on campus were defense and oil, and of the two, oil seemed like the better fit. She took a job with Gulf Oil, based in Houston, analyzing seismic exploration data to help locate oil deposits. But when oil prices took a dive in the mid-1980s and a wave of layoffs began, "the writing was on the wall," Boedecker says. She resigned just three days before her office was shut down in 1985, and set her sights on graduate school that fall at the University of Texas.

"The time was right to go back to school," Boedecker says. "I always had an interest in mathematical modeling, and so I decided to go to grad school for that."

As a graduate engineering student, Boedecker focused on operations research, "or mathematical modeling that represents real world systems," she explains. The modeling she studied "really ran the gamut, from inventory problems to transportation networks. It's really far-reaching," she says.

Which was fortunate, as Boedecker's life was about to become far-reaching. She finished her classwork in 1987, and while working on her thesis, met her future husband in San Antonio. He was in the military at the time. After they married, she took a job with the military as an industrial engineer for the U.S. Air Force in San Antonio, "on the inventory side of operations," she says.

"I did projects to help streamline operations," Boedecker says. "Basically, it involved aircraft parts, getting them where they needed to be, when they needed to be." When her husband was transferred to Germany, she followed him, and for a few years, did not work.

When they returned in 1993, Boedecker started job-hunting. "I didn't set out necessarily to go into the energy industry," she says. "I was looking for any sort of position where I could use my operations research background. The DOE happened to be looking for someone to work on their commercial sector simulation model, which I found out about through a computer system that lists a lot of federal jobs." She got the job, and began work in 1994—right before federal hiring took a dive even more precipitous than oil prices a decade earlier.

"I got in right before they really clamped down," Boedecker says. "I was hired in November of 1994, and a few others were hired after me in January of 1995. But then the hiring freeze went into effect, and they haven't hired since. There have been job cuts every year since, and so the difficulty of getting a job at the DOE increased greatly after I came on board."

Still, Boedecker says, anyone interested in working for the DOE should not give up hope. "It's not impossible to get a job at the DOE," she says. "As we downsize and surpass whatever targets we have on the number of positions, there will be critical areas where work must be done, and if no one is left in the agency with expertise, they will hire. I believe that will happen fairly soon in the EIA. There's been some talk in Congress. They're starting to realize that we're at a barebones level, and have recommended no further cuts."

And the opportunities are varied at the DOE, requiring as varied academic backgrounds, much like opportunities across the spectrum of energy professions, Boedecker says. "It depends on which area you want to go into," she says. "If you want to work on mathematical modeling, then you want to have a very rigorous mathematical background. But in other parts of the industry, they look for different backgrounds."

But Boedecker has found her niche. "I like the DOE, and the modeling work especially," she says. "I like the atmosphere here as well. We work together more as colleagues than in any hierarchical fashion. And I'm one of those people who commutes quite a distance, but it's worth it. If I didn't like the job that much, I wouldn't have stayed so long."

RESOURCES

There are literally thousands of potential resources, as energy is as broad a field as are the people and organizations who use and rely on it. Here are, however, several good places to start your research.

Alliance to Save Energy (ASE). 1200 18th Street, NW, Suite 900, Washington, DC 20036. (202) 857-0666. Http://www.ase.org. A nonprofit coalition of prominent business, as well as government, environmental, and consumer leaders who promote the efficient and clean use of energy worldwide to benefit the environment, the economy, and national security. Website provides information for consumers, educators, and energy professionals and covers their international programs, media information, and job openings with ASE.

American Council for an Energy-Efficient Economy (ACEEE). 1001 Connecticut Avenue, NW, Suite 801, Washington, DC 20036. (202) 429-8873. Http://www.aceee.org. An independent, nonprofit research group dedicated to advancing energy efficiency as a means of environmental protection and economic development. Their wide range of work from conducting in-depth technical and policy assessments and advising governments and utilities, to collaborating with businesses and other organizations and holding conferences is highlighted on their website. Also has links to energy efficiency-related organizations.

American Petroleum Institute (API). A major trade organization representing the oil and natural gas industries of the U.S., including the areas of exploration and production, transportation, refining, and marketing. Website is divided into sections: Newsroom, Resources Center, and Programs and Services. Newsletter, *API Reports*, is also available. 1220 L Street, NW, Washington, DC 20005. (202) 682-8000. Http://www.api.org.

American Solar Energy Society (ASES). A national organization dedicated to advancing both the near-term and long-term use of solar energy for the benefit of U.S. citizens and the global environment. Sponsors the National Solar Energy Conference, publishes *Solar Today* magazine and *Advances in Solar Energy*; publishes white papers; sponsors issue roundtables in Washington, D.C.; distributes solar publications; organizes a Solar Action Network; and has regional chapters throughout the country. ASES is the United States Section of the International Solar Energy Society. Website has many renewable energy links. 2400 Central Avenue, G-1, Boulder, CO 80301. (303) 443-3130. Http://www.ases.org.

American Wind Energy Association (AWEA). Advocates the development of wind energy as a reliable, environmentally superior energy alternative in the U.S. and around the world. Holds annual wind power conference. Although basic in design, website has good coverage of wind energy. 122 C Street, NW, Fourth Floor, Washington, DC 20001. (202) 383-2500. Http://www.igc.org/awea.

Association of Energy Engineers (AEE). 4025 Pleasantdale Rd., Suite 420, Atlanta, GA 30340. (770) 447-5083. Http://www.aeecenter.org. Provides information on the fields of energy efficiency, energy services, deregulation, facility management, plant engineering, and environmental compliance. Offers a full array of information outreach programs, including technical seminars, conferences, books and journals, and buyer-seller networking trade shows. Much available on the website, including a "virtual expo" and links to over thirty other energy sites.

Center for Energy Efficiency & Renewable Technologies (CEERT). A collaboration of major environmental organizations, public interest groups, and clean technology companies working to achieve a more sustainable energy future. Compelling force in key policy-making debates on the local, state, and federal levels. Provides technical support to environmental advocates and clean technology developers. Website links include clean power suppliers, technologies, and global warming. 1100 Eleventh Street, Suite 311, Sacramento, CA 95814. (916) 442-7785. Http://www.ceert.org.

Center for Renewable Energy and Sustainable Technologies (CREST). Operates Solstice, an Internet information service for sustainable energy and development and the Global Energy Marketplace (http://gem.crest.org), as well as a searchable database of more than 2,500 energy efficiency and renewable energy annotated web links. 1200 18th St., NW #900, Washington, DC 20036. (202) 530-2202. Also: 350 Townsend St., Suite 100, San Francisco, CA 94107. (415) 284-6400. Http://solstice.crest.org.

Edison Electric Institute. An association of shareholder-owned electric companies that generate 79 percent of America's electricity. Website includes public information, subscriptions, current and historical information about the industry, and upcoming conventions and expos. Member Net is available for corporate members. 701 Pennsylvania Avenue, NW, Washington, DC 20004. (202) 508-5000. Http://www.eei.org.

The EnviroLink Network. EnviroLink is a nonprofit organization, as well as a grassroots on-line community that unites hundreds of organizations and volunteers around the world. 4618 Henry Street, Pittsburgh, PA 15213. (412) 683-6400. Http://www.envirolink.org.

Environmental Defense Fund (EDF). EDF is dedicated to protecting the environmental rights of all people, including future generations. Website is an excellent resource for information about environmental issues. Includes newsletter (with back issues to 1970), practical action, news releases, program reports, exhibition, annual report, interactive sections, and special sections on energy and global climate change issues. 257 Park Avenue South, New York, NY 10010. (800) 684-3322. Http://www.edf.org.

Global Environmental Options (GEO). Promotes environmental stewardship through sustainable design and development of buildings, communities, and national parks. Utilizes a unique combination of comprehensive Internet resources, training, and hands-on project coordination. 1572 East Bryan Avenue, Salt Lake City, UT 84105. (801) 483-1635. Http://www.geonetwork.org.

National Association of State Energy Officials (NASEO). The nation's leading coalition of state and territorial energy officials from the state and territory energy offices and affiliates from the private and public sectors. Website includes news, events, issues, reference sources, state and affiliate members and links to their websites, and many energy links, including associations, institutes, centers, resources, and research organizations. 1414 Prince Street, Suite 200, Alexandria, VA 22314. (703) 299-8800. Http://www.naseo.org.

National Renewable Energy Laboratory (NREL). The world leader in renewable energy technology development to benefit both the environment and the economy. Website includes Opportunities section with job openings. 1617 Cole Boulevard, Golden, CO 80401-3393. (303) 275-3000. Http://www.nrel.gov.

Natural Resources Defense Council (NRDC). NRDC uses law, science, and the support of more than 400,000 members nationwide to protect the environment. Impressive website covers many topics, and information is accessible in many ways, including articles by topic, bulletins, guides, background information (sorted alphabetically by subject), frequently asked questions, facts, scrapbooks, and *e-Amicus* (journal). Their Air/Energy Program focuses on clean air standards, global warming, transportation, energy efficiency, renewable energy, and electric-industry restructuring. 40 West 20th Street, New York, NY 10011. (212) 727-1773. Http://www.nrdc.org.

Passive Solar Industries Council (PSIC). Resource for passive solar design for residential, institutional, and commercial buildings, as well as product information. Offers professional training, consumer education, and analysis tools nationwide. 1511 K. Street, NW, Suite 600, Washington, DC 20005. (202) 628-7400. Http://www.psic.org.

Renewable Energy Policy Project (REPP). Explores innovative policy, regulatory, and market-based incentive options to promote greater reliance on ecologically sustainable renewable energy technologies. Supports the advancement of renewable energy technology through policy research, including Issue Briefs and Research

Reports. Web links are by subject area and organization type, including international. 1612 K Street, NW, Suite 410, Washington, DC 20006. (202) 293-2833. Http://www.repp.org.

Rocky Mountain Institute (RMI). A nonprofit research and educational foundation with a mission to foster the efficient and sustainable use of resources as a path to global security. The institute creates, and helps individuals and the private sector to practice, new solutions to old problems—mainly by harnessing the problem-solving power of market economics and of advanced techniques for resource efficiency. Website includes frequently asked questions, newsletter, publications catalog, and consulting services. 1739 Snowmass Creek Road, Snowmass, CO 81654-9199. (970) 927-3851. Http://www.rmi.org.

Solar Energy Industries Association (SEIA). The national trade group for commercial enterprises involved in solar energy for over twenty years. Can learn about solar energy, order publications, and get answers to solar-related questions on the website. 122 C Street, NW, 4th Floor, Washington, DC 20001-2109. (202) 383-2600. Http://www.seia.org.

U.S. Department of Energy (DOE). This top federal energy agency has vast resources available on energy. Includes operations offices, national labs and facilities, and power administrations. Website provides news and information, links to other facilities and power administrations, and science arcade. See also: Energy Efficiency and Renewable Energy Network (http://www.eren.doe.gov); Million Solar Roofs Initiative, (http://www.eren.doe.gov/millionroofs); Sandia National Laboratory Renewable Energy Office (http://www.sandia.gov/Renewable_Energy/renewable.html). 1000 Independence Avenue, SW, Washington, DC 20585. (202) 586-5000. Http://www.doe.gov.

U.S. Environmental Protection Agency (EPA). The nation's leading environmental regulator for air, water, hazardous waste, and other issues. Website includes energy/global climate change information and links. People interested in energy might start at the Energy Star Program site (http://www.epa.gov/energystar). 401 M Street, SW, Washington, DC 20460. (202) 260-2090. Http://www.epa.gov.

Part IV

NATURAL RESOURCE MANAGEMENT

11 Land and Water Conservation

AT A GLANCE

Employment:

45,000 professionals in all sectors nationwide (includes some overlap with fields discussed in other chapters)

Demand:

3 to 7 percent growth through 2005

Breakdown:

Public sector, 72 percent (40 percent federal, 32 percent state and local)
Private sector, 10 percent
Nonprofit sector, 18 percent

Key Job Titles:

Agricultural economist
Agricultural engineer
Agronomist
Aquatic biologist
Aquatic toxicologist
Archaeologist
Area ecologist
Biologist
Cartographer
City director of water conservation
Civil engineer
Decontamination specialist
Ecologist
Environmental planner

Farmer
Forester
Geographic information systems specialist
Geologist
Hydrologist
Irrigation specialist
Land acquisition specialist
Landscape architect
Land trust or preserve manager
Lawyer
Marine scientist
Natural resource manager
Oceanographer
Plant scientist
Remediation professionals
River and lake ecologist
Rural sociologist
Soil conservation specialist
Water conservation consultant
Water chemist
Wetland scientist

Influential Organizations:

Center for Marine Conservation
Ecological Society of America
Land Trust Alliance
National Park Service
National Wildlife Federation
Natural Resources Conservation Service
Natural Resources Council of America
The Nature Conservancy
Society for Conservation Biology
Soil and Water Conservation Society
Trust for Public Land
U.S. Bureau of Land Management
U.S. Fish and Wildlife Service
U.S. Forest Service
The Wilderness Society

Salary:

Entry-level salaries range from $18,000 to $30,000 depending on education. With experience and an advanced degree, salaries range from $50,000 to more than $85,000. Average salaries are around $35,000 to $40,000. Be aware, however, that there are large numbers of nominally paid seasonal workers and that volunteers play a crucial role.

Less than 400 years ago, the United States was a great wilderness. Immense stands of ancient forest, a vast prairie of grasslands and bison, millions of acres of wetlands, and miles of pristine rivers and streams defined the American landscape. Today, that original environment is permanently altered. Through the work of today's conservation professionals, however, damaged land and water are being restored, and remaining wild areas are being preserved for the future. As we will see in this chapter, today's conservation professional is also an active manager of the land and water areas she works to protect.

WHAT IS LAND AND WATER CONSERVATION?

In an earlier age, definitions were simple. Conservation was about the protection of wilderness and other "natural" areas, and that was that. Today, things are more complex. It's hard to say where the field of land and water conservation ends and where other careers (e.g., forestry, fish and wildlife, parks and recreation, water quality, planning, and education) begin. The development of ecosystems management, "place-based" environmental protection, watershed planning, and multimedia pollution control have blurred the lines among career areas.

Although the most important goal for most conservation professionals continues to be the protection and management of natural areas, the field has expanded its focus. As Peter Forbes of The Trust for Public Land has written: "Saving land is not enough."

Forbes points out that conservation today "may mean protecting a local pond in one community, a fishing pier in another, and an important cultural symbol in a third." He also suggests a wider mission for the field, as a profession that "helps restore and build a community's relationship with its natural and cultural heritages. . . ."

Whatever definition one uses, land and water conservation involves a wide variety of professionals, as seen by the eclectic list earlier. Conservationists work for a variety of employers, including local park systems, conservation districts, state agencies, land trusts, consulting firms, the federal government, land-owning corporations, and nonprofit groups. Although broad and diverse, conservation work tends to fall into a few major categories, including:

Natural resource assessment and management. Natural resource assessment means inventorying and evaluating flora, fauna, and entire ecosystems, to assess their ecological health and economic value. These assessments are recorded in geographic information system databases for informed decision making. Management of natural resources involves balancing human pressures with the conservation of land and water resources.

Habitat protection and restoration. Protecting fish, wildlife, and plant habitats involves limiting environmental contaminants, (e.g., acid rain, agricultural and urban runoff, and hazardous waste), as well as mitigating adverse human activities, such as ill-planned development, logging, roads, and overuse by recreational visitors. Restoring damaged habitats can mean reforestation,

Conservation professionals work to protect sites as small as an urban garden, and as large as these public lands in Idaho.

decontamination, imposition of strict limitations on human uses, eradication of alien species, and reintroduction of native species.

Preserving open spaces and natural areas. Some professionals work to ensure that land, water bodies, or whole ecosystems are saved from development or extensive recreational use by outright purchase. Nonprofit land trusts generally work on a small scale, whereas professionals at state and federal land agencies designate and manage millions of acres for long-term conservation.

Protecting cultural resources. This includes the preservation of historic buildings and landmarks, saving valuable archaeological sites, and protecting places that have significance for local people.

HISTORY AND BACKGROUND

An organized conservation effort began in the United States around the start of the 20th century with concern for preservation of scenic western lands and issues such as the decimation of bird populations for fashionable clothing. Ladies' hats of the period often featured an entire stuffed bird or copious amounts of plumage from large southeastern waterfowl.

A growing sense that America was in danger of losing irreplaceable wilderness areas (and the values they represented), triggered formation of groups such as the Audubon Society and the Sierra Club, both formed in the 1890s. Then, in the mid-1930s came the ecological disaster of the "Dust Bowl" crisis. Following a severe and sustained drought in the Great Plains, the region's soil began to erode and blow away, creating large dust storms that blackened skies as far south as Texas, and east to New York. Most importantly, the crisis moved opinion in Washington, D.C., where Congress unanimously passed legislation declaring soil and water conservation a national priority.

Since then, land and water conservation has been among the most visible of all environmental fields, in part because the general public remains concerned about development pressures on open lands, recreational access, and loss of natural places. In the past three decades, there has been a dramatic rise in the number of land trusts, the amount of acreage protected as public land, and the number of people who support initiatives for open space, greenbelts, park land, wildlife refuges, watershed protection, and saving agricultural lands.

LEGISLATION

National conservation legislation is one way to track the history and background of the field. Each act created new opportunities and challenges for conservation professionals.

National Industrial Recovery Act of 1935. Established the Soil Conservation Service (now the Natural Resources Conservation Service) to control and prevent soil erosion, reduce flood and sedimentation damage, and improve agriculture. The act authorizes the Secretary of Agriculture, when requested, to assist local agencies with planning and implementation in watersheds of 250,000 acres or less.

Wilderness Act of 1964. Established the National Wilderness Preservation System. The law defines wilderness as a place that lacks noticeable human modification or presence and where the landscape is affected primarily by the forces of nature. It requires that wilderness be protected and managed so as to preserve its natural conditions and allows for consideration of the effect on wilderness from activities on adjacent lands.

National Wild and Scenic Rivers Act of 1968 (WSRA). Establishes a system of areas, distinct from the traditional park concept, to ensure the protection of each river's unique environment. It also preserves certain selected rivers that possess outstanding scenic, recreational, geological, cultural, or historic values and maintains their free-flowing condition.

Clean Water Act of 1972 (CWA). Sets objectives for restoring and maintaining the chemical, physical, and biological integrity of the nation's waters. Also, the act regulates discharge of pollutants and requires federal agencies to avoid adverse impacts from modification or destruction of navigable streams and associated tributaries, wetlands, or other waters.

Coastal Zone Management Act of 1972 (CZMA). Establishes a voluntary program through which states can receive financial and technical assistance to develop a coastal zone management plan for the conservation and environmentally sound development of coastal resources. The philosophy of CZMA is simple: it is more appropriate and less costly to prevent problems than to remedy them. The act also authorizes the National Estuarine Research Reserve System, which now protects twenty-two estuaries nationwide. The 1990 reauthorization establishes a Coastal Nonpoint Pollution Program, requiring each coastal state to develop a program to protect coastal waters from nonpoint sources of pollution.

National Forest Management Act of 1976 (NFMA). Provides a comprehensive planning framework for management of the National Forest System, through the development of management plans for individual forest units. The act's primary focus is to establish land and resource management planning for the effective use and protection of renewable resources and a balancing of uses on forest lands.

Federal Land Policy Management Act of 1976 (FLMPA). This is the organic act for the Bureau of Land Management (BLM) that spells out BLM mandates relating to stewardship, preservation of historic, cultural, and natural heritage, achieving balance between human and resource needs, sustainability, and use of interdisciplinary approaches to management.

Alaska National Interests Lands Conservation Act of 1980 (ANILCA). Increased Alaska's national lands system from one national park, two national monuments, and a few refuges to eight national parks, ten national preserves, four national monuments, nine national wildlife refuges, and twenty-five wild and scenic rivers.

Watershed Protection and Flood Prevention Act of 1985. Establishes the Watershed Protection Program through which the Natural Resources Conservation Service provides financial and technical assistance to local organizations in planning and implementing watershed projects. The 1990 Farm Bill amended the program to allow cost sharing for acquiring perpetual wetlands or floodplain easements for conservation or flood prevention.

North American Wetlands Conservation Act of 1989. Encourages Federal agencies and others to protect, restore, enhance, and manage wetlands and other habitats for migratory birds, fish, and wildlife. The act authorized up to $30 million annually for North American wetlands conservation projects. Because roughly half this amount depends on congressional appropriation, funding may vary considerably from year to year. At least 50 percent of the funding for the act must be used for projects in Canada and Mexico.

Coastal Wetlands Planning, Protection, and Restoration Act of 1990. Authorizes the U.S. Fish and Wildlife Service to make matching National Coastal Wetlands Conservation grants to coastal states for acquiring, managing, restoring, or enhancing wetlands. Funding comes from a tax on small-engine fuel. Grants are provided for property acquisition only if the land will be managed for conservation over the long term. A 50 percent match from state funds is required, which drops to 25 percent if the state has a trust fund for acquisition of coastal wetlands, natural areas, and open spaces.

Water Resources Development Act of 1990. Requires that the goal of the Army Corps of Engineer's water resources development program be "no overall net loss" of wetlands. An action plan to achieve this goal must be prepared by the Corps in consultation with the U.S. Environmental Protection Agency and the U.S. Fish and Wildlife Service. The act also authorizes the training and certification of wetlands delineators.

Food, Agriculture, Conservation, and Trade Act of 1990 (FACTA, commonly known as the Farm Bill). Reinforces and expands conservation provisions begun in the Food Security Act (FSA) of 1985. The main provisions of the FACTA address conservation of highly erodible land and wetlands, and include the Environmental Conservation Acreage Reserve Program, which consists of the Conservation Reserve Program (CRP) and the Wetlands Reserve Program (WRP). There is also a new provision for the Water Quality Incentives Program and for the Integrated Farm Management Program. The "swampbuster" (wetland conservation) provision, introduced in the FSA of 1985 and amended by FACTA of 1990, discourages the alteration of wetlands for agricultural purposes.

Since about two-thirds of the continental United States is privately owned, only active, voluntary support from landowners can guarantee the success of conservation work on private land. Through many of the more recent laws, federal money has been made available to help private landowners voluntarily restore wetlands and riparian areas. These include the CRP; the WRP; the U.S. Fish and Wildlife Service's Partners for Wildlife Program; and the Environmental Quality Incentives and Wildlife Habitat Incentives Program (EQIP, established under the 1996 Farm Bill). In addition, the 1997 Taxpayer Relief Act includes a Brownfields Tax Incentive program, which conserves "green fields" (previously undeveloped land) by encouraging redevelopment of abandoned and contaminated former industrial or commercial sites. Programs such as these create opportunities for private consulting and engineering firms to provide technical assistance for landowners who take advantage of cost-share and tax-break programs.

Local and State Land-Use Plans. Federal laws are crucial, of course. The land- and water-use plans of local governments, however, are among the most influential conservation laws in the nation. Most federal and state laws are focused on the conservation and management of government-owned land. Throughout the nation, the real land-use law is at the local level. This makes elected officials such as county commissioners and city council members among the most powerful forces for conservation in the nation.

ISSUES AND TRENDS

Although the basic goal of the conservation field—protecting land and water resources—remains constant, professionals face constantly shifting circumstances and opportunities. Below are a few of the current issues facing the field.

CONTINUED PRESSURE FROM DEVELOPMENT

Although development pressures on sensitive land and water resources can be found everywhere, they are particularly urgent in the West and Southeast. From 1990 to 1995, ten states increased their population by more than 10 percent. Nine of them were in the West, and the other was Georgia. Land and water resources around popular communities are under incredible pressure, and a great deal of open space, wildlife habitat, and agricultural land is being lost in the Pacific Northwest, the Rocky Mountain states, and the Southwest. In Florida and North Carolina, waves of new people are resulting in large scale losses to subdivisions and mini-malls. In addition, development pressure is being felt in lower-growth states, as well. As more people leave the city for suburbs and small towns, formerly unthreatened areas are being developed. In addition, the strong economy of the last several years has produced a flood of new construction, and desire is strong for larger homes on bigger lots, and for second homes. Coastal areas and vacation spots are particular areas of concern.

FINANCING CONSERVATION PURCHASES AND NONPURCHASE OPTIONS

Finding money to protect land is an essential task for conservation professionals. At some organizations, it is *the* task. People who can successfully arrange bond issues, targeted tax increases, personal and corporate land gifts, and fundraising appeals to protect special areas are always in demand. Fortunately, citizens and professionals are passionately committed to this effort, and trends are strong toward voter approval of well-organized conservation financing campaigns, especially in areas where rapid growth threatens well-loved places that are in imminent danger. For regular updates on creative financing successes throughout the nation, stay in touch with The Nature Conservancy and the Trust for Public Land via their websites.

There will never be enough money to conserve land and water through outright purchase, however, and conservation professionals have developed a wide range of legal methods for placing land in trust, or putting restrictions (voluntary and involuntary) on private owners that achieve conservation ends without public or nonprofit ownership. In applying these techniques, trends are mixed. Although support is generally strong, organized counter forces have developed, which argue that almost any restrictions on private land represent a "taking" under the Constitution, requiring financial compensation, and raising the cost of conservation efforts. Conservation professionals watch legal cases in this area with great interest, and so should you.

GREENWAYS AND TRAILS

Kathleen Blaha, vice president for national programs with the Trust for Public Land (TPL) says that nonprofits and local public agencies have a strong interest in open space that connects communities and gives people access to natural areas. This work involves restoration, land acquisition, environmental education, youth programming, and land-use policy to promote greenways and trails. "These new kinds of parks, which almost every community must have . . . demand different kinds of on-the-ground management skills. You must be comfortable with policy issues that deal with multiple jurisdictions since greenways, rails-to-trails, and riverways often go through many towns and counties," Blaha says.

BROWNFIELDS

Brownfields redevelopment is of growing interest to a large body of state, county, and municipal governments, industries, financial institutions, and community groups. Brownfields are former industrial or commercial sites that have been abandoned, have actual or perceived contamination, and have an active potential for redevelopment for industrial use, or for parks and open space. Conservation professionals are excited about brownfields redevelopment for two reasons. One, because it provides conservation opportunities through the restoration of urban lands. Two, because redevelopment of these properties can help stem urban sprawl and the development of suburban "green fields," such as prime agricultural land near cities.

"In many cases, brownfields are located on waterfronts. There's an opportunity being created for people who have an understanding of real estate techniques, community-based planning, conservation issues, and water quality to do land conservation work in urban areas," Blaha says.

In 1997, President Clinton signed the Taxpayer Relief Act, which included a new tax incentive to spur the cleanup and redevelopment of brownfields in distressed urban and rural areas. The tax incentive builds on the momentum of the Clinton administration's Brownfields National Partnership Action Agenda announced earlier that year, which includes specific commitments from fifteen federal agencies.

One such commitment is the Environmental Protection Agency's (EPA) Brownfields Economic Redevelopment Initiative, which was designed to help states, communities, and other stakeholders in economic redevelopment work together to prevent, assess, safely clean up, and sustainably reuse brownfields. Along with this initiative, the EPA is committed to workforce development and job training partnerships to produce a workforce trained for work on brownfields projects. (For more on brownfields, see chapters 4 and 9.)

INCREASED EFFECTIVENESS THROUGH GROWING COOPERATION

There are an increasing number of cooperative ventures in land acquisition and preservation efforts. Public, private, and nonprofit organizations are working together to increase their effectiveness by leveraging personnel and financial resources through partnerships.

Crane Beach in Ipswich, Massachusetts, is an example. The National Marine Fisheries Service, Trustees of Reservations (owners of the beach), Massachusetts Audubon Society, Natural Resources Conservation Service, and Ipswich Public Works Department have joined forces to restore a 20-acre salt marsh, degraded by a badly engineered culvert beneath the road that gives access to the beach.

As Mark Zankel of The Nature Conservancy (see profile at the end of the chapter) says: "We can't do our work without partnerships. We can't succeed without them." Partnerships allow for a more holistic, ecosystem approach by bringing together multiple scientific disciplines, the local public, and politicians to collaborate on issues that are common to a particular watershed or wetland and transcend state or county boundaries.

Also note that some legislation is specifically designed to encourage such partnerships. For example, since 1972, the Clean Water Act has relied on a partnership between the federal government and the states because solving problems in a body of water such as the Mississippi River requires the collaboration of all thirty-two states in the river's basin.

CONFLICT RESOLUTION

Denise Meridith, director of the Arizona state office of the U.S. Bureau of Land Management, says: "Conflict resolution is a growth industry in conservation. Put emphasis on gaining skills in communication, computer use, facilitation/negotiation, and learning about a variety of land uses. We need to turn away from litigation as our preferred way of resolving conflict." Other land and water conservation professionals agree, especially in an age of growing cultural diversity. Organizations with different missions, different stakeholders, and unique sets of constraints and regulations must somehow sit down at the table together to solve common problems.

INCREASED SOPHISTICATION

The process of managing natural areas is becoming more technical, holistic, and complicated as part of a slow but fundamental change in the manner in which resources are managed. The increase of university degrees in conservation biology is one example of this. Conservation biology programs seek to balance single species understanding with ecosystem issues; the life sciences with the social sciences; and scientific information with political savvy. New types of education, combined with the partnerships mentioned above, point to a more integrated way of managing land and water resources. Think about this in your educational choices. A narrowly defined educational focus, or an inability to work with others on a team, may limit your career potential.

ECOSYSTEM RESTORATION

Land and water conservation professionals are going beyond preserving and managing natural areas. Today's field might entail restoring a damaged ecosystem, significantly altering a natural area, or creating an "artificial" ecosystem. One example of the latter involves engineering wetland areas to serve as "natural" wastewater purification systems. Other projects include restoring prairies, planting local flora along highways, reintroducing wildlife to an area, or getting rid of nonnative wildlife and vegetation. Engineers, biologists, botanists, ecologists, and landscape architects are involved in such projects. Conservationists are unwilling to accept the idea that degraded environments might not be restored to their former ecological health.

USE OF COMPUTERS

Geographic information systems (GIS) are essential for today's conservation work, and they become more sophisticated and easy to use all the time. A GIS is a computerized database application that allows the user to understand complex interactions between human activities and the natural world. In addition to natural features such as rivers, ponds, endangered plant species, and wetlands, GIS systems track the location of underground storage tanks, aquifers, wells, hazardous waste sites, current land uses, demographic patterns, and hundreds of other variables. Because conservation scientists and planners live on such data, GIS has become a crucial tool for all professionals.

Another thing that has changed conservation practice dramatically is the Internet. Because there is such an overwhelming amount of sometimes conflicting and unproven information available, care must be taken in compiling and interpreting data. The BLM's Meridith says: "This had led to changes in the types of people we need, not just people to do manual field work and inventory, but people who have skills in accessing and assembling data, then interpreting it and communicating results. More highly skilled people are needed than ever before."

GROWING CONCERN ABOUT WATER ISSUES

The twenty-fifth anniversary of the Clean Water Act in 1998 seems to have heightened awareness on the parts of nonprofit organizations and government agencies concerned with water. (See chapters 4 and 6 for further discussion.) As a result, new initiatives are being launched and this in turn raises public awareness. "Water quality issues may surpass land protection issues in this decade," TPL's Blaha says. "The public's concern around water quality and health issues creates new taxes, programs, and policies to clean up water sources. Water concerns fund new land protection programs, and demand management plans for public lands and their buffers."

Data from the U.S. Environmental Protection Agency show a real need to focus on protecting our water sources. The EPA reports that 57 percent of the nation's 2,111 watersheds have serious or moderately serious pollution problems. Only 16 percent have good water quality.

LOSS OF AGRICULTURAL LAND

Protecting agricultural land is a particularly difficult task, because small-scale farming can be a marginal economic proposition for many farmers near rapidly growing areas (when compared with selling the land to residential or commercial developers). Simply protecting the land is not enough. It must be protected and maintained in agricultural use. Conservationists help develop markets for local farm products, create "agri-tourism" opportunities, allow development of farm portions to protect the rest, arrange low-interest loans for farm activities, and engage in other creative actions to conserve our agricultural landscape. The American Farmland Trust is a recognized leader in this effort.

CAREER OPPORTUNITIES

Conservation work can be found throughout the environmental world. Look beyond the best-known employers (e.g., federal land management agencies and The Nature Conservancy) when seeking you own niche.

PUBLIC SECTOR

Over 70 percent of land and water professionals work in the public sector, with federal agencies leading the way.

Federal Government. Federal landholding agencies own about 700 million acres of land, roughly one-third of the United States. The federal government is the largest single employer of land and water conservation professionals. Denise Meridith, however, sees the balance shifting. "In the near future, the Feds will not be as dominant in the field. The state governments, nonprofit groups, and private owners, are a growing force," she says. Conservation on federal lands is managed primarily by six agencies within the U.S. Department of the Interior:

- Bureau of Land Management
- U.S. Fish and Wildlife Service
- National Park Service
- Bureau of Indian Affairs
- Bureau of Reclamation
- U.S. Geological Survey

Taken together, the Interior Department employs over 70,000 professionals. Major landholdings are also managed by the U.S. Department of Agriculture's Forest Service. The Forest Service employs 30,000 full-time and 15,000 seasonal workers. The Tennessee Valley Authority, the Department of Energy, and the various components of the Department of Defense round out the federal picture for conservation employment.

One additional agency with a large workforce is the Natural Resources Conservation Service (NRCS). Formerly known as the Soil Conservation Service, the NRCS has a presence in virtually every county in the United States and is a quietly effective force in the conservation field. In 1996, the Service assisted 1.73 million land owners, completed conservation plans on 141.5 million acres, and completed soil surveys on 3.3 million acres. The average field office has 2.5 paid NRCS employees, 2.6 NRCS volunteers, and 2.4 nonfederal district employees for each of the nearly 3,000 conservation districts nationwide. Most of its 11,000 employees serve in the USDA's network of local, county-based offices to reduce soil erosion and pollution from soil runoff and to manage storm water. Other responsibilities include administering federal programs such as the Watershed Protection Program, the Conservation Reserve Program, the Resource Conservation and Development Program, and the erosion requirements of the Farm Bill. The service primarily hires soil scientists, agricultural and civil engineers, and biologists.

The military will be doing more conservation work in the next few years. In addition to the day-to-day management of the thousands of acres of military bases owned by the Department of Defense, Congress has mandated an aggressive program of inventorying the natural resources of the military's landholdings under the Legacy Resource Management Program. This was particularly important in recent years, because inventories were required before unneeded military installations could be closed and sold. In addition, the military is required to comply with the Endangered Species Act and other environmental legislation to which every other landholder is subject. The Department of Defense now practices ecosystem management, as required by the Pentagon on all military installations.

With minor exceptions, the national goal of balancing the federal budget has resulted in downsizing at all of the major federal land and water conservation agencies. Entry-level positions in field offices will still be available, however, since most of the downsizing is occurring at the administrative levels in Washington, D.C. and in regional offices of the land management agencies. Normal attrition and newly funded programs created by Congress will also create employment. Finally, an expected wave of retirees will create new opportunities.

What kind of land and water conservation professionals will find work with federal agencies? Jack Peterson, an Idaho-based executive for the Bureau of Land Management says: "Key current needs include botanists, entomologists, hydrologists, wildlife biologists, riparian/wetland specialists, range management professionals, water rights specialists, and people who are familiar with American Indian–related law."

All federal land management agencies utilize volunteers, hire temporary and part-time workers, and have Student Career Experience Programs (formerly Cooperative Extension). You increase your chances of landing a permanent position if you take one of these avenues to get your foot in the door.

State Government. State governments are becoming increasingly innovative in land and water conservation, sometimes with federal help or prodding, but usually because of popular support on the part of voters. In Colorado, a citizen effort called Great Outdoors Colorado funneled almost $30 million dollars of lottery money to hundreds of conservation, habitat protection, trails, and environmental education projects in its first four years. In Florida, the "Preservation 2000" initiative earmarked $3 billion over ten years for conservation, recreation, and open space. It's now in its eighth year. New Jersey, New York, Massachusetts, and other states have approved bond issues in the hundreds of millions to acquire, protect, and enhance watersheds, parks, and agricultural lands.

State professionals involved in this process include planners (natural resource, urban, land-use, and recreational); general resource managers; resource specialists who offer data and help clarify specific problems; environmental and real estate lawyers, educators; and public involvement specialists. Another type of professional is a facilitator. This individual, not necessarily trained in formal mediation skills, must have independent knowledge and background on the subject in question and must be able to bring together different groups and agencies at the table.

Land and water conservation professionals can be found throughout state government. Look for them in the Departments of Natural Resources, Agriculture, Environmental Protection, Coastal Zone Management, Planning, Fisheries, Wildlife, and Forestry, or in special bodies such as coastal commissions and watershed districts.

A key service of state governments is the administration of natural heritage programs, which were started by The Nature Conservancy (TNC) in the early 1970s. These programs, based on a data center concept, were designed as a means of providing detailed objective information on the patterns and processes of biological and ecological diversity—essentially to guide conservation priorities and strategies of TNC. Today, almost all of these programs are independent entities working in collaboration with TNC and are housed in state government agencies. Some are also located in public universities, and a few are still housed with TNC, who serves as principal network organizer, providing technical support and continually updating procedures, methods, and technologies.

The network covers all fifty states, Washington, D.C., the Navajo Nation, five Canadian provinces, and fourteen countries in Latin America and the Caribbean. The fundamental role of the network is to provide sound scientific information that is made available to the general public. Heritage network data centers are staffed by botanists, zoologists, ecologists, and information managers who piece together facts on the location and status of rare and endangered species and ecological communities in their geographic region.

The Biological and Conservation Data System is an award-winning computer software system developed and maintained by TNC. It manages and analyzes information on location, protection status, ecological needs, condition and rarity of species, and ecological communities. In addition, it tracks land ownership and management. Based on an evaluation of this data, conservation priorities and strategies for protection can be set.

States vary greatly in their involvement in natural heritage programs, and some people wonder whether states will maintain a strong level of commitment to conservation if the economy should decline. If you are considering entering the public sector in this field, follow state funding issues closely.

Local Government. Agencies and citizens are becoming more involved in the conservation and management of natural resources at a local level. However, expect significant variation in the level of activity from region to region and even among neighboring municipalities.

Local government activity takes place on a number of fronts. Towns and regions expend resources to plan where they want to be in the future, developing master plans and working to implement them through zoning and development regulation as well as land acquisition and conservation strategies. The work of some of these planners is outlined in chapter 4.

Outside of the planning department, look for local government conservation workers in the parks and recreation department, water utility, public works department, and other units that manage land or have an impact on it.

Another local presence is conservation districts, known in various parts of the country as "soil and water conservation districts," "resource conservation districts," "natural resource districts," "land conservation committees," and similar names. Regardless of what they are called, these bodies share a single mission: to coordinate assistance from all available sources—public and private, as well as local, state, and federal—in an effort to develop locally driven solutions to natural resource concerns.

There are nearly 3,000 of these districts nationwide, and they are staffed by a combination of local and state personnel as well as federal employees of the Natural Resources Conservation Service (see earlier discussion). They work with individual landowners and units of government to help reduce soil erosion, preserve long-term viability of the land, and limit nonpoint source water pollution. Urban conservation districts work on such issues as storm water management and nonpoint source erosion and toxic pollution from development and redevelopment activities.

In addition to conservation districts, there has been a steady growth in the number of single-purpose agencies and special districts at the local government level. These agencies are created to offer focus, flexibility, secure funding, and better management around specific resources. Park districts, for example, are popular in the Midwest. Water authorities in the Northeast and water management districts in Florida offer great opportunities for land management as well, since many of them own thousands of acres and are charged with protecting watersheds and well-heads.

Indian Nations. Indian nations own and manage significant parcels of land and hire the gamut of land and water conservation professionals. Native land managers employ fisheries biologists, planners, wildlife ecologists, range managers, environmental health specialists, and land restoration staff to deal with the responsibilities of managing hundreds of thousands of acres, mostly in the West. See the Resources section at the end of the chapter for information about the Native American Fish and Wildlife Society, which is an excellent resource for tribal managers and prospective staff people. Contact tribes separately, as each has its own hiring procedures.

PRIVATE SECTOR

Any private company that owns land has a need for land and water conservation assistance. This includes railroads, forest product companies, mining concerns, electric utilities, oil and gas companies, farms and ranches (large and small), real estate developments (commercial and residential), ski lodges, and more. Large corporate landowners, such as utility companies with hydroelectric dams, often open their lands to the public for recreation and have management responsibilities for fisheries, wildlife, watershed protection, and so forth.

Washington Water Power Company (WWPC) in Spokane, Washington, is one example. WWPC owns or controls thousands of acres in Washington, Idaho, and Montana, including nine hydroelectric facilities and miles of transmission lines. The company employs biologists, geologists, foresters, botanists, economists, real estate professionals, GIS specialists, and more—over thirty permanent professionals and ten seasonals in all. The real estate section is one of the larger professional groups, reflecting the need for expertise in land purchase, securing easements, and other legal and financial concerns.

Consulting Firms. Consulting firms are a growing presence in the conservation field, as employers work to keep permanent staff costs down. Conservation agencies and private landowners need help with landscape architecture improvements, site planning, land restoration, environmental assessments, land-use and watershed plans, legal assistance, GIS, brownfields development, land purchase financing, real estate knowledge, environmental impact statements, wetlands delineation and restoration, fisheries management, recreation planning, and other work. The list is long. Consultants to the conservation field range from divisions within full-service environmental engineering/consulting firms to one-person outfits with a focus on a single specialty.

Although the use of consultants is not as prevalent in land and water conservation as it is in fields such as hazardous waste or air quality, there is a growing demand.

NONPROFIT SECTOR

During the 1980s, an increasing number of natural resource management jobs became available with private nonprofit organizations such as nature centers, arboretums, community land trusts, and national organizations such as Trust for Public Land (TPL), TNC, National Audubon Society, and National Wildlife Federation. Then the recession of the early 1990s reversed this trend. Since 1993, a strong economy has again brought an increase in employment in the nonprofit sector.

Nonprofit land trusts are a major force behind land acquisition efforts, working to acquire land outright or purchase easement or development rights on properties. Of these, the largest and best known is probably TNC, which manages more than 1,600 preserves (up from 1,100 in 1993) in 50 states as well as in Canada, the Caribbean, and Latin America. The organization employs more than 2,500 full-time staff people (up from 1,000 in 1993), as well as a seasonal staff.

Beyond national groups such as TNC and TPL, however, are local land trusts. The Land Trust Alliance (LTA), a national nonprofit organization, guides the development of over 1,200 land trusts around the country. About one-third of these are staffed. According to LTA director Jean Hocker, "the number of land trusts being created is starting to slow down, so LTA now focuses on supporting existing trusts to become more sophisticated organizations in terms of land protection and management and taking advantage of government partnerships."

Land trusts are experts at helping landowners find ways to protect their land. Trusts employ a variety of tools, such as conservation easements, that permanently restrict the uses of land, land donations and purchases, and strategic estate planning, to protect places of special scenic, ecological, historic, or cultural value.

Another significant development is the flourishing of statewide and grassroots nonprofit organizations. These groups ensure implementation of state legislation related to growth management, planning, and land preservation. Among them, watershed associations are particularly important. River Network, a national organization in Portland, Oregon, publishes a directory that lists hundreds of watershed-related groups.

At the state and local levels, public agencies are increasingly looking to nonprofits for partnerships. These collaborations involve planning, organizing, environmental education, policy and legislative analysis, real estate work, biological inventories, and scientific projects. It is not uncommon for agencies to provide grants or contracts to nonprofit organizations for direct work that used to be the exclusive province of government employees.

Land and water conservation jobs in the nonprofit sector require a wide range of skills. Blaha says: "The Trust for Public Land is increasingly looking for candidates with commercial real estate experience, public finance experience, legal backgrounds, and always a good understanding of land-use planning and policy issues. Though leadership and communications skills are often mentioned, they become even more important with the increasing number of private/public partnerships, commissions, and task forces that are created to deal with the complexity of addressing land and water management issues in an increasingly interconnected world."

SALARY

Barbara Smith in the Human Resources Management Division at the Natural Resources Conservation Service says that the average natural resource specialist is at the GS-9 to GS-11 level on the federal pay scale ($30,000 to $47,000 in 1998). Entry-level natural resource specialists are at the GS-5 to GS-7 level ($20,000 to $32,000 in 1998), and technicians start as low as GS-4 ($18,000 in 1998). Check with your local Office of Personnel Management (in the phone book under government listings) or their website (http://www.opm. gov) for current pay on the general schedule.

Salaries in state government agencies are roughly similar to the federal salaries above, although there is some variation. Large states, or states with new funding initiatives, may pay more.

Private industry salaries run higher than public sector salaries. Starting salaries for new undergraduates in natural resource management fields were running at $26,000 in 1998. Biologists at major utility companies start at around $28,000 and earn up to $45,000. Lawyers earn from $60,000 to $90,000. Technicians and seasonal employees are paid in the low to mid-20s.

Large, national land trust organizations pay better than one might expect. Science, land protection and data technicians who work both in the field and in the office can earn $25,000 to $35,000, and permanent employees in fields such as ecology, zoology, biology, and botany are paid $40,000 to $55,000. Preserve managers are paid $30,000 to $45,000, and may have assistants who earn from $22,000 to 30,000. Other managers earn $30,000 to $35,000. Real estate lawyers earn $55,000 to $85,000 and legal assistants can expect $25,000 to $35,000. Also look for well-paid jobs in fundraising and operations.

Smaller land trusts, of course, pay less and depend more heavily on volunteers. Fully two-thirds of land trusts have no paid staff at all.

GETTING STARTED

There are many ways to get involved in land and water conservation. A variety of backgrounds not specifically related to natural resource management—planning, environmental education, recreation, and the environmental protection fields—can provide a start. Whatever your starting point is, consider the ideas that are presented in the sections that follow.

EDUCATION

Employers like applicants with a broad-based education—it might be a double major in business and biology or in economics and natural resource management. Hydrology, political science, engineering, planning, marketing, or accounting would also make good second majors depending on your interests. Conservation biology programs are not widely available yet, but are more and more sought after in the federal agencies.

Although technician-type jobs exist for those with two-year degrees or bachelor's degrees, because of competition most professional jobs go to those with master's degrees. There are exceptions, such as opportunities for people who have unique experience and skills.

If you pursue only one undergraduate major, the basic sciences are recommended—biology, botany, zoology, chemistry, physics, and geology. Whatever your major, try to use electives to take courses in a variety of natural resource disciplines.

Although graduate school is a time for specialized training, professionals repeatedly stress that they are looking for applicants who are not overly narrow. They really want people who can think in terms of integrated natural resource management, who are computer literate, and who can communicate well.

Good preparation for a career in land and water conservation would include course work in biology, the ecology of ecosystems and communities, and, possibly, population biology. Course work on public policy as it relates to resource management is also useful, but it should not be pursued at the expense of a hard scientific grounding. Master's degrees that encompass this type of work include natural resource management, ecology, botany, conservation biology, and forestry.

While completing your degrees, do not neglect opportunities to gain volunteer or internship experience. Internships and even some volunteer positions can also be very competitive, but they make all the difference when you are applying for a permanent position. Mark Zankel at The Nature Conservancy says: "If you've had fieldwork experience it's extremely beneficial if you're applying for a stewardship job. Someone who's just spent their whole life taking classes or working inside is just a risk, I think, because fieldwork is hard. . . . I always look to see if a person has identified their skills. Not everyone knows how to read a compass, or read [U.S. Geological Survey] topographic maps, or use a dichotomous field guide for identifying plants, so those are sort of the basics."

ADVICE

Here is a collection of advice from land and water conservation professionals on the keys to getting into their fields.

Use the student career experience program. In addition to universally advising the use of internships to get experience, federal and state agency staff members strongly encourage participation in cooperative education, noting that workers receive all the benefits of federal status during their employment and earn ninety days of noncompetitive eligibility for federal jobs upon completion of their assignment.

Use the student conservation association. For anyone interested in a career with federal land management agencies, a volunteer position through the Student Conservation Association (SCA) is a great way to start. SCA has placed thousands of people in conservation positions over the past three decades and also provides other career services.

Develop legal, real estate, and financial skills. Before an area can be managed, it must be protected. Before it can be protected, it must be purchased or at least have limitations placed on its use. The business aspect of conservation is growing, and these skills are in demand.

Know the "hot" issues. Because job growth in the field often depends on a new funding source, it pays to know what these sources are and gain appropriate academic or practical experience. Review the trends and issues section of this chapter, and talk to people in the field on a regular basis.

Be flexible geographically and take what you can get even if it doesn't pay. "You're going to have to start with something part time, that doesn't pay that great and work your way through it, network and meet people. That's been the most important thing for me. You're not just going to go out and get this great job right out of college. It can be frustrating. The other thing I'd say is you have to be willing to move wherever the job takes you," says Alice Brandon of the Illinois Department of Natural Resources.

Be persistent. "I was told over and over again by people who had the jobs that I wanted at The Nature Conservancy to be persistent. . . . Not unique advice, but it's the truth. It's a competitive field, and it's not without sacrifices, but the benefits are tremendous," says Mark Zankelof of The Nature Conservancy.

SUMMARY

Land and water conservation is a very popular field, and the number of applicants seeking jobs far exceeds the supply. If this is the field for you, getting established will take imagination, persistence, and patience. Go beyond the departments and agencies traditionally associated with land and water conservation—there are conservation jobs tucked away in the most unlikely places.

Employment in land and water conservation will probably always be relatively tight because funds for agencies involved in this field are usually scarce and many applicants want the jobs that do exist. The good news is that the work is strongly supported by the public, and that support is growing. Those who succeed in this field as we enter the 21st century will possess strong, integrated scientific backgrounds, relevant experience, and, above all, commitment.

CASE STUDY

In Defense of the Longleaf Pine: Ecosystem Conservation Finds an Unlikely Laboratory

Conservation professionals are able to increase their impacts by partnering with likeminded people in other organizations. As the following case study shows, non-profits are strong partners to both public and private land managers.

Under a clear, calm, Florida sky, three researchers crouch in the dry under-growth, probing the soil, inspecting plants, jotting down notes. Without warn-ing, the sound of artillery fire punctures the quiet with a thunder of sonorous, bass-drum bangs. No one looks up. With bomb blasts as frequent as bird song, and the occasional F-15 roaring overhead, Nature Conservancy staff working on Eglin Air Force Base in the Florida Panhandle barely notice the distur-bances. As part of a team managing the base's biodiversity, they've gotten used to the noise.

Under a cooperative agreement signed with the Department of Defense (DoD) in 1988 and updated in 1995, TNC and state Natural Heritage Programs have worked with the military on more than 200 conservation pro-jects at 170 bases in 41 states. "The Conservancy can only own so much land— only a fraction of what needs to be protected," says Jeff Hardesty, public lands program coordinator for TNC and one of the key players in the partnership with Eglin Air Force Base.

Just south of Crestview, Florida, one of the ten fastest-growing cities in the country, Eglin Air Force Base stands as an oasis in a desert of development. Its 464,000 acres span three counties. Forests, grasslands, rivers, beaches, and wet-lands cover the great majority of the base, punctuated here and there by wide swaths of cleared land used as bombing ranges. Despite all the humanmade ele-ments and activities on and around the base, Eglin is probably the world's best remnant of longleaf pine forest, an increasingly rare ecosystem that once stretched over 90 million acres from Virginia to Texas. Longleaf pine wood-lands, called sandhills, cover three-fourths of the base and include 10,000 acres of what is believed to be the largest remaining stand of old-growth longleaf pine in the world. In old growth areas, 400-year-old longleaf pines rise 100 feet or more from the sandy soil, their straight, thin trunks topping out in flat crowns of branches tufted with pencil-long pine needles.

Today, longleaf pine ecosystems cover only about 3 percent of their former area, now limited primarily to the coastal plains of the Carolinas, Georgia, Florida, Alabama, Mississippi, Louisiana, and Texas. In the wake of such loss, more than thirty species of plants and animals associated with longleaf pine ecosystems are threatened or endangered. In all, the base contains more than ninety rare or imperiled species. These days the military is out to prove that it is a responsible guardian of these treasures.

Eglin's daunting task is to protect this rich biodiversity while successfully

A field worker surveys boundaries for new state marine parks. Technicians set bronze discs with crucial information stamped on them to coordinate data gathering and set baselines for ongoing environmental surveys.

conducting its primary military mission—developing and testing conventional munitions and sensor tracking systems. "We look at military activities as another type of disrupter, just like wildfires and hurricanes are disrupters," says Rick McWhite, the base's chief of natural resources. "The healthier the system we have, the more disruption it can take without a catastrophic decline in biodiversity. We would never say that our [military] programs don't impact the environment. But we're being responsible by mitigating and restoring areas that we've impacted in the past and by trying to keep [any new] impacts to a minimum."

Eglin managers also have to factor in the thousands of local residents allowed on portions of the base for hiking, hunting, and other recreational pursuits. Pulling these diverse components together into an effective base-wide conservation plan of action is the responsibility of twenty-five staff members of Eglin's natural resources branch.

Of course, the military has its own good reasons for taking serious interest in restoring and maintaining its considerable natural resources. Not the least of those reasons is the need to comply with the federal Endangered Species Act and other environmental legislation. The Legacy Resource Management Program, created by Congress in 1991, also prodded the military to "address urgent issues of biological diversity." Despite the rules and requirements placed on the military by recent legislation, DoD has seized the initiative. Its modus operandi is ecosystem management, a holistic approach to protecting biodiversity that is now Pentagon policy on all installations.

The sheer size of the base has given researchers a chance to move far beyond the territorial restrictions typically inherent in such research experiments. They are amassing large quantities of data from thirty 200-acre plots, scattered in groups of four throughout the base. "This is probably the biggest experimental design in conservation in the United States today," says Louis Provencher, a TNC research ecologist who is leading the project.

Such ambitious ecological experiments don't come cheap. The cost generally puts this type of undertaking out of the reach of conservation organizations, which is why the DoD's funding for such work is so critical. "The work that Eglin has funded is cutting-edge research. Few people have much experience in what Eglin and its partners are attempting to do here," says Jeff Hardesty. "And few agencies have sufficient levels of funding or the commitment to science to support studies of this scale and scope."

Through growing-season burns, the planting of more than 3 million longleaf pine seedlings, the mechanical removal of slash and sand pine, and other activities, more than 200,000 acres were restored to longleaf pine dominance between 1990 and 1995. More significant, the slow but steady loss of forest health and habitat has not only been halted, but reversed. Provencher says, "Eglin has turned the situation completely around."

Lending support to that diagnosis is the base's population of endangered red-cockaded woodpeckers, which increased 6 percent in just two years between 1994 and 1996. "If the red-cockaded woodpecker is there and thriving, you know that you basically have healthy, thriving sandhills," says Carl Petrick, the base's wildlife manager. Because the birds nest only in open stands of mature longleaf pines after painstakingly excavating cavities for their nests, a shortage of old-growth trees can bring dire effects. Even when there are abundant pines ninety or more years old, the woodpeckers will refuse to nest if pines and hardwoods are unusually dense—as is almost always the case in fire-suppressed areas.

Eglin is leveraging both its newly acquired information and its resources by taking part in the Gulf Coastal Plain Ecosystem Partnership, a voluntary partnership among seven major landowners formed in 1995 to sustain 840,000 contiguous acres of longleaf pine habitat in northern Florida and southern Alabama. Recognizing that ecosystems rarely correspond to political and geographic boundaries, Eglin joined Champion International Corporation, the Florida Division of Forestry, national forests in Alabama and Florida, the Northwest Florida Water Management District, and TNC in a memorandum of understanding that encourages the partners to work together to maintain a healthy ecosystem that benefits them all.

The ecosystem, which includes four major watersheds and more than 160 rare or imperiled plants and animals, comprises lands and waters that are managed for purposes ranging from intensive forestry and military training to recreation and water resource protection. TNC, whose 2,700-acre Choctawhatchee

River Delta Preserve is but a small part of the ecosystem, is facilitating the development of joint strategies and helping to coordinate efforts among the partners.

Although the military now realizes and takes a measure of pride in the significance of its natural resources, it didn't always go out of its way to protect them. But compared to land held by other federal agencies, much of the military's lands came out ahead of the game, "kind of by default," says Doug Ripley, a retired Air Force officer now working as a civilian in the environmental division of the Office of the Air Force Civil Engineer. "We didn't muck it up; we put a fence around it and we kept people out. And that ended up being a pretty neat thing for the environment."

Brenda Biondo, a Virginia-based writer, adapted this case study from an article she wrote that first appeared in the September/October 1997 issue of Nature Conservancy *magazine.*

PROFILE

Alice Brandon
Ecosystems Research Associate
Conservation 2000
Illinois Department of Natural Resources
Oregon, Illinois

The nature of conservation work involves collaborative efforts among a variety of disciplines and organizations. The importance of written and oral communication skills cannot be emphasized enough.

Alice Brandon, Ecosystems Research Associate, is contracted by the Illinois Department of Natural Resources (IDNR) on an annual basis through the Nature of Illinois Foundation. Her job is part of a $100 million initiative called Conservation 2000 (C2000), launched in 1995 by Illinois Governor Jim Edgar. C2000 is a six-year statewide initiative to enhance nature protection and outdoor recreation by reversing the decline of the state's ecosystem.

Alice's job is to facilitate, write, and support Integrated Natural Resource/Agricultural Management Plans (INRAMP) in a two-county study area. INRAMP reimburses landowners for up to 75 percent of the costs of implementing plans and is only one part of C2000.

Landowners voluntarily contact the IDNR for assistance in creating an ecosystem management plan for their property. When landowners call, Alice explains C2000, then sends out a letter and a request-for-assistance form for the landowner to complete. This is a step that evolved from early experiences with the program. Alice says, "People don't understand that it takes a lot of money and staff time to write these plans. It's intensive work . . . a serious endeavor. . . . If we're going to put the time into it, we want them to sign the plan."

After landowners indicate serious interest, Alice talks to them about the natural resources on their property and finds out where it's located. Then she contacts natural resource experts from other departments within IDNR and the USDA Natural Resources Conservation Service, pulling together a team to evaluate the property and make recommendations, and obtains aerial maps from the Farm Service Agency.

Alice then coordinates a meeting between her team and the landowner in which they walk the property to see what is there as well as to listen to the landowner's goals. Setting a meeting for the whole team can be tricky given that the biologists and other natural resource experts all have other primary responsibilities, C2000 being only a small part of their jobs. Alice says, "I'm also the liaison between the different biologists. They're not used to working together. This is the first time they've had to do these kinds of (integrated) plans."

One of Alice's biggest frustrations is the three- to six-month turnaround time to write a plan for a landowner due to reliance on experts from other departments and agencies. This time lapse often results in landowners changing their minds about what they want to do, and a loss of momentum or interest in the program.

After the initial meeting, Alice continues to coordinate team activities and meetings. Once she has the team's recommendations, Alice composes a detailed plan, catering to the landowner's goals, which addresses every resource on the property and includes a monthly guide for implementing the plan. The INRAMP is part of a conservation easement requiring that the land not be developed for a minimum of ten years. When the plan is complete, Alice schedules a meeting between the landowner and the team to go through the plan.

Alice's job isn't over after the plan is signed. In keeping with the conservation easement, Alice goes out to take pictures of the property for future comparative evaluations. Further, while she doesn't physically help landowners implement the INRAMP, she does provide support if the landowner has questions or needs technical help.

For example, Alice gets a call from a landowner who signed his plan eighteen months ago. An area of his property has just been accepted into the Conservation Reserve Program (CRP, which was authorized under the Farm Bill). Under the CRP, the landowner commits to a riparian buffer on his stream, so he wants to plant more trees. His agreement under the CRP also requires that a portion of his INRAMP be rewritten. So Alice contacts the team who contributed to the plan to review it and make the changes.

Alice feels that her college education has been an asset to her position with IDNR. She didn't declare her major until her junior year because she didn't want to limit herself to just studying zoology or wildlife biology. Then she discovered a degree program that combined "hard" sciences with social sciences. She says, "It's kind of an unusual degree because it's a multidisciplinary approach to natural resource conservation. I took courses in a lot of different natural resource areas . . . and have this holistic, step-away approach. . . . I look at the land as a whole piece and try to see its place in the greater watershed."

She earned a bachelor of arts in biological aspects of conservation from the University of Wisconsin, Madison, in 1994.

After graduation Alice wanted to do something of service to her country. Her stepfather had worked in the Peace Corps, but she wasn't prepared to make a two-year commitment. The armed forces didn't appeal to her. Then she found out about AmeriCorps. She applied to many different programs, trying to find something in her field. During that time she began volunteering with a wildlife rehabilitator who sometimes had up to 150 animals on her premises to care for. Finally she applied to the Illinois RiverWatch Network through AmeriCorps, and was hired in January 1995.

Alice worked for a year as part of a four-member team, coordinating volunteer monitoring of streams and rivers over a seventeen-county region in southern Illinois and promoting the program. This put her in contact with over 500 citizens and involved training approximately sixty people to monitor streams by teaching them how to identify aquatic invertebrates, take temperature and various physical measurements of the stream, and to evaluate riparian habitat, to assess the environmental quality of the streams. The goal was to have the same volunteers monitor each year at the same time, to establish baseline data on the condition of rivers and streams.

The Illinois RiverWatch Network was sponsored by the IDNR, which is how Alice learned of the opening for her current position. She says: "This is exactly what I got my degree for—to be doing more integrated management and to work from a watershed level. . . . One of the things I really like about it is that it's cutting edge. We're creating the program as we go along. That's one of the things I was [also] really attracted to with RiverWatch. It was the first year of the program. . . . There was a goal . . . [for] . . . what should be done, but there wasn't a whole lot of idea as to how to get it done. So this can be hard, but it's also really challenging because you have a lot of freedom to explore different ways of doing things."

Working with a variety of biologists, Alice discovered gaps in her education where she would like to gain more experience. She wants to increase her botanical, communication, and conflict resolution skills. Eventually, she would like to be capable of making management recommendations to landowners. She is currently applying to graduate programs in plant biology and conservation biology.

Denise Meridith
Arizona State Director
Bureau of Land Management
Phoenix, Arizona

With an increasingly sophisticated public becoming ever-more involved in land and water conservation issues, the role of the Bureau of Land Management has evolved from one of teaching and directing the public to one of facilitation, collaboration, and receiving information, getting groups to work together to solve land and water issues.

Denise Meridith, Arizona state director of the Bureau of Land Management (BLM), has come a long way from her roots in Queens, New York City. Denise is a black woman who decided she wanted to become a veterinarian at age seven. She endured busing to an all-white junior high and high school, as well as insults and ostracism by "keeping her eye on the prize—Cornell University." She followed her dream to Ithaca, New York, and attended Cornell's Agricultural College, a land grant school. There, in the early 1970s, she learned that "women don't become veterinarians," and by the end of her sophomore year she gave up that dream.

Then she met a mentor who didn't tell her what she could or couldn't do. Daniel Thompson, a wildlife biologist, encouraged Denise and she switched her major to wildlife biology. Lucky for the BLM, he didn't tell her that there weren't any female wildlife biologists either!

Upon graduation in 1973, Denise applied to all the federal land management agencies. The National Park Service said they did not hire female biologists. The Forest Service liked her credentials and offered her a job as a secretary. When she accepted a natural resource specialist position with the BLM she was the first woman biologist the agency ever hired, though she didn't know this at the time. Two weeks after graduation, against the odds, she was in Nevada studying desert tortoises and pupfish.

In the last twenty-five years Denise has worked in nearly every BLM program. Today she is responsible for over 14 million acres of land, 8 field offices, and 550 employees. Her position involves a major coordination role and a major external affairs role, dealing with BLM constituents such as the convention bureau and the Arizona Cattleman's Association, as well as with Congress. She says: "It's a pretty exciting job which does vary from day to day. That's what I like!"

Though Denise started her career with the BLM doing fieldwork, her role has become more administrative. Along the way, she earned a master's in public administration from the University of Southern California. She spends a lot of time traveling around Arizona, attending meetings, and talking on the phone. However, she says her job still takes her outdoors "quite a bit." For example, at Thanksgiving she visited the Safford field office and went on a horseback ride into the Aravaipa Canyon. Another recent field office visit involved whitewater rafting. Denise says, "People use it as an opportunity to show me what they're doing. A lot of times they invite members of the local public along and I get to hear from them what their concerns and problems are. Or they'll invite the county commissioner to go, or someone from the local travel bureau. So it's really good because I get to impart and receive information about what's going on around the state."

Right now Denise is excited about the Southwest Conservation Strategy, which proposes to get the various federal agencies working together on common problems. This interagency initiative covers Arizona and New Mexico, and is heavily dependent on local public input. Once a month, state directors from the BLM, the regional forester, head colonels from military bases, and

Denise Meridith, Arizona state director for the Bureau of Land Management, sets out for a day in the field.

regional directors from the National Park Service and the Fish and Wildlife Service come together to discuss key issues. In addition subgroups work on different issues such as endangered species and litigation. Denise says, "We all have our separate missions, separate legislation, and separate problems to deal with, but there are a lot of problems we have in common." For example, the BLM may have one policy and the Forest Service may have another that deals with livestock grazing. This kind of joint effort is the latest management strategy for all those who care about or are responsible for natural resources.

Denise usually starts her day at around 7:00 A.M. On a recent day she met with a group to discuss a program the Professional Golf Association (PGA) is sponsoring to get more inner-city youths involved in golfing. Also at the meeting were a representative from the mayor's office, a private golf pro, a representative from the National Minorities Golfers Foundation, and a representative of the PGA. The city of Phoenix and the BLM both have lands in or near the city that could be developed into "alternative" golf courses. The idea is to provide inner-city children and women with free or low-cost access to beginner-type golf courses, and by doing so, get them interested in management, ownership, and environmentally responsible maintenance of golf courses. "We also have a program called Hospitality Pipeline from which we hope to bring more students of color into the recreation and tourism industry. So that program would be involved with this as well," Denise says.

When Denise arrived at her office after the meeting, she checked messages and followed up. Then she gave a slide talk to the state office employees about a recent trip to South Africa. The BLM was invited there to share techniques in riparian habitat management, allotment, livestock grazing management, and how to get people with different interests to sit down together and work out plans.

The next day she met with representatives from the Tohono O'Odham tribe to talk about a piece of BLM land of spiritual significance that they want returned to the tribe. The group originally approached Denise on the issue two years ago. She told them legislation would be required. Since then they've been working with Congress and various others to draft such legislation. At the recent meeting they discussed some of the implications and future management issues to reach an understanding for the area. The land in question is a remote site for the BLM, but since the tribe is right there, they might be able to provide better safety, search, and rescue, which the BLM is unable to provide. But Denise warns: "It's not going to be without controversy because any kind of change in land status is controversial, but we hope to get the right people talking together."

The thing Denise likes most about her work is being able to give back to the community through such things as providing recreation or environmental education. As her federal career winds down, she sees herself doing more community-based work, either through the state or city government, a university, or even starting her own business related to helping agencies make adjustments and changes and helping them communicate more effectively with the public. "It's always going to be something related to assisting the community and to natural resources. . . . You can't have natural resource management without people and people will not exist without natural resources," she says.

Mark Zankel
Director of Science and Stewardship
The Nature Conservancy, Delaware Chapter
Newark, Delaware

Competition for conservation jobs is very high. Often you have to be willing to take volunteer or low-paying, part-time work for years, and then move every couple of years to advance your career. However, if your heart is in it, be persistent, and it will pay off.

Mark Zankel, director of science and stewardship for the Delaware chapter of The Nature Conservancy, became interested in conservation work when he arrived at Dartmouth College from the suburbs of New York City. He says "When I saw the amazing natural features of New Hampshire it made me realize that I wanted to spend more time there. . . . I spent a lot of time there in the middle of nowhere, and was inspired by the mountains." Mark joined TNC during his sophomore year and says, "from the minute I got the first magazine, I've always wanted to work for The Nature Conservancy."

However Mark, "didn't have the right background," when he graduated from Dartmouth in 1989 with a bachelor of arts in history. "I really thought I wanted to be an environmental lawyer," he says. His first year out of college he worked as a paralegal for a corporate law firm in Washington, D.C. While working there, he also volunteered for the Sierra Club. After seeing millions of dollars spent on legal wrangling, Mark decided that law was, "a bit too removed," and not how he wanted to contribute to conservation.

He moved to Colorado, where he continued doing everything from trail maintenance to letter writing campaigns with the Sierra Club, and got a job with Colorado Public Interest Research Group (Colorado PIRG). After one exhausting year, Mark left Colorado PIRG and worked for a year at an environmental consulting firm in Boulder whose specialty was working with industry on reducing the use of hazardous chemicals in manufacturing processes.

After a few years of continually trying to get more directly involved with environmental issues, Mark realized that, "if [he] wanted to be out on the land [he'd] have to go to graduate school and gain more background and expertise in ecology." Therefore, he entered the University of Michigan's School of Natural Resources and earned a master's degree in resource ecology and management in 1994, specializing in forest ecosystems.

The summer between his first and second year of graduate school, Mark worked as an interpretive park ranger at Rocky Mountain National Park. "I . . . wanted to take a lot of skills I learned that year and test them out. It was great living close to the land and really getting to know the ecology of and the natural features of a place," he says.

During his second year of graduate school Mark focused his job search on TNC. He quickly realized that he would have to be flexible on where he wanted to live if he wanted to work for TNC. He learned of a seasonal ecologist position with the North Carolina chapter of TNC and began working in the Blue Ridge Mountains the summer after he graduated. Over the next twenty months, Mark worked seasonal and contract positions with the North Carolina chapter, while continuing to look for a more permanent position with TNC, doing such things as monitoring rare plants, working on a site conservation plan, and studying the response of shrubby wetlands to wildfire. These jobs, as with all his previous positions, included a lot of communications and public relations work. He says, "I think one thing we've learned in the Conservancy is that we're always doing PR and communications. It's just part of our job."

When he started his current position in early 1996, it was at 60 percent time. Through a series of grants Mark moved back and forth between 60 percent and 95 percent time over the course of a year. In May 1997, his position became full time.

Today Mark is responsible for seven preserves TNC owns in Delaware totaling about 4,000 acres, and helps manage three other areas totaling another 1,000 acres, all with primarily wetland-related species and communities. His time is roughly split between four categories of work: science-based fieldwork, such as biological monitoring and research; maintenance-oriented fieldwork, such as making sure boundaries are posted and gates are in working condition; outreach work with partners, preserve neighbors, and volunteer stewards; and office work, which includes grant writing and budgeting, as well as the conservation planning that is the "backbone" of his job.

On a recent morning, Mark meets with a volunteer preserve steward who sees to the day-to-day management of a TNC preserve while keeping a visible presence on site. This is an annual review to talk about what is and isn't going well, what the volunteer needs from TNC, and where he wants to go with his stewardship. The two walk the site making note of upcoming summer stewardship activities, and look at well sites for the TNC's hydrology research planned for the summer.

Then Mark is off to another preserve to assess damage to the shoreline from recent northeaster storms. This involves walking the preserve to look at the beach and dune community and learn what changes the storm has wrought, as well as scoping out sites for shorebird viewing platforms to be built the next month.

Finally, Mark arrives at the office and spends an hour in a budget meeting. "I guess one of the sad realities of being a steward is that you really have to learn how to budget and account for your money, how to raise money, and how to plan effectively. . . . They don't necessarily teach you that in your college or graduate program," he says.

The rest of the afternoon is spent fine-tuning a collaborative management plan in which TNC is working with the state division of fish and wildlife and a private land trust to manage about 10,000 acres, including nine miles of shoreline. The three partners signed a Memorandum of Agreement to come up with a coordinated management framework that will allow them to manage the land on an ecosystem scale. "Our boundaries run, in many cases, right through the middle of a salt marsh . . . so the boundaries, from an ecological standpoint, are basically meaningless. . . . It's really working well so far," says Mark.

The things that keep Mark motivated from day to day are "spending time on the land that [TNC is] conserving, and working with so many talented, creative, and dedicated colleagues." Looking ahead, he sees the barriers between program areas at TNC breaking down and the science and stewardship positions moving toward project manager positions. He says he may try to move toward such a position, but he'd really like to become a director of conservation programs at a state chapter.

RESOURCES

Listed here are only some of the trade and professional organizations active in the land and water conservation field. Many federal agencies, as well as non-profit and professional organizations offer free on-line subscriptions to a listserv, a bulk-email service, which communicates such things as environmental legislation updates and current issues directly to your email address.

Amazing Environmental Organization Webdirectory. "Earth's biggest environmental search engine." Includes information on land and water conservation and professional associations. Also don't miss the employment section on the webdirectory homepage, which provides links to job listings, descriptions, and agencies specifically concerned with environmental employment. Http://www.webdirectory. com/.

American Rivers. National nonprofit river-conservation organization dedicated to protecting and restoring America's river systems and to fostering a river stewardship ethic. Programs address flood control and hydropower policy reform, endangered aquatic and riparian species protection, western instream flow, clean water, and urban rivers. Offers four, three-month internships each quarter. Website includes links to relevant environmental laws, and extensive list of other river and water-related organizations. 1025 Vermont Ave., NW, Suite 720, Washington, DC 20005. (202) 547-6900. Http://www.amrivers.org.

AmeriCorps. National service program that is a public–private partnership, allowing people of all ages and backgrounds to earn help paying for education in exchange for a year of service. AmeriCorps members meet community needs with services that include turning vacant lots into neighborhood parks, tutoring teens and teaching elementary school students, restoring coastlines, and providing natural disaster relief to victims. C/o Corporation for National Service, 1201 New York Avenue, NW, Washington, DC 20525. (202) 606-5000, ext. 566. Http://www.ameri-corps.org.

Center for Marine Conservation. A nonprofit membership organization dedicated to conserving coastal and ocean resources and to protecting marine wildlife and habitats through science-based advocacy, research, and public education. 1725 DeSales St., NW, Suite 600, Washington, DC 20036. (202) 429-5609. Http://www. cmc-ocean.org/main.html.

Conservation International. Nonprofit organization that protects the Earth's biologically richest areas and helps the people who live there improve their quality of life using science, economics, policy, and community involvement. Works primarily in rain forests, but also in coastal and coral reef systems, dry forests, deserts, and wetlands. Works in twenty-two countries and has over 350 staff worldwide. 2501 M Street, NW, Suite 200, Washington, DC 20037. (800) 429-5660. Http:// www.conservation.org/ciap.htm.

Ecological Society of America. Nonprofit organization of scientists who conduct research, teach, and work to provide the ecological knowledge needed to solve environmental problems. Publishes a bulletin and four research journals that cover current issues, as well as cutting-edge ideas as the field of conservation ecology undergoes transformation. Also publishes *Careers in Ecology* (a pamphlet that is available both on-line and in print). Website has job announcements (under News) and career advice (under Outreach, Education). 2010 Massachusetts Avenue, NW, Suite 400, Washington, DC 20036. (202) 833-8773. Http://www.sdsc.edu/ ~ESA/esa.htm.

Environmental Careers Organization (ECO) Offers paid internships with a variety of conservation employers, as well as other services for conservation career seekers. Offices in Seattle, San Francisco, Boston, and Cleveland. 179 South Street, Boston, MA 02111. (617) 426-4375. Http://www.eco.org.

Habitat Restoration Information Center. Purpose is to facilitate the exchange of information pertaining to the restoration of native plant and animal species and their habitats by providing the educational tools needed to restore the environment. Website lists conferences, workshops, courses, related organizations, federal and state funding, and legislation information, newsletters, journals, and magazines. P.O. Box 1400, Felton, CA 95018-1400. (408) 335-6814. Http://www. habitat_restoration.com.

Land and Water Magazine: The Magazine of Natural Resource Management and Restoration (bimonthly). Published for contractors, landscape architects, consultants and engineers, government officials, and all others involved in natural resource management and restoration. Prints job-site stories, case histories, and information on the latest developments in the industry. P.O. Box 1197, Fort Dodge, Iowa 50501-9925. (515)576-3191. Http://www.landandwater. com/default.html.

Land Trust Alliance. National umbrella organization for land trusts, providing leadership, networking, information, and technical assistance to over 1,200 local, regional and national land trusts across the nation. Website has policy and funding information, list of books for further reading, land trust job postings, and links to other land trust resources. 1319 F St., NW, Suite 501, Washington, DC 20004. (202) 638-4725. Http://www.lta.org/.

National Association of Conservation Districts. Nonprofit organization that represents 3,000 conservation districts across the nation. Pools district experience and develops national policies on a continuing basis. Publishes *The District Leader* (monthly) which covers national conservation issues. 509 Capitol Ct., NE, Washington, DC 20002-4946. (800) 825-5547. Http://www.nacdnet.org.

National Wildlife Federation. Largest conservation organization in the world. Has state chapters and holds an annual meeting. Awards fellowships for graduate study in conservation and sponsors paid internships. Publishes annual *Conservation Directory* ($61.00, available in most libraries), *National Wildlife* magazine (bimonthly), and numerous other publications. 8925 Leesburg Pike, Vienna, VA 22184. (703) 790-4000. Http://www.nwf.org.

Natural Resources Council of America. Federation of national and regional conservation organizations and scientific societies interested in conservation of natural resources. Publishes *NRCA News* and *Conservation Voice* (both bimonthly), which provide information on current events, employment opportunities, state and local conservation issues, member activities, and people in the conservation field. 1025 Thomas Jefferson St., NW, Suite 109, Washington, DC 20007-5201. (202) 333-0411. Website under construction in 1998.

The Nature Conservancy. Nonprofit membership organization. Preserves habitat for rare and endangered plants and animals by buying the lands and waters they need to survive. Publishes bimonthly magazine. Has land and water conservation programs operated by professionally staffed field offices in fifty states. Job-hunt line ([703] 247-3721) is updated each Monday with all jobs available with The Nature Conservancy. Website has searchable job listings under Get Involved. 1815 N. Lynn St., Arlington, VA 22209. (800) 628-6860. Http://www.tnc.org.

River and Watershed Conservation Directory. Printed by the National Park Service. Lists over 3,000 public and nonprofit agencies and organizations directly involved in river and watershed conservation. Obtain a copy for $5.00 by calling (202) 343-3780.

River Network. Nonprofit organization dedicated to helping people organize to protect and restore rivers and watersheds. Also acquires and conserves riverlands that are critical to the services that rivers perform for human communities. Publications are primarily resource guides, but includes the quarterly journal *River Voices*, which offers coverage of river conservation and organization-building topics. P.O. Box 8787, Portland, OR 97207. (503) 241-3506. Http://www.rivernetwork.org/.

Society for Conservation Biology. International professional organization dedicated to promoting the scientific study of the phenomena that affect the maintenance, loss, and restoration of biological diversity. Website is a good place to begin a search for conservation-related employment or information on programs in conservation biology. Http://www.conbio.rice.edu/scb/.

Society for Ecological Restoration. Nonprofit organization dedicated to advancing the science and art of restoring damaged ecosystems in conjunction with preservation and management of key natural areas in order to maintain biological diversity. Offers two main journals, *Restoration & Management Notes* (biannual), and *Restoration Ecology* (quarterly). Website has "employment noticeboard," which has links to other conservation employment websites, job listings, grants, and internships. 1207 Seminole Hwy., Madison, WI 53711. (608) 262-2746. Http://nabalu.flas.ufl.edu/ser/SERhome.html.

Society for Range Management. Professional scientific and conservation organization whose members are concerned with studying, conserving, managing, and sustaining the varied resources of rangelands. Publishes *Journal of Range Management* (bimonthly). 1839 York St., Denver, CO 80206. (303) 355-7070 Http://srm.org/index.htm.

Soil and Water Conservation Society. Advances the science and art of soil, water, and related natural resource management to achieve sustainability. Publishes *Journal of Soil and Water Conservation* (quarterly), and *Conservation Voices: Listening to the Land* (bimonthly). Offers certification in erosion and sediment control. Follow links on website to Natural Resources Research Information, which lists related academic institutions and professional organizations. 7515 N.E. Ankeny Rd., Ankeny, IA 50021-9764. (800) THE-SOIL [843-7645]. Http://www.swcs.org.

Student Conservation Association. (SCA) Nonprofit membership organization that supports internships and volunteers that offer training for conservation careers for high school and college age students, as well as adults. Publishes *Earth Work* magazine (11 times a year), which provides job openings, as well as advice and information on how to break into the conservation field. P.O. Box 550, Charlestown, NH 03603. (603) 543-1700. Http://www.sca-inc.org.

Trust for Public Land. Nonprofit land conservation organization that conserves land for parks, playgrounds, community gardens, and wilderness. Focuses on conservation of land for human needs. Publishes *Land and People* (biannually), which highlights current projects around the country, *On the Land* TPL's regional newsletters (biannually), and *GreenSense*, which offers information on financing for parks and conservation. Website has links to other land conservation resources. 116 New Montgomery St., Fourth Floor, San Francisco, CA 94105. (800) 729-6428. Http://www.tpl.org.

U.S. Department of Agriculture, Natural Resources Conservation Service (formerly the Soil Conservation Service). Works with the American people to conserve natural resources on private lands. P.O. Box 2890, Washington, DC 20013. (202) 720-3210. Http://www.nrcs.usda.gov.

U.S. Geological Survey Biological Resources Division. Works with others to provide the scientific understanding and technologies needed to support the sound management and conservation of our nation's biological resources. U.S. Department of the Interior, Office of Public Affairs, 12201 Sunrise Valley Drive, Reston, VA 20192. Http://biology.usgs.gov.

U.S. Water News. Monthly publication offering the latest news concerning water issues. Coverage includes water supply, water quality, policy and legislation, litigation and water rights, conservation, climate, international water news, and more. Classified ad section has job postings. Print and on-line versions have different articles. 230 Main Street, Halstead, KS 67056. (316) 835-2222. Http://www.uswaternews.com/homepage.html.

The Wilderness Society. Nonprofit membership organization devoted to preserving wilderness and wildlife, protecting America's prime forests, parks, rivers, deserts, and shorelands, as well as fostering an American land ethic. 900 17 St., NW, Washington, DC 20006. 202-833-2300. Http://www.tws.org.

12 Fishery and Wildlife Management

AT A GLANCE

Employment:

More than 37,000 fishery and wildlife professionals and technicians nationwide

Demand:

8 to 10 percent annual growth for wildlife professionals; 6 to 8 percent growth for fishery managers

Breakdown:

Wildlife management:

Public sector, 65 percent (30 percent federal, 35 percent state and local)

Private sector, 15 percent

Nonprofit sector, 5 percent

Education, 15 percent (includes both public and private sectors)

Fisheries management:

Public sector, 50 percent (25 percent federal, 25 percent state and local)

Private sector, 20 percent

Nonprofit sector, 5 percent

Education, 25 percent (includes both public and private sectors)

Key Job Titles:

Animal control supervisor

Aquaculturist

Botanist

Computer programmer/modeler

Conservation educator
Data management specialist
Endangered species biologist
Environmental impact analyst
Environmental specialist
Field crew leader
Field or laboratory technician
Fish and game warden
Fish farm worker
Fishery or wildlife biologist
Fishery or wildlife manager
Foreign fisheries observer
Hatchery manager
Ichthyologist
Limnologist
Lobbyist
Marine biologist or ecologist
Marine resources technician
Museum specialist
Naturalist
Professor (education)
Public aquarium director
Refuge manager
Senior research scientist
Shellfish grower
Toxicologist
Water pollution biologist
Water quality analyst
Wetlands ecologist
Wildlife inspector (at ports of entry)
Zoo director

Influential Organizations:

American Fisheries Society
Conservation International
National Audubon Society
National Wildlife Federation
Society for Conservation Biology
U.S. Fish and Wildlife Service
Wildlife Society
World Wildlife Fund

Salary:

Entry-level salaries range from $22,000 to $25,000 but can go as low as $18,000. Mid-level salaries range from $35,000 to $42,000. Upper-level salaries have a wide range of from $50,000 to over $70,000.

Something about fish and wildlife work attracts a lot of people, people who envision a life tracking elk across mountain meadows or tagging wild salmon on remote rivers. There's no mystery here. People love the natural world and wild animals. Undergraduate biology programs fill up with students drawn by their own experiences in field, forest, zoo, and aquarium; as well as by the powerful images of wildlife photographers, filmmakers, and journalists. It's no coincidence that advocacy groups that protect animals and their habitats have millions of members throughout the world.

The road to a satisfying career in fisheries and wildlife management can be a difficult one, however. Competition for stable jobs in conservation is intense, and colleges generate more qualified people each year. Moreover, many who work long hours at less-than-lucrative pay in hopes of an invigorating outdoor career, end up with an office job. For those who persevere, however, the rewards can be everything imagined. Those professionals we see on *National Geographic* specials really do exist. Why not you?

WHAT IS FISHERY AND WILDLIFE MANAGEMENT?

Management of fisheries and wildlife used to mean maintenance of adequate populations of game fish and animals to satisfy sport-fishermen and hunters. Although this is still part of the profession, the field is now considerably broader. It might be called "ecosystem management" to point out that the concerns of fishery and wildlife managers now extend far beyond the welfare of a few individual species useful to human beings to encompass the flora and fauna of entire ecosystems.

With its broader and more sophisticated responsibilities, the field has grown from one dominated by outdoor biologists with undergraduate degrees to one in which advanced degrees are all but essential. A wide choice of careers are open to you that offer a variety of working conditions. However, biologists and their activities are still at the heart of fishery and wildlife management.

According to the University of Idaho's Department of Fish and Wildlife Resources, fishery and wildlife management are two professions that "are nearly identical in their basic approach to resource management and differ mainly in the type of environment, i.e., aquatic or terrestrial, with which they are concerned. . . . A common saying, and one with a great deal of truth, is that fish or wildlife management is largely people management, since people rely on the same habitats that fish and wildlife rely on, and have large impacts on fish and wildlife habitats."

According to the American Fisheries Society, in the broadest terms, "fisheries science includes genetics, physiology, biology, ecology, population dynamics, economics, health, culture, and other topics germane to marine and freshwater finfish, exploitable shellfish, and their respective fisheries." The Wildlife Society says that wildlife management is broadly construed as "a human effort

Fisheries biologists study stream flows in their work to turn around the decline in populations of salmon and other species.

to maintain or manipulate natural resources, including soil, water, plants, and animals (including man) for the best interests of the environment, whether these interests be ecological, commercial, recreational, or scientific."

Fish and wildlife management professions often involve coordinating management programs with other natural resource activities such as forest management, range management, and land-use planning. A look at the tasks of typical fishery and wildlife management professionals serves as a good definition of the field. The U.S. Fish and Wildlife Service (USFWS) defines these positions as follows:

Fishery biologists study the life history, habitats, population dynamics, nutrition, and diseases of fish. They manage fish hatcheries, propagate various species of hatchery fish, conduct fish disease control programs, gather data on the effects of natural and human environmental changes on fish, and work with other agencies to restore and enhance fish habitats.

Wildlife biologists study the distribution, habitats, life histories, and ecology of birds, mammals, and other wildlife. They plan and carry out wildlife conservation and management programs, determine conditions affecting wildlife, apply research findings to the management of wildlife, restore or develop wildlife habitats, regulate wildlife populations, and control wildlife diseases.

Refuge managers oversee national wildlife refuges to protect and conserve migratory and native species of birds, mammals, fish, endangered species, and other wildlife. Many refuges also offer outdoor recreational opportunities and programs to educate the public about the refuge's wildlife and their habitats.

These are accurate but bureaucratic definitions. The reality behind them is an exciting and world-preserving career.

HISTORY AND BACKGROUND

The modern wildlife management profession in this country can probably be traced to the beginning of the National Wildlife Refuge System, which was begun by President Theodore Roosevelt in 1903 to protect Pelican Island in Florida. This helped stop mass killings of waterfowl for their large feathers, which were prized by northern dressmakers and milliners. Today the system includes 512 refuges and 64 national fish hatcheries.

Scientific wildlife management as a profession in the United States began about fifty years ago. Since then, more and more threats to wildlife have been identified and more species have come under the protection of refuges and human managers.

Modern fishery management began shortly after the Civil War, as New England's rivers, gradually polluted and impounded by industrial development, produced fewer and fewer fish. "Most New England rivers were dammed to produce power for mills to make shoes or textiles," says Paul Brouha, executive director of the American Fisheries Society. "Dams blocked passage for spawning fish such as the Atlantic salmon, striped bass, and shad." In 1870, concern over these declines led to the formation of the American Fish Cultural Association, which later became the American Fisheries Society. The impetus for the organization was to apply science to sustain fish populations.

It was not until establishment of reliable funding mechanisms in the 1950s, however, that the field became a serious and widespread profession. The Dingell-Johnson Act of 1950 led the way by providing continuing allocation of funds to state fishery programs.

LEGISLATION

As is the case with many environmental fields, careers in fishery and wildlife management are driven by laws usually intended to eradicate mistakes of the past, design programs for effective management, and authorize funding. Some of these influential laws include:

Migratory Bird Treaty Act of 1918 (as amended). This act, one of the first wildlife protection laws, implements treaties with Great Britain (for Canada), Mexico, Japan, and Russia for the protection of migratory birds. The act also regulates the taking, selling, transporting, and importing of migratory birds, and provides penalties for violations.

Fish and Wildlife Coordination Act of 1934 (as amended). This act authorizes assistance to federal, state, and other agencies in development, protection, rearing, and stocking of fish and wildlife and controlling losses thereof; surveys of fish and wildlife and the effects of pollution on all Federal lands; and surveys to prevent losses of, and to enhance, fish and wildlife at water-use projects constructed or licensed by the federal government. The act also requires that the costs of constructing, operating, and maintaining measures to prevent or compensate for damages to fish and wildlife caused by a federal project be considered integral costs of the project.

Migratory Bird Hunting and Conservation Stamp (Duck Stamp) Act of 1934. This act requires waterfowl hunters sixteen years of age or older to possess duck stamps and authorizes the acquisition of waterfowl production areas from duck stamp revenue.

Federal Aid in Wildlife Restoration Act of 1937 (as amended—also known as the Pittman-Robertson Act). This act establishes an excise tax on sporting arms and ammunition for wildlife restoration work. States can also receive grants through the act for up to 75 percent of the costs of wildlife conservation activities, including acquisition, restoration, and maintenance of wetlands.

Federal Aid in Sport Fish Restoration Act of 1950 (as amended—also known as the Dingell-Johnson Act). This act establishes an excise tax on fishing tackle sales

A wildlife biologist makes friends with a Northern Spotted Owl in Oregon. Protection of spotted owls under the Endangered Species Act requires the preservation of thousands of acres of forest habitat.

and apportions resulting funds to states for sport fish restoration work based on a formula of land area and the number of resident fishing licenses sold. A portion of funding under this act can be used for aquatic resource education programs.

Fish and Wildlife Act of 1956. This act authorizes the USFWS to acquire lands for wildlife refuges. The act also requires the Army Corps of Engineers to consult with the USFWS to prevent the direct and indirect loss of, or damage to, wildlife resources from a permitted activity. Funding comes from revenues derived primarily from oil and gas leasing through the Land and Water Conservation Fund.

National Wildlife Refuge System Administration Act of 1966. This Act consolidated lands administered by the Department of the Interior through the USFWS into a single National Wildlife Refuge System. The act establishes a unifying mission for the system, a process for determining compatible uses of refuges, and a requirement for preparing comprehensive conservation plans. The act states that the mission of the National Wildlife Refuge System be focused singularly on wildlife conservation.

Magnuson Fishery Conservation and Management Act of 1976 (as amended— also known as the Magnuson-Stevens Act or Sustainable Fish Act). This act frames U.S. fish management efforts. Originally it halted fishing by foreign fleets in U.S. waters, which extend 200 miles out to sea, and encouraged U.S. fisheries to be more active by subsidizing fleet modernization and expansion. Magnuson's weaknesses coupled with "overcapitalization" caused precipitous declines in U.S. fisheries. In 1996, the act was amended to reduce over fishing and "by-catch," as well as to protect essential fish habitats.

Endangered Species Act of 1973 (as amended). This is potentially the most significant and far reaching of all fishery and wildlife protection legislation and a true landmark in environmental management. The act directs the USFWS to determine when a species is threatened with extinction and requires government agencies to take actions aimed at recovery.

National Wildlife Refuge System Improvement Act of 1997. This act formally expands the mission of the National Wildlife Refuge System to include fish, wildlife, and plant conservation, from its previous focus on wildlife exclusively.

This legislative base provides the framework within which fishery and wildlife professionals carry out their work, receive their funding, and measure their success. There are many other federal (as well as state and local), regulations that can affect employment in this field, and more are enacted each year. Make it a point to get acquainted with these before you begin your job search. An extensive list of federal resource laws affecting the USFWS can be found at http://www.fws.gov/laws/digest/reslaws/laws.html. Federal and state wildlife law handbooks are available through the USFWS.

ISSUES AND TRENDS

Knowledge of current issues can point toward areas of increasing employment. Pay attention to local and national news as well as federal and state grants and appropriations to see where funding is going. The sections that follow discuss some of the broad concerns affecting fishery and wildlife managers at the turn of the century.

WETLANDS CONSERVATION

Wetlands, which have been called "the cradle of life" for waterfowl, fisheries, endangered species, countless small birds, mammals, and a wide variety of plant life, are hotbeds of biological diversity. Though the rate of wetland loss is declining, a study by the USFWS released in 1997 showed a net loss of 117,000 acres per year between 1985 and 1995, much of which occurred in highly productive forested wetlands. This is in spite of millions spent on wetland restoration and creation activities.

Identifying, protecting, and restoring valuable wetlands will continue to be

A biologist rides "Partner" into the field as part of the U.S. Bureau of Land Management's Wild Horses and Burros Program in Salmon, Idaho.

a major employment area. Because all levels of government and the private sector are required by law to protect wetlands, employment is widely dispersed and almost any proposed development can trigger the need for wetlands conservation work.

State government employment is sometimes linked to federal action. For example, $10 million in matching funds in wetlands conservation grants were awarded in 1998 from the Department of the Interior, while thirteen states received funds from the National Coastal Wetlands Conservation Grants program for the protection of more than 13,000 acres in coastal lands.

A significant new policy shift was announced by the Clinton administration in conjunction with the twenty-fifth anniversary of the Clean Water Act. The new policy would work for a "net gain" in wetlands instead of the previous goal of "no net loss." To achieve the new goal, several new clean water initiatives are proposed, one of which involves a collaborative strategy between the Department of Agriculture and the Department of the Interior that aims to achieve a net gain of 1 million acres of wetlands by the year 2007. (See also chapter 6.)

ENDANGERED SPECIES PROGRAMS

Continued implementation of the Endangered Species Act is a major issue for fishery and wildlife professionals in the United States. Finding affordable ways to protect endangered, threatened, and rare animals without upsetting political support is a difficult job, but species such as the California condor and the Florida panther depend on it being done successfully. Throughout the world, protection of endangered species is an even larger issue for conservation workers.

Currently, the USFWS lists over 1,000 plant and animal species threatened with, or in danger of, extinction in the United States. This is up from 600 listed species in 1993. In 1997, less than half the species on the list had approved management plans, which leaves a lot of work designing and implementing protection plans for the other half. The proposed USFWS budget for fiscal year 1999 includes a 46 percent ($35.8 million) increase for the service's endangered species program, and many state governments plan increases as well.

Globally, the endangered species picture is much worse. Over 19,000 plant species and 5,000 animal species around the globe are classified as endangered, and many thousands more become extinct each year before scientists have classified them. The current global extinction rate may be 20,000 species per year, or higher.

Conservation International (CI), a nonprofit organization with programs in twenty-two countries, has identified nineteen priority biodiversity hotspots. These hotspots occupy less than 2 percent of the Earth's land surface, but contain a disproportionately large percentage of the planet's biodiversity. Between 66 to 75 percent of the world's most endangered species live in these areas, which are also home to some of the world's poorest people. The tropical Andes, Madagascar, Brazil's Atlantic forest region, and the Philippines top the list. Other sites are found in Indonesia, Central America, Australia, India, and West Africa. Fishery and wildlife management workers in these areas are fighting against remarkable odds with legislative weapons and financial resources that are a fraction of those available to environmental workers in the United States. (For more about endangered species hotspots, visit CI's website at http://www.conservation.org.)

Even in the United States, support of endangered species cannot be assumed. Coming on the horizon is an increased need for professionals to reduce the cost of endangered species protection by designing ecosystem protection plans that protect many species through a few actions. Also, will public support continue as more species qualify for legal protection? Some experts expect confrontations to become more intense as the needs of wildlife conflict with economic realities. Look for increases in employment for people with alternative approaches to conflict resolution and creative species protection plans that save money over conventional approaches.

HABITAT PROTECTION

There are many threats to the health and well-being of fish and wildlife, but the greatest by far is habitat destruction from human activities. Protecting habitat, however, is well beyond the power of fisheries and wildlife professionals alone. As habitat protection philosophies have found their way into laws, regulations, and long-range plans, "new" conservation careers have emerged that require legal, financial, real estate, business, economic development, and related skills to purchase land or control its use. Today's fish and wildlife professional works in close concert with nonprofit land trusts, local planners, business leaders, activists, and government officials to assure that large swatches of land and water are maintained in ecological health as support for fish and wildlife.

Habitat protection efforts create a wide variety of jobs. Passage of the National Wildlife Refuge System Improvement Act of 1997, for example, funded the purchase of more than 50,000 acres of land and created over 200 new hires in biological and maintenance staff.

A popular approach that brings together ecosystem management, habitat protection, and other trends is "watershed planning." Watersheds (areas drained by rivers and their tributaries) are particularly good planning units from an ecological point of view because they often have clear natural boundaries within which distinct plant and animal communities share living space with people. The rise of watershed approaches to conservation is creating more opportunities at nonprofit watershed associations and local government agencies. For more on watershed planning, see chapters 4 and 6.

TOXINS AND WILDLIFE

The publication of Rachel Carson's *Silent Spring* in 1960 first alerted Americans to the harmful effects of DDT on songbirds and other wildlife.

Although DDT (and other "organochlorine" pesticides) are now banned in this country, fish and wildlife continue to be exposed to millions of pounds of pesticides every year. In addition, wildlife habitats are contaminated by oil and chemical spills, illegal dumping, pollutant outflows, and run-off from many sources. Toxins in the environment can have immediate negative impacts, but the long-term effects may be even more insidious.

Concerns about toxins and wildlife create opportunities for toxicologists, chemists, field biologists, biostatisticians, and other professionals. Conservation scientists who study the effect of toxins in the environment must master new technologies.

For example, improvements in remote sensing and geographic information systems (GIS) technology have changed the way fish and wildlife agencies monitor pollutants. "Students coming into the workforce often have the skills to assist with the development of changes made possible by new technologies," reports Paul Brouha, executive director of the American Fisheries Society.

Since 1996, the U.S. Geological Survey's (USGS) Biological Resources Division has administered the twenty-year-old Biomonitoring of Environmental Status and Trends program (BEST). BEST is a monitoring and assessment program that evaluates the exposure and effects of contaminants on species and lands of importance to the Department of the Interior. In addition, the Environmental Protection Agency has an ongoing program of evaluation and publishes an atlas of fish consumption advisories. These are just two of the dozens of organizations that are involved in the study of fish and wildlife.

DEALING WITH NONNATIVE SPECIES

In addition to habitat destruction and toxic pollution, fish and wildlife suffer from the introduction of nonnative species that "out compete" native animals or prey on them. Conservation professionals have a hard time designing strategies to deal with invasive species, which can reduce populations of native species in a remarkably short time. A current example is the zebra mussel, which has spread rapidly into many of the freshwater ecosystems of the eastern United States, wiping out many native mollusks. The zebra mussel was discovered for the first time in North America just ten years ago.

Environmental scientists and managers work to prevent both intentional and unintentional transport of nonnative species through law, regulation, and careful monitoring. Dealing with invasions after the fact is difficult, expensive, and may not succeed.

URBAN WILDLIFE

Employment has increased in urban wildlife areas in the last several years (see also chapter 13), but not as rapidly as expected. The outlook over the next few years is good. It will be enhanced further if the "Teaming With Wildlife" (TWW) legislative package is passed, reports Harry E. Hodgdon, executive director of the Wildlife Society. TWW would place a small excise tax on equipment used for birdwatching, backpacking, nature photography, and outdoor pursuits other than hunting and fishing. This would generate money for states to use toward wildlife-related recreation in protecting and managing "nongame" animals and their habitats. Most wildlife found in urban areas are nongame. Look for job opportunities in previously unexpected places, such as utility companies, local government agencies, and development companies.

MIGRATORY BIRD ISSUES

Over the past several decades, declines in the numbers of many Neotropical migratory bird species have been detected. Scientists have determined that fragmentation of breeding habitat and destruction of tropical forests on wintering grounds are the main causes. Recently, the importance of habitat during the intermediate stage in the annual, three-part life cycle of migratory birds has received attention. Habitat needs of migratory birds has gained worldwide attention through scientific conferences and media coverage.

The conservation of migratory birds and their habitats is an international and interdisciplinary field. Two important initiatives were launched in 1990 in response to growing concerns about declines in bird populations. Partners In Flight is a cooperative effort focusing on the improvement of monitoring and inventory, research, management, and education programs involving birds and their habitats. The Smithsonian Migratory Bird Center conducts research that is translated into recommendations for public and policy action. Both organizations collaborate with a broad spectrum of federal agencies, nongovernmental organizations, state and provincial fish and wildlife agencies, numerous universities, and the forest industry to influence public awareness and affect habitat management decisions.

The primary goal of all involved is to take action now to keep species off the Endangered Species List so as to avoid the risks and costs associated with listing. Accomplishing this goal meshes two of the trends listed earlier: habitat protection across miles of migratory paths and wetlands conservation (crucial to migratory birds). All agree that more basic research on the ecology of migratory birds is necessary. This is a good area for volunteers, interns, and biological science technicians to get field experience.

PUBLIC ACCESS

Federal, state, and private wildlife protection lands are threatened by increasing (and sometimes conflicting) public use demands. As one indicator, over 30 million people visit federal refuges annually and this number is growing. At least one refuge is located within an hour's drive of virtually every major city in the U.S. Sharing wildlife refuges with more and more people requires wildlife managers with a variety of "people skills," in addition to their knowledge of animal and plant needs.

Harry Hodgdon of the Wildlife Society says that although colleges are attempting to broaden the curriculum, it is tough to do that and cover necessary science and technical skills in four years. Students should try to obtain communication, planning, political, and other skills "hands-on" through volunteer and internship experiences, says Hodgdon.

INTEGRATED NATURAL RESOURCE PLANNING

Fishery and wildlife professionals increasingly work with other environmental professionals and agencies to plan, develop, and implement fishery and wildlife programs in conjunction with overall natural resource management plans. For example, the USGS's Cooperative Research Units work closely with the USFWS to identify and address information needs for effective management of fish and wildlife resources. These units conduct research on virtually every type of North American ecological community. Each unit is a partnership among the Biological Resources Division of the USGS, a state fish and game agency, a host university, and the Wildlife Management Institute.

Another example is the U.S. Army Corps of Engineers whose environmental mission requires partnering with local and state agencies, implementing environmental protection statutes, preserving wetlands, and protecting other

Researchers with the U.S. Geological Survey in Woods Hole, Massachusetts, carry out studies for the Stellwagen Bank National Marine Sanctuary Mapping Project. The area is rich in marine life and a feeding area for whales.

natural resources. As more agencies and companies require fishery and wildlife considerations in their work, job opportunities should expand.

MITIGATION FOR HABITAT LOSS

As habitats continue to be fragmented and degraded by agriculture, mining, timber harvest, and development, the parties responsible are required to compensate for the loss. This is accomplished in a variety of ways, including fines that are set aside to fund restoration projects carried out by the organization responsible. "Increasingly we'll see more effective mitigation or compensation for loss, which will require more careful scientific investigation to decide what to compensate for," says Brouha of the Fisheries Society. He goes on to say that this will become a more contentious issue requiring political skills as well as scientific competence.

CAREER OPPORTUNITIES

On the fisheries side, the American Fisheries Society reports that essential fish habitat and watershed restoration will be major employment areas in the next few years. The 1996 reauthorization of the Magnuson Act (see earlier discussion) establishes that essential habitats are near-shore habitats. It also has specific provisions and standards that address treatment of fishing "by-catch," define "overharvest" and require remediation on a specific schedule to bring threatened species of fish back.

The Society says consultants will do much of this work. They will assess the life history of various species subject to harvest, define which habitats are most affected by man, and determine the key parts of those habitats. Brouha says that job seekers should have a good biological background, interpersonal skills, and a knowledge of regulatory frameworks.

Additional trends bode well for fisheries careers. Aquaculture continues to expand and create new hiring both in the private sector and throughout all levels of government. In addition, marine fisheries will need expert help in the coming years. The National Marine Fisheries Service estimates that one of three U.S. fisheries is over fished and the American Oceans Campaign says that fisheries are in decline around the world and some are near collapse. Restoring depleted fisheries carries considerable financial and social benefits, estimated to be in the billions. In many parts of the world, whole communities are dependent on healthy fish populations. Closing areas to commercial fishing is a drastic sign that management changes are needed. It also shows the limits of scientific information on decision making. Scientists have warned for years that certain fisheries were on the verge of collapse, without significant action. Only the concerted action of activists, elected officials, businesspeople, and community members can bring about the action needed. Keep this in mind when plotting your career direction.

On the wildlife side, a 1994 study by the Wildlife Society shows that 45 percent of students graduating with bachelor's degrees in wildlife management obtained employment in wildlife conservation one year after graduating. Sixty-eight percent of those with master's degrees and 89 percent of those with doctorates were employed in wildlife conservation work one year after graduation. But Hodgdon notes that these numbers don't reflect graduates who get jobs in other areas of conservation. "A lot of consulting jobs aren't specifically wildlife related," he says. "They may have more to do with ecological habitat assessments, but someone with a wildlife background would be qualified to do that." With this in mind, things are even better than the numbers report.

The American Institute of Biological Sciences reports that "More and more people are combining their biological knowledge with other professional training. You could consider being a lawyer with an environmental advocacy organization, working to protect endangered species . . . or being a policy analyst, helping government officials develop science-based legislation."

A career in fishery or wildlife management involves long hours of hard work to acquire knowledge and skills, intense competition for employment, and a fierce determination to keep your goals in sight. One wildlife management professional says: "Yes, the field is tight, and if you have only a casual interest there is not a high probability you will get a job. However, the country needs as many people trained in fisheries and wildlife as we can get. I am also of the opinion that 90 percent of the jobs that will exist five years from now haven't been invented yet."

PUBLIC SECTOR

Two-thirds of all fish and wildlife professionals work in the public sector, with federal government employment leading the way.

Federal Government. The federal government is the largest single employer of fishery and wildlife scientists. A survey by ECO of biology employment at federal conservation agencies turned up roughly 7,000 wildlife, fisheries, and "general" biologists at these agencies (see table 12.1). Even this underestimates the influence of the federal government, as these agencies also provide research grants to college-based scientists (and their students) and help set the regulatory agenda that influences the private sector and state agencies.

Table 12.1 Federal Government Employment of Biologist.

	Fish & Wildlife Service	Forest Service	Geological Survey	National Marine Fisheries Service	Bureau of Land Mgmt.	National Park Service
Fishery Biologists	450	381	216	702	73	11
Wildlife Biologists	457	841	234		255	36
General Biologists	1,106	922			375	

Source: Environmental Careers Organization.

Government cost-cutting is keeping employment figures steady or slightly increasing, but all conservation agencies point out that many senior people are nearing retirement age. This will create job opportunities for a new generation. Those who get into the system now will stand the best chance of competing for these positions as older professionals leave the field.

The two largest federal employers are the U.S. Fish and Wildlife Service and the U.S. Forest Service. Other federal agencies employing fish and wildlife professionals include the Bureau of Land Management, the National Marine Fisheries Service, the U.S. Geological Survey, the U.S. Army Corps of Engineers, the Environmental Protection Agency, the National Park Service, the Peace Corps, and the Department of Defense.

The Defense Department's work in environmental protection and conservation is an interesting story. In 1997, Congress reauthorized the Sikes Act of 1960, improving fish and wildlife management through 2003. The act governs nearly 25 million acres of land on over 900 U.S. military installations under the jurisdiction of the Department of Defense (DoD). The earlier law carried no penalties for failure to comply. As a result, management plans were not being prepared or implemented at many locations. The reauthorization requires the secretary of each military department to ensure that sufficient numbers of professionally trained natural resource management personnel are assigned responsibility for developing integrated ecosystem management plans. It also requires the secretary of defense to submit an annual report summarizing the status of implementing these resource management plans.

Carolyn Bohan, assistant deputy director of refuges and wildlife with the USFWS, agreed with other hiring officials about the kind of people agencies are looking for. She says that it's not good enough just to recognize that fish and wildlife should be preserved: "We need economic resource evaluations. If you have studied natural resource economics, you're going to be very valuable. We're always looking for (economists) who really understand the resources." Bohan notes that backgrounds that combine biology with training in real estate or law are also needed throughout the field.

Because so many people begin work in this field with a biology background, job searches are sometimes limited to the "biologist" job title. Look around! Positions such as game or fisheries manager, game or fish warden, park naturalist, research assistant, conservation officer, natural resource manager, and refuge manager offer opportunities to work with fish and/or wildlife, and to draw on fishery and wildlife biology training.

State and Local Government. Every state has a department of game or wildlife and many have separate departments for fisheries management (both freshwater and ocean). Whereas research and policy analysis positions are found in greater concentrations at the federal and university level, state programs tend to be more focused on daily operations and management. In addition, many state programs remain close to the profession's beginnings, with a strong focus on game animals and popular commercial and sport fish. Hunting and fishing licenses remain an important funding source for many programs.

State professionals focus much of their time on population surveys, local implementation of endangered species programs, watershed management, habitat mapping, land restoration, and fish hatcheries. Fishery and wildlife professionals with state agencies often work with other agencies, private businesses, and conservation groups on regional task forces. Providing technical assistance and information to the public is a major part of the job. Important state agencies for fishery and wildlife management include departments of fish and wildlife, forestry, conservation, environmental protection, natural resources, and parks and recreation. The latest trend in state and local programs is creating wildlife habitats on school grounds and in back yards.

States have been developing more comprehensive fish and wildlife management programs in recent years. Part of this is made possible by enlarged databases such as the information collected by Natural Heritage Programs, operated directly by state governments or by The Nature Conservancy. Check out the Natural Heritage Program for your state to gain a quick overview of the status of threatened and endangered species where you live.

State programs have begun to balance their focus on species valued for sport hunting and fishing with nongame species and their habitats. This is aided by the nongame income tax checkoffs available in many states. As mentioned earlier, "Teaming With Wildlife" will generate new funding for states to use toward nongame wildlife management. In addition, some states have passed their own Endangered Species Act.

Finally, many states are increasing expenditures in fish and wildlife education and are expanding educational efforts in major urban areas.

A little-known employment sector for fishery and wildlife professionals is Native American tribal government. According to Patrick Durham, director of technical services at the Native American Fish and Wildlife Society, there are at least 167 tribes with resource management functions, employing more than 1,300 personnel. Durham says that the capacity for tribes to manage their own natural resources is increasing due to the political and structural environment. Durham authored the "Tribal Resources Assistance Handbook," which lists federal programs related to natural resource management on Indian reservations. See the Resources section at the end of the chapter for information on how to obtain the handbook.

PRIVATE SECTOR

Private sector employment in fishery and wildlife management includes a diverse range of occupations, such as work for forest-products firms, utility companies with large landholdings, environmental departments of large companies, consultants, commercial game farms, aquaculture ventures, and the ocean fishing industry.

Private Industry. Mitigation projects are popping up around the country, carried out by utility companies, developers, timber companies, and other businesses with large landholdings. Some are doing these projects with in-house staff, and others are using consultants. In effect, these companies are becoming natural resource management agencies and owners and managers of wildlife preserves. Of these, forest product companies are probably the largest single employer, with utilities second.

Opportunities are increasing at large firms that deal in ranching, mining, and chemical or paper production and with other private sector businesses such as game farming and fish farming. In addition, federal farm policy affects wildlife habitat on more than 400 million acres of private farmland. The 1995 Farm Bill reauthorization has yielded considerable landowner participation. Also, the Conservation Reserve Program, which involves "growing" clean water, wildlife, and other nontraditional "crops," is generating employment opportunities. Look for fish and wildlife-related jobs in agriculture, where retired cropland is being converted to wetlands and wildlife habitats.

In addition to companies that manage natural resources directly, many large corporations have some wildlife/fisheries scientists attached to their environmental, health, and safety departments. These individuals carry out environmental assessments, prepare information for environmental impact statements, respond to spills and other emergencies, prepare reports for regulatory compliance, or hire and manage vendors to perform these services.

There are many employers with one-of-a-kind jobs to offer, such as wildlife ranges, scientific foundations, zoological parks, and hunting and fishing clubs.

Consulting Firms. According to the American Fisheries Society, "specialized consultants constitute a growing niche in the fisheries profession. . . ." Nearly all of the major full-service environmental consulting firms in the United States employ a cadre of fishery and wildlife professionals, usually with significant experience and advanced degrees, to work on contracts with the public and private sectors, as well as with universities. Because consulting firms keep a rigorous eye on costs, employers favor people with broad backgrounds who can be employed on a wide variety of tasks. Scientists who can double as project managers *and* bring in business through strong sales skills, are especially preferred. In addition, there are a large number of small or one-person consulting firms with extremely specialized skills in a specific discipline or type of client.

Commercial Aquaculture. Finally, the dramatic increase in aquaculture, or fish farming, has produced fish stocks requiring staff and controlled by corporations, states, and individuals. Commercial interests see a rapidly expanding future in fish farming and harvesting techniques, both in the United States and in Third World countries. World aquaculture production has more than doubled since 1984 and is expected to continue to increase steadily. Channel catfish farming is the fastest-growing segment of the aquaculture industry in the United States, according to a report by the University of Georgia.

Unfortunately, some existing aquaculture operations are a significant source of chemical and biological pollutants, and farming of carnivorous species such as salmon and trout is resulting in a net loss of fish. Growing one pound of farmed salmon can require three to five pounds of wild-caught fish. The industry needs people who are aware of these problems to employ environmentally sound technologies and practices, many of which are now used on commercial fish farms.

Nonprofit Sector

As is true through much of the environmental field, nonprofit organizations in fishery and wildlife management are but a small portion of the industry when measured in terms of employment. But, as elsewhere, this sector has more impact than its size would indicate. To many, in fact, the name brand nonprofit groups *are* the environmental movement.

Among the important nonprofit organizations working in fishery and wildlife management, the best known are Greenpeace, the National Wildlife Federation, the National Audubon Society, the World Wildlife Fund, the Izaak Walton League of America, and the Sierra Club. These organizations raise funds to purchase habitat or lobby for regulatory changes. They seek fishery and wildlife professionals with excellent communication skills and knowledge of federal agencies and policies.

Beyond the biggest nonprofits, there are literally hundreds of small groups at the state and local level and more are being formed all the time. For example, there are over 1,000 land trust organizations in the country, and dozens of watershed associations, birding groups, animal protection societies, and so forth. Jobs can be hard to find, but they are out there. Use resources such as the annual *Conservation Directory* and your local phone book to track down low-profile employers.

The American Institute of Biological Sciences's brochure, "What Will You Be Doing in 2020?," reports that "the not-for-profit sector is providing an increasing number of jobs." The Institute projects growing partnerships between government, industry, and nonprofits, which may transfer employment from government to the nongovernmental sector as a way of saving government funds and keeping permanent payrolls lower.

If the nonprofit sector is of interest to you, keep in mind that these groups often hire those they know best, including people who have served as volunteers and interns. Use conferences and other meetings to expand your network and keep in touch with hard-pressed nonprofit managers who tend to hire quickly and without lots of advertising.

Colleges and universities hire a significant percentage of fishery and wildlife management graduates with advanced degrees, not only to teach but also for various research projects. However, many of these are temporary positions. The

Fisheries Society says of fishery professionals in academia: "We are seeing a shift from year-long appointments to nine month appointments and also a move away from tenure track positions." This trend is also found in wildlife fields, and in environmental departments generally.

SALARY

Earnings vary with the size and scope of the employer. The private sector generally pays more than federal agencies, federal agencies pay more than state and local agencies, and nonprofits pay slightly below that. In 1997, the Economic Research Institute reported that the average salary for biological scientists with one year of experience was $23,421. Those with nine years of experience averaged $38,962 a year, and those with eighteen years' experience averaged $50,655.

Fish and wildlife salaries in the federal government are an excellent barometer by which to measure your potential earnings in this field. You may earn a little less or a little more in other parts of the public sector and in private business, but federal standards provide you with a pretty good idea of what is possible.

The starting pay for fish culturists or wildlife biologists working for the federal government (measured in "GS" or "government scale" numbers) in 1998 ranges from $19,969 for a GS-5 grade to $24,734 for a GS-7 grade, reflecting a 2.3 percent increase over 1997. The GS scale is adjusted annually and within each grade there are ten steps of incremental pay increases. In addition, there are "locality pay" adjustments for areas of the country where the cost of living is higher.

A person hired at GS-5 is expected to have 4 years of course study above high school resulting in a bachelor's degree and three years of progressively responsible experience such that you are able to plan and organize work, communicate effectively and analyze problems in order to identify significant factors, gather pertinent data, and recognize solutions. A person hired at GS-7 level is expected to have one full academic year of graduate level education, law school, or superior academic achievement along with one year of experience that is in, or related to, the work they're being hired to do such that you have job-specific knowledge, skills, and abilities. Check with the closest Office of Personnel Management or their website at www.opm.gov for current-year pay schedules and to find out about specific requirements for government jobs.

GETTING STARTED

So where do you go from here? As in any career, your formal education is the first step.

EDUCATION

Wildlife and fisheries conservation is both science and art. It requires talent, personal commitment, enthusiasm, sound technical training, and special skills. Beyond the technical and biological challenges, you must also be sensitive to issues of public policy and social values. Both professions cover an increasing diversity of specializations as science continues to evolve. For example, the American Fisheries Society has twenty-one different sections, representing diverse interests such as computer users, fishery law, genetics, and socioeconomics. The organization is actively attempting to integrate nontraditional disciplines into their organization to better understand the interlocking nature of fisheries ecosystems and their management.

Graduates with the best chances of having successful careers in fishery and wildlife management are those who have stressed a broad, ecologically based approach in both their formal education and their work experience. Most professionals recommend an integrated course of study stressing ecosystems as well as fish or wildlife biology. Besides the fact that it prepares you to be a better professional, there is a practical reason for this: you broaden your job options. Some schools now offer a combined undergraduate degree in fishery and wildlife management for that very reason.

The American Fisheries Society lists 50 colleges and universities offering named degrees in fisheries and 117 other institutions that offer fisheries-related programs in North America. The Wildlife Society lists 96 colleges and universities in the U.S. and Canada offering named degrees in wildlife or wildlife major options as well as others that offer courses in wildlife conservation or management. (See the Resources section at the end of this chapter.)

Carolyn Bohan of the USFWS says: "Conservation Biology is a new type of curriculum in which we're very interested. It balances biological life history with ecosystem and biodiversity issues. That's what we're faced with, a balancing of demands on the land base. We still want to see people with classic biologist qualities, but we also want to see a lot of biodiversity and ecosystem study in their educational backgrounds." To help you along, the April 1998 edition of *Earth Work* magazine published a listing of some of the better-known conservation biology departments in the nation, including ones at American University, Clemson, Penn State, San Francisco State, University of Maryland, Michigan, and Minnesota. Illinois State, Purdue, Tufts University, and Wisconsin were also named as schools that have departments with good coursework in the area.

In addition to this focus on interdisciplinary study, advanced degrees are often essential as a passport to careers above the technician or field biologist level. Bohan says that it's common to have people with master's degrees applying for entry-level positions, and Ph.D. candidates also compete for those jobs. She suggests careful selection of schools when obtaining additional skills to add to biological training, such as public administration, economics, or law. Focus on institutions whose curriculum is based on natural resource management. Those, along with universities that attract culturally diverse populations, are the schools on which the USFWS will concentrate recruitment efforts.

Even with an advanced degree and experience you should be prepared to take a low-paying, entry-level position, especially with government agencies. Gene Peltola of the USFWS (see profile at the end of this chapter) says: "It's kind of a catch-22. You can't obtain a permanent full-time position until you obtain government status. I have a friend who has a Ph.D. in water quality and twelve years of research and teaching experience who couldn't get a full-time position with [the USFWS] because he didn't have status. He ended up taking an administrative position for two and a half years. . . . It worked out for him. He was able to get a job as senior water quality biologist after he got the status."

A good possibility for obtaining a permanent fishery or wildlife management job with a federal agency is through a co-operative education (co-op ed) position. The new government term for these positions is the Student Career Experience Program, though most universities still call it Co-op Ed. The USFWS offered sixty-six such positions in 1997. Though this number fluctuates, competition for these positions is intense. Applicants often have related field experience gained through volunteer or other internship programs. If you are fortunate enough to land one of these, however, it will be well worth the effort. Other local, state, and federal agencies also offer this program. While a co-op ed position doesn't guarantee you will be hired, it does allow you to earn money, college credit, and valuable field experience. In addition, upon completion of the program you are automatically converted to government status for 120 days. This means that you can compete for full-time permanent jobs in the federal government that are only open to those who have career status.

Consider how long you want to go to school. If you aren't excited about spending eight or more years of your life after high school continuing your education, you can still work in fisheries or wildlife management. Paul Brouha says: "Inevitably there are going to be a lot of technician jobs. There are associate fish technician degrees from community colleges in some areas of the country." One state supervisor says: "I think students should step back and look again at technicians' jobs. Technicians do the work most students seem to want to do when they originally go into fishery and wildlife programs. They are the ones who get to wrestle with the animals and catch the fish while we biologists are looking at aerial maps and negotiating with foresters."

On the other hand, Brouha says: "It is very difficult to upgrade to a professional series without additional formal education beyond the two-year degree. There's an awful lot of information you need to absorb that can't really be done in two or even four years." However, a two-year degree can be a cost-efficient avenue to a four-year degree, allowing you to attend a less expensive school for the first two years, then get a job working in the field, allowing you to gain experience and support yourself while you continue your education.

Learning does not begin and end in the classroom. An essential part of your education should involve practical field experience. Most colleges or universities will assist you in finding suitable field research projects, summer jobs, internships, or co-op ed positions. You cannot obtain permanent full-time employment without such experience. Not only must you acquire numerous field skills but, given the competition and scarcity of openings, it is also useful to be a known commodity. Many state, local, and federal departments operate under protracted hiring freezes and can rarely create new staff positions. However, there may be latitude to move money around when there is an individual they know and want.

ADVICE

Here is the best of the advice given to us by established professionals in the field, who have faced most of the trials and tribulations you will encounter on the way to your profession.

Develop computer skills. Experience and skills in geographic information systems (GIS), statistics, and computer modeling can be used for such things as tracking wildlife and the migration of pollution. GIS jobs are among the fastest wage growth jobs in the environmental field right now. A good GIS candidate is a little bit environmentalist and a little bit computer geek.

Get some experience. Look for opportunities to do traditional entry-level and seasonal work, such as: conducting surveys, measurements, and other research; assisting a biologist; overseeing the work of seasonal or part-time employees; or interacting with the public regarding fishing and hunting regulations. Other entry-level work includes computer data entry, report drafting, paperwork, statistical analysis, and equipment construction and repair. Use unpaid internships and volunteer experiences if paid opportunities are not available. Don't overlook local, grassroots, and nonprofit organizations. In an ultra-competitive environment, people of equal education are screened out on the basis of their experience. Get as much as you can, at the highest level of expertise available to you.

Join the Peace Corps. Another way to get started in either field is with the Peace Corps. Helping to increase food production in developing countries through growing and harvesting fish is one objective of the Peace Corps. Volunteers work in aquaculture, inland fisheries, and marine fisheries. Besides the hands-on experience, volunteers also receive one-year noncompetitive eligibility for positions with the federal government. Many have used this edge to gain positions in federal fishery and natural resource management.

Use the back door. Use a back door or side door approach to get a job in the field (see example given by Gene Peltola earlier). Take this route with some caution, since there is no guarantee of later transfer and you may become a specialist in another area, limiting your ability to move back to fishery and wildlife management. Obviously, you must also be qualified for your interim position—another argument for a broad-based education.

Get on registers. Look at the federal, state, and even local employment procedures and get on these agencies' job registers as soon as possible, either for job openings or just to be informed of the next test for the position you desire (some tests are held several years apart).

Join professional associations. It is advisable to join and become involved in the professional associations. The Wildlife Society and the American Fisheries Society both have student chapters at universities. Go beyond these chapters to meet active professionals. Both associations offer accreditation for fishery and wildlife professionals.

Know yourself. As you plan your career path, it helps to know your likes and dislikes. Would you rather work with people, plants, animals, or some combination? Do you want to be in the laboratory or outdoors? Resist the temptation to take whatever position is available just because it is available. Initially, of course, you cannot be too picky in this field, but keep in mind your longer-term career goals.

SUMMARY

The popularity of the fishery and wildlife management profession is both a blessing and a curse for the field and those who enter it. Many applicants are overqualified for the jobs they seek, and the frustration of some who struggle to find permanent employment is legendary. Professionals who work for years to gain field experience and knowledge end up behind a desk, while those who are doing the fieldwork complain of low salaries and a limited career path.

Prepare for a career in fishery and wildlife management by focusing on a specific area of interest, while developing highly transferrable skills such as negotiating, consensus building, knowledge of policies, and cutting-edge technology in computers. Advanced degrees are all but assumed in many cases. But the lure of fishery and wildlife management remains strong, and for those with persistence, talent, and creativity, a satisfying career will be the reward.

CASE STUDY

Striped Bass Population Recovery Isn't All Good News

Striped bass show signs of recovering from a serious decline in the 1970s and are once again present in East Coast waters. But the resurgence raises troubling questions about a species-by-species approach to managing wildlife resources.

Autumn on Nantucket Shoals. The black sky embracing the harvest moon warms to a soft purple, then fades to pastel blue with the sunrise. Tide from the east meets wind from the west, setting up crashing, emerald-green waves where sandbars drop off to the deep. Amid the froth, big striped bass ply the rollers, gliding, racing, jumping. In the once fish-rich waters of New England, where species after species has been hunted to the point of collapse and beyond, the striper has returned. This is, once again, a world-class fishery. Everything is picture perfect. For now.

Almost instantly, anglers in the stern of Bob Luce's charter boat, *The Striper*, have action. "Who says there are no big fish?" Luce chortles, as ever-larger bass—37, 39, 43 inches long—come glistening over the side, deep-green backs, lateral stripes, and iridescent bellies flashing in the sun. In a few hours, Luce's charges—a mixed bag of sport fishermen and fisheries officials—land 55 bass, all but one over the minimum legal sport fishing length of 28 inches. All but four are tagged by a state fisheries employee and returned to the sea, in accordance with regulations limiting sport fishermen to one a day.

Without question, striped bass are present in East Coast waters in prodigious numbers, an abundance that is staggering to New Englanders who witnessed the near-fatal decline of the species in the 1970s, when overfishing and pollution drove the striper to the brink. There were only about 5 million stripers then, perilously few to populate a primary range stretching from Maine to the Carolinas. Today there are about 30 million.

Indeed, the resurgence of the Atlantic striped bass is being touted by public officials as a great success story. The Atlantic States Marine Fisheries Commission has pronounced the striper fully recovered and has begun loosening restrictions on annual harvest. The minimum length at which sportsmen may keep fish has been reduced to 28 inches, down from 34 inches in 1996 and 36 inches in 1995. Critics say regulators are moving much too quickly.

Further, government regulators and officials have concluded that overfishing was the overwhelming cause of the striper's decline. Generally, they dismiss the significance of severe pollution of inshore waters in much of the fish's habitat—a conclusion deeply troubling to many researchers, observers, and fishermen outside regulatory circles.

Hardly audible amid the cheering are voices of caution and concern about the striper, and about our ability to recover damaged species. What is worrisome are the size and feeding habits of the fish, even to some who say the striper has recovered enough that restrictions on the catch can be relaxed. "The Division of Marine Fisheries points to spawning numbers, mortality, scientific data. I point to their track record. . . . We don't start managing until there's a collapse," says Bruce Berman, a veteran political operative for environmental causes and director of stewardship of the advocacy group Save the Harbor/ Save the Bay.

"For years, the fish looked real good," says Rusty Iwanowicz, a 27-year veteran of the Massachusetts marine fisheries laboratories, who caught stripers in the great boom of the 1960s, then witnessed the crash in the 1970s and the comeback that began in the late 1980s. "But recently . . . I think they're eating themselves out of house and home."

Iwanowicz's observations, based on thousands of fish he prepares for sophisticated testing in Massachusetts' Gloucester lab, are reinforced anecdotally by fishermen, who say the stomachs of the fish they catch often are empty.

Statistically, their observations are backed by the work of Xi He, a fisheries modeling specialist.

Xi's work shows that weight in relation to age is in a steady decline among stripers sampled in Massachusetts. In 1990, when efforts to restore the fish began to show obvious results, the mean weight of a 12-year-old striper was about 33 pounds. In 1996, the mean weight of a fish that age was less than 25 pounds, according to a Massachusetts striped bass monitoring report prepared by Xi and Paul Diodati, striper expert at the Massachusetts Division of Marine Fisheries.

And there are indications that stripers are feeding heavily on other highly prized resources, such as lobsters and salmon smolts, which have been raised and released at great expense in an attempt to restore that fish to the region's rivers. Researchers don't know why these things are happening, but the size of the fish raises a number of troubling questions: Are today's stripers smaller because too many of them are competing for the available food? Is it because we have overharvested species on which the striper depends, and there is actually less food around for the big fish? Is pollution interfering with the striper's ability to feed?

"Wow! A sow!" gasps a fisherman on Bob Luce's harvest-moon trip off Nantucket, as a companion reels in the biggest striped bass—by far—that he has ever seen. Amidships, Paul Caruso, a former commercial fisherman who now works for the Division of Marine Fisheries, prepares to measure and tag her. But to the surprise of all hands, the striper, which weighs an estimated 22 pounds, already has been tagged, allowing fisheries scientists to trace her history. She had been caught and released in the upper Hudson River on May 16, 1988, when she was seven years old and 32 inches long. In the nine years before her recapture, she grew slightly less than 9 inches. "Of 100 16-year-old fish, this would be at the very low end of the range" of growth in length, says Diodati, who is aboard Luce's boat to help with the state tagging program.

The debate isn't only over how stripers are being managed but over whether the apparent success with this one species is obscuring management practices that still give highest priority to maximizing harvests. Fisheries managers are promoting harvest of alternative species, which are being fished to the point of collapse, says Michael Donovan, an organizer for the Recreational Fishing Alliance, a nationwide group. Prime examples are sharks and monkfish, neither of which was fished commercially until recent years and both of which are now under intense pressure, according to Donovan. Harvests of menhaden, American eel, herring, and mackerel, all important forage for stripers, are increasing. Decimation of those populations easily could do to the striper what the cutting of the bamboo and forests of western China did to the panda.

Awareness is dawning that not just the extinction but the resurgence of a species can produce a ripple effect that spreads through whole ecosystems. Although state and federal agencies continue their long tradition of managing wildlife by species, this awareness is reinforcing calls from independent scientists and environmentalists for whole-ecosystem management. Not only is the species-by-species approach outdated, they point out, it is masking a precipitous decline in species of little-known creatures on which glamour species ultimately depend.

Many fishery and wildlife managers now accept the whole-ecosystem view in principle, but practicing it is a different matter. "Ecosystem management sounds like a great idea," says Paul Caruso, as he finishes tagging a big bass aboard *The Striper*. "But we don't even have enough data for single-species management. To do a whole system, you've got twenty or thirty variables, all with their own cycles, and a lot of them you've got no way to measure."

"It has become a fundamental principle of conservation practice—and should be of fisheries and wildlife management—that no reliable conservation practice can be conducted on a species-by-species basis," says Harvard's Edward O. Wilson, an internationally renowned biologist. "Species cannot exist, fisheries cannot flourish, without the habitat. . . . People should not get the idea that things have turned around," Wilson says. "The reverse is true." Only a few charismatic species that are able to attract broad popular support are coming back, he says. The general outlook is grim for fish, land animals, and plants alike.

Charles A. Radin, staff writer for the Boston Globe Magazine, *adapted this case study from his magazine feature story of October 1997.*

PROFILES

> *Tom French*
> *Assistant Director*
> *Natural Heritage and Endangered*
> *Species Program*
> *Massachusetts Division of Fisheries*
> *and Wildlife*
> *Boston, Massachusetts*

State natural heritage programs protect species that are not hunted, fished, trapped, or commercially harvested. The Nature Conservancy started its Natural Heritage Programs in the 1970s to keep inventories of wildlife in each state. In Massachusetts, this program protects 175 species of vertebrate and invertebrate animals, as well as 250 species of plants, all considered at risk.

Tom French's profile is one of only three from the 1993 edition of The Complete Guide to Environmental Careers *that we retained for this 1998 edition. We learn in this profile that a few things have changed for Tom in five years, but he is as excited about his work as ever.*

Wildlife management professionals caution new entrants into the field not to expect glamour and drama in their careers, but there are some professionals who make even their desk jobs look exciting. Tom French is one of those. In his capacity as assistant director of the Natural Heritage and Endangered Species Program for the Massachusetts Division of Fisheries and Wildlife, he has the kind of busy management position that you would expect, complete with long hours.

What you might not expect, however, is to see Tom on television, rappelling down the side of an office building to rescue a baby peregrine falcon in need of medical attention, or far above the ground on an old iron catwalk, netting young barn owls from the interior of a building sealed off for reconstruction.

"I enjoy being outside and getting dirty and being involved in projects," says Tom. "That is what I was trained for. But the better I got at it, the more administrative responsibilities I took on as I moved up. Now my position is essentially an administrative job. But that doesn't mean I don't have pet projects that allow me to keep my hand in and have fun. I have good staff who help ensure that the administrative needs are met, but the team is small enough that my skills as a field biologist are still needed."

Tom's program is responsible for the protection of 173 species of vertebrate and invertebrate animals and 254 species of plants that are considered rare, threatened, or endangered in Massachusetts. This includes species as diverse as bog turtles, a plant called the small whorled pogonia, the bald eagle, the piping plover, and the American burying beetle.

Tom says he traces his consuming interest in animals "back as far as I can remember." His youthful interest in catching frogs and turtles and playing in the creek gradually evolved into a career—but he started early. Tom went from earning a sixth-grade science project award for a display of animal skull brain capacities to working as a collector at a vertebrate museum during his first week as an undergraduate student in biology at Georgia State University in Atlanta.

Tom worked in the museums at each of the three universities he attended, including Georgia State University, where he earned his degree in biology; Auburn University, where he earned his master's degree in zoology; and Indiana State University, where he obtained his Ph.D. in ecology and systematics. Having focused his graduate research on shrews, the smallest mammals in the world, Tom now spends much of his time at the other end of the size scale, working with whales. Tom chairs the Northeast Whale Recovery Plan Implementation Team. This is a group of eminent whale biologists and staff from a wide variety of state and federal agencies who serve to advise the National Marine Fisheries Service on how best to help save the northern right whale, among others, from extinction.

Tom credits much of his success in getting this and a previous great job as a zoologist with The Nature Conservancy to a résumé that shows a variety of career-related summer jobs and experiences and an early track record of publishing. "I coauthored my first scientific papers in a small regional bird journal when I was an undergraduate student, and I continued to publish mostly short articles throughout my college career," he says. His broad-ranging interests have now resulted in papers on focused areas of mammalogy, herpetology, ornithology, entomology, and archaeology. His level of comfort in an array of different fields makes Tom an ideal administrator. It does not, however, protect him from the work load. "I usually have four or five large projects, like work plans or contracts, that make up my work expectations for the day when I get to the office, but the reality is that most of my time is taken up by brush fires and emergencies, usually on the phone." Other activities during the day may include "a frighteningly small amount of creative time, a law enforcement issue or two, tons of meetings, and lots of networking." There may also be calls about rabies, oil spill hazards to wildlife, or special wildlife collection permits, all of which fall into Tom's domain.

To ensure that all of these responsibilities are met, Tom has assembled a varied team of fourteen professionals. He points out, however, that "not a single one of them has a traditional wildlife management degree." The program includes the state ornithologist, the state botanist, two computer and data management experts, and two environmental reviewers who review proposed development projects for their likely impacts to wildlife, among others. Four of the fourteen have doctorates, and most of the rest have master's degrees.

These varied talents are put to the test on most days by the range of issues the department must address. A recent emergency involved the report of a large dead whale floating about seven miles offshore. Since this was thought to be a critically endangered northern right whale, Tom was asked by the National Marine Fisheries Service to help secure a location to which the carcass could be towed so that a careful necropsy could be performed by the New England Aquarium. This is the only way biologists might learn why this great whale had died. Tom succeeded in getting the U.S. Fish and Wildlife Service to agree to let the U.S. Coast Guard tow the whale to a beach on Parker River National Wildlife Refuge. To everyone's surprise and minor embarrassment, the whale turned out to be a 60-foot long and more than 60-ton fin whale rather than a right whale. A necrospy was still in order. Then Tom coordinated the removal of the 16-foot-long skull and the skeleton, which was donated to Harvard University. This is a good example of the interagency cooperation that is often needed to get a job done, and just another day at the office for Tom French.

Beverly Houten
Hatchery Supervisor
Pyramid Lake Fisheries
Sutcliffe, Nevada

Since 1905, more than half of the Truckee River has been diverted out of the river's basin for a federal reclamation project, resulting in a drop of 80 feet in the water levels of its sink, Pyramid Lake. When the water dropped, a sand bar blocked spawning grounds and native fish populations plummeted. Much of the economy of the Pyramid Lake Paiute Indian Reservation is centered on fishing and recreational fees. In the 1950s the tribe began collaborating with the state of Nevada to restore the Pyramid Lake Fisheries. They tried everything they could think of to get the water back in their lake, but nothing worked until they sued the government in 1967 over the endangered Cui-ui (KWEE-wee), once a primary source of food and livelihood for the Paiute Indians. Bringing back the Cui-ui required the restoration of its habitat—Pyramid Lake.

Beverly Houten of the Pyramid Lake Paiute Tribe in northwest Nevada oversees the production of Lahontan Cutthroat Trout, which nearly became extinct in the 1930s and Cui-ui lakesucker, an endangered prehistoric species that evolved in the lake and claim it as their sole habitat. Working in this remote desert location, Beverly and her staff of two get involved in every aspect of the hatchery including incubating eggs, rearing fish, minor construction, plumbing, and conducting tours for school children. Beverly also shows the facility to fishermen, who stop by when the fish in the lake aren't biting.

What Beverly loves about her job is that each day brings something different. "I'm out here where I know I'm doing something right, something for the tribe, by increasing the fish population in the lake." Historically the Cui-ui was a staple of the Pauite who called themselves Cui-ui-Ticutta, the Paiute name for Cui-ui eaters.

Work at the hatchery is based on the needs of the fish and can vary with the seasons. "During the spring months, the Cui-ui spawning run starts," Beverly says. The adult Cui-ui journey out of the slightly alkaline and saline waters of Pyramid Lake and head up the delta seeking fresh water in which to spawn. Through coordination with the Reno office of the U.S. Fish and Wildlife Service, gill nets are set in the delta area to capture the Cui-ui, and hatchery personnel are sent to pick up males and females for spawning.

"Back at the hatchery, we sort the males and females into holding troughs," Beverly explains. "The females are injected with carp pituitary hormones to stimulate the final maturation of the eggs. After that, we check them every day. Usually, by the third or fourth day, you just touch the stomach and the eggs shoot out! By this time, the males have released their sperm and we can propagate, using a hatching jar made by hatchery personnel. Finally, we put the eggs up for incubation."

Beverly has no formal education in fisheries biology. She learned everything she knows about fertilizing and growing fish on the job. She began working at the Pyramid Lake Hatchery twenty years ago and worked her way up, starting as a fish culturist. Currently she oversees two hatcheries, one for rearing the Lahontan Cutthroat Trout and the other for rearing Cui-ui.

Beverly says: "You can't go to school and learn this stuff. What we do here, raising large fish, didn't come from a book. This is the only place in the world where the endangered Cui-ui are found. There is no book written on this species." Beverly and her staff attend conferences related to fisheries management, but Beverly maintains, "all the people here on the reservation that work for fisheries have gotten all their training right here." If anything goes wrong, Beverly and her subordinates must know the systems inside and out. Experience and familiarity are more advantageous than biology degrees under these circumstances.

Beverly speaks with pride as she talks about changes in the hatchery over the last twenty years. "We've done feed studies for postlarvae Cui-ui, including yearlings, to see what is suitable. In the trout hatchery, we've modified the incubation station. Previously we had reused water flowing into the trays. Now we have direct well water flowing through the system. This helped our fungus problem among the eggs. So that is something good that I've done while I've been here."

Beverly's boss, Paul Wagner, says that under Beverly's care the survival rate of Cui-ui eggs to larvae went from 10 to 50 percent in certain groups, to 50 to 80 percent for most groups. Similarly, the cutthroat trout went from 50 percent to 90 percent survival for some groups and the size of the fish doubled! When asked why, Paul says very simply: "Care. Pride."

Through the efforts of the Pyramid Lake Hatchery, the Cui-ui are making a comeback. In 1995, there were 697,008 male Cui-ui and 901,430 females, according to the best estimates by scientists. In 1985 there were only 20,704 males and 34,304 females. There is talk of delisting the fish; however, Cui-ui are a long way from meeting the requirements that would take them off the endangered list. Beverly voices concern: "I really don't know how that will go. If they get fished out again then we are back to where we started."

Gene Peltola, Jr.
Wildlife Biologist/Pilot
Selawik National Wildlife Refuge
U.S. Fish and Wildlife Service
Kotzebue, Alaska

In addition to biology, analysis, report-writing and budget proposals, wildlife management is an increasingly political job that incorporates federal, state, and local ideas about how wildlife and their habitat should be managed.

The Selawik National Wildlife Refuge stretches across northwest Alaska, just above the Arctic Circle. As unbelievable as it may seem, the 3.2 million-acre refuge is one of the smallest refuges in the state. Among the five U.S. Fish and Wildlife Service employees at the refuge, only one is a wildlife biologist. If that isn't difficult enough, he has two distinct job titles—wildlife biologist and pilot. Welcome to the world of Gene Petola, Jr.

A Native Alaskan, Gene was born and raised in Bethel, located in southwest Alaska. His ancestors are primarily Tlingit Indian and Yupik Eskimo. Subsistence hunting and fishing were an active part of his childhood. He says: "As far back as I can remember, I've known I wanted to be involved with wildlife. . . . It was, and still is, a significant part of my life. I wanted to make sure that my children and grandchildren would have the same opportunities (to hunt) that I had."

During his senior year of high school, Gene was accepted at Humboldt State University where he majored in wildlife biology. Two days after his high school graduation, he began a paid seasonal position as a biological technician at the Yukon Delta NWR in Bethel. He worked with songbirds, monitored seabirds, and studied the productivity of the arctic nesting goose. Gene spent two seasons there during college before obtaining a co-op ed position at the refuge through the University of Alaska at Fairbanks, where he finished his degree in wildlife management with a focus on research.

With the co-op ed position came more responsibility. From mid-May through September, Gene worked at the refuge. Back at school, he analyzed the data he gathered and generated a report. He returned to Bethel for a month over spring break and then went back to school again. The work-and-school seesaw of cooperative education was perfect for Gene. Not only did he earn course credit when he was working, but he received a preference when it was time to compete for a full-time position with the federal government

Upon graduation in May 1991, Gene was offered a position as wildlife biologist at the Yukon Delta National Wildlife Refuge. In the fall of 1991, he transferred to Selawik NWR continuing as a wildlife biologist. In spring of 1994, after attaining his private pilot's license with 200 hours of flight time, he applied for a wildlife biologist/pilot trainee position at the refuge. He was hired and began work under his current title after completing the agency's pilot training program.

Gene's job requires decisions that are just a little different than the ones most professionals deal with. On a recent weekend, for example, he flew off to retrieve radio collars from two moose. "There was a place I could have landed with a decent margin of safety," he recalls. "But I didn't feel comfortable leaving the aircraft out for an extended period of time at 15 to 20 degrees below zero while I hiked over to the animals."

His solution? "I found the location with the plane, then headed out there—400 miles—by snowmobile. It took two days to get in, but getting there with the aircraft would have been pretty marginal—just doable."

Depending on the time of year, Gene's duties vary. During the dark winter months, when northwest Alaska gets less than two hours of daylight, most of Gene's time is spent in village and staff meetings, working on reports, writing responses to his regional office, requests for permits, seasonal hires, fuel contracts, and helicopter contracts for capture work to get ready for the field season.

Gene normally conducts annual moose surveys in the fall. This involves five to ten days of aerial surveys with four light aircraft, as well as logistical planning. It's a challenge getting fuel from Fairbanks or Anchorage to the refuge cabin, which is located 85 miles from refuge headquarters in Kotzebue. In the fall, a moose survey yields gender and age data on the moose. This requires snow cover and a week or so of good flying weather. If a fall survey can't be done due to snowstorms or lack of snow cover, it is conducted in the spring. Spring surveys yield adult to calf ratios rather than gender and age since most of the bulls drop their antlers by then.

By early April, northwest Alaska gains enough daylight to get in an eight-hour flight day for moose capture operations and deploying radio collars on wolverine. This involves coordinating a spot aircraft to find them, and helicopters, which get low enough to "dart" the moose so that radio collars can be put on the animals for a moose study along the Tagagawik River. This allows

Gene to assess distribution and movement along the drainage to see whether upstream sport hunting is affecting downstream subsistence hunting. Wolverine are captured using live traps or immobilization darts.

In late spring Gene does bear den surveys to determine the population for both sport harvest and subsistence harvest. With an annual series of surveys he is able to perform a "nearest neighbor" analysis to come up with a den density. He uses that as an index for the population. This is a technique developed for bird work, which he has adapted to bear study in order to avoid a more costly projection method that would eat up the whole station budget on one species.

Seasonal employees arrive the last week of May for safety training. By the third week in June "melt-off/green-up" has begun and field crews are deployed. This year the field crews are working in previously unsampled areas to test the accuracy of the vegetation map. Four years of on-the-ground wildlife sampling have identified a wide variety of different species on the refuge. This "ground tested" information is combined with satellite data for a more complete picture.

As summer ends, Gene works on budget requests and proposals for the next fiscal year, which begins in October.

Hunting season opens in September. Gene gets involved by conducting overflights with a Fish and Wildlife Service law enforcement officer. When there's an opportunity to land on a lake, river, or gravel bar near a camp, the two go up and talk to the hunters, and the officer checks licenses.

Even the best job has less enjoyable aspects. For Gene, it's paperwork and politics. He says: "When I started working for the Fish and Wildlife Service I had this vision of going out and working with the animals. What I didn't realize is that, especially in Alaska, there are a lot of politics involved in wildlife management. There's a lot of people management as opposed to working with animals."

What does Gene like most about his work? "I enjoy working with animals. As a wildlife biologist, I try to provide the best data I can to managers who make the resource decisions. I feel like I'm contributing to making sure that people are still able to enjoy Alaska's resources, whether it be watching a bear or hunting caribou." Gene's ultimate goal is to manage the Yukon Delta Refuge in Bethel. At 31 years old, he's in no rush.

RESOURCES

American Fisheries Society. Promotes scientific research and enlightened management of resources and encourages a comprehensive education for fisheries scientists and continuing on-the-job training. Offers professional certification and job listings. Among others, the society publishes *Fisheries* (bimonthly), and the *Journal of North American Fisheries Management* (quarterly). *American Fisheries Society Guide to Fisheries Employment* (1996), book coauthored by Tracey Hill. 5410 Grosvenor Ln., Suite 110, Bethesda, MD 20814-2199. (301) 897-8096. Http://www.esd.ornl.gov/societies/AFS/.

American Institute of Biological Sciences. Nonprofit organization, originally established under federal charter in 1947. Profices advisory and other services to the federal government, academia, and industry through Scientific Peer Advisory Review Services (SPARS). Diverse membership represents the full spectrum of biological sciences. Publishes *BioScience* (monthly). 1444 Eye Street, NW, Suite 200, Washington, DC 20005. (202) 628-1500. Http://www.aibs.org.

"Aquanet." Website that serves as a clearinghouse of information relating to aquatic environments. Includes a diverse collection of services, databases, news, and editorials. Http://www.aquanet.com.

Center for Marine Conservation. A nonprofit membership organization dedicated to protecting marine wildlife and its habitats by reversing the degradation of oceans through science-based advocacy, research, public education, and promotion pf citizen participation. 1725 DeSales St., NW, Suite 600, Washington, DC 20036. (202) 429-5609. Http://www.cmc_ocean.org.

Chronicle Guidance Publications. Corporate publisher most noted for its occupational briefs that profile a wide variety of environmental careers, including wildlife biologists, fish farm workers, oceanographers, and hydrologists. 66 Aurora St., Moravia, NY 13118-1190. (315) 497-3359. Http://www.chronicleguidance.com.

Conservation International. International nonprofit organization that works to protect ecosystems and the people who live within them. Works in twenty-two countries throughout the world, with a staff of 350 people. Excellent website with information about endangered species, maps, ecotourism resources, and well-selected links to global conservation sites. 2501 M Street, NW, Suite 200, Washington, DC 20037. (202) 429-5660 or (800) 429-5660. Http://www.conservation.org.

Defenders of Wildlife. Promotes the preservation of wildlife, particularly endangered species, through education, litigation, research, and advocacy. Conducts public education and runs an activist network. Publishes *Defenders* (quarterly). 1101 14th St., NW, #1400, Washington, DC 20005. (202) 682-6400. Http://www.defenders.org.

Environmental Defense Fund. Nonprofit membership organization. Leading advocate of economic incentives as a new approach to solving environmental problems, including water and wildlife issues. 257 Park Avenue South, New York, NY 10010. (800) 684-3322. Http://www.edf.org.

Habitat Restoration Information Center. Facilitates the exchange of information pertaining to the restoration of native plant and animal species and their habitats. Excellent resource for environmental laws, restoration organizations, government agencies and funding sources, newsletters, magazines, and educational materials. P.O. Box 1400, Felton, CA 95018-1400. (408) 335-6800. Http://www.habitat_restoration.com/.

National Audubon Society. Conserves and restores natural ecosystems, focusing on birds and other wildlife. Offers internships. Publishes *Audubon* magazine and *American Birds* (both bimonthly). 700 Broadway, New York, NY 10003. (212) 979-3000. Http://www.audubon.org.

National Marine Fisheries Service or (NOAA Fisheries) is part of the National Oceanic and Atmospheric Administration. It administers NOAA's programs that support the domestic and international conservation and management of living marine resources. 1315 East-West Hwy., SSMC3, Silver Spring, MD 20910. (301) 713 2239. Http://www.nmfs.gov.

National Wildlife Federation. Largest conservation organization in the world. Has state chapters and holds an annual meeting. Awards fellowships for graduate study in conservation and sponsors paid internships. Publishes annual *Conservation Directory* ($61.00, available in most libraries), *National Wildlife* magazine (bimonthly), and numerous other publications. 8925 Leesburg Pike, Vienna, VA 22184, (703) 790-4000. Http://www.nwf.org.

Native American Fish and Wildlife Society. Nonprofit membership organization that serves tribal governments and the conservation professionals that work on tribal fish and wildlife programs. Excellent newsletter and other publications, including the *Tribal Resources Assistance Handbook*. Programs for Native American youth and students. 750 Burbank Street, Broomfield, CO 80020. (303) 466-1725. Http://www.nafwsprd@iex.net.

Office of Personnel Management. Has information on jobs in all government agencies. Get the GS salary scale at www.opm.gov, by clicking on "what's hot" or by looking in the phone book under government listings to call the OPM near you. USAJOBS provides access to the Federal Jobs Database of worldwide opportunities. Offers full text job announcements, answers frequently asked federal employment questions, and provides access to electronic and hard copy application forms. Http://www.usajobs.opm.gov. (912) 757-3000, TDD Service at (912) 744-2299.

Peace Corps. Recruitment Office, 1900 K Street, NW, Washington, DC 20526. Or call (800) 424-8580 for the Peace Corps office nearest you. Http://www.peacecorps. gov.

Society for Conservation Biology. International professional organization dedicated to promoting the scientific study of the phenomena that affect the maintenance, loss, and restoration of biological diversity. Website is good place to begin a search for conservation-related employment or information on programs in conservation biology. Http://conbio.rice.edu/scbl/.

Society for Ecological Restoration. Nonprofit organization dedicated to advancing the science and art of restoring damaged ecosystems in conjunction with preservation and management of key natural areas in order to maintain biological diversity. Offers two main journals, *Restoration & Management Notes* (biannual) and *Restoration Ecology* (quarterly). Website has "employment noticeboard," which has links to other conservation employment websites, job listings, grants, internships. 1207 Seminole Hwy., Madison, WI 53711. (608) 262-2746. Http://nabalu.flas. ufl.edu/ser/SERhome.html.

U.S. Fish and Wildlife Service. The service manages more than 500 national wildlife refuges. U.S. Department of the Interior, 1849 C Street, NW, Washington, DC 20240. (202) 208-4131. Http://www.fws.gov.

U.S. Geological Survey. Has jurisdiction over the Biological Resources Division, which conducts research on fish and wildlife and their habitats. The USGS's Northern Prairie Wildlife Research Center annually employs between fifty and sixty seasonal biological science technicians. 807 National Center, Reston, VA 20192. (703) 648-4460. Http://www.usgs.gov.

The Wilderness Society. Nonprofit membership organization devoted to preserving wilderness and wildlife, protecting America's prime forests, parks, rivers, deserts, and shorelands, and fostering an American land ethic. 900 17 St., NW, Washington, DC 20006. (202) 833-2300. Http://www.tws.org.

The Wildlife Society. Nonprofit scientific and educational society dedicated to sustainable management of wildlife resources and their habitats. Offers professional certification. Has student chapters. Publications include the *Journal of Wildlife Management* (quarterly), the *Wildlife Society Bulletin* (quarterly), and *The Wildlifer* a bimonthly newsletter that contains information on job opportunities, career notes, and conservation issues. 5410 Grosvenor Ln., Suite 200, Bethesda, MD 20814-2197. (301) 897-9770. Http://www.wildlife.org.

World Wildlife Fund. Nonprofit membership organization with global presence. Mission is to conserve nature and ecological processes by combining fieldwork and policy making to preserve genetic, species, and ecosystem diversity, and by promoting actions for sustaining natural resources. 1250 24th St., NW, Washington, DC 20037-1175. (202) 293-4800. Http://www.panda.org.

13 Parks and Outdoor Recreation

AT A GLANCE

Employment:

240,000 parks and recreation workers nationwide, overwhelmingly at government agencies

Demand:

10 to 20 percent increase expected in recreation administration through the year 2005; 4 to 6 percent annual employment increase overall, including seasonal workers

Breakdown:

Public sector, 80 percent
Private sector, 15 percent
Nonprofit sector, 5 percent

Key Job Titles:

Administrator
Archaeologist
Biologist
Botanist
Campground director
Concession manager
Ecosystem restoration expert
Ecotour guide
Environmental interpreter
Geologist
Historian
Landscape architect

Maintenance manager
Museum director
Natural resource manager
Naturalist
Outdoor recreation manager
Park planner
Ranger
Wildlife biologist

Influential Organizations

The Ecotourism Society
National Association of State Parks Directors
National Park Service
National Parks and Conservation Association
National Recreation and Park Association
U.S. Bureau of Land Management
USDA Forest Service

Salary:

Base starting salaries for federal rangers vary from $20,000 to $30,000. Experienced individuals draw salaries of $30,000 to $40,000. State and local park salaries start as low as $10,000 annually, but vary widely by locale. The average is around $20,000. Top salaries for senior executives and entrepreneurs fall in the $75,000 to $100,000 range.

Many of today's environmental professionals can trace their career to a memorable childhood experience at a park, summer camp, zoo, aquarium, adventure tour, or nature center. The appeal of a life in the park is dramatically illustrated by the thousands of people who apply each year for the opportunity to *volunteer* to work at Yosemite, Yellowstone, Acadia, and the other jewels of our national parks system.

Parks and recreation workers are the people who create and maintain these special places, and who heighten our experience of forests, canyons, beaches, lakes, and mountains. The familiar park ranger, in full uniform and hat, is one of the most durable images in the conservation world.

Perhaps that is why many people look to the parks first when they think about environmental careers. If you are one of those people, there are surprises ahead. Parks and recreation work is a rapidly growing field that goes far beyond the most visible jobs to embrace dozens of different professions.

WHAT IS PARKS AND OUTDOOR RECREATION?

Parks and outdoor recreation is a complex field. One agency, the Indiana Department of Natural Resources, lists sixty-seven distinct positions needed to operate the state's parks and recreation programs. The text that follows discusses the major parks professions.

*The chance to live and work in some of America's most beautiful places makes a
parks career extremely competitive.*

ADMINISTRATION

Parks and other outdoor areas are physical and organizational entities that must
be managed just as any other agency or company. To do so requires skilled people in the areas of budgeting and finance, public affairs, procurement and contracting, personnel management, overall management, and related support services. Specialists in management information systems are especially needed at
park agencies.

INTERPRETATION

Interpreters are the park personnel whom the public is most likely to see. The
most visible, perhaps, is the park ranger. Rangers are involved in law enforcement, protecting both the natural resources and park visitors. They also are
responsible for education, maintenance, and planning and executing recreational programs for visitors. In small park systems, a ranger might handle all
of these functions; elsewhere, specialists handle the diverse functions. Thus
there are park police, interpreters, recreation planners and programmers, maintenance staff members, and natural resource managers. The ranger position is
currently undergoing reexamination and change. In some cases, new categories
are being created to reflect a need for specialization and targeted skills. Law
enforcement, for example, is generally given over to a particular group of
rangers. In other cases, ranger positions with narrow definitions are being

altered to encourage more generalists who are equal parts scientist, teacher, manager, emergency medical provider, and more. The ranger position is discussed in greater detail later in this chapter.

NATURAL RESOURCE MANAGEMENT

Maintaining the ecological health of our parks while allowing for growing numbers of human visitors is not an easy job. Parks are "natural" areas, but they are also carefully monitored and managed. In fact, the more natural a park area strives to be the more likely we are to find employment for foresters, range managers, fishery and wildlife biologists, ecologists, soil scientists, and others. Many of these professionals are covered in more detail in the other conservation chapters of this book.

RESEARCH

Public lands, including parks and recreation areas, are repositories of biological information, gene pools, endangered and threatened plants and animals, and general species diversity. They are ideal natural research facilities, both for direct management purposes and for larger conservation questions. Popular areas of current research include climate change, fragmented habitats, preferred human uses of the parks, nonpoint source pollution, and "boundary issues," where park wildlife spills over into the human communities that abut our parks.

Some areas receiving study at the National Park Service include the connec-

Staff people from The Resource Center in Chicago, Illinois, visit the site of a former vacant lot, now a much needed playground.

tion between UVB rays and the disappearance of amphibians, human impacts on natural and cultural resources in parks, and what factors influence the vulnerability of habitats to nonnative plant invasions.

SITE OPERATIONS AND MAINTENANCE

Whether parks and recreation facilities are maintained in a roughly natural state or are intensively managed facilities, their maintenance and upkeep are formidable and chronically underfunded tasks. Daily maintenance of a park's buildings, roads, trails, interpretive facilities, bathrooms, camp areas, beaches, playgrounds, signs, and natural areas takes the lion's share of a park's budget and staff. Small armies of landscape architects, horticulturalists, property managers, laborers, technicians, seasonal workers, interns, and volunteers are required to keep our parks in the condition we expect. Park administrators regularly list the need for greater maintenance budgets as a major priority.

HISTORY AND BACKGROUND

The United States is blessed with one of the largest collections of federal, state, local, and privately owned parks and outdoor recreation areas in the world. It was not always that way, however. Our parks are the result of hard work on the part of activists, citizens, elected officials, and others, primarily in this century. A few highlights of our federal parks history include:

- Yellowstone National Park, the oldest national park in America, was established as a federal reservation in 1872 and placed under control of the U.S. Army.
- The Lacy Act, 1894 (amended in 1900) gave the army authority to forcibly stop interstate shipment of wildlife, bringing damage to wildlife and other park resources under more control.
- National Park Service Organic Act of 1916 created the National Park Service as a civilian agency. The act clearly defines the mission of the Park Service as preservation. It charges the new agency with conserving scenery and natural and historic objects as well as wildlife in the national parks and also requires the Park Service to provide for the public's enjoyment of the parks while protecting them for future generations. Finally, the act empowers the secretary of the interior to contract for recreational services.
- The Wilderness Act of 1964 (as amended in 1968 and 1970) establishes wild buffer zones around national parks to insulate them from nearby human activity. The National Park Service administers over 38 million acres of land protected as wilderness under this act.
- General Authorities Act of 1970 brings all areas administered by the National Park Service into one National Park System. The act states, "these areas derive increased national dignity and recognition of their superb environmental quality through their inclusion jointly with each other. . . ."
- National Parks and Recreation Act of 1978 requires all park units to have management plans that include four items: measures for the preservation of the area's resources; type and intensity of development for public enjoy-

ment; visitor carrying capacity and implementation commitments; and proposed boundary modifications with explanations as to why they are
required. The act further requires the secretary of the interior to submit
annual detailed programs for the development of facilities, structures, or
buildings for each unit of the system consistent with management plans.

- The Alaska National Interest Lands Conservation Act of 1980 set aside
large tracts of land in Alaska for new national parks with thirty-five new
wilderness areas comprising more than 56 million acres. This act more than
tripled the National Wilderness Preservation System.

Other laws govern the national historic sites and cultural resources that are
a part of the National Park System. These include the Antiquities Act of 1906;
the Historic Sites, Buildings, and Antiquities Act of 1935; the Archeological
Resources Protection Act of 1979; and the National Historic Preservation Act
of 1966. Additional natural resources and recreation legislation of interest to
parks professionals includes the Outdoor Recreation Act of 1963; the Land and
Water Conservation Fund Act of 1965; the Wild and Scenic Rivers Act of
1968; the National Trails System Act of 1968; the National Environmental
Policy Act of 1969; the Clean Air Act of 1970; the Clean Water Act of 1972;
and the Endangered Species Act of 1973. This is only a partial listing. Be on
the lookout for new legislation that could affect the increase or decrease of job
opportunities. A good source on the World Wide Web for new legislation that
covers both federal and state laws is "Newslink" Environmental at http://
www.caprep.com. The Natural Resources Defense Council's "Legislative
Watch" at http://www.nrdc.org/field/state.html, is another good source.

Where do parks professionals work? The National Park System now includes
some 375 parks that encompass over 83 million acres and serve 275 million visitors annually. But the federal park system is dwarfed in numbers of parks and
visitors by state and local park systems. There are over 5,500 state parks alone.
Though difficult to determine, the number of local recreation sites is estimated at around 100,000.

ISSUES AND TRENDS

More than ever before, professionals are struggling with issues of balance
among competing uses for our beloved parks and outdoor recreation spaces.
Some of the leading concerns are outlined below.

INCREASING IMPORTANCE OF RECREATION ON "NONPARK" LANDS

The U.S. Bureau of Land Management, the Forest Service, and a wide variety
of private and public landowners manage millions of acres of land. In the past,
these lands were overwhelmingly used for ranching, timber production, mining, and agriculture, or they closed to the public for safety and liability reasons.

That is no longer the case, especially in the West, where outdoor recreation
is rapidly becoming the number one use of many public lands. Look for recre-

ation career opportunities at agencies and companies that are catching up to this change.

NEED FOR URBAN PARKS AND OPEN SPACE

As much as parks professionals love the great western parks, nearly everyone agrees that the parks of greatest importance to the majority of Americans are urban parks, whether they are run by federal, state, or local agencies. Advocates for people of color and low-income people take the argument further, noting that parks and open space are often lacking in poorer neighborhoods or are not accessible by public transportation. Activists fight for a reallocation of resources to disadvantaged areas. Van F. Anderson, director of professional services with the National Recreation and Parks Association, says: "The parks people use, and need the most, are the ones closest to where they live. Seventy-one percent of the population in the U.S. lives within walking distance of a park or playground. Expanding and maintaining this base is a crucial piece of business."

Some urban groups are focusing on smaller and smaller pieces of open space. Glenda Daniel, urban greening director with the Open Lands Project in Chicago, says: "Beyond the issue of having a place in neighborhoods where people can go, the biggest concern is having a *safe* place where you can take your kids to play." Daniel focuses on reclaiming vacant lots from gangs, cleaning them up, putting up fences, and installing plants and benches. "The goal is to create a lot of little pocket parks scattered all over the city so that seniors, families, and babysitters can safely take children there to play," she says.

According to Richard Heath, executive director of the Boston Greenspace Alliance, the need for urban parks does not necessarily translate into action. He claims that urban areas are the last places to be reached by the environmental movement. "With few exceptions, the big environmental organizations aren't addressing urban parks at all," says Heath.

DEMOGRAPHIC CHANGES, THE DISABLED, AND A NEW GENERATION

Profound demographic changes will require new approaches to park placement, management, and hiring. With its current growth rate, the population of the United States will double in about seventy-five years. Half of that growth will come from recent immigrants and their children, with trends indicating that minorities will collectively exceed the Anglo population sometime in the next century. This indicates a critical need for multilingual employees to serve and involve these growing population segments, build support networks for the future, and offer park experiences that are meaningful to people from varied backgrounds.

Another pressing need is to make parks more accessible to those with impaired mobility, for two reasons. First, parks must often comply with the Americans with Disabilities Act, which requires sweeping, expensive, but necessary changes. Second, park managers are looking ahead to meet the needs of aging baby boomers (born between 1947 and 1961). Millions of boomers will want parks that serve the needs of the elderly and will exert political pressure to make it happen.

Another audience is the children of baby boomers (born between 1964 and 1981). "Generation X" participates in outdoor recreation to the same extent their parents did at the same age. However, since there are fewer individuals in this group, they don't represent the same demand for outdoor recreation as the baby boomers. Generation X'ers are continuing the trend started by baby boomers—more frequent short trips and fewer long vacations, creating a demand for more and better recreation closer to home.

In the next ten years, parks will also have to work at attracting children born after 1981, often referred to as the "millennial generation." Initial indications are that young children participate in outdoor activities at a 10 to 20 percent lower rate than did the baby boomers and the generation X'ers at the same age. This is a cause for concern because a lack of interest could affect political support for our parks. The millennial generation is composed of high proportions of ethnic and/or socioeconomically disadvantaged children who live in inner cities. These children must be reached at home through educational activities in their schools.

APPEAL OF TRAILS, BIKE PATHS, AND LINKED PARKS

What is a park? Does it have to be a boundaried place, with open space or recreational facilities inside? In fact, a park could be an old rail bed that is now a multiuse path for bikers, skaters, horseback riders, cross country skiers, and hikers. It could extend for ten, twenty, fifty, or two hundred miles. According to the Rails-to-Trails Conservancy, there are nearly 1,000 "rail trails" throughout the United States, creating a "park" experience that travels through towns, cities, open lands, forests, and more. These narrow parks are incredibly popular with the public and more of them are certainly possible and desirable. In addition to rail-trails, the public clearly loves the existing network of hundreds of miles of outdoor trails and wants more of them. Finally, park planners recognize the need to connect existing parks and open space through scenic road ways, trails, paths, and protected land to create uninterrupted "greenways." These projects create career opportunities for people with real estate, legal and financial backgrounds, political organizing skills, planning and design knowledge, and engineering ability.

URBAN WILD PLACES

Wetlands, rivers, seacoasts, meadowlands, forests, and old farmlands are being protected to give urban residents wilderness experiences close to home. The new Boston Harbor Islands National Park (formerly a state park) is one example. With a simple boat ride, residents of a metropolis of 2.5 million people can put the city behind them.

The country's Urban National Forests (those located within 50 miles of populations greater than 1 million people) provide unique management challenges and opportunities. As urban sprawl continues to affect a broad range of forested ecosystems, an increasing number of national forests within the system are facing social problems such as crime, vandalism, arson, and traffic congestion in addition to more traditional recreation and resource management concerns. "Social science skills are needed to address human behavior more often than technical skills to modify resource conditions," says Brent McBeth, resource group leader at Uinta National Forest near Salt Lake City, Utah.

Too Many People?

Whether a park is close to where people live, or far away, many are being "loved to death." Recreation visits to units of the National Park System increased 30 percent between 1977 and 1994, while the U.S. population increased only 18.7 percent, and many popular state parks have traffic jam conditions on summer weekends. At many popular parks, reservation systems for controlling access are already in place, and getting stricter. Many are calling for increasing entry, parking, and other fees to both cover costs and reduce use. Expect growing conflicts when park managers must limit autos, close trails, raise prices, or turn people away from "our" parks. Parks professionals with creative solutions to controlling park use without triggering public resentment are needed.

Balancing Increased Access with Ecosystem Preservation

What are parks for? Closely related to the issue of growing park use is the question of balance among different park uses. Should some parks be set aside for quiet contemplation while others are full of golf courses, tennis courts, swimming pools, concert areas, ice skating rinks, formal gardens, education exhibits, hiking trails, and restaurants? Or, should each park have a little of both? If a park supports threatened plants and wildlife, should the habitat needs of those wildlife supersede human use? Should beaches close when piping plovers are laying eggs? These questions have always been a part of park planning and management. Today, however, they are more pressing than ever. There are opportunities for managers who can address balanced use by spreading different types of parks throughout an overall system, without creating too many inequities of access. Students with an interest in policy may want to take up these questions in class and through internships.

Outside Threats

Outside threats to parkland health, such as development on park borders, acid rain, water pollution, and the introduction of foreign species, also command the attention of outdoor recreation professionals. As stated in a list of challenges the National Park Service faces, "parks are not isolated islands, they are a small part of the larger ecosystem." Ecosystem management is a long-term, cooperative venture. Park personnel are becoming more active in working with their neighbors (both public and private) to identify common interests, develop common goals, and devise compatible solutions to issues of individual or common concern in order to lessen outside threats. They are also engaged in public relations and media strategies. All of these issues point to a need for park professionals who have excellent diplomacy and negotiating skills. Interpretive staff members who previously were concerned only with helping people enjoy their visits to the park now participate in education programs designed to make visitors aware of the park's health.

PRIVATE OWNERSHIP OF PARK-LIKE RESOURCES

What happens when private individuals or organizations own and manage parks and other open space? Is the public served? Beaches and golf courses are examples of this concern. In many towns, the largest managed open spaces are private country clubs, which are off-limits to most residents. Many states and towns have done a poor job of preserving waterfront property, turning unnecessarily large tracts over to personal beach houses, private resorts, hotels, and other private uses. Even when park lands are owned by environmental nonprofit groups, access can be limited to those who are members or who can afford steep usage and parking fees. Career opportunities exist for people who work for private entities and for those who craft solutions that increase public access to private lands.

ECOTOURISM AND ADVENTURE TRAVEL

An undeniable bright spot in the private sector for recreational services is the growing field of ecotourism and adventure travel. More and more people are looking for a vacation experience that offers rigorous hiking, biking, and camping or that teaches visitors about local ecology and anthropology. Organizations such as the nonprofit group Earthwatch send volunteers around the world to work on environmental monitoring projects and other scientific work. Other companies send people rafting down whitewater rivers, exploring coastal wetlands, swimming with the dolphins, watching whales, or exploring tropical rainforests. Do a quick web search using the keyword "ecotourism" to find several leading companies.

NEED FOR INCREASED FUNDING AND MORE
CREATIVE REVENUE STREAMS

The scarcity of funding for outdoor recreation at the federal, state, and local levels is a persistent, significant problem for park professionals (see the case study at the end of this chapter). Due to limited budgets and workforces, both the National Park Service and a coalition of Urban National Forests say they spend more time and money managing people than protecting natural resources. While they recognize the need to correct this imbalance and put resource protection first, a backlog of infrastructure repairs continues to grow and affect the safety and enjoyment of visitors. Both organizations continually work to streamline operations, raise funds from private investors, and heavily utilize volunteers to help bridge the gap between their needs and the resources available, but clearly more funding is needed. Although the park system has expanded (thirty-nine new sites since 1984), budget increases and the number of employees have not kept pace. Partnerships with local governments and community groups have become necessary to the survival of our national parks.

The USDA Forest Service is the "number one provider in America of the outdoor recreation experience," according to James Lyon, head of the USDA. An audit of the Forest Service by the General Accounting Office shows that 74 percent of its contribution to the gross national product comes from outdoor recreation, especially from camping, fishing, and hiking, yet Congress allocates only 2.5 percent of the Forest Service budget to recreation. The Forest Service is addressing the lack of recreation funding through a three-year program authorized by Congress to collect fees at fifty sites where previously access was free. One hundred percent of the money goes to the unit where the fees are collected to offset recreation impacts through public education, increased law enforcement presence against vandalism, and improvements to user facilities such as toilets, trails, and roads. Over the next five years, the government will reappraise cabin sites in the national forests for the first time in two decades. In many cases, owners of prime cabin sites will have to pay rents five to twenty times higher than what they currently pay, the Forest Service says.

The National Parks and Conservation Association (NPCA), which advocates for national parks, has been working on concession reform legislation since 1989. According to an article from the July/August 1997 issue of *National Parks* written by Wendy Mitman Clarke, "NPCA said studies show that the National Park Service receives an average 2 percent return from private businesses operating within the parks, when states and other entities receive at least 12 percent from businesses operating in their parks." The article adds that conservative estimates indicate that concession reform could generate $50 million annually. In 1996 an extreme measure, corporate sponsorship of national parks, worked its way into legislation and continues to be discussed, illustrating how serious the problem of national park funding is, writes Clarke. A host of other creative funding solutions exist to alleviate tightly stretched budgets.

All of the comments above for national parks and recreation lands are equally applicable to other levels of government. Certainly, most local parks are financially strapped and in need of help simply to maintain basic infrastructure.

ENTREPRENEURS IN STATE GOVERNMENT

Decreasing budgets, growing maintenance backlogs, and increasing attendance at state parks are resulting in more and more entrepreneurial enterprises. In 1993, Texas instituted an "entrepreneurial budget system" (EBS), which allows parks to keep as much as 35 percent of the revenue they generate beyond their target goal. Under this incentive-based program, if park managers spend less than their allotted budgets, they can keep the difference, increasing their budget for the following year. Historically, individual parks kept none of the revenue they generated for their own use and there was no advantage to saving money, because if parks didn't spend their annual budget, it was reduced the following year. Texas is still working some bugs out of the EBS, but even if the program doesn't ultimately work, the idea behind it is here to stay. Other states, such as California, South Dakota, and Arkansas, have similar programs. In Ohio, entrepreneurial programs, including user fees, raised park revenue from $12 million to $24 million in six years, although 59 percent of their budget still comes from the state. New Hampshire and Vermont state parks are completely self-supporting. This points to the importance of business skills for park professionals. National parks that, until recently, were unable to raise fees, charge fees for new programs, or market their natural resources, may soon follow this trend out of necessity.

INCREASING PROFESSIONALISM

The outdoor recreation field has become increasingly professional. There is less patronage hiring, fewer old-boy networks, and more national job listings. More people enter the field with specialized training rather than learning on the job. Bill Sanders, ranger careers manager with the National Park Service, says: "We're moving away from an experiential base to an education base in natural or cultural resources in parks." As the field becomes more sophisticated, employees also need skills outside of natural resource management or recreation programming, including written and oral communication, management, and budgeting.

CAREER OPPORTUNITIES

Opportunities in parks and outdoor recreation in the United States vary greatly from one facility to another and from smaller systems to larger ones. The Detroit park system, for instance, has a different mix of personnel from that of Yellowstone National Park. Still, all agencies hire rangers and law enforcement professionals, interpreters, maintenance and recreational program personnel, and administrative staff members.

PUBLIC SECTOR

Parks and outdoor recreation specialists are overwhelmingly employed by federal, state, and local government agencies. There are important differences, however, among these levels of government.

Federal Government. Working at a national park is often presented as the career path of choice for those entering the parks and outdoor recreation field. The National Park System encompasses two broad categories: historical parks, which are found primarily in the East, and large western parks, which exhibit the characteristics and hire the rangers commonly known to the public. As we have seen, the National Park Service, with about 15,700 full-time workers, employs a relatively small percentage of park and recreation professionals. Many of the service's employees work in maintenance. This doesn't stop people from applying in droves, therefore it's worth talking about the Park Service's most well-known position—the park ranger.

The definition of "ranger" is so broad that many people consider the term meaningless. The National Park Service lists the functions of a federal ranger as supervision; conservation management; natural resource management; interpretation; protection and law enforcement; forest fire control; predator control; traffic control; accident investigation; and even folk art demonstration. Ranger careers manager Bill Sanders says: "The ranger occupation is divided into two main career fields: resources protection rangers and resources interpretation rangers." However, interpretative rangers are expected to be able to jump in and act as the logistics manager for a fifty-person rescue team, and likewise, rangers on the protection side are expected to be fully skilled and capable on the interpretive side.

Although federal park rangers are the image many have in mind when they consider an outdoor recreation career, breaking into the Park Service as a ranger is not easy (see Jackie Henman's profile at the end of this chapter). "People who really get the jobs have held temporary or permanent (nonranger) jobs within the system. Most rangers find a back-door way into the park ranger position, whether it's driving a shuttle bus, working for the Student Conservation Association, or working as a visitor use assistant," says Bill Sanders, ranger careers manager for the National Park Service.

But even seasonal jobs are difficult to get. The number of applicants far outnumbers the positions available every year, particularly at the larger, more popular parks. Some positions are filled by experienced seasonal employees who have worked previously for the National Park Service. Further, even those seasonal employees who have years of experience have difficulties getting hired as a permanent employee. Applicants who have federal status and veterans of the armed services are given preference over those without federal status, even if they are less experienced or educated. The Park Service is unlikely to increase the number of rangers it hires until 2005 to 2008, when older employees will retire in large numbers.

Although national parks come to mind first, the public finds outdoor recreation opportunities on many other federal lands as well, including national forests, wilderness areas, wildlife refuges, and scenic rivers. These lands are managed by federal agencies that are often overlooked by job seekers. Table 13.1 illustrates that the Bureau of Land Management, the USDA Forest Service, the Fish and Wildlife Service, and the nation's state parks offer many

Table 13.1 Employment at Selected Agencies with Parks and Recreation Programs

Organization	No. of sites	No. of acres	Permanent employees	Seasonal employees
National Park Service	375	83 million	15,729	5,548
National Forest Service	900	191 million	30,000	15,000
Bureau of Land Management	140	270 million	8,760	1,900
Fish and Wildlife Service	719	90 million	7,000	N/A
State Parks	5,541	11.8 million	18,980	28,579
TOTAL EMPLOYEES			80,469	51,027

Source: Environmental Careers Organization.

more sites and more opportunities for employment than does the National Park Service. The number of employees includes those employed as rangers as well as a variety of other positions, such as researchers, wildlife biologists, administrative personnel, land acquisition experts, museum staff, design and construction personnel, maintenance, trade, and craft positions.

In 1997, the Forest Service hired 500 new permanent employees, mostly in clerical or technician positions. However, by 1999 the agency expects to decrease their permanent workforce by 1,000. Brent McBeth notes, however, that "There are a lot of employees who have been with the Forest Service 15 to 20 years, so while all national forests are currently reducing their workforces, in the next five years or so a lot of employees will be retiring." Advertised seasonal vacancies with the Forest Service vary from 5,000 to 10,000 positions annually, but many of the more than 15,000 seasonal employees return non-competitively to their temporary positions each year.

The Bureau of Land Management has recreation staff in all states and field offices. They hired 175 new employees in 1996 and estimated 150 to 200 new hires in 1997 and 1998. Given that they employ over 8,700 permanent employees, their hiring rate is at about 2 percent per year.

The following are three good ways to learn of job openings in federally managed parks:

- Contact your local Office of Personnel Management (OPM), where they will explain what is available and how to apply. Or visit the OPM website at http://www.usajobs.opm.gov.
- Target a geographic area or even a particular park and contact park superintendents at a specific location to find out about vacancies.
- Visit http://www.fedworld.gov/jobs/jobsearch.html, the federal jobs search engine that lists both seasonal and permanent jobs.

Seasonal employment requirements for national parks can be accessed on the web at http://www.NPS.gov/pub_aff/jobs.htm. The filing period for winter employment is June 1 through July 15. The filing period for summer employment is November 15 through January 15.

State and Local Government. All of the federal agencies combined provide far fewer opportunities for parks and outdoor recreation professionals than do the state parks and recreation agencies and numerous state forests, scenic rivers, and wildlife refuges. There are over 100,000 state, county, and municipal parks in this country.

Although it is not well publicized, employment in state park systems is growing despite hiring freezes in many state governments. The National Association of State Park Directors Annual Information Exchange for 1997 reported over 50,000 state park employees, including 28,000 "wearing uniforms." Only 22,000, however, were full- and part-time employees. Over 28,000 were seasonal workers.

Towns large and small all have parks, and in large cities the park system is often run by a major department. Consider as well the numerous regional and county park systems. Small municipal park systems deserve careful consideration by aspiring parks professionals, for many reasons. First, competition is less, therefore your odds are better. Second, staffs are smaller and there are opportunities to learn a wide range of new skills through responsible work very quickly. Third, in a smaller community, you are face-to-face with clients who are also your neighbors. You learn very rapidly what the public wants and is willing to pay for, either through taxes or user fees. Fourth, traditional recreation is mixed with environmental protection at the town level—you can find yourself dealing with wildlife issues one day and planning a softball tournament the next. For those who love variety, local parks management is an excellent choice. Fifth, educational requirements to do senior-level work are often less rigorous at the town level. No one is likely to say that you can't take charge of the biological inventory because you lack a master's degree. Finally, if you choose to stay in a local system, the chance for advancement to managerial ranks (without sacrificing daily work in the field) is greater.

State and local park and recreation systems bear the brunt of the need discussed earlier to provide for urban populations. Many park professionals work in inner-city or suburban parks where they educate citizens about conservation issues. Environmentalists in urban systems often need social intervention skills as substance abuse, gangs, vandalism and other crimes become increasingly common in and around parks.

Most states have recreation and/or park associations that provide networking opportunities.

PRIVATE SECTOR

Private sector employment in parks and outdoor recreation is growing, as more government agencies contract out services to businesses, and as entrepreneurs find new ways to meet the public demand for understanding and enjoying the natural world.

Recreation Services and Privately Owned Facilities. Visit the towns around any large park, recreational area, forest, or wilderness and you will find dozens of businesses catering to visitors. Outfitters and guides for hiking, fishing, whale watching, white-water rafting, kayaking, rock climbing, and mountain biking crowd these "gateway communities," employing local residents and aspiring outdoor recreation workers from throughout the nation. Many of these businesses have formal contracts with government agencies to provide services that might otherwise be delivered by government workers.

In addition to companies around public lands and parks, entrepreneurs have created a growing number of privately owned recreation facilities that employ outdoor recreation workers. Most of those tend to be "artificial" environments that are specifically designed for particular outdoor sports. These include golf courses, marinas, resorts, camps, and ski lodges. Together, revenues for private sector outdoor recreation activities easily exceed $5 billion, and the employment impact on surrounding communities generates even more jobs for those at hotels, restaurants, and so forth.

Many of the most exciting jobs in outdoor recreation are now in the private sector. In fact, the popular face of recreation is beginning to shift; from the government park ranger in a "Smokey the Bear" hat, to a private employee guiding a raft full of people down a white-water river. Popular environmental magazines such as *Sierra* are full of ads for these companies, and more are created every year. The downside of private sector recreation work is that employment is overwhelmingly seasonal, limiting long-term career possibilities. In addition, the field is extremely competitive, requiring business owners to keep costs (including labor costs) under control. Finally, the ability of customers to spend money on outdoor recreation opportunities rises and falls with the overall economy and is affected by the weather. Boom and bust cycles are common in the business.

Ecotourism and Adventure Travel. Ecotourism, run by both private businesses and nonprofit agencies, is one of the fastest-growing sectors of the recreational field. The Ecotourism Society's 1998 *International Membership Directory* lists 1,400 ecotourism professionals from fifty-five countries, representing nearly forty professions, who are ready to transport vacationers to nearly any part of the globe for the environmentally correct time of their lives. The expansion of this field means that jobs are available, and according to Chris Bresnan of the National Recreation and Parks Association, more students with environmental education backgrounds are being absorbed by this field.

Ecotourism and adventure travel has been touted as a sustainable economic development strategy to replace ecologically damaging industries such as logging, poaching, certain types of agriculture, and mining. Ecotourism advocates suggest that people living in and around tropical rain forests, for example, can build an economy based on visitors who come to climb catwalks through the forest canopy, walk carefully constructed trails, take photographs of wildlife, and even volunteer time for environmental and scientific projects. Guests, of course, would also need lodging, food, transportation, and more.

Almost any kind of threatened environment is a candidate for ecotourism—the savannahs of Kenya, the barrier reefs of Australia, the forests of Vermont, the mountain peaks of Nepal and Kathmandu, and the rain forests of South and Central America, Africa, and Asia. Even the European farming landscape supports a growing ecotourism industry, as the German government provides subsidies to farmers who open their properties as "bed and breakfast" sites to preserve a farming landscape that might otherwise be lost.

Unfortunately, the definition of "ecotourism" remains in dispute, and the power of tourism for ecological protection is unclear. Will the growth of ecotourism create more places such as the carefully designed conditions on St. John's in the American Virgin Islands, or will the growth of visitors bring pressure for uncontrolled growth in the form of more roads, motels, restaurants, souvenir shops, night clubs, bus tours, and strip developments? Moreover, is ecotourism a Hobson's choice for native people—environmental destruction through logging and agriculture or cultural destruction through dependence on wealthy foreigners?

Although the risks are many, sensitive ecotourism is possible and has a place in the economic plans of developing nations and rural areas everywhere. The need is great for talented entrepreneurs and recreation professionals who can turn the promise of ecotourism into a reality.

Nonprofit Sector

There are hundreds of nonprofit organizations providing park-like places and outdoor recreation to the public, although most of them have limited staffs, and many are run primarily by volunteers. Nonprofit organizations such as land trusts and birding/wildlife groups often own conservation land in particularly beautiful places that is offered to the public for swimming, walking, wildlife observation, picnicking, and so forth. These include large, well-known groups such as The Nature Conservancy and The National Audubon Society, but are more likely to be small, local outfits known only to neighbors, members, and the committed.

This country is also home to hundreds of nonprofit summer camps and nature centers whose lands are used as parks by paying customers (in season) and by local residents (out-of-season). Don't overlook the many seasonal opportunities for naturalists, educators, and camp counselors at these camps and centers. Add to your seasonal experience by getting to know the management and fundraising challenges of these operations. It will increase your appreciation for the hard work that goes into keeping these facilities open and thriving, and it will increase your skill base.

Finally, zoological parks (called "zoos" by most of us) are a great employer of aspiring parks professionals, and some are run as nonprofit organizations. Zoos have a special place in most park systems and offer great opportunities for people who want to work with wildlife, but do not want to live in a remote area. Although competition is intense, and volunteer status is nearly always a prerequisite for future employment, zoos have a regular need for educators, interpreters, and similar professions.

Other nonprofit groups work to protect and enhance our parks systems. The National Parks and Conservation Association and the National Recreation and Park Association, for example, provide invaluable information tailored to suit the needs of this field. In addition to carrying out such information programs, they also lobby for improvements in parks organizations and espouse new techniques and programs that will benefit both their members and the environment. Local park organizations, with names such as "Friends of the Park," need talented organizers and fundraisers to provide citizen support for financially strapped parks and recreation programs.

A particularly interesting form of nonprofit recreation organization intersects with the ecotourism movement. Organizations such as Earthwatch in Watertown, Massachusetts, organize teams of vacationing volunteers to carry out scientific monitoring projects and environmental restoration activities, while exploring the beauties of the rain forest, coastal areas, arctic lands, anthropological digs, and more. See the Resources section in chapter 3 for more about these opportunities.

SALARY

Traditional entry-level positions in parks and outdoor recreation are fairly uniform in salary, and no one goes into parks and recreation to get rich. Most professionals in the field, however, feel that there are other nonmonetary payoffs and truly love their work.

Interpretive, ranger, and recreational positions offer starting pay in the range of $20,000 to $30,000, depending on college degrees and experience. (See the other conservation chapters in this book for additional salary information on related careers.) To check current federal pay ranges for these positions and others, visit http://www.opm.gov, and click on "what's hot."

Average annual pay for experienced rangers is $35,000. Since 1994, all federal salaries have been augmented by "locality pay" for areas where federal pay is out of step with the cost of living.

Seasonal employment in entry-level positions is likely to pay $300 to $350 per week. Seasonal federal positions in interpretation are graded between GS-2 and GS-7, and those in law enforcement are graded between GS-3 and GS-7, depending on education, skills, and experience. This means that these positions may pay as little as $16,000 per year. Seasonal employees who have been working for some time can make as much as $300 per week, though with few, if any, benefits.

The mean salary for a field unit employee in state parks is a minimum of $19,299 and a maximum of $31,360, with some states paying lower than the minimum and higher than the maximum, according to the 1997 National Association of State Park Directors' Annual Information Exchange. The mean salary for a field supervisor was a minimum of $37,764 and a maximum of

$51,174. Field unit managers (probably the best guide to mid-career state parks salaries) were paid a minimum of $26,919 and a maximum of $44,846.

Jobs in the nonprofit sector yield salaries roughly comparable to federal salaries, while private positions can be somewhat more lucrative for managers and about the same (or less) for seasonal people. Salaries in the federal parks lag behind private sector annual earnings.

Many park employees function as specialists in their respective fields. See the other conservation chapters for further information on salaries in land and water conservation, forestry, and fishery and wildlife management.

GETTING STARTED

Because parks positions are often in high demand, getting hired will require more effort and careful planning than in other segments of the environmental field. Careful consideration of your educational plans is essential.

EDUCATION

There are so many different careers in parks and outdoor recreation that it is impossible to note one particular way to prepare for such a career. Furthermore, professionals say that it is difficult to specialize until you get a job, and they recommend against attempting to specialize as part of under-graduate training.

The National Park Service careers webpage recommends the following areas of major study for both undergraduate and graduate education: natural resource management, natural or earth sciences, history, archaeology, anthro-pology, park and recreation management, social or behavioral sciences, muse-um sciences, business or public administration, and sociology. Debbie Byrd, chief ranger at Sequoia and Kings Canyon National Park, says she looks for a combination of education and experience, but the real tie-breaker for her is a service-oriented attitude. She says that the future park superintendent isn't nec-essarily the person with a natural resources education background. Brent McBeth, resource group leader with the National Forest Service, says the most popular degree among his recent hires is in park and outdoor recreation plan-ning, however, he pointed out that recreational use is just one of the many areas of the Forest Service. There are over 300 baccalaureate, over 280 associ-ate, and over 100 graduate degree programs in parks and recreation in the United States. The National Recreation and Park Association has helped devel-op standards of accreditation for four-year programs and accredits 98 out of more than 300.

You need specific skills and a careful strategy to get your first job in parks and outdoor recreation. However, you also need a broad arsenal of skills and education to have a successful career in the field. One way to choose a field of study is to decide where you want to work and query that organization about its educational requirements.

If you are fairly certain of your long-term goals, there exist some distinct career paths that you can work toward as an undergraduate. If your major interest is in natural resource management or research, a hard science background with a strong ecological base is recommended, and a master's degree is probably needed. If state park management and administration is your ultimate goal, a degree in recreation and parks management, perhaps combined with some hard sciences, is a good path. These are not the only ways to get started in these subfields, but they are among the most common.

No matter what their educational background may be, most parks and outdoor recreation professionals start at the bottom and work their way up, specializing as they go along. To advance your career, it is important to have held some of the entry-level jobs, especially those that entail contact with park visitors; most administrators were once rangers, interpreters, or foresters. This speaks for a broad-based education designed to develop a variety of skills, both technical and interpersonal.

With the exception of some specialized positions, a master's degree is not absolutely necessary and probably will not guarantee the raise in salary that it can in other fields. Parks and outdoor recreation professionals view a graduate degree as a way to specialize later in a career or as a way to broaden oneself, as well as a complement to an undergraduate degree. For example, if you have a B.A. in a hard science, you might consider a master's degree in management.

Whenever possible, gather expertise in additional areas such as communications, writing, fund-raising, negotiation, and computer applications. Knowledge of a foreign language, especially Spanish, is often valuable to your parks and recreation center. In addition, the application form for the position of seasonal park ranger, besides focusing on law enforcement and medical and safety experience, asks about outdoor skills (e.g., hiking, rock climbing, and canoeing); leadership and ability as a tour guide; experience in dramatic arts; operation and repair of equipment (e.g., chain saws and fire-fighting equipment) and vehicles (e.g., farm equipment and boats); knowledge of archaeological and historical preservation; and ability to work with people of varying ages, abilities, and backgrounds.

ADVICE

The tougher the job market, the more useful it is to heed those who have preceded you. It is important to actively gather and consider the advice of professionals in the field as you embark on, and progress in, your career.

Get as much experience as you can. Experience is absolutely a prerequisite for getting jobs beyond the entry level in parks and outdoor recreation. One way to gain valuable experience is to attend a school that has a cooperative education program with the agency for which you would ultimately like to work, or regularly receives internship opportunities. If you do a good job, you might be hired full time on completion of your degree.

The breadth and professionalism of your work experience is important.

Think carefully about what you most want to learn and gear your part-time, seasonal, or volunteer positions toward that goal. If you are interested in parks administration and management, gain experience on management issues, not biological inventories. Consider starting your career at the state or local level, where competition is not as harsh and opportunities are more likely to be tailored to your desires.

Master needed computer skills. Parks management, like all other environmental work, is finding more and more uses for the power of computers. Visit a government or private parks employer near you, learn about their computer systems, and then master them. Having hands-on knowledge of geographic information systems, advanced databases, and other uses will help immensely and make you competitive over those who lack these skills.

Start with seasonal work. The entry-level job in the parks and outdoor recreation field is the seasonal position. Few people are hired for full-time jobs without previous seasonal experience. Seasonal positions are found in all areas of park operations, and include jobs as interpreters, law enforcement workers, park rangers, laborers, researchers, and recreation programmers. When possible, seek the highest level of seasonal work that you are competitive for. Try to avoid having only the most common skills, gained by doing the most common tasks.

Use your college classes and projects to help employers. Consider the many issues and trends listed at the beginning of this chapter. Parks and recreation managers and professionals are seeking innovative solutions to these problems and also want to know what people in other parts of the country are doing to resolve them. Why not write a paper on an issue of interest to you in cooperation with the local parks director, or with data from a national urban forest? The staff will get to know you as a smart professional, you will provide valuable information on a problem of real interest, you will probably have more fun and, as an added bonus, earn a better grade! Ask professors for help on using this advice.

Understand the priority problems of parks that interest you. Every park, park system, ecotourism outfit, and nature center has specific problems. People who take a little time to understand what they are and think about proposed solutions are way ahead of their competitors. Is the park overrun with a particular nonnative species? Is it trying to provide more environmental education on the same budget? Perhaps it wants to increase attendance by people of color. Seek employment at those parks that have problems that you feel strongly about.

SUMMARY

Parks and outdoor recreation breaks down into five broad categories: administration, interpretation, natural resource management, research, and operations and maintenance. Demographic shifts are bringing changes to all parks and outdoor recreation organizations. The multiple, simultaneous, and often conflicting pressures of reduced budgets, special needs, endangered species, demands for urban recreation, low salaries, and other issues present parks and recreation organizations with both demand for, and obstacles to, change.

Salaries will increase somewhat, and demand for well-trained professionals will expand this area more strongly through 2005. However, competition for jobs will continue to be fierce and only the most persistent and qualified applicants will find permanent employment. Education and especially seasonal experience are extremely important for the competitive job seeker.

CASE STUDY

Boston's Emerald Necklace

Today's parks and recreation professionals must reach beyond park boundaries to form partnerships with individuals and organizations who have a stake in the health of our parks, as illustrated by this case study from Boston.

Between 1878 and 1895, Frederick Law Olmsted designed and built an interconnected series of parks throughout the city of Boston that has been dubbed "The Emerald Necklace." The premiere landscape architect of his day, Olmsted was the designer of some of America's most treasured open spaces, including New York's Central Park. More than 100 years after its creation, the parks of the Emerald Necklace remain a vital resource for Boston, as well as a challenge for parks and recreation professionals who struggle to maintain the Olmsted legacy while meeting the needs of a diverse population in the 21st century.

The Emerald Necklace comprises nine parks connected by parkways that form a 1,000-acre chain of greenspace that weaves through and around the heart of Boston. Olmsted designed six of these parks: Back Bay Fens, Muddy River Improvement, Jamaica Park, Arnold Arboretum, and Franklin Park. He also created a series of connecting parkways (Fenway, Park Drive, Riverway, Jamaicaway, and the Arborway) to link with Commonwealth Avenue and the existing Boston Common and Public Garden. The Common and Public Garden, at the heart of old Boston, are now considered part of the "Necklace."

By the late 1970s, much of the Emerald Necklace was overgrown and neglected. In fact, a few parts still are. In the 1980s, however, there was a renaissance of interest in Olmsted parks across the nation, and public demand for restoration began to grow. In Massachusetts, this took the form of a 1983 statewide bond bill called the Olmsted Landscape Preservation Program. The bond issue provided crucially needed funding and began the process of restoring the Emerald Necklace parks. Since then, "tens of millions of dollars have been spent on capital improvements to the parks," says Fran Beatty, senior landscape architect for historic parks with the City of Boston Parks Department.

The renaissance of the Emerald Necklace didn't just happen. It was made possible by years of grassroots efforts, according to Richard Heath, executive director of the Boston Greenspace Alliance. "A constituency of residents had been forming since 1975 to focus sustained attention on the parks of Necklace," Heath says. "The Franklin Park Coalition, the Fenway Alliance, and others are largely responsible for this success. Without these activists, there would have been no pressure for the preservation program."

Each park has its own set of management issues and serves a diverse range of recreation needs. One of the biggest challenges, however, is for the four distinct public agencies who are responsible for managing different pieces of the Emerald Necklace to do so in such a way that the public sees a seamless park system. Those agencies are the Boston Parks Department, the Metropolitan District Commission (MDC), the town of Brookline, and Harvard University. When the Emerald Necklace Master Plan was completed in 1987 after two years of public process, "nobody was talking to anybody," says Beatty. "We are leap years away from that point in time now," Beatty continues, "The Boston Parks Department maintenance director talks to the Brookline and the MDC maintenance directors. Now we have a group of people who are willing to work together for the greater good." This cross-agency cooperation and partnering is one of the essential elements to the successful restoration and continued operation of the Emerald Necklace.

The two volume Emerald Necklace Master Plan is, in part, a guide for three of the managing public agencies: the city of Boston Parks Department, the town of Brookline, and the MDC. In 1996, these three organizations signed a memorandum of agreement in which they formally agreed to share resources, coordinate efforts, and work on joint projects. The fourth managing agency, Harvard University, is not included in the master plan. Harvard manages the plant collections of the Arnold Arboretum, while the city of Boston owns the park and is responsible for the infrastructure of roads, boundaries, walls, and utility lines. According to Beatty, the Arboretum collections are in good hands with Harvard: "They have sustained a high level of maintenance at the Arboretum. They also have a computer database which chronicles all the plant diseases they've encountered and every treatment that has been applied to the plants and how they responded." The main reason Harvard is able to maintain the Arboretum at a higher level than the other parks is they have a professional management staff and a park-specific maintenance crew.

Much like the problems plaguing our national parks, underfunded operations and research combined with an overburdened staff in the Boston Parks Department is a chronic problem. As Beatty says: "You can have all good intentions, but resources are stretched tight." There are only two certified arborists responsible for the whole city of Boston. Horticulturists tend the public parks and squares over the whole city. But there are no arborists or horticulturists solely dedicated to the Emerald Necklace parks. "We need to be creative about attracting an endowment so that we can operate off of the dividends and hire horticulture crews which are so necessary to the health of the Necklace. Many of the plantings have not been maintained at all, but somehow they've retained their basic shape and survived," says Beatty. The ongoing challenge evolves into a question of who will manage the endowment and make sure that cross-jurisdictional issues are resolved at a policy level and a consensus level among the managing agencies. Currently funding for the parks owned and managed by the Boston Parks Department comes from the city's budget, as well as a variety of private sources, trust funds, and state and federal grants. The Olmsted Landscape Preservation Program provides funding through the state department of Environmental Management.

The $25 to $30 million spent on the Emerald Necklace parks in the last ten years ($10 million spent on the Boston Common alone) focused primarily on the "furniture" of the parks, which was a term Olmsted used to refer to the buildings, bridges, benches, gates, fountains, and fences. According to Beatty, this part of the park system restoration was relatively easy to implement, because identifying broken bridges or fences is straightforward, whereas identifying ecological problems is a little more involved. "Everything is an evolution . . . now that we've done the capital work the challenge for the future is to improve the ecology of the Emerald Necklace," says Beatty. Currently the two big ecological concerns are the health of the Muddy River and restoration of the system's woodlands.

The Muddy River was designed as a drainage way for the park system, however two main obstacles to that purpose have necessitated an examination of the river's health. The first problem involves the river's flat grade and shallow depth, which results in a lack of velocity. The second concern is the presence of tall reeds, called phragmites, which have grown across the river at several points, further impeding the water flow. The Boston Parks Department is working with the surrounding communities and the U.S. Army Corps of Engineers to develop a list of options for remediation from which a course of action will be decided on.

"The Army Corps has been involved in the Muddy River issue for the last four or five years," says Beatty. They've hired water quality experts and soil experts to determine what drains into the river and evaluate the sediment in the river for contaminants to better determine clean-up requirements and associated costs. The goal is to create a system of water where fish can live and to limit what drains into the river so that it's as clean as it can be. "Restoring the river to ecological health is not the only goal of the project," Beatty notes. "From a process point of view, the Emerald Necklace has some unique concerns," he explains. "Because it is an historic landmark, we must chart a course between conservation laws and preservation laws, which don't always overlap perfectly."

The woodlands restoration initiative, the other primary ecological concern, is still in its infancy. The first step in putting the understory back into the Emerald Necklace is to get all the parks on a computer mapping system to identify existing conditions and track changes to the forested areas of the system. According to Heath, The Emerald Necklace Conservancy, an initiative of the Boston Greenspace Alliance, was created to focus sustained attention on the two-volume master plan, unite and enlarge the constituency for the Emerald Necklace, and identify alternative sources of funds for Emerald

Necklace maintenance. "The Conservancy established a steering committee in August of 1996 which included the [Boston] Parks Department. It identified the forests of the system as the single biggest maintenance issue for which the least resources were available. Franklin Park was selected as the pilot project because, at 110 acres, it is the largest contiguous stand of trees in the park system," Heath says.

In August 1997, the University of Massachusetts–Amherst Forestry Department was selected by the Greenspace Alliance, in consultation with the Boston Parks Department, to conduct the initial survey and prepare the computer base. Field work began in October 1997. The first step was to lay out sixty, one-tenth-of-an-acre plots in which all trees over 4 inches in diameter were inventoried along with understory conditions. According to Heath, "The Franklin Park Coalition provided volunteer help for all the field work." When completed, the computer based maps will be contributed to the Boston Parks Department. Identification of funding sources is underway to begin a phased implementation project in cooperation with the parks department. This geographic information system mapping project is an example of the public/private partnerships that have existed in the Emerald Necklace for over twenty years.

Finally, an issue that all parks face is how to balance preservation and public access. In the Emerald Necklace, the most difficult areas are the Boston Common and Jamaica Park, according to Beatty. In 1990 the first edition of the Boston Common management plan was published to provide guidelines on how events that take place on the Common are run. It was developed through public process and provided for crowd control, clean up, and restoring of the land to the condition it was in before the event.

Jamaica Park is another story. Beatty describes the issue bluntly: "It has become so popular that everyone wants to be biking and rollerblading on the paths. It's really overburdened. I think Jamaica Park needs a rest at the moment, but what are you going to do? Put up a fence? Where would people go? If we could at least make the path around Ward Pond (part of the Muddy River improvement) walkable, people could go there instead of Jamaica Park. It is wild and overgrown, and we need to reclaim some of it, but there is a constituency that advocates for the wildness. Compounding the issue is people coming from outside the state to use this regional resource. It becomes an issue of democracy and equal access. Some people don't want to consider the communal aspect of their public parks which requires that their use of the park doesn't impinge on someone else's use. A management plan to address the Jamaica Park issues is up and coming."

The responsibility for implementing the restoration of Olmsted's park design master plan is daunting for both the community and the Boston Parks Department. Olmsted's plans and intentions for the Emerald Necklace have had to be modified for modern times; the automobile alone has created dramatic changes. Beatty says: "A lot of people quote Olmsted, but few really know what he'd do. One really has to be inside Olmsted's ideology to be able to get out there and try to do it. As much as possible we'll try to recapture the visual aesthetics he was after."

Olmsted's intent for park usage was that they be democratic places where people of all classes could come together in pursuit of a common interest. Beatty believes that the demographics of usage in Franklin Park and Jamaica Park (J.P.) are living up to Olmsted's wish. "J.P. really has a multiethnic and socioeconomically diverse visitor population. That sociology of place that he was seeking happened." Olmsted had a fervent belief in the value of natural scenery near densely settled urban centers. That belief transcends the 120 years since Olmsted began designing the Emerald Necklace, and is evident in the high value Americans place on urban parks today.

PROFILES

Jackie Henman
Park Ranger
Sequoia and Kings Canyon National Parks
Three Rivers, California

Park rangers perform a variety of duties every day. They can be called into any situation requiring immediate attention, and must draw on skills from a wide range of disciplines.

Jackie Henman is a front-country ranger at Sequoia and Kings Canyon National Parks. Like most park rangers, she had an early desire to get into the profession. "When I was in [the] fourth grade I had to write an essay about what I wanted to be when I grew up. I wrote that I wanted to be a forest ranger because I liked being off by myself in the woods. Nothing could be farther from the truth than that! My friends and relatives think I spend my days hiking over hill and dale. But no, it's very much a people-oriented line of work."

Jackie has two undergraduate degrees, a bachelor of arts in French from Kansas University, and a bachelor of science in Outdoor Recreation with an emphasis in Environmental Interpretation from Colorado State University. Her early work with the National Park Service (NPS) was on the interpretation side rather than the ranger side. Her first seasonal job was in Rocky Mountain National Park at the Alpine visitors center. She worked for the NPS five seasons while she was at Colorado State, including an internship one season at Olympic National Park in Washington.

After graduating from Colorado State she endeavored to get a permanent job with the NPS for about six months. She says: "It's tough to go from seasonal to permanent because you have to get federal status." Finally a former supervisor at Rocky Mountain National Park told her of a mail and file clerk job open at the park. He petitioned the hiring supervisor to hire Jackie, giving her "that magical federal status."

Her next job was at Grand Canyon National Park as assistant supervisor at the Yavapai Museum where she worked for four years. Then, ready for a new challenge, she began applying for ranger jobs. She was hired at Mount Rushmore, where she worked for a year and a half. During that time she took a ten-week program at the Federal Law Enforcement Training Center.

In 1993 Jackie was hired at Sequoia and Kings Canyon National Park. She is a patrol ranger with a dual function to protect the resources and the visitors. She emphasizes that resource protection is a major part of her job, as well as the most satisfying. Resource protection involves a wide range of duties from educating visitors on why they can't chop down trees for their fires, to hiking a bear cub five miles into the backcountry in a cage, to surveillance of caves and other natural resources to catch resource violators.

At Sequoia/Kings Canyon a lot of time is spent on (black) bear management. At any given time there are six or seven problem bears. Jackie keeps mental tabs on where they are and what they're up to so as to determine which one(s) are responsible for breaking into cars or interacting with visitors. She says: "The hardest thing I ever had to do was destroy a bear I was really fond of. We have techniques to avoid getting attached to the wildlife, but this bear was very personal to me because I spent so much time trying to protect her, keeping people away from her so she wouldn't become more aggressive."

All rangers have special projects for which they're responsible. One of Jackie's projects is writing a reference manual for new employees called *Ranger Operating Procedures*. But this is just a small part of what she might be doing on a given day.

A recent day begins for Jackie with changing the bandage on a mule who had gotten wrapped in barbed wire a few months earlier. She enjoys working with the "stock," about seventy head of horses and mules. On this day she helps out by feeding them. Next she checks the location of some cattle that have trespassed into the park. Then she begins routine patrols. While on patrol she sees several bears, a lot of deer, and "a beautiful coyote." She stops to watch the coyote at a distance for a while, trying to determine whether it might become a problem coyote. She says: "It always alarms me when a wild animal doesn't run away when you're stopped nearby." Finally she arrives at the office and works on administrative tasks lingering from the summer patrol staff she supervised. She tells the person in charge of snow surveys when she will be available to help him. Then a visitor who was cited for having loaded firearms in a motor home comes in. He proves that he has paid the citation and Jackie returns his weapons to him. She also writes a report on a coworker over a domestic problem from the night before.

Most of the entry-level to journeyman-level NPS employees are required to live in park housing. Like any small community, domestic problems arise and need to be addressed. She says that working and living in isolation from urban areas, you get close to coworkers because you live, work, and socialize with them.

Jackie says: "We're at the convenience of the government and have to be stationed in the park so that we can respond to emergency situations." She cautions: "If a person considering this career wants a nine-to-five job and their weekends to be their own, they should be warned off this job."

One of the reasons Jackie loves her job is that no day is typical. At any moment a call from dispatch can change the course of a day. These call-outs involve everything from helping a disabled vehicle, to helping put out a wild-land or structural fire, to flying into the backcountry to help someone who is lost, injured, or sick. Jackie likes being able to help people in need.

Jackie says that most park rangers get into the profession because of some physical, spiritual, or emotional connection to the resources that makes it very soul-satisfying work. A successful park ranger must have that strong desire to protect something close to their hearts to put up with the demands of the job. Jackie describes the job of a park ranger this way: "It's not just a career, it's a way of life."

Rick Trostel
Guide
Alaska Discovery
Juneau, Alaska

Ecotourism is a rapidly expanding field. An ecovacation allows people to spend their leisure dollars seeing some of the most pristine places. This helps the environment by providing the often-remote surrounding communities with alternatives to exploitation of natural resources for economic growth and survival.

Rick Trostel of Alaska Discovery, a wilderness adventure guiding company, has had a lifelong "love affair with the wilderness experience." He began guiding trips after his freshman year at Oberlin College, which ranged from seven days, to a thirty-five-day combination canoeing, backpacking, rock climbing trip. But he traces this love affair all the way back to his conception: "I have observed my parents nudging and winking when they talk about a kayak trip they took . . . about nine months before I was born," he says.

During senior year in high school Rick took a trip with Outward Bound. The summer between high school and college, he went on a three-week canoe trip in northern Ontario, offered as a three-credit biology class on the natural history of the north woods. Rick rates this as "one of the peak experiences of [his] life—socially, spiritually, and physically."

Throughout college the affair continued. He majored in biology because it was a "real" field that would prepare him for a "real job in the real world." But Rick confesses that his course selection depended on whether he could get outdoors during the labs. In addition to summer guide jobs, while in college he gained related experience as an intern at an environmental education center, and teaching a course called "Wilderness Philosophy, Policy and Practice" as part of Oberlin's experimental college. Among other things, Rick trained and guided his students on a week-long trip in the Smokey Mountains. He says: "This was a more powerful experience than any course I ever took with the exception of the freshman canoe trip."

After graduation, Rick worked as a docent at a natural history museum. He also worked for the YMCA as a wilderness guide and naturalist before going into the Peace Corps where he served as a forestry volunteer in the Domincan Republic. After more than three years Rick returned to the states.

It wasn't long before his wilderness love affair took him to a remote Eskimo village in Alaska to teach school. "I thought I'd died and gone to heaven in Manokotak," Rick says, but his wife felt too isolated being a 400-mile plane ride from Anchorage!

After spending two unfulfilling years in Minnesota, Rick and his family moved to Juneau where he and his wife got jobs as elementary Montessori teachers. Rick learned of the opportunity to work at Alaska Discovery from a parent who also works there. After two trips as an apprentice, he was leading trips of his own, "thrilled to be back in the business."

Most of the trips Rick guides are about a week long. A typical trip has ten guests. Most are in their thirties and forties, but have ranged from thirteen to seventy years old. Skill levels range from no camping experience at all, to recently summiting Mount McKinley.

On the day a group arrives, Rick meets his assistant at a small warehouse in Juneau where they pack food and equipment for the trip and confirm charter and commercial transportation for the trip. This done, he greets his group of "guests" (as he calls them) at their hotel, and holds a pretrip meeting. His goal is to help the guests feel relaxed and ready for their plunge into the wilderness, discussing "everything from potty procedure and bear safety, to last minute gear questions." The next morning everyone gets fitted for rain gear, rubber boots, and personal flotation devices (pfd) before setting off, usually on chartered boat or float plane.

A typical day in the field begins at 7:00 A.M. for Rick, though it varies depending on a variety of factors, such as tides, route for the day, exertions of the previous day, and nature of the group. Rick says he isn't a "morning person," but hits the ground running and doesn't stop until 11:00 P.M. or later. First he packs his personal gear, takes down his tent, and puts his things on the beach, estimating where the tide will be later when it is time to load the boats. This enables him to turn full attention to the group for the rest of the morning preparations. He begins getting breakfast for the group, which can be as simple as granola or as involved as french toast made from fresh-baked bread with sausages. He warns: "In my work, if you don't like cooking, then you don't like a large part of what I do." Guests often help out with the food preparation.

During breakfast Rick discusses the details of the day, covering such things as suggestions for packing kayaks, or what to look for in terms of wildlife and geology, generally expanding on the itinerary he laid out at dinner the previous evening. While his assistant helps the guests get their gear packed and down on the beach, he does dishes with the help of a couple of guests, packs up the kitchen, and sets aside lunch provisions in a duffle bag that will be readily accessible.

By 10:00 A.M. the group is usually on the water. Rick's responsibilities on the water include keeping the six kayaks "in reasonably safe proximity" and to share his enjoyment of the ride. He continually emphasizes that they are in no hurry to get there because they're already there. The group has periodic "floating powwows to discuss things as mundane as potty stops or as sublime as Leopold's land ethic." Rick says he often finds himself in the role of bartender or psychiatrist, listening to people's life stories. "There are few things I enjoy more than paddling a beautiful fjord, learning about how people live and conduct their lives in other parts of the world."

In the late afternoon the group arrives at their next campsite. Rick and his assistant help everyone find suitable tent sites. Then they set up the kitchen and cook dinner. While cooking dinner, Rick makes a batch of bread for the next day's lunch, which is baked after the dishes are done.

During dinner Rick tells the group what to expect the next day and brings up any issues requiring group decisions, such as an early start to catch a favorable tide, or a side trip to some point of beauty. Rick also makes a point of checking in with guests to see that things such as equipment, pace, and food are meeting their expectations. After dinner he always makes a little time for himself, going off to play his trumpet to relax.

On the last day of the trip, equipment is readied for transport. Once back in Juneau, the guests are taken to hotels, then Rick and his assistant go back to the warehouse to take care of leftover food, kitchen equipment, and gear. Then he submits receipts and a trip report to the Alaska Discovery office. That evening, he often sees his guests one last time for a farewell dinner at a restaurant in Juneau.

Ironically, the main drawback for Rick is loneliness. He misses his family and they miss him when he is gone for a week or two at a time. Also, after the intense social contact of a wilderness trip, he says goodbye to that group of people and starts all over with a new group. People who spend more time per year as a guide than Rick, and who don't have a spouse and children, may find it hard to sustain relationships with significant others due to extended separations. He says an introverted person might fare better with the loneliness factor. However, the intense social contact with people requires a wilderness guide to be communicative and able to effectively manage a wide range of personalities and skill levels with patience, caring, and diplomacy. Rick also says that the pay isn't great but, on the upside, you can't beat the view from his "kitchen" and "office"!

Why does he do it? Rick says: "As a naturalist, I am aware of the details of the natural environment around me. . . . I constantly engage my guests and myself in ecological, geological, and biological questions." But this is not the primary reason why he guides people into the wilderness. He says: "The spiritual element is my essential goal as a naturalist. I would be tickled if my guests could tell the difference between a Marbled Murrelet and a Pigeon Guillemot by the end of the trip, but I would be moved more by their love of the environment that supports these birds—a love that would move them to conserve this home for Murrelets, which is also a place of spiritual renewal for us humans."

Diana Foss
Conservation Scientist III
(Urban Biologist)
Sheldon Lake State Park and
Wildlife Management Area,
Nongame and Urban Program,
Wildlife Division,
Texas Parks and Wildlife Department
Houston, Texas

Jobs at parks located in and around urban centers differ from jobs in rural wilderness areas, primarily in terms of heavier visitor contact. This offers frequent opportunities to "make a difference" for the environment by educating ever-increasing numbers of visitors who live within minutes of parks.

Diana Foss, urban biologist at Sheldon Lake State Park and Wildlife Management Area, was introduced to her profession through her father's work as a geologist. "My family went on long vacations wherever he worked. . . . We spent many hours hiking and camping. . . . Along the way, I learned about endangered species and that many of the actions humans take may cause the reduction in wildlife populations."

In high school, Diana decided on a career in public environmental education, hoping to help solve environmental problems by educating people as to what causes them. She was impressed by the work of women in the field such as Joan Embery (San Diego Zoo), Dian Fossey (gorilla research), and Jane Goodall (chimpanzee research), reasoning that if they could do such fascinating work, she could too. However, after researching possible career tracks, she learned that it was difficult to get field-research jobs due to limited government funding. The summer she graduated from high school, Diana and her family followed her father's work to Alaska where they "spent the summer trailing through the tundra after him. It was fantastic!" she says.

Diana began college, majoring in zoology, at Texas A&M University. At the end of her sophomore year she was "tired of looking through microscopes all the time and wanted more hands-on opportunities with wildlife." She changed her major and graduated with a B.S. in wildlife and fisheries sciences, taking such courses as mammalogy, ornithology, ichthyology, herpetology, ethology, botany, organic chemistry, and astronomy. She broadened her technical and scientific training by taking several parks and recreation coursesto learn such things as trail design, park interpretation, and presentation style.

During college, Diana assisted several professors with various research projects and wildlife studies. She recalls one study where she "had to count thousands of blackbirds each evening at a roost site." She also volunteered at the local science museum, Brazos Valley Museum, where she worked at odd jobs, such as cleaning stuffed specimens and cataloging slides. The summer after her junior year she completed an independent research course in which she compared the results of a controlled burn in a prairie ecosystem at Armand Bayou Nature Center.

The summer after graduation Diana worked as a summer camp teacher back at Brazos Valley Museum, which included a creek with nature trails. She was responsible for creating and teaching nature-related activities to six- to eight-year olds, during week-long summer camps. Also during that summer, a former professor told her about a job as an education director at the Texas Zoo, a native animal zoo. She was hired and worked there for ten years. Her duties included designing education programs, conducting field trips to natural areas for students, organizing a volunteer program, and creating native plant areas on the zoo grounds.

Diana left the zoo in 1993 to accept her current job. The program in which she works began that year as well. As a result, her duties constantly change. Like other environmental professionals in this section of the book, each day is different for Diana. Because she works in an urban area, "most of [her] time is spent with people, not with wildlife."

A recent day for Diana begins at 8:30 A.M. She responds to phone and email messages, does paperwork, and prepares materials for a 10:00 A.M. fishing clinic and upcoming meetings. A school bus arrives at 10:00, and she introduces the students to Sheldon Lake State Park with a standard safety lecture. Then she acquaints them with the equipment and techniques before taking them to the fishing pond. She, along with other park rangers and volunteers, assists the students with untangling lines and unhooking fish. At 11:00 she leaves the clinic "in the park ranger's capable hands, and wash[es] the fish smell off her hands."

At 11:30 she meets committee members from a local school, as well as with representatives from the U.S. Fish and Wildlife Service, Natural Resources Conservation Service, and County Extension Service to plan the development of a school-yard habitat. She walks the site looking at soils, sun/shade patterns, drainage patterns, and accessibility for wildlife and students to determine the types of habitats possible for the site. The meeting results in an action plan.

At 1:00 she gives a seed-planting demonstration to 128 students at a local elementary school. They are participating in the "Growing Wild" program to create butterfly and hummingbird habitat on their school grounds by planting species chosen for their food benefit to both caterpillar and adult butterfly, as well as hummingbirds.

At 3:00 Diana meets with city planners and architects to discuss the renovation of a city park. She suggests the use of native plant species to reduce the amount of maintenance needed, as well as to provide food and shelter for wildlife.

At 4:30 Diana gets back to her office, catches up on paperwork, and prepares information packets, requested by phone and visitors, for mailing the next day. At 5:30 she is able to "relax, enjoy the sunset, and take some time to 'smell the flowers' by weeding the Wildscape Demonstration Garden." This area requires routine maintenance to remain beautiful for park visitors. Diana enjoys gardening and working after hours when Houston's heat and humidity are lower and the park is quiet.

The least enjoyable part of the job for Diana is the paperwork, for which there never seems to be enough time. In addition, she regrets not having more time to conduct wildlife research programs. Her favorite part of the job is seeing the results of her efforts. "I work with people every day, encouraging them to gain knowledge and perhaps change their attitudes about various wildlife issues. When a parks department establishes a new piece of wildlife habitat, or a when a child experiences the joy of seeing a butterfly land on a flower he or she grew in the classroom, that's when I see that I've made a positive difference."

RESOURCES

Contact individual government agencies for information on application processes for full-time and seasonal employment, or contact the nearest Office of Personnel Management. Information on cooperative education programs can be obtained from agencies and schools. Each agency can provide materials that acquaint you with the agency's objectives, the range of full-time and seasonal jobs available, and the application process.

Amazing WebDirectory for Parks and Recreation. "Earth's biggest environmental search engine." Http://www.webdirectory.com/Parks_and/Recreation.

American Association for Leisure and Recreation. Supports members in the development of leisure programs. Sponsors educational programs at conventions. Publishes information sheets on twenty-five separate careers in parks and outdoor recreation. 1900 Association Drive, Reston, VA 22091. (703) 476-3472. Http://www.social. com/health/nhic/data/hr1300/hr1393.html.

American Recreation Coalition. Works on public/private partnerships to enhance and protect outdoor recreational opportunities and the resources on which such experiences are based. Conducts research, organizes and conducts national conferences and meetings, and disseminates information through newsletters, columns, and other mediums. Monitors legislative and regulatory proposals that influence recreation and works with government agencies to study public policy issues that will shape future recreational opportunities. 1225 New York Avenue, NW, Suite 450, Washington, DC 20005. (202) 682-9530. Http://www.funoutdoors.com/arc.

The Ecotourism Society. Unites conservation and travel worldwide by assisting professionals who are working to make ecotourism a genuine tool for conservation and sustainable development. Offers training, education, and internships. Maintains a bookstore of relevant publications. P.O. Box 755, North Bennington, VT 05257. (802) 447-2121. Http://www.ecotourism.org.

National Parks and Conservation Association. A private citizens' organization dedicated to promoting and improving national parks. Provides extensive membership services, publishes *National Parks* (bimonthly), and organizes local groups near national parks (NPCA Park Activist Network). Also has job listings. 1776 Massachusetts Ave., NW, Washington, DC 20036. (202) 223-6722. Http://www. npc.org.

National Parks Employment Data. Book listing over 130 national parks, preserves, monuments, and seashores, as well as over 750 employers. Sections on federal employment, private sector employment, and how and where to apply. Interviews of current and former park employees and personnel managers. List of the thirty employers most likely to hire you, as well as job search and resume help. 124 North San Francisco Street, Suite 100, Flagstaff, Arizona 86001. (520) 779-5300. Http://www.gorp.com/nped.

National Park Service. For jobs in national parks, preserves, monuments, recreation, and wilderness areas, search for "cool works" on the Web. P.O. Box 37127, Washington, DC 20013-7127. (202) 208-4747. Http://www.coolworks.com/showme/natprk.htm.

National Recreation and Park Association. Association of parks and recreation professionals and citizens' advocates. Holds annual meetings and conducts professional development activities. Provides technical and general information in publications and periodicals, including *Parks & Recreation* (monthly); *Employ* (nine times a year), which is designed to assist individuals in preparing for the job search; and *Parks and Recreation Opportunities Job Bulletin* (twenty-two times a year). A Job Mart is held at the association's annual conference. 2775 S. Quincy St., Suite 300, Arlington, VA 22206-2204. (703) 820-4940. Http://www.nrpa.org.

Outdoor Recreation Coalition of American. Preserves and promotes human powered outdoor recreation industry. Has a government affairs page on current legislative and policy issues. Compiles industry research and information in its *State of the Industry* report. Sponsors an international conference of outdoor recreation and education. P.O. Box 1319, Boulder, CO 80306. (303) 444-3353. Http://www.orga.org.

Student Conservation Association. Develops internships in natural resource management for students at various levels. P.O. Box 550, Charlestown, NH 03603. (603) 543-1700. Http://www.sca-inc.org.

U.S. Department of the Interior On the Web. The DOI Automated Vacancy Announcement Distribution System (AVADS) provides electronic access to job listings, updated each Thursday. Gives application guidelines for each agency within the DOI. Http://www.info.er.usgs.gov/doi/avads/index.html.

14 Forestry

AT A GLANCE

Employment:

Over 80,000 environmental professionals work on forest issues, including 60,000 foresters and forestry technicians. The forest products industry as a whole generates over 1.6 million jobs in the United States.

Demand:

High growth (10 to 20 percent through 2005) for foresters and conservation scientists; low growth (1 percent or less) for forestry technicians and general workers

Breakdown:

Public sector, 40 percent (23 percent federal, 17 percent
  state and local)
Private sector, 48 percent
Nonprofit sector, 2 percent
Education, 10 percent

Key Job Titles:

Aircraft pilot
Arborist
Archaeologist
Biologist
Botanist
Civil engineer
Consulting forester
Ecologist
Forest entomologist

Forester
Forest hydrologist
Forest manager
Forest pathologist
Forestry technician
Horticulturist
Natural resource manager
Procurement manager
Soil conservationist
Range conservationist
Recreation manager
Urban forester
Urban planner
Wildlife biologist

Influential Organizations:

American Forests
American Forestry Association
Association of Consulting Foresters
International Society of Arboriculture
Rainforest Alliance
Sierra Club
Society of American Foresters
USDA Forest Service
The Wilderness Society
World Resources Institute

Salary:

Entry-level salaries range from $18,000 to $32,000; more experienced forestry professionals earn $35,000 to $50,000. Top salaries range from $60,000 to over $100,000 for senior managers.

Preservation and careful management of the world's forests is one of the most important goals of the environmental professions, and for good reason. Healthy forests are crucial to the Earth's ecological health. The Sustainable Forestry Working Group reminds us that "Forests provide habitats for fish, mammals, insects, plants, and humans. Forests hold water, and hold it back, providing steady supplies to cities downstream and preventing floods, mud-slides, and soil runoff that fill streams and ruin fish runs. They provide non-wood products and jobs from medicines to hunting and other forms of recreation. Finally, forests are necessary for absorbing carbon dioxide and are essential to reversing global climate change."

Nearly one-third of the United States is forested, with about two-thirds of forests classifed as "timberland." Of this land, 59 percent is owned by private, nonindustrial concerns (a big surprise to many people). 14 percent of timberland belongs to the forest products industry, and 27 percent is owned by federal, state, and local governments.

No issue in the environmental world is more filled with controversy than forestry. There is even debate about what a forest *is*. The Working Group mentioned earlier asks: "Thousands—perhaps millions—of trees, many of them identical clones, carefully planted in neat rows: is it a farm or a forest?" Whatever it is, plantation forestry is the present and the likely future. The U.S. Forest Service has even published studies suggesting that more major wildlife species thrive in the young plantation forests than in old growth environments.

Forestry abounds with such claims and counterclaims. Activists of various stripes exchange dueling data that show that U.S. forests have declined to a shadow of their former glory (measured by the remaining "old growth" forests) *or* that the total amount of forests today is only 20 percent less than the forests we had when the Mayflower arrived (using broader definitions).

Behind the controversies (or because of them), something remarkable is happening in forest management. The head of the U.S. Forest Service (tellingly part of the Department of Agriculture) now embraces policies that would have been rejected out-of-hand just a few years ago. Multinational forest companies launch serious efforts to be certified as "sustainable" foresters, and giant utility and petroleum firms work with environmental groups to plant millions of trees in an effort to earn credits toward slowing global climate change. Central American nations move to protect large tracts of forest for parks and wilderness areas. The idea of an actual ban on commercial logging in our own national forests is seriously considered by many legislators. These are exciting times for forestry professionals.

WHAT IS FORESTRY?

"There are five traditional management uses of the forest: timber, water, wildlife, recreation, and grazing," says Greg Smith, director of science and education for the Society of American Foresters. "In the past, timber received most of the attention. A few years ago, there was a shift toward considering integrated uses of the forest. Now, the primary focus of forest management is on the sustainable management of a variety of goods and services derived from forests, only one of which is timber. Foresters now look at managing for the whole property rather than harvesting timber at the expense of degrading other resources. They are striving for a good balance."

Michael Dombeck, head of the U.S. Department of Agriculture's (USDA) Forest Service, is emphatic that forestry, conservation, and environmental protection must work together. Dombeck, a Ph.D. fisheries biologist, says that the Forest Service will balance its activities so that "no Forest Service program will have dominance over another. Timber is not more important than minerals, fisheries and wildlife, or recreation. Nor is wildlife and fisheries more important than timber, minerals, recreation, or range management."

Once characterized by a small number of professions (e.g., the jack-of-all-trades forester, the timber cruiser, and the fire fighter), forestry today is a diverse, specialized profession. Though "forester" and "forestry technician" are still by far the most prevalent job titles in the field, a big employer such as the Forest Service lists over 200 separate occupations, including aircraft pilot, civil engineer, ecologist, human resource developer, law enforcement officer, soil conservationist, surveyor, and more. When we talk about forestry, then, we're talking about all professionals who work on forest issues—not just foresters.

Forestry includes urban work—creating and preserving trees in urban areas and protecting nearby forests that protect critical watersheds. It requires specialists in fields such as entomology, forest genetics, forest hydrology, soils, planning, and forest economics. A great deal of forestry work is done throughout the world on tropical reforestation projects, as well as harvesting operations. Forestry now also includes professionals who provide recreational opportunities and assure the health of fish, plant, and wildlife habitats.

"There has been a shift away from pure forestry and a move toward ecology, adding people like ecologists and terrestrial or aquatic biologists" to the occupations needed to manage a forest, says Ken Holtje, ecosystem management program leader with the U.S. Forest Service.

Finally, forestry today is also about understanding people and their interactions with the forest. Greg Smith says: "now there is a definite social science

Forestry today includes the identification and protection of endangered plant and animal species, requiring the help of biologists, botanists, and other professionals.

component which includes rural sociology, archaeology, cultural appreciation, economics, and more."

HISTORY AND BACKGROUND

Obviously, forest use has been practiced for thousands of years. People have been cutting, clearing, burning, gathering from, and otherwise using the world's forests since the dawn of civilization. Europeans began developing professional approaches to forest management at a time when Americans could still afford to view forests as a seemingly inexhaustible resource.

In the 1800s, forest practices in the United States for the most part amounted to disorganized pillaging without regard for sustaining timber production, much less water quality or wildlife habitat. The U.S. Land Office was responsible for federal lands, but lack of funding and skilled workers (made worse by corruption) rendered management virtually impossible. Indiscriminate abuse of forests was one of the many excesses that helped create the conservation movement in the 1890s. New forestry legislation was one response.

Professional forestry in the United States might be said to have started in 1893, when Gifford Pinchot opened an office in New York City and called himself a consulting forester, based on his training in Europe. His ideas so impressed presidents William McKinley, Grover Cleveland, and Theodore Roosevelt that he was able to transform the nation's forest practices and help establish the Forest Service. The changing mission of the Forest Service is a reasonable guide to the history of forestry in America generally.

For sixty years, forest management was driven by "science for economics" and was primarily about timber harvest and fire protection. Beginning in 1960, as the environmental movement grew, forestry in the United States began its evolution to a complex, multiple-use focus.

A review of our forestry legislation over the last century clearly shows the changing history of forest management approaches.

Forest Organic Act of 1897. This act began to make a science of forestry. It authorized the president to establish national forests to provide "favorable conditions of water flow, and to furnish a continuous supply of timber. . . ." Although the act sets some strict limits on timber harvesting, the statute provided no forest management guidelines.

Agricultural Appropriation Act of 1905. This act put the force of law behind forestry by giving foresters the authority to enforce violations of forest regulations. The Forestry Division then changed its name to the Forest Service. By 1909, the service controlled 148 million acres and had become a highly regarded government agency. Pinchot, whose ideas still guide much of what we consider forestry to be, wrote: "Conservation is the foresighted utilization, preservation, and renewal of forests, waters, lands, and minerals for the greatest good of the greatest number of people for the longest time."

Multiple-Use/Sustained Yield Act of 1960. This act formally established a multiple use policy by stating "outdoor recreation, range, timber, watershed and wildlife and fish" shall be subject to multiple use management. It was intended to give each of the listed resources equal status in the eyes of federal resource managers. The terms of this act supplement and refine the Forest Organic Act; redefine the functions of the National Forests; explicitly recognize wilderness as providing a habitat for wildlife, as well as opportunities for hunting, fishing, scientific research, and other enjoyment of the outdoors; and establish that the management of all these uses is a part of forestry.

The Wilderness Act of 1964. This act created the National Wilderness Preservation System with an initial endowment of 9.1 million acres of national forest lands. Congress expanded the system to almost 91 million acres through dozens of separate laws. By the end of 1989, the Forest Service administered nearly 33 million acres of wilderness, which must by law retain its "primeval character and influence, without permanent improvements or human habitation, and be protected and managed so as to preserve its natural conditions. . . ."

Endangered Species Act of 1973 (ESA). A revolutionary piece of legislation that has dramatically affected forest management practices in the United States. The ESA is designed to protect endangered plants and animals and the habitats on which they depend. This legislation established two categories for species at risk. "Endangered" species are those that are deemed to be at immediate risk of extinction and probably cannot survive without direct human intervention. "Threatened" species are found in abundance in some areas, but are declining in total numbers. Finally, conservation professionals also try to track "rare" species that do not yet fall under the ESA's protection.

The ESA has played a major role in recent forest management history. When the United States used the ESA to protect the Northern Spotted Owl, which lives throughout the heavily forested areas of the Pacific Northwest, the result was a collision between environmentalists and loggers that shook the world of forestry. It was several years before an uneasy balance was reached in the form of a settlement between commercial forestry operations, activists, government agencies, and local communities. Carrying out logging activities that do not threaten species protected under the act is one of the most difficult tasks faced by foresters today and one of the "drivers" that creates employment for environmental professionals in the field.

Forest and Rangeland Renewable Resources Research Act of 1978. This act authorizes the agency to conduct and cooperate in research to generate knowledge about protecting, managing, and using the renewable resources of forests and rangeland.

Cooperative Forestry Assistance Act of 1978 (as amended). This act authorizes cooperation and assistance to nonfederal forest landowners in forest management, timber production, insect and disease control, and fire prevention.

International Forestry Cooperation Act of 1990. This act authorizes the agency to work overseas and to provide technical and financial assistance for its international cooperative activities and research.

To access full texts of legislation, use the University of California's GPO gateway to the Government Printing Office at http://www.gpo.ucop.edu. In addition, you can find summaries of legislation affecting public lands at http://www.habitat-restoration.com.

In addition to federal legislation, be aware of state and local laws that affect management of private forest land. Find out about state legislation through "Newslink" Environmental's web links at http://www.caprep.com. There are over 600 state and local forest regulatory laws enacted across the U.S., 90 percent of which were enacted in the past ten years.

ISSUES AND TRENDS

Forestry is a rapidly changing field with a heavy crosscurrent of political, economic, financial, and technological trends that affect employment opportunities. Ten of these trends are outlined below.

MULTIPLE-USE FORESTS

As we have seen, forestry today is about managing our forests for multiple uses. This is easier said than done, as increasing (and conflicting) demands are placed on forests. According to the Food and Agricultural Organization of the United Nations, world demand for timber products will nearly double by 2050. In this country, demand for forest products will reach 25 billion cubic feet *annually* by that time, up from 18 billion in 1991.

These increases in production must happen while recreational and other uses of our forests are increasing. The Forest Service, for example, is now the "number one provider in America of the outdoor recreation experience" (exceeding the Park Service), according to James Lyon of the USDA.

In response to these changes, as well as recent legislation, Forest Service chief Michael Dombeck is restructuring the agency "in key areas such as: stream-side condition and health, water quality, watershed health, soil stability, noxious weed management, and endangered species habitat management and protection." These government actions are mirrored by similar policies in the private sector and at state and local agencies.

Each one of the concerns stated earlier (e.g., water quality and endangered species) would have been listed as a separate "issue and trend" a few years ago, calling for special (and separate) kinds of professionals. The trick today is to solve many concerns through integrated actions.

ECOSYSTEMS MANAGEMENT

One approach to achieve that integration is through ecosystems management. Ecosystems management is a five-year-old initiative at the Forest Service that calls for a more ecological approach to forestry. It is a hierarchical system of managing landscapes by ecological units, according to Ken Holtje, ecosystems management program leader in the eastern regional office. The objective of ecosystem management is to "maximize biodiversity in each ecosystem." The concepts of ecosystem management are being used to revise land management plans written in the early 1980s and issued in 1985 or 1986. The Forest Service is required to write new land management plans every fifteen years.

PROTECTING OLD-GROWTH FORESTS

Saving our remaining old-growth forests has given rise to numerous political battles. The case study in this chapter is about one such battle—over the Tongass forest in Alaska. Other examples are found throughout the nation, however. In the Pacific Northwest and northern California, there is fierce debate about how much old-growth forest to protect, and how best to do it. In the Northeast, activists have fought for years to protect portions of the 26-million-acre Northern Forest, which stretches across Maine, New Hampshire, Vermont, and New York. There are several reasons for aspiring forestry professionals to follow these battles, but here's an important one: to track whether or not environmentalists, government agencies, and the timber industry choose cooperative or adversarial approaches to problem solving. These high profile efforts have a domino effect throughout the environmental community and (as discussed in chapter 1) cooperative and voluntary efforts can create completely different employment patterns than those brought on by lawsuits and tight regulation.

CITIZEN INVOLVEMENT AND ACTIVISM

The need for forest management plans has helped fuel citizen activism on forest issues. Andy Stahl, a forester with the Sierra Club Legal Defense Fund in Eugene, Oregon, observes, "Several years ago, a small cottage industry cropped up whose mission was to appeal forest management plans proposed for the 156 national forests managed by the Forest Service. Now, citizens get involved by working with local organizations to devise their own management plans, lobbying their Washington representatives to push for action." Citizens of all stripes have opinions, and not all of them belong to the Sierra Club. A good example of an opposing view is the Quincy Library Group (QLG), which is composed of citizens who presented a management plan to the Forest Service for two national forests in California. The QLG plan, though touted as a consensus bill, is opposed by most environmental groups since it would more than double logging in a third of California's Sierra Nevada forests, destroying up to a quarter million acres of ancient forests.

Concerns about plans vary by region and involve below-cost timber sales, construction of roads in wilderness areas, clear-cutting of timber rather than selective harvesting, logging of old-growth timber, monoculture plantings in areas that previously had a variety of trees, and lack of wildlife protection, among others.

THE BUSINESS OF SUSTAINABLE FORESTRY

Forest products companies are under intense pressures. Costs alone are a sizable issue. Regulation and other factors will push production costs up by nearly 25 percent over the next thirty years using conventional logging practices. According to the Sustainable Forestry Working Group (which includes representatives from forestry companies, prominent forestry schools, the World Bank, and others), the wood products industry is going through a historic transition. Environmental laws and community pressure has made many past logging practices impossible to continue. In response, innovators throughout industry, academia, and the activist world are creating "sustainable forestry."

What is "sustainable forestry"? No single definition has emerged, but the general objectives seem clear. According to the Working Group, sustainable forestry means "making investments in research, mapping, planning, and training. It means managing . . . resources in ways that may raise initial costs but pay off in more efficient operations, less waste, and a better bottom line over the medium and longer terms. It means having neighbors . . . who are partners, rather than adversaries. It means being a leader in setting standards that optimize . . . environmental returns, rather than waiting to be regulated by outside forces."

In practice, sustainable forestry favors new logging practices over clearcuts, for example. It calls for large amounts of replanting relative to that harvested, assuring that loggers will plant more trees than they cut. Watersheds are to be rigorously protected, as are known bird and wildlife habitat needs. Time between harvests may be lengthened. Some forests of Weyerhaeuser Company (the world's largest private owner of standing softwood timber) are suggestive of what sustainable forestry might look like. Through the use of high-yield "plantations," the company produces quality wood on substantially fewer, continually regenerated acres, with a claim of much greater sustainability and less ecological damage.

ENVIRONMENTAL CERTIFICATION AND "GREEN" LABELING

Consumers of wood products—corporations, governments, and individuals—are skeptical of claims from individual companies that their products are produced in sustainable ways. They are even more skeptical when "green" claims come from the companies themselves. In response, certification and labeling programs have sprung up. So far, no certification program has been accepted by the industry as a whole. The Forest Stewardship Council (created in 1993 by environmental groups) certified some 2.3 million hectares of forest land as "sustainable" in its first three years, but this is just .5 percent of the world's woodlands. The Rainforest Alliance's "Smartwood" program is another certification attempt, along with a general set of principles developed by the American Forest and Paper Association. Don't expect sustainable forestry to really take off as a job creator until there is a more universally accepted certification and labeling program, perhaps from the International Organization of Standards (ISO).

GLOBAL CLIMATE CHANGE AND POLLUTION

Concern over global climate change impacts forestry in two ways. First, deforestation contributes to global warming by reducing the capacity of our planet to deal with increased levels of carbon dioxide and other greenhouse gases. Second, increases in atmospheric pollutants have negative impacts on forests. The first problem points to a need for preventing high rates of forest destruction (especially in tropical areas) and for tree planting programs to keep up with forest loss.

The second concern points to a need for scientific study. Models project an increase in global mean surface temperature of 2 degrees between 1990 and 2100, well above the 1 degree found to change growth and regeneration of many tree species.

A statement on forest health made by the USDA Forest Service in 1996 said that in the Appalachian Mountains, acidic cloud moisture had been associated with increased winter injury to red spruce. Acid rain results from the release of sulfur and nitrogen compounds from motor vehicles and from the burning of fossil fuels by electric power plants and other industries. Deposits of these compounds from the atmosphere may affect forest soils, causing changes in the calcium-to-aluminum ratio or loss of nutrients.

Many trees weakened by pollutants have died from subsequent insect attacks. Even though the source or identity of particular pollutants or the manner in which they damage trees is not fully understood, few can argue with the results: from 1986 to 1991 tree mortality increased by 24 percent. The need for more information about the affects of pollutants on forests is one reason for the trend toward a broader ecological component to undergraduate education.

Staying abreast of the latest research makes job seekers more competitive. Research continues to focus on interactions between atmospheric chemistry and the biological world, responses of terrestrial and aquatic ecosystems to global climate change, and the relationships between human activities and global climate change.

URBAN FORESTRY

Although mixed-use forests in urban areas cover more acres than all of the land managed by the Forest Service, they are currently dwindling. In urban areas nationwide, only one tree is planted for every four removed. More than 80 percent of the nation's population is concentrated in densely populated areas, bringing up issues such as widespread erosion, increased polluted runoff and flooding, and loss of open space and wildlife habitat to urban sprawl. This increases the complexity of managing forested areas where urban and rural publics meet, according to a list of urban national forest issues.

In addition to the aesthetic value of urban trees, they help purify the air, provide shade and moderate temperatures, improve water quality, and reduce flooding. As part of the trend toward concern for environmental issues closer to home, municipalities are increasingly hiring foresters and arborists to help maintain urban greenspaces to legal and public standards, according to Smith at the Society of American Foresters.

SMALL FORESTED AREAS IN PRIVATE OWNERSHIP

It's easy to focus on the big guys—the federal government, Weyerhaeuser, and so forth. Much of the nation's forestland, however, is owned by thousands of private landholders. Look for opportunities in consulting and at local government agencies to help these landowners better manage forestlands to comply with regulations and maximize returns for small logging efforts.

INTERNATIONAL FORESTRY

Increasing concern about global deforestation and the lack of forestry management in many less developed countries creates new opportunities for those interested in international forestry. Both government agencies and timber companies need foresters to help shape forestry management practices abroad. For example, the federal government collaborated with USAID Brazil from 1992 to 1997 to carry out a program on fire and environmental change in tropical ecosystems and to strengthen forest management technologies and practices in Amazonian forests. The Peace Corps has markedly increased the size of its forestry program in recent years and conducts many reforestation projects in Third World countries. And, of course, multinational corporations have tree plantations throughout the world.

CAREER OPPORTUNITIES

Employment prospects for foresters have been rather cyclical and are tied closely to the overall economy and the demand for forest products. There are three factors that permit cautious optimism. First, demand for forest products continues to grow. Second, many in the current generation of foresters are nearing retirement age. Third, the number of students entering forestry programs is closely balanced with the number of jobs available.

According to the Society of American Foresters' Greg Smith, the broad field of forestry has expanded greatly in the last decade. In response, educational

A surveyor with the Department of the Interior defines boundaries for future studies in the national forest lands of southeast Alaska.

programs have evolved curricula that allow graduates to pursue a variety of employment opportunities, from forest management to environmental consulting. Undergraduate programs surveyed reported that the overwhelming majority of their graduates find employment in industry and the majority of the balance go to graduate school. Schools are seeing an increase in employment of their graduates by private consulting firms. A very small percentage find government jobs.

An entry-level position in forestry can lead to several different career paths managing larger parcels of land and supervising the foresters assigned to these parcels. You might move to a corporate office or develop a specialty. Some possible specialties include database development, forest entomology and pathology, forest economics, forest hydrology, forest recreation, silviculture, planning, fuels management and fire suppression, bioengineering, forest ecology, contract administration, public relations, and soil science. Many of these specialties require an advanced degree. Given the amount of basic forestry that must be learned in college, it is difficult to do much specialization as an undergraduate.

Entry-level jobs in state and federal agencies often involve foresters in recreation, wildlife, and watershed management. This might mean talking to hikers, campers, and hunters; carrying out trail maintenance, or conducting wildlife and plant surveys.

Forestry technicians, who usually have two-year degrees that prepare them with a broad base of technical skills and knowledge of forestry, serve as timber cruisers, recreation area custodians, fire dispatchers, tree nursery workers, tree maintenance staff members, research aides, and log scalers. In short, they spend most of their time in the field. They can advance to such conservation-focused management positions as refuge managers, fish and game preserve managers, and forestry consultants. Many prominent professionals begin their careers as forestry technicians, receiving excellent field experience, before moving on to professional positions. You will almost certainly need a bachelor's degree (or more), however, to move up.

PUBLIC SECTOR

Although the public sector employs only 40 percent of environmental professionals in the field, government agencies play a leadership role in defining allowable practices and in managing millions of acres of public land.

Federal Government. The U.S. government employs 26 percent of the professional foresters in the United States. The majority of these work for the Forest Service in the Department of Agriculture, including 5,000 foresters and nearly 7,000 forestry technicians. The next largest federal employer of foresters is the Department of the Interior, which employs foresters in its National Park Service, Bureau of Land Management, and U.S. Fish and Wildlife Service. Significant numbers of federal foresters also work for the Natural Resource Conservation Service, Peace Corps, and the U.S. Army Corps of Engineers.

Substantial growth took place in federal forestry during the 1970s, creating a large group of professionals moving through their careers in a rather homogeneous age group. As these people begin to reach retirement age in the late 1990s, increased hiring will take place. However, "forester" positions will be fewer as some retirees are replaced by more specialized forest managers, while others are cut due to workforce reduction plans.

In October 1992, the Forest Service workforce had 35,085 employees. In August 1996 the permanent workforce was 30,436. By 1999 the agency is projecting a permanent workforce of approximately 29,000 employees to manage 191 million acres in 156 national forests. The seasonal employment level goes from about 3,000 in January to over 15,000 in July.

Still, there are about 11,000 professional positions in the Forest Service that typically require education or training equivalent to a bachelor's degree or higher. Examples include accountant, microbiologist, civil engineer, forester, geologist, and wildlife biologist. Most entry-level positions accepting applications from the general public (applicants without federal status) are posted in the office with the vacancy, the local state employment office, and the nearest Office of Personnel Management Employment Office, which can be located on the World Wide Web at http://www.usajobs.opm.gov.

In addition, check out Fed World, a federal jobs search engine, at http://www.fedworld.gov/jobs/jobsearch.html. A recent search for the word "forest" turned up ninety-four open positions that included seasonal/summer positions as well as such permanent positions as wildlife biologist (4), forestry technician (10), realty specialist, botanist, fishery biologist (3), soil scientist, general biologist (6), sustainable development coordinator, range conservationist, and recreation specialist.

State and Local Government. State and local governments, though employing 17 percent of forestry professionals, are among the fastest-growing segments of the industry. Demand for forestry employees will be spurred by a continuing emphasis on environmental protection and responsible land management. Urban foresters are increasingly needed to do environmental impact statements in urban areas and to help regional planning commissions make land-use decisions. At the state level, more numerous and complex laws have created demand for more foresters and conservation scientists to deal with environmental regulations. Also, the nationwide Stewardship Incentive Program, funded by the federal government, provides money to the states to encourage landowners to practice multiuse forest management. Foresters will be needed to assist landowners in making decisions about how to manage their forested property.

PRIVATE SECTOR

Nearly half of all forest professionals work in the private sector at large multinational corporations, smaller regional companies, and hundreds of small firms and consulting businesses.

Forest Products Companies and Other Corporations. Private sector firms employ 45 percent of all professional foresters, and this continues to grow. Forestry giants like Weyerhaeuser and Georgia Pacific are, of course, the employment leaders, but many smaller firms hire substantial numbers of environmental workers. While the forest products markets experience boom and bust cycles, forestry employment with most companies has largely stabilized in the 1990s according to Dave Mumper, director of environmental affairs at Weyerhaeuer (see profile at end of chapter).

Private sector companies manage forests for lumber and pulpwood, produce paper and other wood fiber products, supply forestry equipment and materials, and provide care for urban parks and forests. Private owners of timberland, both industrial and nonindustrial, are likely to employ an increasing number of foresters due to an increased sense of responsibility to protect the environment and manage their land.

Although private sector companies have increased attention to plant and wildlife protection, water quality, and so forth, innovative forestry work in the private sector is focused on increasing productivity, profitability, and new products. Private forestry businesses (like their agricultural counterparts) are investing heavily, for instance, in genetic research and the search for trees that grow quickly, resist pests, and produce quality wood. Professionals with these interests will be well rewarded. Companies are also searching for innovations in logging practices that can keep the cost of harvesting reasonably low, while protecting the environment and complying with regulations. Finally, private firms are seeking help in increasing the amount of "waste" wood that is used or recycled profitably.

Nonforestry companies are also hiring forestry workers, especially in urban areas. An innovative federal program, in fact, helps prepare entry-level workers for forestry work in the private sector.

The Urban Forestry Job Corps program, begun in 1993, addresses a national shortage of tree trimmers and other urban forestry workers nationwide. Utility companies are a significant employer. ACRT Environmental Services developed the program, which has retrained some loggers and miners whose jobs have disappeared. Students from the program receive offers from private tree care companies, as well as others.

Consulting Firms. Although consulting firms have never employed large numbers of foresters, they have experienced significant growth in recent years. Forestry consultants work with private landowners to acquire standing timber, make volume estimates, and authorize purchases. Consultants also develop forest management plans for privately held lands, and provide assistance to government agencies.

NONPROFIT SECTOR

Forestry in the nonprofit sector is a very small segment of the field, perhaps accounting for 2 percent of the total number of professionals. This segment includes industry associations, as well as forestry professionals within larger environmental organizations and the academic community.

Although small in number, forestry researchers are extremely influential, especially those academics who teach at prominent forestry schools such as the University of Washington and Oregon State University. Government and industry alike look to researchers in the university community to find new approaches to common problems, and frequently carry out their own research and development through grants to principal investigators and graduate students.

Activists at environmental organizations are also professionally influential beyond their numbers and salaries. The number of paid forestry professionals at the Sierra Club, Environmental Defense Fund, American Forests, Natural Resources Defense Council, and local groups may be small, but anyone in the timber industry will tell you that these advocates play a large role in determining the disposition of millions of forested acres. Don't be put off by limited job opportunities if you want to pursue an activist career in forestry in the non-profit sector.

SALARY

A 1997 salary survey conducted by the Society of American Foresters shows average salaries of experienced foresters ranging from $35,000 to $45,000. The results of the survey also showed:

- Entry-level salaries ranged from $18,000 to $25,000.
- Salaries for field positions fell between $20,000 and $35,000.
- Salaries for mid-level positions averaged between $35,000 and $45,000.
- Top management salaries ranged from $50,000 to $70,000, but go as high as $100,000 in the private sector.

Entry-level positions in private sector forestry range from $24,000 to $32,000. Larger companies tend to pay higher starting salaries than do smaller companies. Consulting firms sometimes pay entry-level foresters a lower base salary, but offer a commission type arrangement with financial incentives to bring in customers. In the private sector, an M.S. degree will command a slightly higher starting salary.

GETTING STARTED

Before you decide on a career path in forestry, decide how much time you think you want to spend in the field. Because of technological advances, today's forester is moving out of the forest and into the office. Much of the work of foresters has become less labor-intensive or has been farmed out to forestry technicians. Where maps and surveys were once used, computers, aerial photography, remote sensing from satellites, and computerized geographic information systems now do a quicker and more accurate job.

Consequently, today's forester must have a high degree of skill with computers, statistics, and accounting, along with good interpersonal skills. The latter are necessary because foresters are not only communicating more with a variety of colleagues and coworkers, but are also in the public eye more than ever before. Their job increasingly entails public relations and public education.

EDUCATION

Education curricula are constantly modified to reflect employer needs. Previously the education of foresters was biologically based. As mentioned earlier, in response to increased multiusage, education is now trending toward the appreciation of the role of social sciences in managing biological resources and toward a broader ecological education. Curricula modifications are primarily science-based to keep up with advancements in science and technology, though computer technology is also an area where programs have been expanded. Computers are used extensively, both in the office and in the field, for storage retrieval. Analysis of this information is required to manage forestland and its resources. According to Ken Holtje with the Forest Service, GIS is one of the areas where they have done more hiring.

Fourteen states have either mandatory licensing or voluntary registration requirements that a forester must meet to acquire the title "professional forester." Getting licensed usually requires a four-year degree in forestry, a minimum period of training time, and passing an exam.

Associate Degree Education. The Society of American Foresters accredits twenty-five two-year forest technology programs across the United States. An associate of applied science degree (A.A.S.) is usually a combination of science-based education, professional preparation, and hands-on experience that qualifies graduates for employment as technicians, professional assistants, and supervisors in private and public organizations.

Good preparation for a program in forest technology includes strong math, science, computer, and communications skills. Outdoor/woods and shop experience are also helpful. Good coordination, the ability to lift heavy objects and to climb steep slopes, and general fitness improve the students' prospects for success in the job market. Women and minorities are particularly successful in obtaining jobs and are urged to apply.

An A.A.S. degree can serve as a foundation for a B.S. degree at most schools, if further education is your goal. It can also prepare the student to enter the job market at the middle-management level doing forest inventory, vegetation mapping, land surveying, harvest planning, road engineering, fire and pest control, wildlife habitat management, outdoor recreation, soil and water conservation, and more.

Undergraduate Education. Foresters have a tall order to fill. As one forester acknowledges, "We are trying to pack into four years of school what realistically should take seven." This is where experience and graduate school increasingly come into the picture.

Most foresters obtain a B.S. from one of the forty-eight forestry schools accredited by the Society of American Foresters. As with the A.A.S. degree programs, most schools require students to hold at least one field position. Do not, however, limit your fieldwork to the bare requirements—obtain as much experience as you can. This not only will help you direct your interests and studies in the field, but also will make you more attractive to prospective employers.

Keep in mind that all schools, even those that are accredited, are not created equal; it is quite legitimate to ask professionals about a school's reputation. Many schools have a tendency to specialize either in a particular application of forestry (e.g., forestry management, recreation, economics, forestry engineering, ecology, and urban forestry) or in the type of forest in the region in which the school is located. Decide whether you are interested in a particular focus or want a more general background. Finally, spend some time comparing the courses offered and required by the various schools.

Specialization. There is no consensus on specialization in forestry education. Some employers are looking for broadly educated graduates, and for a pull toward specialization once a forester starts working. Other employers want to see an inclination toward a specialty before they hire. Some foresters feel that undergraduates can hurt themselves by being "a mile wide and an inch deep." Others told us that specializing early in a career can limit your options before you have a chance to learn about the field and make career decisions based on experience. The latter camp advises that specialization be left to graduate school.

One approach is to get a minor or possibly a second major in addition to your forestry degree. This could be in a technical area—soil science, wildlife, or surveying—or might be oriented more toward liberal arts—business, economics, political science, or computer science. A similar route is to pursue one of the forestry tracks offered by many schools, such as forest economics, management, or hydrology.

Field Experience. As is the case with all natural resource management professions, seasonal or part-time work experience is necessary to obtain a full-time job. Your first experience may be as a volunteer. Use this as an opportunity to test out various types of forestry work, build up skills, make contacts in the profession, and collect letters of recommendation. Many graduates are employed in seasonal jobs upon graduation and gain permanent employment within two to three years.

A variety of volunteer, internship, and seasonal work programs are available through government agencies, nonprofit organizations, and universities. You may want to consider broadening your work experience with a stint in a nontraditional setting, such as doing policy work with a nonprofit organization, research with a botanical garden, or interpretation with a park system. Formal cooperative education programs with state and federal agencies offer you the best odds of getting full-time, entry-level employment upon graduation.

Graduate Education. Many forestry specializations now require graduate study. A graduate degree is also an opportunity to broaden your skill base. For example, foresters may go back to school to obtain an M.B.A., a master's degree in public administration, and even a law degree.

A master's degree will probably be required later in your career. Whether it helps early on depends somewhat on the demand for foresters. One employer in industrial forestry points out: "There is currently an abundant supply of foresters. One way to choose is to see whether they have a master's degree. In the last few years, two of every three persons we have hired have had graduate degrees." Undergraduate programs in forestry reported about 15 percent of their graduates go straight to graduate school.

ADVICE

Forestry leaders from business, government, the activist community, and academia have different perspectives on their common profession. Here is some advice for aspiring foresters from those who are building the sustainable forestry of today.

Learn the business aspects of forestry. Regardless of your future employment desires (government, private, academic, or activism) you will do well to understand forestry as a profit-making activity. How does it work? What are the pressures on profitability? How can environmental protection and sound business work together? What innovations can you propose in the areas of recycling, reuse, toxics use reduction, harvesting practices, revenue from recreation, retaining forests for water and atmospheric protection, or new products? Economic "drivers" may ultimately be as powerful as political, legal, and regulatory ones as a means of protecting forests. By understanding the inner workings of the forest products business and markets, you will be in an excellent position to suggest improvements.

Study ecosystems management. We've seen that ecosystems management is crucial to multiple use forestry. Choose undergraduate and graduate programs which have strong faculty in this area.

Consider urban forestry. If urban forestry interests you, you can prepare by completing a traditional undergraduate forestry program. However, you may want to attend one of the growing number of schools that have special programs for urban forestry or find a school that offers a minor in urban forest management. The urban forester must be able to identify and know the characteristics and requirements of literally hundreds of types of trees. Urban foresters must also be well versed in entomology, pathology, herbicide and pesticide applications, communications, landscape architecture, federal, state, and local statutes, and public relations.

Much of the work on urban trees is performed by arborists and horticulturists. Most prepare for these professions by combining a two-year technical degree and on-the-job training or by completing a four-year program.

Get experience—develop real world skills. If you want to compete successfully for jobs in forestry, you must unearth opportunities to develop some of the skills specific to forestry, such as inventorying and timber cruising, grading lumber, identifying species, using aerial photographs and maps, administering contracts, and controlling pests. Demonstrating your knowledge of these hands-on skills is your best assurance of obtaining an entry-level job.

Master the computer. Because forestry involves determining conditions and planning uses for large areas of land, it is particularly well suited to computer-aided tools such as geographic information systems. Look for opportunities to become familiar with these systems and get over any "computer phobia."

Training employees to use these systems can be costly and inefficient, so your experience will be attractive to potential employers.

Learn communication and management skills. Everyone we spoke with emphasized the need for the same short list of skills—strong verbal and written communication, ability to organize work into an effective plan of action, listening and consensus building, ability to motivate, and educating others. Does this sound like you?

Love the forest. It may sound corny, but in the end, forestry professionals are happy and successful because they are drawn to the forest and have a passion for it.

SUMMARY

There are a wide range of professionals working on the issues of forestry. Prospective foresters should have a strong grasp on policy issues and on the increasingly numerous and complex environmental regulations that affect many forestry-related activities. The demand for other life and social scientists will increase relative to foresters as timber programs are de-emphasized at the federal level.

Continued research into the potential effects of atmospheric pollution and climatic change on terrestrial ecosystems will result in the development of methods to mitigate the negative impacts of climate change on forests.

Communities and their expectations for their trees and forests will continue to evolve, as will developments in forest health. Both will influence access to, and supplies of the goods and services of our nation's forested lands. Cross-jurisdictional, collaborative forest management plans based on the interrelated issues of community expectations and forest health are the keys to the sustainability of both.

CASE STUDY

Tongass National Forest

Preservation of old-growth forests has been a controversial issue in the western United States for many years, often pitting industrial logging concerns, native subsistence interests, tourism, and conservationists against one another.

The Tongass National Forest, stretching 500 miles up the southeast "leg" of Alaska from Ketchikan to Yakutat, represents the largest remaining temperate rain forest on the Earth. It is home to more than 300 species of wildlife (including the largest concentrations of bald eagles anywhere); "temple trees," some of which reach up to 200 feet and are 800 years old; and, of course, about 100,000 humans. Wild and ancient runs of salmon return each year to the Tongass, providing food for eagles, bear, and other wildlife, as well as world class commercial, sport, and subsistence fishing.

Created in 1902, when President Theodore Roosevelt set aside 4.5 million acres in the archipelago, the Tongass was expanded in 1908. Today, at 17 million acres, it is the largest national forest in the country.

This primeval forest has been a battleground between those who want to continue logging in the remaining old growth trees (which make up only 4 percent of the Tongass), and those who want to prevent this from ever happening. And yet, that's too simple. The struggle is over jobs and the economy, values and lifestyles, and subsidized industry and the free market. Each side works furiously to dispel the "myths" of its opponents. This has resulted in "facts" about the Tongass that vary by as much as 50 percent, depending on who is reporting them.

Environmental professionals play a major role in the debate over the Tongass. Foresters, biologists, hydrologists, economists, attorneys, policy analysts, community organizers, and more work on the issue at state government agencies in Alaska, the Forest Service and other federal agencies, tribal governments and native corporations, private timber companies, trade associations, activist groups, and (crucially) congressional and legislative staffs. Journalists and academics follow the fray with great interest.

Debate today centers on the 1997 Tongass Land Management Plan, approved by the U.S. Forest Service after years of bitter fighting. The plan tries to strike a politically acceptable balance that will expand wilderness while subsidizing new road construction; protect most of the old growth while allowing some cutting; assure the guaranteed subsistence rights of Alaskan natives; protect wildlife and water quality through expanded "buffers" and other means; make Alaska's congressional delegation and legislature happy; keep the Clinton administration out of court; remove subsidies that may encourage the Ketchikan Pulp Company to cut trees for which there is no market; and assure that the area's economy, which (depends on tourism, commercial fishing, and sport fishing over logging) continues to grow.

The result? Over thirty appeals are now pending against the plan from all sides! Although most agree that the plan is a "quantum leap" over previous ones (especially scientifically), the debate rages on. What's at stake here anyway?

Why save a temperate rain forest? Temperate rain forests, are one of the rarest and most biologically productive ecosystems, covering just 0.2 percent of the Earth (compared with tropical rain forests which cover about 10 percent). The Alaska rain forest represents about one-third of the world's remaining old-growth temperate rain forest and contains the largest pristine stands. In the lower forty-eight states, 95 percent of old-growth forests have been logged.

Since time immemorial, traditional gathering of subsistence foods has been a way of life for Alaska natives. These rights are guaranteed by federal law and subject to strict formulas. Nonnative immigrants to the Alaskan wilderness also rely on harvest of wild game and fish. Eighty-five percent of rural households in Southeast Alaska harvest some kind of subsistence food. Nearly one-third of rural households in the region supply half their need for fish and meat by hunting and fishing. Other species depend on high-volume, old-growth forest as their primary habitat, including the Alexander Archipelago wolf, brown bear, and Queen Charlotte goshawk.

Timber harvesting (especially through clear-cuts) converts large old-growth forests into second-growth stands that have a lower habitat value. All trees are logged in a clear-cut, regardless of age or size. At first the increased light gives rise to an abundance of new vegetation. But twenty to thirty years later, new trees close in, creating a dense thicket of small trees that severely limits light on the forest floor and kills understory growth. This lasts for at least 200 years until old-growth conditions begin to naturally redevelop. While logging companies generally replant a sufficient number of trees, the Forest Service's management model is based on a 100-year rotation. So stands that have been clear-cut can be cut again in 100 years and will never regain old-growth characteristics unless they are left alone for centuries.

About 10 percent of Tongass old-growth has been clear-cut, but this amounts to more than half of the best timber stands, which are also the best wildlife habitat. One million acres have been logged since 1954, most of it in the last ten years.

Jobs vs. conservation. The fight over the Tongass yields dire predictions of economic collapse if conservationists have their way. But the economy in the Tongass region has grown an average of 2.5 percent annually since 1988, despite a decline in timber industry employment at an average annual rate of 5.7 percent. Mill closures in Sitka and Haines disrupted the communities for a short time, but both have experienced economic recoveries.

Just as timber is only one of the uses of national forests under the Multiple-Use/Sustained Yield Act of 1960, it is also only one part of the Alaskan economy, ranking fourth below the private industries of tourism, commercial fishing, and sport fishing in the number of people it employs. All of these industries are closely linked with the well-being of the Tongass. Salmon are at the core of southeast Alaska's ecosystem and economy. Tourism has increased over 20 percent annually in southeast Alaska since 1988, but that phenomenal growth will be limited by clear-cutting in the Tongass. Jim Gould writes in *Outside* magazine (August 29, 1996): "A recent survey by the Alaska Institute for Sustainable Recreation and Tourism found that of the 437 bays and coves in the Tongass most suitable for boat-based nature tourism, 54 percent were impaired."

Alaska-based conservation groups advocate for sustainable management rather than a ban on logging. They also say that thousands more jobs could be created with a smaller harvest if more value were added to the timber. In the Tongass, a majority of the timber is exported as round logs, lumber, or cants (squared off logs) to the Far East where it is processed into higher value products and exported back to the U.S. In Alaska, about four jobs per million board feet are generated, compared with twelve jobs per million board feet in California, Washington, and Oregon. Reductions in timber harvest resulting in the loss of jobs could be relieved by the development of local wood-processing. Perversely, U.S. law requires only minimal U.S. processing of logs cut on public lands.

The battle over the Tongass started at the turn of the century. One hundred years later, we're still struggling.

PROFILES

Susan Peitzmeier Romano
President
Wildland Research and Management, Inc.
Macomb, Illinois

Consulting foresters are a small but growing segment of forestry professionals. In addition to technical and scientific backgrounds, they must have business, sales, and marketing skills as well as an entrepreneurial spirit to succeed.

Susan Peitzmeier Romano, founder and president of Wildland Management and Research, says her first memory of the forest was hunting Morel mushrooms with her family every spring. Susan was "very taken by the forest. It's a completely different world," she says. From this came her aspiration to be a scientist who would contribute "practical and useful" knowledge to the real-world management of our most valuable resources—our forests.

Susan worked her way through college, starting at Western Illinois University in her hometown. When she completed the preforestry program, Susan transferred to Southern Illinois University in Carbondale where she continued work on a bachelor's degree.

Though it took her longer than the traditional four years, Susan was able to gain valuable field experience during her undergraduate years, alternating work with school. She paid her tuition by working as a crop scout for Pfizer-Genetics Seed Corn and as a forester trainee with the USDA Forest Service, among other positions.

In 1984, Susan received her B.S. degree in forest resource management. She went to work for a paper company in Kentucky, evaluating timber stand data and writing management recommendations. Within months Susan realized that she would need more education to accomplish her goals. She returned to Western Illinois University and pursued a master's in biology with an emphasis in botany.

During the course of her master's program Susan developed a wide array of practical skills, working such jobs as staff forester for Illinois Forest Products; landscape designer for Timberhill Nurseries; soil conservation aid for the

USDA Soil Conservation Service (now the Natural Resource Conservation Service); soil technician for the McDonough County Soil Survey; and project assistant in the Department of Biological Sciences at Western Illinois University. As if that weren't enough, she also got married and had two children.

After receiving her master's degree in 1990, Susan worked for the Illinois Natural History Survey, where she gained extensive experience in monitoring wetlands to determine the relationship of wetland communities to environmental factors. While there she presented award-winning research on the reestablishment of submersed aquatic plant species. Susan says: "It was a great job. I could be on the river just about every day, and I was pursuing my research interest while trying to come to some good practical ways of managing that natural resource."

Next, Susan worked at the Illinois River National Fish and Wildlife Refuge. Her experience there led directly to the decision to form her own forestry consulting company in 1994.

Susan's broad experience with federal, state, local, and private agencies is precisely what a consulting forester needs. In the course of her business, Susan works with all these constituencies, and knowing how they operate is an advantage. In addition, it allowed her to develop many of the wide-ranging skills encompassed in the forestry profession.

When she founded Wildland, the start-up money for the business came from her teaching salary at Spoon River college, where she taught a course in environmental ecology. Today she owns her own equipment such as chain saws, pruning equipment, a tree-planting machine, and a four-wheeler with an herbicide sprayer. Each year she adds equipment, which she calls "toys." She employs two full-time foresters, and hires two interns each summer to help with timber stand improvement, just one of the services her company offers.

Susan's clients are primarily private landowners. However, Susan does work with state district foresters as well through a cost-share program called the Illinois Forest Development Act, which levies a 4 percent tax on all timber sales. The money goes into a collective account and is disbursed back to landowners when they want to improve their forests. For example, if an individual wants a forest stewardship plan written, he or she can obtain funds through this program. The landowner might then call on Wildland to write a comprehensive ten-year plan and make recommendations on how to manage the land. The state cost-share program helps support Romano's business.

Wildland's tree planting business is partially supported by another economic incentive program, the Conservation Reserve Program (CRP). This federal program encourages landowners to convert their marginal farmland, bottomland fields, and old pasture ground, back into timber.

Susan says the hardest part of getting where she is today has been learning how to run a business. She received help from the Small Business

Administration and the Association of Consulting Foresters. On being a small business owner Susan says: "It's very important that you give back to the community."

On a recent day, Susan began work at 7:00 A.M. with a meeting at Macomb's parochial school in her capacity as education commissioner. When she returned to the office, a logger called her out to a job site to introduce him to a landowner whose timber he would begin harvesting that day. Then she was back in the office working on a management plan for a client. About noon, she drove two hours for a timber sale evaluation in which she "cruised" the timber for a client, walking through it to determine if there was enough value for a timber sale. She recommended a harvest and helped plan some of the details. Then she returned to Macomb for another meeting.

Susan's business roughly corresponds with the seasons, with timber sale administration, harvest marking, and pruning in the winter; tree planting and herbicide application throughout the spring; and timber stand improvement in the summer. She writes forest management plans throughout the year.

There are many things that Susan loves about her work but she says: "My underlying motivation is a true love for the forest."

Dave Mumper
Director of Environmental Affairs
Weyerhaeuser Company
Tacoma, Washington

The private sector timber industry employs nearly half of all forestry professionals, with a full range of environmental specialties. Weyerhaeuser is one of the world's largest forest products companies.

"I grew up in southern California, right up against the mountains, and I spent a lot of time up there. I thought, 'Boy, I would like to work up there for the Forest Service,'" recalls Dave Mumper, director of environmental affairs for timber industry giant Weyerhaeuser Company.

"I was, and am, very environmentally oriented," he says. "I was very interested in what the Sierra Club was doing on environmental issues, and I knew I was going to escape Los Angeles!"

Mumper escaped to Humboldt State University, "in the heart of the redwoods," just north of Eureka, California, where he earned a bachelor's degree in forestry. He earned a master's degree in forestry economics from West Virginia University and then faced the rare and delightful task of deciding which of many job offers to accept. "Weyerhaeuser was the example held up all the way through school as [a company that was] making an attempt to practice and invest money in good forestry," he says.

In his first assignment for Weyerhaeuser, Mumper worked out of Coos Bay, Oregon, doing timber inventory and appraisal work. "What hit me [in that job was that] I am a people person, and I was spending day after day in the woods looking at trees and bushes. . . . I decided I had to be around more people."

By 1971, Mumper was chief forester for Weyerhaeuser's Snoqualmie tree farm, some 40 miles east of Seattle. There, his job was indeed much more of a people-oriented occupation. "I spent 70 percent of my time convincing people in Seattle that what we were doing was okay and that more than likely this would still be a tree farm fifty years from now and not a development." Mumper went back to the woods in the late 1970s as a logging manager at Weyerhaeuser's Twin Harbors tree farm, but again he "missed the exposure to people."

When a corporate job became available in 1984, Mumper became a people person once again at company headquarters in Tacoma, first as manager of timberlands resources, and more recently as director of environmental affairs. He has worked extensively with wetlands, which appear on every tree farm owned by Weyerhaeuser.

His specialty is one that barely existed in timber companies a few years ago: identifying and resolving timber controversies and developing effective compromises. "There are a lot of people in forestry who say the very last thing they want is to be involved in politics. That means there are a lot of technical graduates who have only one piece of what they need to be successful in the environmental arena. The people who have an appreciation for, and have worked on, both the politics and the science of forestry have an advantage that I would not trade for anything."

These days, Mumper divides his time about evenly between meetings outside the company, during which he keeps up on the latest issues, and meetings within Weyerhaeuser in which he disseminates that information to the people who need it. Recently he was involved in the stewardship of a conservation partnership between Weyerhaeuser and the Environmental Defense Fund (EDF). The two organizations worked together on a parcel of forest in North Carolina referred to as the Parker Tract and a remnant of the East Dismal Swamp. Weyerhaueser worked closely with EDF to identify some nontimber values, including some rare forms of wildlife habitat. Through this partnership they were able to accommodate their forestry needs while protecting the most critical habitat on the tract. Says Mumper, "these types of cooperative partnerships will change how companies and the environmental community do business in the future."

"I enjoy being involved in the resolution of controversy," Mumper says. "If you can't walk up to an industry person and an environmentalist without having an uncontrollable urge to take a side, then you probably shouldn't get into this line of work. It puts a burden on you to look at creative solutions.

"I think the thing that gives me the most satisfaction is to take an issue that seems to be going nowhere and move it a little bit so people's eyes light up and they say, 'Yes, this is moving in the right direction.'"

Lisa Burban
Urban Forestry Coordinator
USDA Forest Service
St. Paul, Minnesota

Legislation often indicates employment opportunities, as when the 1990 Farm Bill increased funding for urban forestry programs in the USDA Forest Service from $2.5 million to over $20 million.

Lisa Burban was in the right place at the right time in February 1990. She had a B.S. degree in forest management, and was working on her M.S. degree when she successfully applied for a cooperative education job with the USDA Forest Service. That job evolved into her current position as an urban forestry coordinator with the Northeastern Area of the Forest Service.

Lisa was introduced to urban forestry through her summer job while she was an undergraduate at the University of Illinois in Champaign/Urbana. She worked for the Village of LaGrange Park every summer, learning how to identify trees, as well as the proper way to plant, trim, and prune them. She also gained first-hand knowledge of Dutch Elm disease, that is, how to recognize it and come to terms with removing the large trees. Dutch Elm disease started in the early 1970s in the Chicago area. It was an epidemic that raised awareness and justified urban forestry in Illinois, according to Lisa.

A lot of the work in this municipal setting required her to deal with the residents. "In urban and community forestry you're right out there with the people every day, so it requires good people skills. It takes a certain kind of person to be on the hot seat when you want to take down a tree that everybody loves." This experience serves her well in her current job, which is collaborative by nature.

When Lisa was an undergraduate (1984–88), there were only a few courses offered in urban forestry at the University of Illinois. By the time she was in graduate school at the University of Minnesota, St. Paul, she knew she wanted to be an urban forester. She created an urban emphasis in her program by taking such courses as urban entomology and urban pathology to supplement what she didn't get at Illinois.

Lisa's school ethic consisted of three main ideas—get good grades, get experience, and be active in school. While she was an undergraduate she sought to work for the head of the Department of Forestry, doing library research work as well as working at the Illini Plantations, where she learned to use a chainsaw and did brush clearing and general forestry work.

As a graduate student Lisa was a teaching assistant for an urban forestry class, and eventually taught the class herself. In addition to her teaching assistant job and her thesis work, Lisa helped write an assessment of Minnesota's urban forests with the Minnesota Shade Tree Advisory Committee. Last but not least, she began working twenty hours a week in her cooperative education position with the Forest Service.

Lisa's region includes seven midwestern states. In each state she works with the state urban forestry coordinator to establish programs funded by federal money and communicates issues and concerns between the state and federal forestry groups. Getting in on the ground floor of the urban forestry trend, Lisa was able to influence the formation of state urban forestry councils, and get involved in writing the first state urban forestry management plans for some states. Part of the satisfaction she gets from her work is being able to look back and see that she has helped make a difference for the urban environments where 80 percent of the population lives.

When Lisa began working with the Forest Service there were about fifteen state coordinators. In the eight years since then, all fifty states have met the criteria for funding under the 1990 Farm Bill. The bill requires each state to have a full-time state urban forestry coordinator, a state urban forestry council, a strategic plan, and volunteer coordination capacity.

When the state urban forestry councils began forming they focused on street tree management and park tree management. Now that the councils are beginning to revise their management plans, the focus is shifting from street trees and park trees to a broader perspective on natural resources management around cities. Water quality, air quality, and economic issues relating to trees and jobs are becoming stronger areas of interest, according to Lisa.

In addition to stewardship of her seven states, Lisa is a member of the Federal Urban Forestry Team, which meets several times a year, and she recently took on expanded duties and a new job title, disaster assistance coordinator, for twenty northeastern states. This opportunity is a result of Lisa developing an area of expertise in disaster planning and preparation. This niche that she's carving out for herself is something she did not foresee: "Who'd have thought an urban forester would get into something like that?" she asks.

In 1993 Lisa coauthored a book with a former professor from the University of Illinois, John Andresen, called *Storms over the Urban Forest.* The book grew out of their experiences when they were called in to assess the loss after a tornado hit several communities just south and west of Chicago. The two saw a need for technical information on disaster planning and preparation. At first they were going to write a pamphlet about their experience, but the project evolved into the book. Lisa says: "I feel very passionately about being prepared for disasters."

As a result of the book, doors have opened for both authors. Lisa chaired the National Storms Conference two years ago and is collaborating on next year's conference. She has developed other workshops and conferences across the country on natural disaster planning and management.

In the next five to ten years Lisa would like to develop her new job responsibilities as well as stay involved with her state urban forestry coordinators, working from the broad perspective of ecosystem management. She would also like to become a national expert in disasters.

At thirty-one, Lisa has been fortunate throughout her career and she knows it. She says she's never been stopped from trying new things. "In my agency you can be like [me], or maybe not. I work for a person who is an entrepreneur in government." Lisa credits her mentors with giving her the freedom to try new ideas, "a ton of flexibility," and allowing her to design her own job.

RESOURCES

Amazing Environmental Organization Webdirectory for Forestry. "Earth's biggest environmental search engine." Http://www.webdirectory.com/Science/Agriculture/Forestry/.

American Forest Foundation. Mission is to encourage long-term stewardship and sustainable use of natural resources through the Tree Farm System (www.treefarmsystem.org) and outreach education. 1111 19th Street, NW, Washington, DC 20036. (202) 463-2462. Http://www.affoundation.org/About.

American Forests. A national citizens' conservation organization devoted to trees, forests, and forestry. Publishes educational materials on forests as well as *American Forests* magazine (quarterly) and *Proceedings of the National Urban Forestry Conferences* (every other year). Internship program. Web info about other programs and list of publications on forest policy. P.O. Box 2000, Washington, DC, 20013. (202) 955-4500. Http://www.amfor.org.

Association of Consulting Foresters. Sets standards for professional consulting forester, publishes *The Consultant* (quarterly). 732 N. Washington St., Suite 4A, Alexandria, VA. 22314. (888) 540-8733. Http://www.acf-foresters.com.

Conservation Directory (annual). Comprehensive information on public and private organizations concerned with environmental conservation, education, and natural resource management. Call (800) 477-5560 or look on the web at Http://www.igc.org/nwf/news/consform.html.

Directory of the Forest Products Industry. A comprehensive listing of forest products industries (including sawmills, wood treatment plants, and plywood mills) by state and province. Includes addresses, products and volume, and names and telephone numbers of key personnel. Miller Freeman Publications, Circulation Department, P.O. Box 7339, San Francisco, CA 94120. (800) 848-5594. Http://www.mfi.com.

Forest People. A personnel recruiter that works exclusively within the forest industry. Website has job listings and links to other forest industry websites. Forest People International Search Ltd. 800-1100 Melville St., Vancouver, BC V6E 4A6. (604) 669-5635. Http://www.corp.direct.ca/forestpeople/.

Forest Service Employees for Environmental Ethics. Nonprofit organization existing to "forge a socially responsible value system for the Forest Service based on a land ethic which ensures ecologically and economically sustainable resource management." Publishes *Inner Voice*, a newspaper with inside information about what the Forest Service is doing (good and bad) and the on-line *E-Activist* to provide timely updates on legislation and other issues related to protecting the environment and reforming the Forest Service. Important part of website is links to other sources. P.O. Box 11615, Eugene, OR 97440. (541) 484-2692. Http://www.afseee.org.

International Society of Arboriculture. A scientific and educational organization devoted to the dissemination of knowledge in the care, preservation, and research of shade and ornamental trees. Prints a listing of colleges and universities offering forestry and other arboriculture courses. Publishes bimonthlies *Journal of Arboriculture* and *Arborist* News. P.O. Box 3129, Champaign, IL 61826. Http://www.ag.uiuc.edu/~isa/.

IRIS: Forest Products Industry Directory. Web search engine with over 2,500 active sites including job listings. Http://www.primusweb.com/forest/.

National Arborist Association. Publishes *The Reporter* (monthly). Meeting Place Mall, Route 101, P.O. Box 1094, Amherst, NH 03031. (603) 673-3311. Http://www.natlarb.com.

National Association of State Foresters. A nonprofit organization representing directors of state forestry agencies. Maintains a "Directory of State Foresters" and publishes a monthly newsletter, *Washington Update*, available on-line to keep state foresters up to date on important policy, legislative, and legal issues affecting forest management. Website has links to forestry and environmental groups, federal agencies, and other natural resource agencies. 444 N. Capitol St. NW, Suite 540, Washington, DC 20001. Http://sso.org/nasf/nasf.html.

National Council of the Paper Industry for Air and Stream Improvement, 260 Madison Ave., New York, NY 10016. (212) 532-9000.

Opportunities in Forestry Careers, by Christopher M. Wille (1998). Details how you can become a forestry professional. Published by VGM Career Horizons, 4255 W. Touhy Ave., Lincolnwood, IL 60646-1975. (847) 679-5500.

Peace Corps. Volunteer to help restore and maintain forest resources in Asia, Africa, the Pacific, South America, Central America, and earn one year of federal status, without which you cannot apply to most vacancies in the federal government. There are former Peace Corps volunteers working in most national forests and parks. (800) 227-4675. Http://www.peacecorps.gov.

Society for Municipal Arborists. Professional Association for urban arborists and foresters. Publishes a membership magazine. Write c/o Norma Bonham, 7000 Olive Blvd., University City, MO 63130. (314) 862-1711. Http://www.urban-forestry.com.

Society of American Foresters. National organization representing various segments of the forestry profession, including public and private practitioners, researchers, administrators, educators, and students. Publishes *Journal of Forestry* (monthly) and *Forest Science* (bimonthly). Other publications include *So You Want to Be In Forestry*. Accredits undergraduate and graduate forestry programs (write for a list of institutions). 5400 Grosvenor Ln., Bethesda, MD 20814. (301) 897-8720. Http://www.safnet.org/index.html.

Timber Harvesting (monthly). Each January issue contains a listing of personnel employed by the wood supply and forestry departments of all major pulp and paper companies and industrial timber firms in the United States. Hatton-Brown Publishers, P.O. Box 2268, Montgomery, AL 36102. (334) 834-1170. Http://www.forestind.com/timberharvesting/index.html.

Urban and Community Forestry Resource Materials Guide. Lists the most useful resources for individuals and communities interested in urban or community forestry. Http://www.ag.uiuc.edu/~forestry/guide/sec1.html. Guide developed by Patrick Weicherding, Ph.D., University of Illinois, Department of Forestry, Urbana, Illinois 61801.

USDA Forest Service. Has responsibility for 155 national forests, and employs about 15,000 forestry professionals involved in management and research directly related to forestry. Website has volunteer information and an employment homepage. P.O. Box 96090, Washington, DC 20250. (202) 205-1765. Http://www.fs.fed.us.

Index